Pulitzer's Gold

PULITZER'S GOLD

A Century of Public Service Journalism

Revised and Updated Edition

Roy J. Harris Jr.

For Nancy & Rob, long live public service journalism!
Roy Ha...

Columbia University Press
New York

Columbia University Press
Publishers Since 1893
New York   Chichester, West Sussex
cup.columbia.edu
Copyright © 2016 Columbia University Press
All rights reserved

Library of Congress Cataloging-in-Publication Data
Harris, Roy J., 1946–
Pulitzer's gold: a century of public service journalism /
Roy J. Harris, Jr.—Revised and updated edition
pages cm
Includes bibliographical references and index.
ISBN 978-0-231-17028-4 (cloth: alk. paper) — ISBN 978-0-231-17029-1
(pbk.: alk. paper) — ISBN 978-0-231-54056-8 (e-book)
1. Journalism—Awards—United States.
2. Pulitzer Prizes—History. I. Title.

PN4798.H37 2016
071'.3079—dc23
2015016644

Columbia University Press books are printed on permanent
and durable acid-free paper.
This book is printed on paper with recycled content.
Printed in the United States of America

c 10 9 8 7 6 5 4 3 2 1
p 10 9 8 7 6 5 4 3 2 1

COVER DESIGN: Archie Ferguson
COVER IMAGE: Used by permission of the Pulitzer Prizes

References to websites (URLs) were accurate at the time of writing.
Neither the author nor Columbia University Press is responsible for URLs
that may have expired or changed since the manuscript was prepared.

To journalists who will mine Pulitzer's gold in the future

and those who have gone before.

And in memory of one in particular: my dad.

CONTENTS

CONTENTS

ACKNOWLEDGMENTS

This new edition of *Pulitzer's Gold* makes me grateful on a whole new level. First, for the readers—journalists, nonjournalists, students, and teachers—who urged me to keep researching these exemplary stories. I especially appreciate how they encouraged me to use the 2016 centennial of the Pulitzer Prizes as a platform for heralding the future of public service journalism while honoring the past. Second, my thanks go to Columbia University Press and editor Philip Leventhal for bringing *Pulitzer's Gold* "home" to the school Joseph Pulitzer chose to administer his prizes.

The original forces behind *Pulitzer's Gold* stayed as strong as ever: my wife, Eileen Carol McIntyre, and my sisters, Ann O'Keefe Brewer and Judy Wolman. My sons Dave and R.J. and the spirit of their mom helped me keep my focus on youthful readers. My stepson, Jesse Laymon, and his wife Vicki promoted that goal too. I lament the passing of so many original supporters, notably John S. Carroll and Bill Thomas of the *Los Angeles Times*, Selwyn Pepper and Wayne Leeman of the *St. Louis Post-Dispatch*, Bob Greene of *Newsday*, and Gerald Boyd, Jim Naughton, and Ben Bradlee. I miss them, but their faith in this work still nurtures me.

The backing of the Poynter Institute—which first came from Jim Naughton and Karen Dunlap—remains my bedrock in the era of Tim Franklin. Bill Blundell, bureau chief extraordinaire from my *Wall Street*

Journal years, returned to help me rinse the manuscript clean of clichés. (Sorry, Bill.) And Bob Woodward's support continued to inspire me for this edition.

At the Pulitzer Prizes, outgoing administrator Sig Gissler; his successor, Mike Pride; and Edward M. "Bud" Kliment all granted me generous access to the archives and made me feel a part of their prestigious Pulitzer club. And, of course, there is no *Pulitzer's Gold* without the many journalists who shared their golden stories with me. I am honored and privileged to be able to continue retelling them.

REINTRODUCTION

Refining *Pulitzer's Gold*

The centennial of the Pulitzer Prizes in 2016 casts a new light on the journalism that is honored with their most coveted award: the gold medal for meritorious public service. Through all the changes that a century has wrought within news organizations—changes both technological and cultural—winners of this one annual Pulitzer Prize have continued to exemplify an eternal force in quality reporting: the drive to dig for the truth and present that truth persuasively to a publication's audience.

With so much uncertain about the future of journalism today, the study of these "stories behind the stories" still has tremendous value. The back stories offer lessons in public service reporting at the highest level and show how society benefits from that reporting. They show how journalists are adjusting their approach to fit new times and new technologies. Plus, as pure newsroom adventures, they make exciting and rewarding reading.

This new edition of *Pulitzer's Gold* adopts a celebratory tone, as befits 100th birthday recognition. Twenty-first-century winners get the most attention while the decades of interplay between the Pulitzers and history become an even stronger theme.

The 2014 Pulitzer Gold Medals certainly represented a case of the media and history intertwined. One prize was awarded to the *Washington Post* and another to the *Guardian-U.S.* website for the public service of analyzing government documents that detailed extreme and hidden levels of administration surveillance of American citizens. Controversy still rages over the *Post* and *Guardian-U.S.* working with stolen material, leaked separately to their news organizations by the former National Security Agency contractor Edward Snowden. The *Post* and *Guardian-U.S.* reporting recalled the prize awarded in 1972 to the *New York Times* for its work analyzing Daniel Ellsberg's stolen, secret Pentagon Papers—in that case recounting the deception of the public by several administrations related to Vietnam policy. That honor to the *Times* long has been considered among the Pulitzers' finest moments.

Among other landmark Public Service Prizes in this century was another to the *Post* in 2008 for graphically exposing shameful conditions for injured war veterans at Walter Reed Army Medical Center. That work still resonates as other Veterans Administration scandals have arisen. Two Gulf Coast newspapers, the *Times-Picayune* of New Orleans and the *Sun Herald* of southern Mississippi, not only survived but thrived by serving their communities during the worst American hurricane season on record: 2005's summer of Katrina. And the *Boston Globe*'s shocking exposure of priests as sexual predators and a cover-up of their crimes by the Catholic hierarchy has continued to ignite Church investigations and reforms since that 2003 Pulitzer was awarded.

Going further back, the most famous gold medal of all is arguably the best known of the Pulitzer Prizes: the *Washington Post*'s 1973 prize honoring the Watergate coverage led by Bob Woodward and Carl Bernstein. But usually the Pulitzer links to history are more obscure, even if their effect was powerful. As early as 1921, the now-defunct *Boston Post* won for exposing Charles Ponzi as a financial charlatan. Its reporting made the "Ponzi scheme" a metaphor for the get-rich-quick mania of the Roaring Twenties while helping coin a popular term for a type of fraud we still know today.

The book's focus on this stellar reporting from the past has won *Pulitzer's Gold* fans among journalism teachers. "Many scholars have argued that aside from the Watergate era and the muckraking period, there was little investigative reporting taking place in the 20th century," wrote Indiana University's Gerry Lanosga in one review of the original edition. "Harris's research reveals that investigative reporting has been a persistent force in American journalism, though he does not remark upon that important finding."[1] So let me remark here: Yes, this century of Pulitzer winning by news organizations proves that public interest journalism—usually by teams of reporters and editors—has powerfully served communities and remains a potent force for good.

A danger that cannot be ignored today, however, is that serious financial pressures within the news business could force American public service reporting to *become* history. When *Pulitzer's Gold* was first published, the *Economist's* 2006 "Who Killed the Newspaper?" cover story was fresh in my mind.[2] Somewhat overstated in its headline—yet still too close for comfort—it talked of "once-great titles" then facing a possible digital death. It quoted a Carnegie Corporation report that asked if the American press was "up to the task of sustaining an informed citizenry on which democracy depends."[3] The *Economist* story was prescient in some ways—calling attention, for one thing, to the fast-growing online presence of the *Guardian* in the United States.

Traditional newspapers, still at the center of the Pulitzer journalism awards, have continued losing readers since then amid steadily worsening finances. And more ownership shifts and many more stumbles in combining online and print operations lie ahead. Yet the examination of recent Pulitzer Public Service Prize winners reveals inspiring successes by reporters and editors—often as they overcome newsroom turmoil with ingenuity, energy, and the efficient use of technology. Those achievements deserve attention too, and they get it here.

After preparing a riveting series that explored how frequently South Carolina women are murdered by men in their lives, Charleston's *Post and Courier* in 2014 broke what was once a cardinal rule of newspaper publishing. It put the entire project on the Internet in advance, making it available to social media before its five parts ran in the daily print version. The *Post and Courier*—whose 2015 gold medal work is discussed in the afterword—thus found a much larger national audience for the serious issue of spousal abuse.

What of the challenges to the Pulitzer organization itself? Such questions range from its role in making the media overly award-conscious[4] to the fairness of its treatment of women journalists.[5] But mainly the prizes must improve their ability to recognize the best American journalism in a fast-changing media world. And that mission still involves encouraging excellence by example, as Joseph Pulitzer intended when he created the prizes in the will he left when he died in 1911. The Pulitzers moved slowly to accept online material, first allowing entries from "digital-only" enterprises in 2009.[6] Only in 2015 was magazine work allowed to enter Pulitzer competition in the investigative and feature writing categories, even though all such journalism competes among the mushrooming number of readers who get their news from computer and cell phone screens.

Sometimes, news organizations have learned business lessons while in the middle of their award-winning work. "Hurricane Katrina was our great digital wakeup call," says the *Times-Picayune* editor Jim Amoss, who led the staff's remarkable coverage after the storm drove the newspaper from its New Orleans headquarters. Without access to presses, it had no choice but to publish online only, something the Pulitzer board noted in awarding the 2006 *Times-Picayune* prize. "Two years ago, when we shifted our focus to digital journalism and reduced home delivery to three days, it was a dramatic change," Amoss said in 2014. "But those days of Katrina had already blown open the window to our future. Whether they're getting their news from the *Times-Picayune* or from our website, NOLA .com, our readers have a voracious appetite." Staffers "know we need to satisfy it, at all times and on all platforms."[7] And the addition in recent years of a second publication in town, the *New Orleans Advocate,* has brought competitive pressure too while giving online and print readers even more resources.

The long-term swing away from print, however fast it moves, is sure to continue based on the economics of print and digital, according to Paul Steiger, the former *Wall Street Journal* managing editor who became the founding editor of the not-for-profit, Web-based investigative powerhouse ProPublica in 2007. Steiger, whose reporters often collaborate with newspapers on projects, says, "In the next recession I would be astonished if many more papers didn't close their print editions. I hope it's not soon."[8]

Of the 103 gold medals awarded through 2015, *Pulitzer's Gold* examines the latest sixteen in detail. Reaching back to the earliest prize in 1918, it then follows a trail of winners up through today. The cases chosen represent their historical era particularly well or spotlight important reporting styles or trends in coverage. Other winners get briefer treatment in the appendix. As much as *Pulitzer's Gold* is about the past, it is designed to serve journalism's future. And that future is its students. In a March 2014

Yale seminar, Bob Woodward got an encouraging result when he had the class study the dramatic *Washington Post* Walter Reed reporting—Pulitzer Gold Medal–winning work that embarrassingly caught the military hospital system unprepared to treat the soldiers coming back from the Iraq and Afghanistan wars. "Students were blown away by the work, and the emotional impact after seven years is undiminished. Some almost cried," he says, adding: "It is one thing to talk abstractly about the importance of living in the scene, spending months and picking hard targets invisible to some. It is another to have this powerful example. These great works of journalism can live on and do not exist just in some dust-covered binder or museum."[9]

This book exists to inspire current and future journalists with just such examples.

Roy J. Harris Jr.
Hingham, Massachusetts
October 2015

(For instructors, students, and book groups, a study guide is available at http://pulitzersgold.com/studyguides.php.)

PART I

Gold for a New Century

CHAPTER I

A MEDAL FOR ALL SEASONS

2013–2014: From Police Speeding to NSA Spying

Put the data you have uncovered to beneficial use.

—ADVICE IN A FORTUNE COOKIE GIVEN TO THE *WASHINGTON POST*'S
BART GELLMAN, OCTOBER 27, 2013

To the investigative reporters Sally Kestin and John Maines, a radar gun seemed a fitting tool for getting the drop on police they suspected of recklessly speeding. An October 2011 video had gone viral on the Internet, showing off-duty Miami officer Fausto Lopez being chased at 120 miles per hour and pulled over at gunpoint by a Florida state trooper. The video—taken from the trooper's dashboard—gave the reporters an idea for a story for their newspaper, the Fort Lauderdale–based *Sun Sentinel*, about cops who drive dangerously fast. "We saw this kind of thing all the time, and we thought it was the tip of the iceberg," says Kestin. "The challenge was proving it."[1]

So at five o'clock in the morning, just before a police shift change, she and Maines stationed themselves on a turnpike overpass, armed with a $120 Bushnell Speedster III radar gun purchased on Amazon.com. A staff videographer filmed the action as Maines beamed the device at onrushing cars below, hoping to catch other off-duty officers in the act. "Bad idea," Maines says now. "With the radar gun you can't really tell which car on a busy highway at rush hour is giving you the reading. And you can't see if it is a cop or not, because all you can see is headlights." Then a morning rainstorm blew in. The videographer had gear to protect his camera and himself. "We did not. So we got wet."

The pair's next effort to document reckless police driving and to precisely measure the excessive speeds turned out to be wildly more successful for them—as well as considerably drier. Getting access to records from the transponders in nearly four thousand police vehicles, they used the data to meticulously calculate speeds at specific times on specific routes, concentrating on nearly 800 cases in which cars reached speeds between 90 and 130 mph. From the spreadsheet they created, interactive charts and maps were drawn up showing cops' speeding patterns along individual stretches of highway. Crafted to be accessed directly by readers online, the material would accompany the series of articles they began envisioning.

Three months later, the three-part *Sun Sentinel* "Above the Law" series vividly illustrated how speeding south Florida cops often terrorized the roadways, sometimes causing death and destruction while rarely getting them cited for their offenses. Because of the stories, 163 officers from nine departments would be disciplined by the end of 2012. And Officer Lopez was fired after it was shown he routinely drove faster than 100 mph while off duty. On April 16, 2013, the coverage won the *Sun Sentinel* the Pulitzer Prize for Public Service, with the Pulitzer board noting how the ingenious measurements had been used "to curtail a deadly hazard": the serious injuries and fatalities that the paper showed had been caused in 320 cop-caused crashes over seven years.

"Big Casino"

The tale of the *Sun Sentinel*'s recovery from its reporters' soggy turnpike misadventure to win America's top journalism honor in 2013 earns the newspaper a place in the proud century-long tradition of the Pulitzer Prize for Public Service.

But so does the strikingly different case of the public service awards in 2014: rare separate honors for the *Washington Post* and for the online *Guardian-U.S.* news site of the British *Guardian* newspaper. In the glare of global media attention—and bitter controversy—articles in both the *Post* and the *Guardian-U.S.* examined the widespread secret surveillance of Americans being conducted by intelligence gatherers at the National Security Agency. Drawing on highly classified documents that the former NSA contractor Edward Snowden had stolen and leaked to reporters, the two publications described the domestic spying that had sprung from antiterrorism laws passed after the September 11, 2001, attacks on New York's World Trade Center and Washington's Pentagon.

The ten decades of Pulitzer Public Service winners represent a truly eclectic body of work, beginning with breakthrough World War I coverage and a 1920 scoop that exposed the Boston confidence man Charles Ponzi and winding in an impressive trail of journalism through American history. From the Roaring Twenties, the Great Depression, and the post-World War II era of social change, the Pulitzer trail runs through a golden age in the 1970s that includes coverage of the Pentagon Papers Vietnam archive and the Watergate break-in. In more recent years gold medal winners have exposed major scandals in the Catholic Church and at Walter Reed Army Medical Center, to name only two. Along the way, Public Service Pulitzers also recognized numerous examples of extraordinary local or regional reporting—like the *Sun Sentinel's*—giving that type of journalism welcome exposure in the national spotlight. Issues explored ranged from civil rights and women's rights to the environment to corporate crime. And for nearly all this public service journalism, newsroom teams of reporters and editors played a huge but often unsung role.

Newspaper pioneer Joseph Pulitzer—the benefactor of the prizes and no stranger to controversy himself—took a broad view of public service both in his publishing career and in the award program he established. As detailed in Pulitzer's will, a "gold medal costing $500" was to be given each year for "the most meritorious and disinterested public service rendered by any American newspaper." First among the three journalism awards he envisioned, the Public Service Prize alone was for a news organization rather than individuals. (The other two awards, first given out in 1917, honored a reporter and an editorial writer, bringing them prize money of $1,000 and $500, respectively.[2])

Today there are fourteen journalism categories covering news and opinion writing, photography, and cartooning. For each, except the Public Service Prize, $10,000 in cash now accompanies the award. Including seven nonjournalism prizes recognizing arts and letters, twenty-one Pulitzers in all are awarded in a typical year, though this varies if more than one prize or no prize is given in a category.[3]

The Pulitzer Prize board picks the winners. Its nineteen members are a diverse assortment of top-ranking print or online journalists, along with academics from around the nation. Board members meet for two days in April in the Columbia Graduate School of Journalism's World Room, named for the long-gone New York newspaper once owned by Joseph Pulitzer. There in the Morningside Heights area of Manhattan the members typically work to choose one of three finalists selected in each category by "nominating juries." The juries are also diverse and often have past Pulitzer winners in their ranks. They meet for three days, a month before the board's session.

While much has changed in the Pulitzer selection system in a hundred years, the Public Service Prize remains relatively the same. It still takes the form of the Joseph Pulitzer Gold Medal, just under three inches in diameter, bearing Benjamin Franklin's profile on one side and a shirtless Franklin-era printer working his press on the reverse. Columbia commissioned the original design from the Massachusetts sculptor Daniel Chester French, later known for his seated Abraham Lincoln statue in the Lincoln Memorial on the National Mall in Washington, DC.[4] Though now gold-plated silver instead of solid gold—and valued at about $2,000—the Pulitzer Medal continues to be awarded each year to one news organization, except in the circumstance of dual winners, as in 2014. The lack of prize money hardly tarnishes the medal's appeal among winning publications.

"That's Big Casino. It's the cream of the cream. It's the one you want to win if you have a choice," was the way it was put by the *Washington Post* executive editor Ben Bradlee Sr., who was associated with arguably the most famous of all journalism Pulitzer Prizes.[5] That was the public service award won by the *Post* in 1973, primarily for Bob Woodward and Carl Bernstein's reporting of events after the break-in at Democratic National Headquarters in the Washington office building known as Watergate.

For any organization, winning the Pulitzer Gold Medal is a historic moment. The 2014 medal was the *Post*'s fifth, tying it with the *New York Times* and the *St. Louis Post-Dispatch*—but one behind the six won by the *Los Angeles Times*. And the online *Guardian-U.S.* became the first Public Service Prize recipient without a print edition, as well as the first to be affiliated with a publication outside the United States. (The British

Guardian newspaper dates back to 1821; it changed its name from the *Manchester Guardian* in 1959.)[6]

Generally, Pulitzer board members pondering public service candidates look for measurable impact in the community, whether in the publication's immediate locale or the nation as a whole. Government action in response to news coverage—a law passed or a wrongdoer charged, for example—carries special weight.

In the language of today's prizes, the Pulitzer medal recognizes winners for meritorious service "through the use of its journalistic resources which, as well as reporting, may include editorials, cartoons, photographs, graphics and online material." And this has focused recently on Internet-based presentation techniques.

Often the award reflects exemplary reporting that comes out of a gripping news event. The medal in 1957 honored Little Rock's *Arkansas Gazette* for bringing sanity to the community chaos at a time of court-ordered school desegregation. The 9/11 terrorist attacks provided the backdrop for the winning *New York Times* coverage, which helped a horrified nation cope. And after Hurricane Katrina's devastation of the Gulf Coast, the *Times-Picayune* of New Orleans and Mississippi's *Sun Herald* each won in 2006 for work that helped hold their battered communities together.

Indeed disaster coverage qualifies as a public service genre all its own. In 1948 the *St. Louis Post-Dispatch* won for an investigation of a fatal coal mine explosion in Centralia, Illinois, that revealed payoffs to state officials and inspection lapses. (The Pulitzer bar is high for catastrophe stories. "You shouldn't automatically win the prize because a plane hits a building in your town," says former Pulitzer board member Michael Gartner. "That's when you're supposed to do a good job.")[7]

In terms of overall subject matter, two of every five medals awarded since the Pulitzers began involve exposing some kind of government wrongdoing on the local, state, or national level. One in five has been for exploring human rights abuses or other social ills. And increasingly the Public Service Prize has acknowledged environmental journalism, which accounts for about one of every ten awards.

The style of prizewinning journalism varies widely. Behind some awards are multipart team writing projects like the *Sun Sentinel*'s. But many other gold medals over the years have recognized a news organization's incremental coverage of events. The *Washington Post*'s Watergate reporting, which Bob Woodward now half-jokingly describes as "boring," is a prime example.[8] It was built on gradual, relatively small-scale discoveries made over months of investigating. Only taken together did the stories expose the clear involvement of Richard Nixon's White House in the crime and its cover-up.

News organizations big and little compete against each other for the gold medal. And board members sometimes seem to display a fondness for small-town entries, perhaps because of the sheer gall it takes for tiny newsrooms to challenge authority. The board also appreciates ingenious reporting methodology. As part of an investigation that won for the *Wall Street Journal* in 2007, a reporting team calculated the infinitesimally low probability that companies were playing by the rules in pricing their executive stock options year after year—revealing how some corporations cheated shareholders and sparking regulatory reforms. The *Sun Sentinel*'s methodology also intrigued the Pulitzer board, just as it had impressed readers.

SunPass and Shoe Leather

Even as she and her partner were being drenched at that turnpike overpass, Sally Kestin was pondering a much better plan for documenting off-duty police speeding. A veteran of thirteen years as a *Sun Sentinel* investigative reporter, she had written a year earlier about lax controls on south Florida cops. But the paper's investigative "I-Team," as an economy measure, had been in what editor Howard Saltz calls "a state of dormancy"—restricted to helping on other stories rather than launching its own projects.[9] (The paper's owner, the Chicago-based Tribune Company, was in the middle of a three-year bankruptcy from which it emerged at the end of 2012.) After his hiring in 2011, Saltz quickly returned the I-Team to full investigative status through a reallocation of duties that did not involve adding staff.

A reader of her earlier police stories suggested to Kestin that electronic transponders, routinely installed in police cars as part of Florida's SunPass toll-collecting program, could yield raw data—precisely down to a hundredth of a second—showing when each passed through a turnpike toll gate. Gaining access to the toll records, Kestin thought, could be a first step to calculating the frequency of police speeding and would allow Kestin and Maines to calculate speeds based on the distance and time from one toll location to the next.

SunPass officials at first declared the raw data proprietary but quickly relented after the paper argued that police department secrecy was not warranted. Kestin and Maines got more than one million records from 3,915 transponders in the vehicles of a dozen police agencies. To calculate speeds, all that was missing were precise distances between tollgates—distances the state could not provide. Rather than use their own imprecise car odometers, the paper sprang for a $150 Garmin Edge device that was accurate to within a few feet. After a month of tracing routes and creating a master Excel spreadsheet, the reporters saw that the numbers pointed to a clear trend of rampant police speeding, with other official data establishing that much of it was on off-duty time.

Early on, Kestin interviewed former police and state troopers who had been sources for previous stories, asking about the cop culture they lived through. Some sources told the reporters they were on the right track, she says. For one thing, "professional courtesy" was often extended to cops even after serious violations. The two of them, working with the investigative editor John Dahlburg, drew up a plan to broaden the work into a three-part series. They knew they had to work quickly because of the continuing statewide interest in Fausto Lopez's arrest video. After the first-day overview, they would look at recent victims of the speeding cops, using their anguish to help humanize what might otherwise be just a numbers story. Part three would examine the police officer speeding culture and how it might be changed. The database specialist Dana Williams researched seven years of accident records, establishing that the number of cop-caused accidents had climbed into the hundreds in recent years. For the second installment—eventually titled "Ruined Lives"—eight dramatic cases were identified, including that of a fourteen-year-old girl killed when a Broward County sheriff's deputy, driving 87 mph on a call to assist with a minor traffic stop, struck a Honda Civic where the girl was a passenger in the back seat.

Part three—headlined "Why? 'Because We Can'"—detailed the negligible penalties for cops caught recklessly driving; only one officer had gone to jail and for only sixty days. Another angle of the story became the special treatment cops got when caught speeding, with only 12 percent being ticketed when crashes resulted from an offense compared to 55 percent in similar cases involving other motorists. "The investigation combined technology and data with old-fashioned shoe-leather reporting," according to Kestin and Maines. "Obtaining the SunPass data was just the first step."

With Dahlburg and Metro editor Dana Banker, in early January they took the plan for the series to associate editor Willie Fernandez, whose duties included carrying out Saltz's plan to restore the paper's investigative function. The human drama behind the speeding cop stories immediately grabbed Fernandez, as did the shock of police malfeasance. "These are the people who we hired to uphold the law, and they were the biggest offenders," he says. "The irony of it is incredible."[10]

When the first story drafts came in, they needed work—mainly to bring out that human element of the damage these accidents caused. Revisions helped, and the work of assembling interactive graphics and videos added to the effect on the reader. Saltz was amazed with the copy he saw. "It's a database that does not lie, and a methodology that is perfect," he says. "We knew right away that we had the potential to open some eyes in the community. In fact, we couldn't wait to publish."

But there was more to do. The police agencies had not been contacted for comment; the I-Team wanted its documentation to be solid first. Now Kestin made the calls and visited Miami police Major Delrish Moss with a four-inch stack of reports documenting speeding cases. As Kestin handed one report to Major Moss, the newspaper videotaped the exchange as he thumbed through it—then caught him as he saw the stack. "Wait," he says with alarm on the recording. "All of these are ours? Wow."[11]

On February 12, a story headlined "For Cops, No Limit" ran along with a sidebar detailing the *Sun Sentinel*'s speeding calculations for the now infamous Officer Lopez. In one year he had averaged speeds of at least 90 miles per hour on 237 days, hitting 100 mph or higher nearly half the time. And coverage of the issue continued even as the instances of improper police speeding plunged 84 percent by year-end, as measured by the paper's own methodology.

FIGURE I.I The front page on the day of the first story of the *Sun Sentinel*'s February 2012 series, "For Cops, No Limit." *Source*: Used by permission of the *Sun Sentinel*, © 2012.

A Pulitzer Dark Horse

After all the year's stories were in, the paper put together its submissions for the 2013 Pulitzer Prizes, entering both the public service and investigative reporting categories while also submitting to other national contests that are judged earlier than the Pulitzers. The series did less than glowingly in those first competitions—earning runner-up status in the American Society of News Editors, Investigative Reporters and Editors, and Scripps Howard Foundation contests.

By February 2013, when the entry reached the Pulitzer jury, it faced serious competition among the sixty-seven public service submissions. But the seven Pulitzer jurors loved it, forwarding the entry to the Pulitzer board as one of the three nominated finalists. Others were a *Washington Post* study of flawed U.S. Justice Department forensics and a project by the online investigative operation California Watch that detailed shocking abuses—including rapes and beatings by staff members—at five California state centers for the disabled. The California Watch reports by Ryan Gabrielson produced significant reforms at the centers. The *Post* forensics stories by Spencer Hsu had led to a review of more than twenty thousand criminal convictions across the country.

One jury member, Peter Bhatia, editor of Portland's the *Oregonian*, notes the "every-person appeal" of the *Sun Sentinel* series. "We all say when we see a speeding cop, What's that about?"[12] And these stories explained it. "When I first saw the entry I was skeptical," says Reuters managing editor Paul Ingrassia, the jury chair. He remembers thinking: "Big deal; a bunch of cops are speeding. So what? Then, I saw the results: the deaths and damage. And it was so innovative, and yet not a project that, from the start, was trying to win a Pulitzer. The reporters didn't overhype it. It was written dispassionately—without any sense of chasing a prize. It's great to get recognition from your peers, but journalism is about the readers."[13]

Pulitzer board deliberations are steeped in secrecy. But the board chairman at the time, Paul Tash, recalls each of the three public service nominees having supporters before the final vote. "All the work was admirable, and the prize could have gone to any one of the three," he says. Why was he personally impressed by the Fort Lauderdale entry? "The elegant construction of the *Sun Sentinel*'s work stood out," says Tash, who is chief

FIGURE I.2 The *Sun Sentinel* reporters John Maines (left) and Sally Kestin (arms raised) celebrate the Pulitzer announcement with the staff. *Source*: Used by permission of the *Sun Sentinel.*

executive of both the *Tampa Bay Tribune* and the Poynter Institute journalism training center. "They started with anecdotal reports of crashes, and they found a way to test it using technology."[14] Such qualities may have helped the police speeding story get the majority vote that the Pulitzer board requires for an entry to win.

In the newsroom, winning the *Sun Sentinel*'s first Pulitzer felt especially sweet. For one thing, the Pulitzer announcement had been something of a surprise because "Above the Law" had been largely off the radar of the earlier journalism awards. More important, says Saltz, "It demonstrated to the staff that we were back. For years it was like we had dropped off the face of the earth, and staffers lost confidence in themselves." Giving newsroom morale a boost is one reason he had reinstituted the I-Team. The speeding cops story had been its first new project. Saltz especially likes how the gold medal goes to an entire news organization rather than just the reporters whose names are on the stories. An extra morale boost came from spreading credit to everyone.

So what was his contribution as head of the newsroom? "My genius was to say 'Okay,'" he says laughingly. The project had filtered up to him from the investigative team through a chain of other editors before he first saw it. "Actually, I challenged the math. I know that journalists are notoriously bad at math," adds Saltz. "It withstood every challenge that I threw at it."

2013—The *Sun Sentinel*, Fort Lauderdale, Fla., for its well documented investigation of off-duty police officers who recklessly speed and endanger the lives of citizens, leading to disciplinary action and other steps to curtail a deadly hazard.[15]

Sharing Secrets

If the *Sun Sentinel* was a dark horse for the 2013 Public Service Pulitzer, the *Guardian-U.S.* website and the *Washington Post* became front-runners for 2014 almost as soon as their first blockbuster stories started appearing. "I thought it was a slam-dunk because in many ways this was the biggest story of the year, and clearly a huge public service," says Paul Steiger, a former Pulitzer board member, veteran *Wall Street Journal* managing editor, and founding editor of the investigative website ProPublica. "And these two news organizations had done the major work, with considerable reporting to back up the documents they had been given."[16]

But in the newsrooms of both the *Post* and the *Guardian-U.S.*, nothing was automatic in the weeks leading up to their first stories—appearing within a day of each other on June 5 and 6, 2013. In a competitive flurry, reporters and editors rushed to assemble and confirm their drafts, based on the extraordinarily detailed and complex files that Edward Snowden, a former NSA contractor, had provided.[17]

Both publications were aware that what they left *out* of their stories—because its publication might truly threaten national security or put lives at risk—was perhaps more critical than what they published. (In the final days before the first stories ran, each news organization gave the government a chance to argue that publication of certain information was too sensitive—much as the *New York Times* had done forty-two years earlier in preparing its Vietnam-era revelations about the Pentagon Papers for publication.) One element in the *Guardian–Post* competition was perhaps unique to Pulitzer-winning journalism: the rival news organizations both had the same journalist, the documentary filmmaker Laura Poitras, on their teams. That stemmed from Poitras in January 2013 being the first media person with whom Snowden made contact, communicating through a strict encryption procedure and hiding his identity at that point. "How this story unfolded," Poitras acknowledges, "does not fit into a neat newsroom story."[18]

Snowden, who in late 2012 had failed to link up with his first choice of media contacts, the *Guardian-U.S.* opinion columnist Glenn Greenwald, viewed both Poitras and Greenwald as potential recipients of his stolen government material. From their past work he knew they were sympathetic with his outrage over extreme levels of government spying on Americans. Conveniently the two journalists knew each other through their common board membership in a press freedom foundation. Snowden also considered them outside the mainstream media, which he distrusted in part because he believed such organizations too cautious—delaying, neutering, or killing sensitive stories after vetting them with those being challenged. While there was one story from his trove of documents that Snowden wanted to go public right away—about a secret NSA program called PRISM—he generally planned to give his entire file to chosen reporters and let them and their editors decide what to publish and what to hold back. "In one of Snowden's early emails he told me that the evidence he would provide would be too much for one journalist," Poitras says, and she started thinking of possible collaborators, with Greenwald at the top of her list.

Her own encryption skills—which she developed when U.S. authorities started routinely monitoring her gear and her notebooks when she traveled—made Poitras especially useful in Snowden's plan. "Ironically, being targeted by the U.S. government for my reporting was the best training to prepare me for working on the NSA story and communicating with Snowden," she says from her home in Berlin. "By the time Snowden reached out I had been through seven years of security training."

The anonymity of her source raised worries about whether he was legitimate, even as he described the huge archive of secret documents that exposed widespread U.S. spying on Americans. So in February she met in New York with Barton Gellman—a former *Post* reporter then working at a foundation—seeking advice on how to confirm that the documents were real and piquing his interest about the mystery source.[19]

Scarier Than Iraq

Poitras was aware of the historic debate dating back to the Pentagon Papers about how the media should deal with secret documents. "I knew very well the risks that whistleblowers take and the government's intimidation to stop publishers from working on national security issues." But other worries were personal, she says. "The six months from January to June 2013 were the most frightening and stressful of my life. It was much more scary than the eight months I spent in Iraq [making a 2006 documentary]. I knew that if the sources were legitimate, they were at great risk, and so was I."

For the *Guardian-U.S.* and the *Post*, another kind of angst began in May. Poitras and Greenwald stayed in regular contact. But when Snowden told Poitras that he thought it time for one particular NSA story to be published, she also reached out to Gellman. The story related to a program code-named PRISM, which allowed the agency to tap directly into the databases of nine U.S. Internet companies: Microsoft, Google, Facebook, AOL, Apple, Yahoo!, Skype, YouTube, and Paltalk. The race was on to be first with an NSA story.

At the *Guardian-U.S.*, a website that had grown to sixty journalists since opening in 2011, Greenwald had been hired as a columnist by editor in chief Janine Gibson, who was looking for impact writers to bring it visibility. A former constitutional lawyer who was already popular online, writing from his home in Rio de Janeiro, "Glenn was such a powerful presence on the Internet I was worried he would overshadow the *Guardian* brand," says Gibson. "But soon, it was very clear he was a fantastic fit. Working with him was challenging, but brilliantly so."[20] The arrangement called for Greenwald to post his own *Guardian* columns unedited, but anything that could have legal consequences "or posed an unusual journalistic quandary" would be processed by editors.[21]

Gibson had not expected Greenwald to be a reporter, but his conversion began when Greenwald "rang me up one day and said I have this huge story; it's the biggest intelligence leak ever," according to Gibson. "And I said get on a plane." Greenwald, who at the time held about twenty-five of the secret NSA files, arrived with Poitras in Gibson's offices on May 31.[22] Gibson knew that Bart Gellman had reconnected with the *Washington Post* and was also interested in the NSA files. But the *Guardian* editor remembers getting the feeling that Poitras "was suspicious of whether the *Washington Post* would ever publish." Gibson says, "I felt she was suspicious of me, too. But Glenn has a relationship with Laura, and I have a relationship with Glenn. So it worked out." The editor adds, "The thing about the *Guardian* is we don't get too hung up on the way things are supposed to be. Our approach is embracing the new." In this case that "new" involved making New York–based *Guardian* veteran Ewen MacAskill a third member of the Greenwald-Poitras team. MacAskill would accompany them to Hong Kong, where Poitras and Greenwald had made plans to meet with Snowden.

"A story of this kind can be quite capsizing for an organization," says Gibson. So the *Guardian* took care to make sure everything it published on the NSA documents would be solid. Concerns about objectivity "were why we put in Ewen in the first place, and why all our stories were written and constructed by a team of editors here," she says. "We questioned every single word, making sure we didn't overreach, and justifying every single claim where a legal case could be made." Greenwald may have had free rein with his columns, "but when somebody writes a news story, that goes through the Guardian process. It's the work of many, many people." Looking back she adds, "Most of the stories had several bylines, and even when it's Glenn alone, it's gone through many levels of process."

The *Guardian* began preparing two stories based on NSA documents: first a story that Greenwald singled out as particularly shocking, on the government collecting the phone records of millions of citizens from Verizon under secret court order. The second story was about PRISM—the piece Snowden had wanted out first. While the *Guardian-U.S.* team traveled to Hong Kong, Gibson would help manage getting comment from the administration and doing the final editing.

Not a Good Time to Be Freelance

After contact between Gellman and Laura Poitras had been renewed in May 2013, a period of three-way trust building began among the two of them and the still anonymous Edward Snowden. "Laura and I had to worry about whether we were being set up," says Gellman. "Snowden saw me as the corporate newsroom guy, and worried that the story would be too hot for a card-carrying member of the mainstream media."

Gellman had practical concerns about handling secret documents like the PRISM files he had received. His decision to reconnect with the *Post* alleviated that problem by providing him with legal protection and the backing of a news organization he respected. Poitras agreed to participate with him. And Gellman won Snowden over to the idea by explaining how boldly the paper had published previous stories on government surveillance. "I told him I'd take the story elsewhere if the *Post* and I could not agree on what should be done. I meant that," says Gellman.

"It was clear I didn't want to be Bart Gellman, freelance reporter, with a story like this." Even the process of verifying classified documents could create legal liability for an individual journalist while company lawyers could more easily deflect such concerns. "I'd made my home at the *Washington Post* for many years," he says, "and I trusted the leadership there." The former leadership anyway; Gellman had never met the *Post*'s new executive editor, Martin Baron, hired from the *Boston Globe* a few months earlier. So the reporter placed a call to the *Post* assistant managing editor for investigations, Jeff Leen. Leen had worked with Gellman on stories about Vice President Dick Cheney that had won Gellman and Jo Becker the 2008 National Reporting Pulitzer.[23]

Gellman's call to Leen came on a Sunday, May 19. "So I was completely not in work mode," Leen recalls. "I was surprised to hear from him, and frankly a little annoyed. He was very secretive and cryptic." Then came the conditions Gellman said the *Post* would have to accept. "It's going to have to go in the paper in forty-eight or seventy-two hours—that kind of thing. My mind was reeling a bit at all the demands." But he knew Gellman. "It's like E. F. Hutton: You listen," Leen says. "Also, there was a faint note of fear in his voice. And that scared *me* a little bit." Leen suspected that NSA documents were involved.[24]

Several meetings were quickly planned with *Post* editors, including one with Baron, just coming back from vacation. It was arranged for Gellman to enter the *Post* building unseen to avoid office speculation. "The first stop I made was with Don Graham," says Gellman. "I knew this was going to be a very tricky story, with high stakes for the paper." The reporter assured himself that the Graham family, which still controlled the *Post* at the time, would support a project the editors approved.[25]

At the first meeting with Baron, Gellman made his pitch to a small group of editors and lawyers. Gellman described "*a* document and *a* story, and I said it was possible that there would come a time when there would be more." But there would be many more questions, he knew, beyond "How many stories are there?" Gellman was asking an editor he had never met to approve a story from a source whose name could not be revealed. The *Post* would have to grant legal protection to Gellman and to Poitras, whose byline might also be appearing in a rival publication competing for the story. Plus a new security and encryption system was needed in a locked room used for nothing else. "I felt like I was making preposterous demands," says Gellman, "and I was thinking, '*I'd* probably throw me out.'"

But Baron was riveted. "My initial reaction was that I was surprised that the U.S. government was doing this," he says of the PRISM material. "It was a sensitive subject, in that it involved national security matters. It was also highly consequential, in that it could have legal consequences for us, and it raised significant public policy issues." And, says Baron, who is often given to understatement, "I'm always glad when somebody's coming to us with a story that might be good."

As for approving a joint Gellman-Poitras byline, "It was unusual, but this was an unusual story, in unusual times," Baron says. So he signed off on it. "Bart felt she deserved a byline as a result of the access she provided. I didn't see any particular reason we shouldn't include Poitras on the byline. And it was the right thing to do."[26] At a subsequent meeting, Poitras got her first experience of Baron, Jeff Leen, and other *Post* newsroom players. "I remember Marty joked that he wanted to meet me, before risking the institution," says Poitras, who felt acknowledged for bringing it the PRISM story.

As the editor Jeff Leen and Gellman began preparing the *Post*'s PRISM story, Leen had the strange sense that he and Gellman "were just picking

FIGURE 1.3 The *Guardian-U.S.* website breaks its first story based on Edward Snowden's stolen, secret NSA files. *Source*: Used by permission of the *Guardian-U.S.*

FIGURE 1.4 The *Guardian-U.S.* team of Ewen MacAskill (left), Glenn Greenwald, and Laura Poitras traveled to Hong Kong in early June 2013 to meet source Edward Snowden. *Source*: Used by permission of Laura Poitras.

up where we left off after the Cheney series." With two differences: first, only a handful of staffers knew Gellman was even in the building. Second, "I knew this could be the biggest story I've ever seen. And it turned out to be. These documents were really the crown jewels of American intelligence gathering," Leen says. "We also knew that this was an issue that was ripe for public debate." A number of legislators had been calling for months for more transparency on domestic surveillance. "And it was about a system that has grown so big that a contractor like Snowden is in a position to get this information."

But as the PRISM story entered its final editing stage, the *Guardian*'s June 5 Verizon story appeared.[27] "We realized, Now we're in a race to get our story out," says Leen, who knew a *Guardian* PRISM story could appear online any time and beat the *Post*. Shifting to high gear, the *Post* brought Gellman into the main newsroom to work with Leen in his office. For the first time, staffers knew their old colleague was back. "This was investigative reporting on deadline on a very complicated subject," says Leen. At the same time, the *Post* sought comment from the government for inclusion in the story while Baron reviewed drafts from his own office. The *Post*'s PRISM story beat the *Guardian*'s by a matter of minutes.

"Transcending Newspaper Rivalry"

June 5 and June 6 were just the start of a months-long effort by both publications to break down the Snowden archive of NSA documents into segments that would align with the *Guardian*'s and the *Post*'s reporting priorities.

After the *Guardian-U.S.* ran its own PRISM story by Greenwald and MacAskill, it moved on to a June 9 profile of the twenty-nine-year-old Snowden, running this along with an interview that Poitras filmed in Hong Kong.[28] Snowden was no longer anonymous. This was followed on June 17 by a Snowden question-and-answer session on the website theguardian .com.[29] One jewel of its coverage was its "NSA Files Decoded" feature, a video discussion that made surveillance a personal issue for readers.[30] (Poitras, meanwhile, compiled her footage from the *Guardian*–Snowden interviews for use in a film to be called *Citizenfour*, after the code name he had used in reaching out to the filmmaker. In February 2015, *Citizenfour* would win the Academy Award for Best Documentary.[31])

The *Post* published a Gellman profile of Snowden on June 10. Gellman's first in-person Snowden interview would not appear until that December 24, when the reporter visited him in Moscow, where Snowden had relocated after leaving Hong Kong in June.

Among the major exclusives the *Post* reported from the NSA files was an August 30 exploration of the fiscal 2013, $52.6 billion "black budget" for U.S. spy agencies, which the article said had "built an intelligence-gathering colossus since the attacks of Sept. 11, 2001." Still, according to the *Post* they "remain unable to provide critical information to the president on a range of national security threats."[32] The article by Gellman and the staffer Greg Miller was accompanied by an elaborate Web-based breakdown allowing readers to delve into certain expenditures of the Central Intelligence Agency, the National Reconnaissance Office, and the NSA.[33]

In a lighter vein, Gellman was dining with his family at a Chinese restaurant not long after that when his partner handed him a fortune cookie

FIGURE 1.5 The fortune from a cookie opened at Bart Gellman's table during an October 2013 family Chinese dinner in New York. His partner Dafna Linzer handed it to Gellman, saying, "I think I got your cookie." *Source*: Used by permission of Barton Gellman.

saying she had gotten his fortune by mistake. "Put the data you have uncovered to beneficial use," it read.

"In terms of working with the *Guardian* and the *Washington Post*, I think both organizations have done extraordinary reporting," says Laura Poitras of her peculiar relationship with competing publications on a critical story. "On a personal level, it has not been easy. I am an independent journalist without an organization behind me. I published with the *Guardian* and the *Post* on a freelance basis. Neither organization offered institutional support for things like legal fees, travel costs, and computer security. At the moments of highest risk, I was very much on my own."

As the seven public service jurors assembled at Columbia's Graduate School of Journalism in March 2014 to consider the sixty-nine entries in the category, they were well aware of what the *Guardian* and the *Post* had written over the past eight months. But according to the *Buffalo News* editor Michael Connelly, the jury chair, careful reading was given to all submissions. "What you worry about is overlooking something of merit because it didn't get national attention," he says.[34] The Pulitzer board asks jurors for three nominated finalists, and the jury picked *Newsday* as one for the Melville, New York-based daily's use of digital tools and in-depth reporting to expose shootings, beatings, and other misconduct by some Long Island police. The Pulitzer board had already ruled that the *Guardian-U.S.* qualified to enter for the prizes despite its parent newspaper being in the United Kingdom. Though the awards are for American media, its U.S.-based newsroom and separate online *Guardian-U.S.* site made it eligible.

In Connelly's view, the power of the *Guardian* and the *Post* stories had already created "a shared sense that this was a big deal, a big year. It was exciting," he says. "You knew whatever you did you were doing something important." After reviewing all entries, the jurors listed both the *Guardian* and the *Post* along with *Newsday*, leaving it to the Pulitzer board to decide whether to give two public service prizes or one. The jury addressed each of the *Post* and the *Guardian* entries in a four-paragraph note. (*Newsday* got one paragraph.) The first three identical paragraphs said the stories were "published nearly simultaneously" as part of "an unprecedented moment in journalism." The final paragraph differentiated the *Guardian*'s and the *Post*'s NSA coverage in language that the board would echo in naming the two publications the gold medal winners. In the jury nominations, only Bart Gellman was mentioned by name.[35]

Janine Gibson sees wisdom in the Pulitzer board's decision to honor both her publication and the *Post*. "It's really one of those stories that transcends newspaper rivalry. It's been quite a solidarity thing," she says. And in a way, she notes, "the role of the press had become almost as big a deal as the role of the surveillance."

The Pulitzer choice was nearly as controversial as the stories themselves. Beyond those who simply viewed the *Post* and the *Guardian-U.S.* as traitorous for working with Snowden's stolen documents, some critics took issue with the specific decisions made at the *Post* and the *Guardian* about which files to make public and which to hold back. The *Vanity*

Fair columnist Michael Kinsley wrote in his *New York Times* review of Greenwald's book *No Place to Hide*: "It seems clear, at least to me, that the private companies that own newspapers, and their employees, should not have the final say over the release of government secrets, and a free pass to make them public with no legal consequences."[36] His review also stirred a storm of debate.

The media authority Jay Rosen of New York University pointed to what he sees as a weakness in the Pulitzer system exposed by the process of selecting these winners. Designed to recognize American news organizations or individual journalists, the prizes had no way to acknowledge Snowden's role and especially his choice of the journalists who would receive the NSA files. "In my view," wrote Rosen, "that decision—through collaboration [to] release stories in the press vehicle 'closest to those individuals whose privacy has been invaded'—won the Pulitzer today."[37]

The Pulitzer board's selection of the *Post* and the *Guardian* focused on the public service involved in preparing important material in a way that had value for readers. In that way, it was quite similar to the board's decision in 1972 to honor the *New York Times* with a gold medal—not for dumping the stolen government Vietnam War archive on the public but for meticulously analyzing the government deceptions within those so-called Pentagon Papers. Thus the board had "already crossed that bridge about being willing to give the prize based on stolen documents," former Pulitzer board member Geneva Overholser told PBS *Newshour*'s Gwen Ifill in commenting on the two 2014 gold medals. "It was awarded to the most affecting story of this year, in my view. This story had enormous impact. . . . The president himself has said there need to be steps taken in terms of kind of reining in the National Security Agency."[38] And even beyond the review ordered by the White House, as Bart Gellman sees it, the U.S. government at all levels "acknowledged that too much had been kept secret and a debate on the boundaries of surveillance was overdue." A federal appeals court ruled the collection of telephone call records unlawful. And indeed, in the wake of the NSA disclosures "privacy became a market force for the first time since Internet revolution."[39]

In choosing its public service winners, the 2014 Pulitzer board specifically recognized the *Post* for "authoritative and insightful reports that helped the public understand" and the *Guardian* for "helping through

FIGURE I.6 Bart Gellman (center) is congratulated by the *Washington Post* executive editor Martin Baron in an office celebration on the day of the 2014 Pulitzer Prize announcement. *Source*: Published by permission of the *Washington Post*.

aggressive reporting to spark a debate." It is possible, then, that the work of the *Post* on the Snowden story eased the way for the Pulitzers to honor the *Guardian* with a prize that it otherwise might not have gotten. Janine Gibson believes part of her publication's Pulitzer acknowledgment came because "the *Guardian* as an institution took an enormous amount of risk." She adds, "I hope it gives other institutions confidence and succor."

As for the *Post*, Marty Baron was reminded of the Catholic priest stories that won the same prize eleven years earlier for the *Boston Globe* when he was editor there. In giving the May 2014 commencement speech at his alma mater, Lehigh University, he said that in Boston, "one of the world's most powerful institutions was held accountable." Meanwhile, "There is nothing more powerful in our society than the federal government. . . . Do American citizens get to determine how much privacy they're entitled to? Or does government decide all that for us—in secret—as long as it can assert national security as its rationale?"[40]

2014—The *Washington Post* for its revelation of widespread secret surveillance by the National Security Agency, marked by authoritative and insightful reports that helped the public understand how the disclosures fit into the larger framework of national security.

and

2014—The *Guardian-U.S.* for its revelation of widespread secret surveillance by the National Security Agency, helping through aggressive reporting to spark a debate about the relationship between the government and the public over issues of security and privacy.[41]

CHAPTER 2

THE MOST PRIZED PULITZER

The "Germ of an Idea" Takes Root

> I think I am safe in saying that the members of the Board . . . consider
> the gold medal for public service as easily the most important prize of the
> year. I feel certain that they share my belief that my father so regarded it.
> Journalistic public service was my father's passion.
>
> —JOSEPH PULITZER II, PULITZER BOARD CHAIRMAN, 1940–1955

For those who follow the journalism Pulitzer Prizes each year, mention
of the Public Service Gold Medal probably conjures such famous work as
the *New York Times*'s Pentagon Papers coverage and the *Washington Post*'s
Watergate reporting, honored in 1972 and 1973, respectively. In a way,
those two reporting efforts rise like twin peaks above the majestic range
of great stories whose news organizations have been honored through the
twentieth century. At the beginning of a new century, exactly thirty years
later, two more summits stand out: the *Times*'s response to the terrorist
attacks of September 11, 2001, and the *Boston Globe*'s remarkable revelations about the sexual abuse of young parishioners by Catholic priests.
Taken together over the one hundred years of prizes, though, the entire
succession of gold medals has dramatized—and often seemed to predict
uncannily—the course of national events. Indeed, the famous 1960s-era
definition of the American newspaper as "a first rough draft of history"—
usually attributed to the late *Post* publisher Philip Graham[1]—could just as
well describe the work honored with the Public Service Prize.

The first gold medal honored the *New York Times* for its coverage of
World War I, marking America's turn from isolationism. Three years later,
one recognized a newspaper's exposé of scam artist Charles Ponzi that fore-
cast, in a way, the nation's economic malaise of the 1920s. As the Great
Depression began, Pulitzer Prize–winning publications unearthed cases of

municipal corruption and other crimes and called attention to the heroic efforts of farmers to counter the Dust Bowl's effects. In a campaign by the *St. Louis Post-Dispatch* to clean its hometown's air—the public service winner in 1941—one sees early signs of the environmental movement that would eventually sweep the country. The old *Chicago Daily News* won in 1963 for reports on birth control services, an early look at one of a number of social issues getting attention from the press. And with the Pentagon Papers and Watergate disclosures, of course, a new era of public skepticism about government arrived. Perhaps scandals described in more recent gold medal stories—the Catholic priest exposé (2003), mismanagement of the Walter Reed Army Medical Center (2008), and rampant government spying on Americans (2014)—will be seen one day as predictors of another age of reforms stemming from public attention brought by the media.

Often the Pulitzer board's selection recognizes a news organization's courage in blowing the whistle on those with the power to harm the messenger. The 1927 prize acknowledged Ohio's *Canton Daily News*, whose editor Don R. Mellett was murdered for his criticism of local politicians too close to a criminal gang. In 1953, the board chose the *Whiteville News Reporter* and *Tabor City Tribune*, two North Carolina weeklies that took both fiscal and physical risks by exposing a local revival of the Ku Klux Klan. A case in 1978 involved a small California weekly, Marin County's *Point Reyes Light*, which took on the locally based Synanon cult. The paper intensified its fight after a lawyer who opposed Synanon was bitten by a rattlesnake that group members had stuffed in his mailbox.

Of course, the year's gold medal winner hasn't always glittered so brightly, especially in the early years when the Pulitzer Prize was struggling to establish an identity. The 1919 Public Service Prize to the *Milwaukee Journal* hailed the paper's opposition to "German-ism" during World War I when the *Journal* argued for schools to stop teaching the German language, for example. Some other early public service honorees basically submitted a range of their best stories without a central theme. (Newspapers also slowly learned what qualities it took to produce a gold medal winner. In 1929, the *Cleveland News* submitted the work it had done to simplify its headline styles. It lost.)

Ask winners about the value of awards like the Pulitzers and they will toss in a few caveats. "We don't write for prizes," says *New York Times* publisher Arthur O. Sulzberger Jr., whose newspaper has nonetheless won five gold medals between 1918 and 2004. "We are delighted to win them but our journalism is aimed at enhancing society, not winning prizes,"[2] he reiterates.

The cult of self-congratulation that some see in the proliferation of press awards, and to some extent the Pulitzers, certainly has its critics. Among those who find flaws in the Pulitzer process itself, few had sterner reservations than Ben Bradlee, who became a celebrity after the *Washington Post*'s Watergate Pulitzer and the *All the President's Men* phenomenon. In a 1995 autobiography the then-seventy-five-year-old editor declared that "as a standard of excellence the Pulitzer Prizes are overrated and suspect." The opinion, he said, is based on observations from his service on the Pulitzer board from 1969 to 1980: "It is this board, political and establishmentarian, that clouds the prizes. Mind you, it's better to win them than lose them, but only because reporters and publishers love them. In my experience, the best entries don't win prizes more than half the time."[3] In later years, though, he found the gold medal to be relatively pure. "The Public Service Prize is what it says it is," Bradlee claimed. "The Public Service gene is very strong in all good journalists."[4]

The McClatchy Company has long prided itself on having that genetic structure. Before its 2006 purchase of Knight Ridder, McClatchy boasted of having five Public Service Prizes, and the Knight Ridder acquisition added significantly to its stable of papers with Pulitzer-winning traditions. "The Pulitzer Prize, particularly the Public Service Prize, resonates in terms of recruiting talent," says Gary Pruitt, who at the time was McClatchy's chief executive officer. "Those things don't happen by accident; they're a reflection of commitment of resources on a sustained basis."[5]

A Statesman for the Press

The wide appeal of the prizes would have pleased Joseph Pulitzer, who had what he called "the germ of an idea" in August 1902 for a system of awards to honor the best of both American journalism and arts and letters. At Chatwold, his secluded summer retreat on Maine's Mount Desert Isle, he dictated his thoughts: "My idea is to recognize that journalism is, or ought to be, one of the great and intellectual professions; to encourage, elevate,

FIGURE 2.1 The Chatwold estate near Bar Harbor, Maine, with its "tower of silence," right. At Chatwold, Joseph Pulitzer developed the idea for the Pulitzer Prizes. *Source*: Used by permission, *St. Louis Post-Dispatch*.

and educate in a practical way the present and, still more, future members of that profession, exactly as if it were the profession of law or medicine."[6]

Two years later, he inserted a $500,000 bequest to Columbia University for the prizes into his will. It was part of a $2 million overall gift that also endowed a journalism school at Columbia. In 1912, the year after Pulitzer died at age sixty-four aboard his yacht *Liberty* in Charleston Harbor, the university got the journalism school running. That established the framework, under the terms of the will, for a system to consider entries from 1916 for the new Pulitzer Prizes. The first prizes were awarded at Columbia's commencement in June the next year.

The Pulitzer Prizes in journalism were a revolutionary notion. Not that the thought of a major awards program was so unusual. Sweden's first Nobel Prizes had been awarded in 1901, just before Joseph Pulitzer dreamed up his own system of awards. The Nobels were globally celebrated as a way of honoring scientific and literary achievements and of furthering the cause of peace. And in 1896, the modern Olympic organization had resurrected the ancient Greek Games, bestowing gold, silver, and bronze medals on the world's sports heroes. (Indeed, preparations were heating up for the 1904 Olympics in Pulitzer's old hometown of St. Louis, where the Hungarian immigrant had settled in 1865.)

What was outlandish about the Pulitzer Prizes was the thought of prais-ing *journalism* at the turn of the century. Newspaper work was a suspect occupation at best as practiced by most of the publications of the day. That had certainly been true at Pulitzer's own *New York World* as recently as the late 1890s, when it was the epicenter of that shameful period of press his-tory known as yellow journalism. That term for rampant sensationalism, in fact, had gotten its name from one of Pulitzer's many *World* innova-tions, the first comic strip, known as "The Yellow Kid."

Joseph Pulitzer's career had started brilliantly. In 1878 he had merged two small papers into the *St. Louis Post-Dispatch*, which was a hugely suc-cessful operation when he left its day-to-day management five years later and moved to New York to take over the *World*. At both papers he pro-moted investigative reporting and campaigns against government corrup-tion, part of a broad strategy designed to appeal to the masses of average readers. The approach produced handsome profits and Pulitzer's ability to spur prolific readership gains by combining hard-hitting journalism and public promotions became a model for other publishers.[7]

One such Pulitzer promotion made the *World* the leader in raising money for a pedestal on Bedloe's Island in New York Harbor, without which France's gift of a dramatic "Statue of Liberty" would have remained only a dream. Its erection had been unpopular among wealthy New York-ers, but the *World* taunted the rich for their unwillingness to finance the construction and promised to publish the name of every contributor, no matter how small. Circulation soared as a result.

Then came a darker period for Pulitzer and journalism. When an all-out war for New Yorkers' pennies broke out among newspaper publishers, Pulitzer reacted desperately in an effort to keep his circulation high. Com-peting with William Randolph Hearst at the *New York Journal*, among others, Pulitzer's *World* carried absurdities and exaggerations in the news pages. It was a nasty, no-holds-barred conflict as well, particularly when Charles A. Dana of the *Sun* turned on Pulitzer personally and labeled him "Jewseph Pulitzer" and "Judas Pulitzer [who has] denied his race and reli-gion." (It was a thinly veiled attempt by Dana to turn both anti-Semitic readers and Jewish readers against the *World*.) The proliferation of sensational news accompanied chauvinism of the worst kind, winning the *World*, the *Journal*, and other papers a place in journalism infamy for having helped foment the Spanish-American War.

Pulitzer was pained by the descent of his papers even though he clearly had allowed it by sacrificing his principles to hold onto circulation. After the war he quickly restored sanity in the newsrooms. But he was tortured in other ways. His health, never very good, deteriorated seriously. He became nearly blind and extremely sensitive to noise and suffered from debilitating nervousness and depression.

FIGURE 2.2 Joseph Pulitzer I, nearly blind, strolls along Fifth Avenue with oldest son Ralph of the *New York World*. *Source*: Used by permission, *St. Louis Post-Dispatch*.

He had also become an absentee publisher, controlling from afar the activities in the twenty-story, gold-domed *World* building with which he had graced lower Manhattan. (As the 1880s ended, it was the tallest skyscraper in the city, eclipsing Dana's humble *Sun* offices across the street.) Pulitzer began spending nearly all his time at Chatwold—equipped with a stone "tower of silence" where he could concentrate deeply—and his other homes in the United States and Europe, and eventually aboard *Liberty*.

He became a statesman for the press, championing the newspaper's role in preserving democracy by giving readers all the facts. In an article for the *North American Review*, composed the same year as his will, Pulitzer wrote:

> Our Republic and its press will rise or fall together. An able, disinterested, public-spirited press, with trained intelligence to know the right and the courage to do it, can preserve the public virtue without which popular government is a sham and a mockery. A cynical, mercenary, demagogic press will produce in time a people as base as itself.[8]

In those later years, he made sure his own papers—the *Post-Dispatch* and the *World*—followed that creed. The "platform" he wrote when he stepped down from the editor job in St. Louis proclaimed that the paper should "always fight for progress and reform" and "always oppose privileged classes and public plunderers."

Another Pulitzer comment presaged, in a way, what the *Washington Post* was to do almost sixty-five years later in winning its 1973 gold medal. A 1909 letter he wrote to the *World* editorial page editor Frank Cobb expressed Pulitzer's thoughts on Theodore Roosevelt's support of the Panamanian revolution, which preceded the completion of the Panama Canal by American industry. The *World* had argued that $40 million in improper payments were made along the way: "If this is to be a government of the people, for the people, by the people, it is a crime to put into the hands of the President such powers as no Monarch, no King, or Emperor has ever possessed. He has too much power already. . . . I would rather have corruption than the power of one man."[9]

Nobels and Pulitzers

A near recluse as his maladies intensified and he entered his mid-fifties, Pulitzer contemplated his mortality. He began envisioning a personal legacy—one that would recognize his lifelong devotion to newspapers and the role he believed they should play in democratic society. The spirit of philanthropy was in the air, stirred by vast gifts to benefit the public good from industrialists like Andrew Carnegie, who was very public about the need for the rich to give back to society. But Swedish munitions mogul Alfred Nobel may have seemed a better model to Pulitzer, providing both inspiration and a model for his benefaction.[10]

Some historians have suggested that Pulitzer and Nobel indeed shared a hidden motivation for their desire to take on worthy causes. According to this view, the Nobel Prizes designed by the inventor of dynamite and the blasting cap were sparked by a macabre happenstance in 1888. That year, some French newspapers mistakenly reported Nobel's demise after they confused him with his brother Ludvig. "Le Marchand de la Mort Est Mort," one paper proclaimed: "The Merchant of Death Is Dead." Seeing how he was fated to be remembered, these accounts suggest, a horrified Nobel changed his life overnight—much in the manner of Dickens's Ebenezer Scrooge on that ghostly Christmas Eve. Eventually, by devoting part of his fortune to the commemoration of great world achievements, he saved his reputation for posterity.[11] Whether Pulitzer acted out of a need for redemption for earlier career sins is likewise open to speculation. But he also designed his prizes to be established after his death and made them part of a grand benefaction, in combination with a bequest he envisioned as creating the first university-based school of journalism. (As it turned out, the University of Missouri's journalism school opened in 1908, giving it that distinction by four years.)

Columbia had been Pulitzer's first choice as a home for the journalism school and the awards, largely because of his love of New York and its place as the center of the publishing universe. (He had briefly considered Harvard, until that school responded coolly to the idea.) Pulitzer's will dictated that the awards in journalism and letters would exist "for the encouragement of public service, public morals, American literature, and the advancement of education." In his negotiations with Columbia president

Nicholas Murray Butler, Pulitzer was particularly insistent on giving control of the prizes to a special new board that would be dominated by newspaper editors. The group originally had the name Advisory Board of the Columbia School of Journalism, even though its main responsibility was always to be for the prizes.[12] (In 1950 it became the Advisory Board on the Pulitzer Prizes and then in 1979 simply the Pulitzer Prize Board.)

Neither the plan for the school nor the plan for the prizes was popular with Pulitzer's aides. One of them, Don C. Seitz, suggested a better investment for the $2 million: "Endow the *World*. Make it foolproof." There was some prescience in the recommendation. While the paper would turn out some great journalism in the two decades after Pulitzer's death, it would finally be run into the ground by sons Ralph and Herbert, who sold it to Scripps-Howard in 1931 and watched it disappear. But the deal for the bequest was sealed with Columbia's president Butler, and the will was signed on April 26, 1904. Columbia was required to prove to the new advisory board that the journalism school had functioned successfully for three years before the money for the prizes would be established.

Including the journalism prizes with related awards to honor American novelists, historians, biographers, and dramatists was a clever stroke on Pulitzer's part. The association of lowly newspaper work with achievement in fine arts did indeed help elevate the press. The timing was just right, too, for innovations like the prizes and university-based journalism schools. Early in the twentieth century, Pulitzer's own papers in New York and St. Louis were helping create what was called the New Journalism, turning away from the pure sensationalism and political bias of the past and emphasizing fairness and balance instead. At the same time, the papers launched crusades to right various public wrongs on the readers' behalf.

The first advisory board contained a handful of powerful newspaper editors and was chaired by Pulitzer's son, the thirty-five-year-old *World* editor Ralph Pulitzer. Only two of the eleven editors or publishers on the board worked outside the Northeast—one from the *Post-Dispatch* and one from the *Chicago Daily News*. Besides Columbia's Butler and Ralph Pulitzer, the board included John Langdon Heaton of the *World*, Edward P. Mitchell of the *Sun*, Charles Ransom Miller of the *New York Times*, St. Clair McKelway of the *Brooklyn Eagle*, Melville E. Stone of the Associated Press, Samuel Calvin Wells of the *Philadelphia Press*, Samuel Bowles of the *Springfield* (Massachusetts) *Republican*, and Charles H. Taylor of the *Boston Globe*. Early on a rule was established calling for editors to step out of the room whenever their own papers' entries were considered.

The original designations for the annual awards adopted language from the Pulitzer will, including a description of the medal for "the most dis-interested and meritorious public service." The Reporting Prize was for "the best example of a reporter's work during the year; the test being strict accuracy, terseness, the accomplishment of some public good command-ing public attention and respect." The reference to terseness, long since removed from the reporting description, is worth a chuckle in this day of multipart, multipage entries that sometimes tax even jurors' ability to get through them.

While the first board was guided by Joseph Pulitzer's terms and seemed intent on honoring his memory by selecting high-quality winners, it had few submissions to work with in the early years. That was true even though Columbia advertised for entries. The infrastructure that had been designed for the prizes was weak, leaving much of the judging in the hands of Columbia professors. They were assigned to look through entries and pass on their recommendations to the board. In one of his histories on the Pulitzer Prizes, John Hohenberg suggested that Columbia president Butler wanted the *faculty* to make the final selection of winners, with the board doing the nominating. Hohenberg, who was Columbia's administrator of the prizes from 1954 to 1976, noted that the journalists of the advisory board soon took charge of the final designation of prize winners. They have never relinquished that task. And as the jury system evolved, smaller panels of journalists eventually took the job from professors.

The length of service on the board was not limited during the early years of the Pulitzer Prizes, and a number of members stayed on for more than a decade. Several strong factions developed over its early decades, opening the board of those years to charges that it was something of an "old boy network." Ralph Pulitzer's younger brother, Joseph Pulitzer II, editor and publisher of the *Post-Dispatch*, joined the board in 1920 for what was to be a thirty-four-year stay, spending the last fifteen years as chairman. He was a modest man who was generally happy acting as moderator while the powerful editors around the table expressed their opinions. But his devotion to his father's principles was a beacon for the board, and that grounding in Pulitzer family values continued when his own son, Joseph Pulitzer III (known as Joseph Pulitzer Jr.), took over as chairman after JP II died in 1955. JP Jr. retired in 1986 and left the board without a Pulitzer as chairman for the first time in seven decades.

A Juror Makes a Difference

Almost from the beginning, the Pulitzer boards were steeped in secrecy, which they believed was necessary to allow for a candid discussion of candidates. Until recent years, the board did not identify entries that had been finalists and said next to nothing about the selection process.

In 1985, the late *Los Angeles Times* media critic David Shaw, a student of the Pulitzer Prizes and a winner himself, wrote about the power struggles that had played a role in past board choices for prizes and described some of the board's selections as capricious. But Shaw wrote that in the late 1970s a nine-year maximum term limit and other board-instituted reforms had improved the process. Since then, he wrote, "although some prizes are still won (or lost) for reasons other than journalistic merit—sentiment, tradition, geography, luck—no one man (or group of men) dominates the Pulitzer board today. Voting blocs shift constantly, depending on the issues involved in any particular award or procedural question."[13]

Jurors today infuse the Pulitzer process with energy. They view jury duty as an honor—"Pulitzer juror" looks very good on a résumé—and value a networking experience that inspires them to bring their best to the historic World Room. The room is dominated by the ninety-square-foot "Liberty Window," a blue stained glass representation of Lady Liberty raising her lamp between the globe's two hemispheres. Columbia received the memorial to Joseph Pulitzer's Statue of Liberty campaign after the *World* building was torn down in the 1950s to improve access to the Brooklyn Bridge.[14]

Although Howard Weaver first served as a public service juror in 1988— the first of his three times on that particular panel—he remembers the experience as though it were yesterday. "I was just gaga to be there," says Weaver, then an *Anchorage Daily News* editor whose work had been part of a gold medal project about Alaska's Teamsters Union a dozen years earlier, when he was twenty-five. Now here he was, debating the best public service of the prior year with a distinguished panel of reporters and editors from around the country, faced with the job of narrowing about one hundred entries to three.

In the process of selecting finalists—including the eventual winner, the *Charlotte Observer*, for its exposé of the PTL television ministry's misuse of funds—Weaver was involved in a heated discussion about the publication that would be the jury's third pick. His position won out, he says. "It was one of those moments when I realized how important the jury work was," he says. "And I also realized, here's this kid editor from Anchorage, Alaska, who made the difference. If I'd been slightly less passionate, the nomination would have gone the other way."[15]

The old jury system of passing around "clip books" with paper entries from newspapers gave way years ago to laptops for reading entries—now submitted electronically, of course. However, there is still no formal fact-checking capability within the entry judging system—something that has

FIGURE 2.3 Pulitzer Prize jurors in the 2014 judging meet under the "Liberty Window" that dominates the World Room of the Columbia Journalism Building. *Source*: Used by permission. Photo by Thomas E. Franklin.

hurt the journalism Pulitzers over the years. In the worst-case scenario of an undetected Pulitzer fraud, the *Washington Post* returned the 1981 Feature Writing Prize of reporter Janet Cooke after it learned that she had made up her story about a child hooked on heroin. Since then, skepticism has played a much greater part in the judging process for both jurors and Pulitzer board members.

But former board member Geneva Overholser, for one, maintains that it would be hard to improve on a Pulitzer selection system that puts the task in the hands of the nation's top editors, backed by academics familiar with journalism. "I challenge anyone to think of a better way to recognize extraordinary journalism. The record speaks for itself," says Overholser, a celebrated journalism educator who cites among her own proudest moments her acceptance of the 1991 gold medal for the stories written for the newspaper she edited at the time, the *Des Moines Register*. "It's like that wonderful Churchill statement about democracy being the worst form of government, except for every other form of government."[16]

In 2014, the nineteen-member Pulitzer Prize board was chaired by Paul Tash, the chairman and chief executive officer of the *Tampa Bay Times* who also chairs the board of trustees of the Poynter Institute, the school for journalists. The Pulitzer board contained editors and publishers from large and small media outlets all over the country, from New York, Miami, and Washington, D.C., to Sioux Falls, South Dakota; Davenport, Iowa; and Dallas, Texas. There was a playwright, a magazine writer, and faculty members from the Massachusetts Institute of Technology and the University of Pennsylvania, along with Columbia president Lee C. Bollinger and Columbia journalism dean Steve Coll, who is a former *Washington Post* reporter and editor.[17]

When the winners are announced at exactly 3:00 p.m. on the first Monday after the April board meeting, the administrator traditionally steps to a lectern in front of the Liberty Window to "sprinkle fairy dust on people and change their lives forever," as former administrator Sig Gissler once put it when he presided over the old-fashioned press affair of the type he liked. Within a few minutes of the announcement, a package of information about winners and finalists is made available online.

When word reaches the dozen or so winning newsrooms, of course, cheers go up and champagne corks pop—if editors have learned of a prize in advance or have taken a chance on purchasing bubbly just in case. At many other news organizations, though, the mood is somber as the official word goes to finalists that there will be no prize for them that year.[18] One such "Pulitzer Day" at the start of the twenty-first century was like no other, though. Even as *New York Times* staffers celebrated a record one-year haul of seven prizes—including the coveted Public Service Gold Medal—they felt an enormous pang of sadness.[19]

CHAPTER 3

A NEWSROOM CHALLENGED

2002: The *New York Times* and 9/11

> I have seen reporters crying at their telephones, even as they summoned the
> professional discipline to keep reporting, keep writing until the task was
> done. They were inspired and sometimes driven by an awareness of what
> these pieces had come to mean to the grieving families and friends and to
> that larger community of Americans who mourned for all the World Trade
> Center victims, strangers to them or not, just as in an earlier day their
> parents mourned for the dead of Pearl Harbor.
>
> —*NEW YORK TIMES* EXECUTIVE EDITOR HOWELL RAINES,
> ON THE PREPARATION OF "PORTRAITS OF GRIEF"

Before work one morning, Gerald Boyd was relaxing in the barber chair.
Then the world changed. The haircut was in preparation for a special dinner party that night. Just five days into his new job as the managing editor of the *New York Times*, Boyd would be joining the new editorial page
editor Gail Collins and the executive editor Howell Raines at the home of
the publisher Arthur Sulzberger. It was also primary election day—a nice
little exercise for a Metro desk with the extraordinary talent of the *Times*.
But certainly there seemed to be nothing on the horizon that warm late-
summer morning to jeopardize dinner at the publisher's.

The barber was Haitian and spoke French and Creole and little English.
Boyd liked it that way. "We didn't have to engage in conversations, and he
could do his business without talking about world affairs," Boyd said. To
catch a breeze, the shop's door was open. "Someone walked in and yelled
to the barber, 'Have you heard about the plane that crashed into the Twin
Towers?'" The words were hardly spoken when Boyd leapt from under the
scissors. "I ran out with the smock still on, fishing money out for him,

saying, I have to go. He didn't understand what I was saying. He said he wasn't finished."

The barbershop was sixty-five blocks north of Times Square, where the newsroom was in desperate need of its new managing editor. Boyd tried the subway: no service. "Police action at the World Trade Center," the announcement said. He stopped a gypsy cab willing to make the trip. His fifty dollars and his constant urging for the driver to ignore the speed limit—"If you get a ticket, I'll pay," Boyd shouted—paid off. In fifteen minutes he was in the office. On a newsroom television he was able to watch early film of the second plane hitting, eighteen minutes after the first strike.[1]

The Culture Kicks In

An outsider looking at the job ahead for Boyd, Raines, and other *New York Times* "masthead editors" might see September 11 as a nearly uncoverable local, national, and global story. But Boyd, who for eight years had served as an assistant managing editor and then a deputy managing editor before assuming the managing editorship the prior week, saw a ritual play out that was no less amazing because it was expected. At least, it was expected at the *Times*. "The culture of the *New York Times* kicks in, and that culture is that certain things become automatic," he said. The A-book—the paper's first section—was immediately opened up, its ads cleared out. That happened on any huge story: the Berlin Wall coming down, the first Gulf War, or the earlier 1993 attack on the World Trade Center. The A-book had been opened a dozen times since Boyd had been in management.

Planning his staff's day under such pressure, his mind adjusted with each new shock. "As we watched the tube it was soon clear that we were dealing with an incredible story. But what struck me most about it—and it's kind of strange—was when I learned that Air Force One had been zigzagging." Having been a White House correspondent, he knew all that was done to keep the president's plane insulated from the world outside. "I always felt extremely safe, and if they were taking these extreme measures, it made it even more frightening."

Boyd made two decisions within minutes. One was to pull all the staff that had been assigned to cover the election—essentially everyone on Metro staff—and recapture the space in the paper that was dedicated to the primary. It was a bit of a gamble but paid off quickly when the crush of events forced the vote's cancellation. ("When I made the call I didn't know that," he noted.) The decision had given the paper a head start. The second order was to create a series of meetings for the day to coordinate coverage "and get a handle on what the nature of the story was." That call had been made easier given the rapid unfolding of events: the Towers collapsed; thousands were feared dead downtown; the president made a statement that it was a terrorist attack; the Pentagon was hit; and another plane crashed in Pennsylvania (after initial, erroneous reports saying it was in Ohio). "We knew four planes had been used as guided missiles," Boyd recalled. "That was basically enough for us to begin staking the outlines of that report."

Freeing the A-book of ads had created some immediate needs. "You had twenty or thirty pages that were open. How do you package those pages? And again the culture of the paper was such that we knew how to do that," Boyd noted. "The need first of all is to break down the pages—four pages on collapse of the buildings, four on victims. . . . What we had learned to do was to have a packaging meeting that did these kinds of things—to deal only with design, presentation and look"—keeping design decisions away from the news meetings. "We weren't reinventing the wheel." Amid the chaos, it was a reassuring thought. The questions had been asked before, even if the scale might have been different: "How do we coordinate a Washington staff, a foreign-bureau staff, and Metro staff? And how much overall space to commit?"

As staffers tried to focus fully on the "battlefield coverage" they were suddenly engaged in, personal worries crept in. Boyd was no exception. With phones not working in the city, he could not contact his wife, who worked in the same area as an editor at *Essence* magazine. "Was she at the World Trade Center or in the vicinity?" he wondered. It would be five o'clock before they finally got in touch.

He led the 11:00 a.m. news meeting. "We didn't talk about stories. We talked about what we knew, what we needed to know, and how we'd get there. Then we came back around noon." That meeting covered story assignments. "Then we had a 4:30 news meeting, and right after that we had our design people begin to lay out the pages." Editors assembled for a photo meeting an hour later and then for a design meeting. "We had incredible art, and a whole lot of it," said Boyd. Page layouts went on until about eight o'clock. He was home by 4 a.m.—without a thought, of course, for the canceled Sulzberger dinner party.

With staffers the caliber of the *Times*'s, great notes were pouring in along with the great pictures. When reporter David Barstow heard about the attacks, he was driving back from Pennsylvania, where he and another writer had been covering a Little League baseball scandal involving an over-age player from the Bronx. With the tunnels and bridges into the city closed, they took the Tappan Zee Bridge north of the city and then went south into the Bronx until traffic allowed them to go no further. "I jogged from 243rd Street down to 168th Street, then took the subway to the news-room," says Barstow. By 8:30 p.m. he was at Ground Zero, having avoided the police who were assigned to keep reporters and others away. He spent the next several days there, he says, "feeding stuff back to the newsroom from the American Express Building while dodging the cops, who were constantly doing sweeps to get reporters like me out of there."[2]

Because such enterprise was going on all around the managing edi-tor, this assessment by Boyd may not sound quite so incredible. "The first night was, in a way, the easiest night," he said, "once we learned the dimensions of the story." Again, that *Times* culture was guiding reporters and editors. Tougher newsroom decisions were ahead.

Breaking Through the Abstraction

Christine Kay would also never forget the incongruous little scene that got her to bolt for the office without a thought. The enterprise editor for Metro was on her sofa at home in Chelsea with a cup of coffee. She planned to report to work a little later than usual because of the expected late demands of the primary coverage. Her eye half on the TV, she saw what appeared to be some strange movie: a plane, the flames in one of the Twin Towers. "I jumped up and literally ran the twenty blocks north to the office to watch the second plane hitting," she says. "And we all started to work."[3]

A former *Newsday* editor who now reported to the *Times* Metro edi-tor Jonathan Landman, Kay had been editing a piece on adult homes for the mentally ill. On September 11, it was set aside. She has little recollec-tion of what her hour-to-hour actions were that first day, except that she marshaled forces for Landman and served as a contact for reporters at Ground Zero and throughout the city. Gradually she began to focus on the victims, taking charge of each missing-person report in those first few days. The identification of the dead would come much later.

Times culture or no *Times* culture, there were really no precedents for the scope of this catastrophe when it came to the newspaper dealing with victims. Not in peacetime, anyway. "I was here for TWA 800," Kay says, recalling the July 17, 1996, air disaster that killed 230 people off the coast of Long Island. But those victims were known as soon as the passenger list was in hand. September 11 offered few comparisons. "We had no idea what we were facing," she says. "For the first three days I was coming in to a budget line that said Zero-Zero victims; Zero-Zero firefighters." That meant that even rough estimates of the dead were lacking, both among those who happened to be in the World Trade Center and those among the first responders trying to save them.

The TWA crash did suggest some obvious approaches to editors looking to help readers grasp a mass-death situation. Even if there are hundreds of victims, "you start writing about them in real ways, intimate ways," Kay says. "You write about the group of school kids who were going to France. You write about the neighbors who were killed, or the husband and wife, or the girls who were left behind. You find small ways to report on it, and there is an immediacy about it." But in the collapse of the Twin Towers, there were untold thousands of lives lost—with an emphasis, in those early days, on the "untold."

In her role advising Metro on how to develop victim coverage, the challenge was finding an approach that would speak to readers and reduce what she calls the "abstraction" of so many deaths all at once. She tried to plan something, but there was little time. Thoughts of something like "Portraits of Grief," though not yet by that name, floated to her first on the breeze that carried so many sad, desperate flyers. Posters pleading for information about the thousands missing had started to appear all over the city. A reporter did one story on the phenomenon. "I started to pick them up and collected them next to my desk in that week," Kay recalls.

"I know people want to hear that we had this thoughtful conversation and sat in a room for three hours, and came up with this magical approach," she says. "But that is not what happened." What did happen was that the pressure built from day to day with the thought that "for better or worse, we had to do something about the victims." The challenge for Kay and other editors was to find the time to discuss the various options for their paper to make these victims become real people for readers and to reduce the abstraction of the still-unknown death count. "We'd steal five minutes here and five minutes there," she says. "In one stolen five minutes, it came up that thumbnail sketches had been used before." The *Times* and others had used them in writing about the 168 victims of the 1995 Oklahoma City federal building bombing, for example. Kay thought a different approach was needed here. She discussed various alternatives with reporter Janny Scott. Previous mass-death treatments were "too telegraphic," Kay says. "They had birth date, where they went to school. . . . They weren't impressionistic." And impressionism, rather than obituary-style detail, was needed to help readers see these victims as real people. Two hundred words seemed a good length to Kay and Scott.

Kay had edited the "Public Lives" profiles that ran in the second section, where she had sought to build impressions of the subjects by using a single character element—a hobby, a passion—and building on it. "I thought one of the most successful things about them was when they luxuriated in one little tantalizing tidbit," she says. To qualify for such a public-life study, the person, sometimes a celebrity, had to be elsewhere in the news. "The reader got a very intimate profile—a very distinctive, often one-interview profile that made you feel like you were inside the room with them," says Kay. Maybe something like that could work. But could it be reduced to two hundred words?

The time came for a Metro meeting. "Jon laid some approaches on the table," says Kay. One was the telegraphic bio approach. "Both Janny and I thought that would be very unsatisfying and mind-numbing." Hanging over the editors was the uncertainty of the total count. "We still thought there were ten thousand to twenty thousand dead, and if the goal was to make that less abstract, the bios weren't going to do it."

There was another thought: "What if these people aren't really dead?" The profiles, whatever they were, would have to avoid the feel of an obituary. Kay was after a sense of lives interrupted. "So we thought, 'What if you just choose one aspect of life? What if you focus on this one woman gardening, one man taking his daughter to ice-skating lessons, or maybe smoking cigars?'" Indeed, the definition of the new profile approach grew as much from what it would *not* be. "These are not obits, and this is not about death. This is not about professional achievement. These are not people who would ordinarily appear in the *New York Times* obituary page."

The editors' thinking about a style for the profiles began to take on the feel of a mission to Kay—to design something that would work with the overall coverage approach evolving around them. That coverage reflected "a level playing field," she says. "People who were in the upper echelons of these [investment] trading groups were to be treated in the same way as the dishwashers at Windows on the World."

It was Friday morning, September 14. "I grabbed this bunch of missing posters, which was really handy because they had photographs on them, and I took Janny Scott and five other reporters into Jon Landman's office," says Kay. "It was very important that they happened to be some of the best reporters in the place. We divided up the posters and they went at it."

On Saturday the first series of mini profiles—not yet "Portraits"—ran under the heading: "After the Attacks: Among the Missing." Below that was the kicker line "The Names" and below that was another headline: "Snapshots of Their Lives with Family and at Work." These paragraphs introduced the first day's collection:

It has been four days since the World Trade Center was destroyed. Thousands of people who were in the towers at the time are assumed to be dead. But the official body count stands at 124, and the medical examiner has identified only a few dozen victims. It could be months before many of those killed can be officially confirmed dead.

In the meantime, there is the interminable registry of the missing, nearly 5,000 people whose friends and families have reported their names to the police in the hope that they are alive. With each passing day, those hopes grow dimmer. They are fathers, daughters, fiancés and best friends. Bond traders, boxing aficionados and chefs. People expecting babies, planning their weddings, hoping for promotions. Firefighters and police officers who raced to the scene after the first jet crashed. And people who set off for work on a dazzling September morning and met with something unimaginably horrible. Here are glimpses of some of those lives.

The next day, on September 16, the rubric "Portraits of Grief" made its first appearance over the profiles. The top half of the page was devoted to a picture layout of the posters and below was the text.

Who had come up with the "Portraits" name? Lots of ideas were bandied about, all avoiding use of "the dead." With the posters in mind, Howell Raines had tossed out "The Street Art of Despair." It was a starting point. As desk editors used the typical process of free association, the word "portraits" seemed to stick and variations like "Portraits of Despair," "Portraits of Sorrow," "Portraits of Mourning," "Portraits of Grief," and "Portraits of Loss" made the rounds. Recalling the process in an in-house newsletter, Patrick LaForge, then an assistant Metro editor on the night shift, said he flipped "a mental coin" and made "Portraits of Grief" the front-runner. "I wasn't in love with the phrase, but I figured we could change it." The next day was his day off, so LaForge suggested in an e-mail to the next night's desk editor that he think up something else. "Then I went for a bicycle ride, fell, and broke my thumb," wrote LaForge. He was in the emergency room and missed the editor's reply. Things had been so hectic in the newsroom that editors had just continued using "Portraits of Grief."[4]

Birth of "A Nation Challenged"

Well into the first week after the attacks, managing editor Boyd maintained the office meeting routine. It was built around four daily news sessions, with one devoted to layout. But it quickly became clear that the A-book format wouldn't work for the long haul. "We were throwing ads out of the A-book at considerable cost to the paper, so the issue became how long do we want to do this," he said. Advertisers paid $100,000 per page for the A-book. There were no notes from the *Times* business side or from the publisher, Boyd said, but editors were aware of the costs and began looking for an alternative that could be applied right away.

"What was obvious was the need for stories to be packaged together," Boyd said. And a fifth section couldn't simply be added because the *Times* had a physical limit of four sections capable of carrying the prior day's news. Besides the normal *Times* A section—including foreign and national coverage—there was a separate Metro section, a Sports section, and a fourth section that varied according to the day (Science on Tuesdays, for example).

As war began raging in Afghanistan and other reports with ties to 9/11 sprouted around the globe, the nation, and the nation's largest city, the range of stories was vast. Having space for it all was vital. "We wanted an open section—a section without ads—so that we could present the most impressive displays," said Boyd. "The question became what section do we do this in." As the masthead editors met, there was a huge, if unspoken, worry: if "A Nation Challenged" ended up sharing an editor's section, that editor could lose a front page to the new report.

A brainstorm by the *Times* assistant managing editor Tom Bodkin, though, solved the problem of "losing" the page. He proposed that Sports and Metro share a section, but in a peculiar way. Sports would keep its "front" on the back page—upside down, so that readers would have to flip the section and read toward the center. With that minor adjustment, Sports readers had their accustomed front pages while "A Nation Challenged" stood alone, devoid of ads, with two-page spreads for display inside.

On the first Monday after 9/11—the regular meeting day for Boyd and Raines with the publisher—they showed a mock-up of the section to Sulzberger. It was a hit. The section heading "A Nation Challenged" had been proposed by veteran assistant managing editor Allan M. Siegal. As Siegal recalls it, "I scribbled a few possible section rubrics on a scrap of paper and caught Howell Raines on his way out of the office and asked him to choose." "A Nation Challenged" had been Siegal's favorite too, he says.[5]

In determining the mix of stories in the newly named section, the guiding principle was to augment and complement what was appearing on page one. "We looked at the stories we had fronted. Then we thought about the front of A Nation Challenged, and how we could use that to make different points journalistically," said Boyd. The approach accommodated each wrinkle as the nature of this gigantic story morphed—war in Afghanistan, anthrax-laced mail, the flow of local profiles. The new section gave editors an accepted alternative to use. Without the section, a major article would probably start with five column inches on page one and jump inside. Did writers feel it was a step down to lose that small front-page display and instead to see their stories fronted on "A Nation Challenged"? "There may have been that feeling

A Nation Challenged

L   B1

TUESDAY, SEPTEMBER 18, 2001

The New York Times

Stress From Attacks Will Chase Some Into the Depths of Their Minds, and Stay

By ERICA GOODE

For some, the ultimate legacy of last week's events will be memories that gradually turn malignant, as dangerous as any cancer.

No one can predict precisely how many they will be, but experts say it will not be everyone, nor even a majority of the people most closely affected by the terrorist attacks. Researchers who study the psychological impact of war, torture, violent crime, terrorism and natural disasters say that what stuns them is not their debilitating effects but rather the resilience of the human spirit.

"Over time, most people will be

O.K.," said Dr. Robert Ursano, a professor of psychiatry at the Uniformed Services University of the Health Sciences in Bethesda, Md. Dr. Ursano is an expert on the effects of terrorism and disasters.

One large survey of Americans and their mental health found that of those who said they had been exposed to trauma, about 25 percent developed the hallmarks of posttraumatic stress disorder. Experts said that figure might provide a rough estimate for those traumatized by the attacks in New York and Washington.

Other researchers, including Dr. Edna Foa of the University of Penn-

There may not be immediate signs of lasting symptoms.

sylvania, have come up with higher numbers for the victims of rape and other forms of physical assault, of at least in the first few months after a trauma. In such studies, which began following victims immediately after the event, up to 50 percent of the subjects showed acute symptoms of post-traumatic stress a month later,

when a diagnosis of post-traumatic stress disorder can first be made. Three months afterward, the numbers had dropped to about 30 percent. After a year, up to 25 percent continued to experience difficulties.

But researchers say the people who develop lasting symptoms are not always the same as those who show immediate signs of extreme distress. And because of the tragedy's size, its resemblance both to natural disasters and to war, and its human toll, researchers say it is impossible to generalize past findings to what lies ahead.

"We don't have a precedent for anything like this," said Dr. Rachel

Yehuda, director of the post-traumatic stress program at Mount Sinai Medical Center and the Bronx Veterans Affairs Medical Center.

Perhaps the only thing experts can say with any certainty is that people most directly exposed to death, injury and loss are at highest risk. Those who do develop post-traumatic symptoms will relive last week's events in nightmares, flashbacks and images their minds cannot suppress. Any reminder — a television replay or the sound of a siren — may send their bodies on a physiological roller coaster. They may start at loud noises, sleep badly, strike out in irrational anger or try to avoid places

or people that trigger memories.

Some will be unable to grieve normally, their mourning stalled in a mental canyon where screams still echo. Some will be too fearful to walk down the street. Some will take pills. Some will empty bottles into despair.

Some of those most to come, experts said, will be to identify and help those headed for trouble. Those efforts will be aided by scientists who are beginning to piece together a new understanding of traumatic disorders.

Terror, panic and grief are not new

Continued on Page B11

With Flags and Doffed Caps, Baseball Resumes

Baseball resumed yesterday after a week of canceled games. A Marine Corps color guard took part in a ceremony as the Phillies and Braves began their game in Philadelphia.

Technology Will Play Bigger Role In Security

By WILLIAM GLABERSON

Security experts are describing a new kind of country, where electronic identification might become the norm, immigrants might be tracked far more closely and the airspace over cities like New York and Washington might be off limits to all civilian aircraft.

Yesterday, Attorney General John Ashcroft outlined several proposals, saying, "We must strengthen our laws to increase the ability of the Department of Justice and its component agencies to identify, prevent and punish terrorism."

The proposals Mr. Ashcroft described included measures that would give law enforcement officials expanded electronic surveillance powers, added search authority and new powers to seize assets of suspected terrorists.

Congress has already begun to act on proposals to make wiretapping of computers easier, and a flood of measures is expected that would loosen restrictions on what will effectively be domestic spying.

Legal experts say the courts are unlikely to impose many restrictions on Congress's security decisions. As a result, they say, the country could adopt security measures as stringent as its people will tolerate politically or support financially.

Security experts say technology has presented almost limitless possibilities, including national electronic identification cards.

"Each American could be given a 'smart card' so, as they go into an airport or anywhere, we know exactly who they are," said Michael G. Cherkasky, president of Kroll Inc., a security consultant.

"The technology is here." Mr. Cherkasky said. "These cards in industry are going to spread, and then it's going to spread very rapidly elsewhere."

Such cards, with computer chips, would have detailed information about those they were issued to and would identify them when read by a computer. The cards could be coordinated with fingerprints or, in a few years, facial characteristics, and be programmed to permit or limit access through turnstiles to buildings or areas. They could track someone's location, financial transactions, criminal history and even driving speed on a particular highway on a given night.

Critics say that electronic identification cards combined with other measures could usher in an era of surveillance and suspicion.

Civil libertarians were a major battle ahead because an anxious public may now seem too willing to trade some freedoms for greater safety.

It is not clear, said Bruce Ackerman, a law professor at Yale University, whether that acceptance would continue if people perceived themselves as being searched and watched frequently. Professor Ackerman said some of the proposals being discussed, like increased video surveillance, would threaten anonymity.

"It is a profound affront to be metered and measured," he said. "And that is, I think, the debate of the future."

Legal experts say the civil libertarians will find little sympathy in the courts. In World War II, they noted, the United States Supreme Court approved the internment of Japanese-Americans, a decision that constitutional scholars now widely consider to have been wrong.

When the country is facing war or wartime threats, judges tend to slide in the direction of security, even if it limits freedoms, said David A. Strauss, a law professor at the University of Chicago.

"If history suggests anything," Professor Strauss said, "it suggests

Continued on Page B5

After a War Starts at Home, the Guard Prepares to Take It Abroad

By C. J. CHIVERS

Lt. Col. Mario T. Castagliola sat on a park bench in the mottled shade of Hope Garden yesterday, inside the perimeter of the World Trade Center security area. He was clean-shaven and intent in camouflage fatigues, but he smoked one cigarette after another, right down to the filter, and his right knee bounced uncontrollably as he spoke. He ground the jumpy knee, ground the filter into fluff and dared the suggestion of a smile.

"I've got twitches now I never had before," he said, and then wiped his

reddened eyes.

One week after two airliners slammed into the World Trade Center, members of New York's National Guard, many of whom have been at the impact area continuously since the hours after the towers toppled to the streets, have come to realize that they occupy a unique position in the response to the most deadly terrorist attack in American history.

In the near term, they are much like the police and firefighters who also crowd the rubble, a pool of labor for the vast rescue and security effort.

In the long term, however, they are something more. They are soldiers, and long after New York City's public safety personnel resume something like a normal schedule, they will be preparing for war.

Colonel Castagliola, the commander of the 101st Cavalry Squadron, a tank battalion from Staten Island, admitted to feeling shell-shocked by the things he and his 300 soldiers had seen and done in the most ghastly week of their lives. And yesterday, speaking in the soft and measured tones of a man trying to contain his emotions, he said that he was prepared now for the next phone call:

the one that might send his battalion overseas.

"I don't want to speculate," he said. "It's one thing we're not ever supposed to do. But I think if we do go to war, then those soldiers who have witnessed this thing firsthand will be motivated for the extraordinary sacrifices ahead."

The past week has tested New York's 17,000-member National Guard in a way it has not been tested in modern memory. Three battalions of part-time soldiers rushed to the impact area a week ago, and almost all the soldiers who showed up have not left. They are from the First

Battalion of the 69th Infantry Regiment, out of the Lexington Avenue armory on Manhattan's East Side; the First Battalion of the 258th Field Artillery Regiment from Jamaica, Queens; and from Colonel Castagliola's unit, the 101st Cavalry.

They have posted themselves to the fragile edges of exhaustion. Even before receiving notification that Gov. George E. Pataki had activated them for duty, hundreds were already en route to their armories. Some even bypassed the staging areas and went directly to ground

Continued on Page B7

Support for Arabs and Muslims in U.S.

President Bush listened to Yusuf Saleem of the Muslim American Society, second from right, yesterday at the Islamic Center of Washington. Mr. Bush denounced domestic attacks on Middle Eastern people. Page B5.

Blair and Chirac Heading To U.S. to Discuss Crisis

By JANE PERLEZ

WASHINGTON, Sept. 17 — As some European allies began to express caution about the administration's plans for military action, the leaders of France and Britain were preparing to arrive here this week to show solidarity and discuss with President Bush their contributions to a coalition against terrorism.

In an unusual move, the European Union called a special summit meeting for the end of the week to work on ways of pooling resources to combat terrorists.

With France's president, Jacques Chirac, planning to arrive on Tuesday and Britain's prime minister, Tony Blair, hastily arranging a visit for Thursday, the administration has already defined the different kinds of support, from rhetorical to military, that it needs from members of the coalition it is trying to build.

Senior officials said that one country they expected to contribute troops was Britain, the United States' strongest ally and a country that last an estimated 300 citizens in last Tuesday's attacks. The administration has also not ruled out participation by troops from other European allies. The administration has also plainly stated, though not

stressed, that the United States reserves the right to act unilaterally despite the expressions of support.

Secretary of State Colin L. Powell said last week that even with the strong support from NATO and the European Union, the administration would not feel constrained in its military decisions.

The 18-member NATO alliance has said it will regard the attack on the United States as an attack on all the allies if the Bush administration determines that the attack was "directed from abroad." While the administration has pointed an accusing finger at Osama bin Laden, the Islamic militant based in Afghanistan, it has not yet made that formal determination.

Mr. Chirac, whose visit was already scheduled, has turned his Washington trip into a two-hour session with President Bush and his senior foreign policy advisers as the White House on Tuesday evening. The French leader has said that if the United States takes military action, "France will be its aide."

But France is at the start of a presidential campaign and despite the outpouring of overwhelming

Continued on Page B2

FIGURE 3.1 Tuesday, September 18, 2001, the first day the *New York Times* "A Nation Challenged" section ran. *Source*: Copyright © 2001, The New York Times Company. Reprinted by permission.

in the beginning," Boyd said, "but not later on." No single editor ever ran "A Nation Challenged." Boyd called the section "a collaboration of numerous editors" over which he and Raines retained the final say.

Besides "Portraits"—the purview of the Metro staff—a feature that was Raines's invention also took root within "A Nation Challenged." Described by staffers as "all known thought," this journalism form allowed significant issues to be featured in a special, cerebral way. "'Portraits' spoke to the heart and All Known Thought spoke to the mind," according to Boyd. "It proved especially valuable because it became an anchor, and it allowed us to spend a day exploring an issue, like a history of al Qaeda, and produce a comprehensive story that explains it." With all the open pages, the third "anchor" became art—large, well-packaged photos that told a story all by themselves. That the *Times* ended up winning Pulitzers for breaking news and feature photography in addition to public service was an indication of that success.

A Portrait of "Portraits"

As a daily facet of the section, "Portraits of Grief" took on a life of its own. While missing posters still prompted some vignettes, gradually employee lists from companies at the World Trade Center and lists of firefighters and police became available for reporters to use in assembling the profiles. The size of the operation grew. "It became this huge machine. We had ten to thirteen reporters working on it non-stop," says Kay.

Reporters volunteered to contribute, some even coming from Washington, D.C. to play a part. The items' short length was deceptive. Emotion aside—and it rarely was—they were hard to write. "They were exhausting and absolutely overreported," says Kay, noting that often multiple sources were consulted to get the information right. "There was no glamour here. It was something you didn't have a byline on." Instead, writers' names appeared in a credit box, not even connected to the particular portrait they produced. Yet 143 reporters participated in the project, some for a day or two, others through much of its fifteen-week run.

Subscribers from around the country turned to "A Nation Challenged" first thing after the paper arrived. Or last. One of the many readers that wrote to the *Times* in praise of "Portraits" said she could not drop off to sleep at night without having read them. Jeff Bray of Sioux Falls, South Dakota, wrote: "Nothing—and I mean NOTHING—I have ever read in my life has moved me as much as these riveting windows into the lives of ordinary people." At least one paper, the *Oregonian* in faraway Portland, ran "Portraits" in their entirety.[6] Christine Kay summarizes the feature as delivering this message: "My God, New Yorkers are just like the rest of us. They take their kids ice-skating, and they like Bart Simpson, and they play soccer. Those New Yorkers, they're really Americans."

Still, as one of its editors, Kay did hear complaints—from relatives of those featured in the columns. "Some were upset that we weren't talking about more traditional things," she says. "We weren't talking about the accomplishments, but things that they perceived to be trivial or prosaic. Or a mother was upset that we took what the daughter-in-law remembered, or vice versa." Editors would explain that the idea had been to focus more "on the passion than the professional accomplishment."

Most were moved by the collective power of "Portraits," however. Howell Raines wrote in the book *Portraits 9/11/01*: "These lives, bundled together so randomly into a union of loving memory by those terrible cataclysms of September 11, remind us of what Walt Whitman knew: 'The United States themselves are essentially the greatest poem.'" Metro editor Landman "resisted any suggestion that we abandon our rhythm of a page or two pages every day until the end of 2001." Raines added: "Among the reporters, another kind of democracy—the democracy of craftsmanship—came into play. Often, on so huge a story as the World Trade Center disaster, the writing of shorter pieces falls to younger reporters. On the 'Portraits' project, it became an emblem of pride to join in the largely anonymous labor of creating these pieces; some of our most senior correspondents insisted on participating."[7]

From an editor's view, there were some rules to consider. "We tried never to mention that day," says Kay. Balance was important from item to item. "You certainly didn't want too many Bart Simpson lovers and too many cigar-smoking stockbrokers in the same day." To help achieve balance without being "formulaic," as Kay puts it, a large backlog of "Portraits" was collected in the first month and then grouped to be run. "It was the ultimate group effort," says Kay, who is still stunned by the how "Portraits" came together. A group effort, that is, in every case but one.

In a bizarre footnote, disgraced *Times* reporter Jayson Blair was later to become entwined with "Portraits of Grief"—even though he had not written a single vignette. In the report prepared by the *New York Times* analyzing Blair's errors during his time at the paper before he was discovered in 2002 to be fabricating articles, it was disclosed that he had begged off doing assignments for "Portraits." A cousin of his had died in the Pentagon bombing, he said. It turned out, however, that the cousin had been another of his fabrications. "It's too ugly to even go there," says Christine Kay, who does not like to talk about Blair. (Blair resigned after his false reporting was revealed.)

David Barstow was on the team assigned to look into Blair's record at the newspaper and thus learned early about the cousin's invention. "That tidbit about Jayson hit a very deep nerve inside this building," Barstow says.[8] "Blair gamed that situation," was how Gerald Boyd put it. "At

FIGURE 3.2 The *New York Times* managing editor Gerald Boyd steps to the microphone with publisher Arthur O. Sulzberger's encouragement on the day of the 2002 Pulitzer Prize announcements. To the right, executive editor Howell Raines looks on. Others present include Jonathan Landman (behind Boyd) and, next to him, Thomas Friedman. *Source*: Copyright © 2002, The New York Times Company. Reprinted by permission.

the publisher's insistence, we put together a list of all *Times* employees throughout the building, to find out who had lost relatives in the attacks. And it was in that sense we were told about Jayson." The *Times* treated employees who had lost loved ones compassionately and Blair benefited— especially when he started being caught in a series of reporting mistakes and was given special treatment because of his supposed loss of a cousin. In the wake of the Blair plagiarism scandal, Boyd and Howell Raines both resigned from the *Times* in June 2003. (Boyd, fifty-six, died of complications from lung cancer in November 2006, a few months after being interviewed for this book.)

While the gold medal was among the record seven Pulitzers garnered by the *Times* that year, the celebration among editors and staffers was muted.[9] "I had very mixed feelings," said Boyd. "I had seen first-hand the extraordinary job that the staff of the *Times* had done. I knew how difficult it was on people. I knew reporters who lost friends in the Twin Towers. I knew of people who had been down in Battery Park when the Towers collapsed and barely survived. And I knew of people who went to Afghanistan for us and had incredible medical problems that they're probably still trying to deal with." Still, "I also felt that the world had changed in a fundamental way. And so in that sense, all of this was more than just journalism. It wasn't about prizes." For Christine Kay, there was less conflict. "You want to know my personal thoughts? I wish they'd canceled the Pulitzers. Certainly one felt good about the effort and how 'Portraits' became this national touchstone. But I think everyone would rather not be standing there at all."

Few metropolitan news organizations will ever confront a challenge like 9/11 and its aftermath. But many will face the shock of a sudden community crisis that requires total staff commitment at a moment's notice—whether a raging storm, a horrific accident, or a major crime. In such instances, "A Nation Challenged" may offer some lessons. "Editors should understand that inspiration comes from a lot of different places, and you've got to have a mechanism that encourages people," said Boyd. The section and its "Portraits" feature served to inspire staffers just as it inspired readers. "I was always amazed how on a given day, someone I never would have thought of would have a brilliant idea. There was really a belief that people could be heard."

In his mind, the *Times*'s performance also underscored the value of avoiding the kinds of severe retrenchments that weaken a staff's ability to react to major events. "As executives and editors try to balance the cost of good journalism with the need for profits, they should think about a couple of things," said Boyd. When "A Nation Challenged" began, "the circulation of the newspaper went up 100,000 copies. The public was saying, 'If you are relevant, if you are trying to address things we care about, and if you are doing it in a way that provides quality, we'll come along.'"[10]

2002—The *New York Times* for "A Nation Challenged," a special section published regularly after the September 11th terrorist attacks on America, which coherently and comprehensively covered the tragic events, profiled the victims, and tracked the developing story, locally and globally.[11]

CHAPTER 4

EPIPHANY IN BOSTON

2003: The *Globe* and the Church

In fact, the investigative staff of the Boston Globe has done the Catholic Church an enormous favor. . . . They were the good guys, the guys in the white hats as opposed to the bad guys in the red hats.

—FATHER ANDREW M. GREELEY

Every new editor likes to make a splash the first day on the job. But Marty Baron's inaugural Monday morning story meeting at the *Boston Globe* on July 30, 2001, would hit with all the force of one of those rare summer hurricanes that sweeps up the Atlantic Coast to hammer New England.

The Florida-born Baron—forty-six at the time and a twenty-five-year newspaper veteran—had held senior editing posts at the *Los Angeles Times* and the *New York Times* before returning to his native state to serve the last eighteen months as the executive editor of the *Miami Herald*. There he had been on a fantastic roll. The *Herald* had won national praise for its aggressive handling of the Florida vote count debacle in which the presidential race between George W. Bush and Al Gore teetered on a review of "hanging chads" and other ballot peculiarities. In pursuit of the story, the *Herald* sponsored its own recount and launched legal challenges, running up a bill of $850,000 for its owner, Knight Ridder. Then, in April, the *Herald* had received the 2001 Pulitzer Prize for breaking news reporting for "balanced and gripping on-the-scene coverage" of the Elian Gonzalez affair.[1] Young Elian's story had riveted the nation twelve months before when federal agents seized the boy from his Miami relatives to reunite him with his Cuban father.

Along with prizes, Baron's management of such high-profile work had won him editor of the year recognition from *Editor and Publisher*. No wonder Baron was atop the list being kept by the *Globe*'s then-owner the New York Times Company for the plum assignment of running one of the nation's premiere papers. The *Globe*, which blankets New England with a daily circulation of more than 400,000, is also one of America's most honored publications. The *Globe* or its staff members had won an extremely respectable total of sixteen Pulitzer Prizes since its first prize in 1966.

Despite Baron's own impressive press clippings, the new editor tended to be the type of manager who makes a low-key first impression, asking questions rather than calling shots. At sessions like this editorial meeting— which Matthew Storin, his predecessor, had established as the standard day-starter—the main order of business was a critique of the morning's paper and a review of what stories were in the works. And Baron was content to use his first meeting for that purpose.

The *Globe* had been flown down to Baron in Miami for about a month, so he was familiar with some of its running coverage when he first walked through doors of the paper's huge brick Morrissey Boulevard complex south of downtown. One continuing story involved the legal case of a defrocked Catholic priest named John J. Geoghan, accused of sexually abusing children years earlier. A court filing that had managed to escape a judge-ordered confidentiality order—and that had been written about in the *Globe* only after it first appeared in the rival tabloid, the *Boston Herald*—suggested that Cardinal Bernard F. Law had been involved in keeping Geoghan active in the priesthood for years. The document said that Law had transferred Geoghan to another parish in 1984 after the priest had been accused of molesting young people in his care.[2]

While the Geoghan stories were not particularly prominent, two consecutive Sunday pieces by the *Globe* columnist Eileen McNamara caught Baron's eye in the week before the meeting.[3] They piqued his curiosity both about his new paper and about the Massachusetts court system. McNamara had noted that a Church-requested seal on the Geoghan case prevented the public from peering "into corners of the Church that the cardinal would prefer to keep forever in shadow." Baron was somewhat surprised by the response of the assembled editors as he ran down a list of possible stories and got to the Geoghan case. There wasn't any follow-up planned, they said. The paper seemed stumped by the court's confidentiality order.

The editor, however, had just come from a state in which so-called Sunshine laws tended to keep the media from being shut out. "I mentioned that I didn't know what the laws of Massachusetts are, but in Florida there's a more expansive public records law, and an inclination to make everything public. I asked whether there had been any consideration given to challenging the confidentiality order in court," Baron recalls. "There was some silence, and the answer was no."

He could certainly see why his new subordinates might be reluctant to pursue a major Geoghan article that lacked documentary support from court filings or interviews with the parties involved. Such coverage would be nearly devoid of the detail necessary to make the case come alive. "Of course I was looking for interesting stories," says Baron. "But I find people just arguing with each other to be pretty dissatisfying. It's important to get beyond the 'he-said, she-said' quality of news reports, to what actually happened, to what the underlying truth is." To do the Geoghan case that kind of journalistic justice would mean detailing the actions of the abusers, how their crimes had impacted the victims, and how the Church hierarchy had responded, for starters.

That day, a call went out to the *Globe* attorney Jonathan M. Albano asking him to look into the prospects for getting the court seal lifted. By mid-afternoon Baron had summoned to his office the paper's two top investigative editors: Ben Bradlee Jr., the deputy managing editor for projects and investigations, and Walter V. Robinson, the head of the Spotlight Team of investigative journalists and also its chief reporter. The subject was Geoghan: both the possibility that the paper might try to open up the court files and that Spotlight might begin looking into the circumstances surrounding the priest's alleged abuse of young parishioners.[4]

Bradlee and Robinson were among the paper's most widely experienced and respected editors—and were the keys to launching any major investigative project. Affectionately known to the staff as Robby, Robinson was a graduate of the Catholic Boston College High School just across Morrissey from the *Globe* and had joined the paper after graduating from Boston's Northeastern University in 1974. He had covered numerous major local, national, and international beats, including as the Middle East bureau chief during the 1991 Gulf War and as the White House correspondent under presidents Ronald Reagan and George H. W. Bush. Bradlee—a seasoned reporter and editor who had spent the last nine of his twenty-three years at the *Globe* managing the paper's special projects—had investigative work in his blood. He was the son of the *Washington Post* editor of Watergate Pulitzer Public Service fame.

The *Globe* owned two gold medals among the sixteen Pulitzers on its trophy wall. The 1966 prize had honored its service through a campaign that kept a politically connected jurist from being appointed as a federal judge. Then, in 1975, the paper's coverage of Boston school desegregation had been cited.

The "Prospecting" Begins

Baron's idea about trying to get the court records unsealed and investigating Geoghan's life as a sexual predator struck Bradlee and Robinson as particularly courageous because of its potential to embarrass the most powerful institution in their heavily Catholic city. Also, the decisiveness and speed with which the new editor had called such a critical meeting with his investigative leaders were a gust of fresh air blowing from the editor's office. While such snap sessions might seem normal in many newsrooms, in previous *Globe* administrations such a Baron-Bradlee-Robinson session probably would not have taken place without a half-dozen other editors being marshaled as well, and possibly even with publisher Richard Gilman being consulted. It was the *Globe*'s culture.

It also crossed Robinson's mind, he later wrote, that actually pursuing such a story would represent "the assignment from hell: a newspaper's investigative team pointed at the city's—any city's—preeminent sacred cow." The Boston archdiocese, in addition to being almost paranoid about what it perceived as "negative press," was known for extreme secretiveness in matters concerning its priests. So, Robinson thought, Spotlight would face a seemingly insurmountable obstacle: "How do you breach an institution that has neither the obligation nor the inclination to make its records public, nor to discuss how it operates?"[5]

Bradlee and Robinson enthusiastically agreed that Spotlight should take a look at whether to pursue a Geoghan project, however. That meant starting with a team process that Robinson calls "prospecting." The initial session with Bradlee and Robinson was only a discussion, as Baron puts it, about going beyond a document search "and actually embarking on a broader investigation of the whole case, apart and parallel with the legal action." A call on whether to pursue the story would be made later when the results of Spotlight's prospecting were in. While the lawyers began to study what the chances were for a motion challenging the confidentiality order in the Geoghan case, the scene shifted that afternoon to the tiny suite of offices—purposely made hard to get to from the newsroom one floor above it—that the Spotlight Team calls home. (Bradlee's office was upstairs, in the newsroom.)

Spotlight itself was one of the oldest standing investigative units among U.S. newspapers. Created in 1970, it was largely modeled on the "Insight" teams of the London *Sunday Times*, although some ideas had come from visits with members of the "Greene Team" at *Newsday.* The Long Island, New York, paper had launched the team concept under veteran investigative reporter Bob Greene.[6] On the *Globe's* trophy wall, Spotlight was responsible for two of the sixteen Pulitzers, both of them for investigative reporting. One, in 1972, for exposing corruption in the suburb of Somerville, had also been a public service finalist in the year that the *New York Times* won the gold medal for its work with the Pentagon Papers.

If the unit itself had a long history, the 2001 edition was relatively new. Only Matt Carroll, the team's computer-assisted reporting specialist, had been there more than a year. Robinson had taken the team leader job just after the 2000 elections, drawn to the job partly by the prospect of being able to hand-pick two reporters to fill vacancies on a squad of four members, including himself.

Looking for complementary skills and personalities—and steering clear of the "substantial egos" that he had seen infect the investigative ranks at some papers—he had selected state house reporter Michael Rezendes and legal affairs writer Sacha Pfeiffer. As it turned out, that meant that the new Spotlight was made up of four native Bostonians, all of whom happened to have Roman Catholic upbringings. (Robinson, though still having some Church-related associations, jokes that he is more of a "collapsed Catholic.")[7]

Rezendes remembers that on the afternoon of July 30, Robinson called the team into his office and told members about the discussions upstairs. They agreed to do some more reporting, short of engaging in a project at that point. "The idea," says Rezendes, "was to look at how many others besides Geoghan there might be."[8]

Spotlight typically came up with its own ideas. Says Robinson: "We go to the editors and we say we want to look into 'A.' We don't actually launch a project on 'A' until we've done enough of what I call prospecting to determine that we can get 'A.' Can we get documents? Can we get people to talk to us? Is it worth Spotlight's effort?" Working this way, Spotlight rolled out three or four major projects a year along with a few shorter-term stories. A Geoghan investigation would hardly be typical, of course. For one thing, Spotlight had been asked to check things out by the paper's new editor. That gave it special weight. For another, all the team members were clear—even without having done any reporting—that the story had the potential to dwarf any previous Spotlight project.

Rezendes had never known anyone personally who claimed to have been abused. Still, he says, "I remember having the thought, long before I got on the Spotlight Team, that clergy sexual abuse was an epidemic." And Pfeiffer had a particular professional interest in the subject. In her coverage of the courts, she had written occasional spot stories about suits that had been filed by lawyer Mitchell Garabedian on behalf of Geoghan's victims. In those stories, though, the detail was extremely thin, leaving to the imagination what awful specifics of child abuse were sealed away in the court filings.

The team members also were aware that stories about Geoghan and a Church cover-up of clergy sexual abuse were hardly new. Indeed, along with the story the *Herald* had broken about Cardinal Law's awareness of Geoghan's history, reporter Kristen Lombardi of Boston's weekly *Phoenix* had focused on the priest and some of his victims earlier in the year. No documentation at that point had backed up the suggestion that the Church was coddling Geoghan or other accused priests, however. Mostly Spotlight was curious about how far Geoghan's sexual abuse had extended and whether the problem went much beyond the case of one bad apple.

Prospecting involved total immersion in the topic: starting with calls to lawyers, known victims, the relative handful of experts in the field of clergy sexual abuse, and any priests or Church officials who would discuss the situation, off the record or on. In terms of previously reported cases, the team reviewed a scandal that had involved abuse allegations against

Father James R. Porter in the early 1990s. The charges and resulting news stories had rocked the Fall River diocese in the southeast corner of Massachusetts. His case, heavily covered by the *Globe* at the time, also stirred up a storm of press controversy within the Church. At one point, in fact, Cardinal Law had called down "the power of God" on the media—and especially the *Globe*—for suggesting in its Porter stories that sexual abuse by priests was a problem wider than *that* one bad apple.

A Green Light for Spotlight

"After several days of rummaging around we came upon people who told us that Geoghan was the tip of the iceberg," Robinson says. "I remember at the time saying to my wife, 'What if it was ten or twelve priests? What an extraordinary story that would be.'" The Church's own studies showed that pedophilia was a problem among no more than 0.5 percent of priests, or one of every two hundred, about the same as the population as a whole. But what Spotlight was hearing suggested a problem more insidious among the 650 priests in the archdiocese than the occasional bad apple infecting the clergy's barrel. Perhaps far more insidious.

Robinson reported first to Bradlee, then to Baron: "We hadn't advanced the ball much on Geoghan," he told them, but the team had heard reliably that Geoghan was one of many. And Geoghan was unusual not for the number of his victims, but "because his case had actually gotten to the lawsuit stage in court, whereas a large number of other cases had been quietly settled in chancery court."

Baron immediately gave the green light to Spotlight. Albano, the leader of the *Globe* legal team, provided arguments for and against trying to unseal the documents, calling the chance of success about fifty-fifty. "Those are actually pretty good odds for newspapers," says Baron, "so we decided to go to court." He had called publisher Richard Gilman before the decision to pursue the reporting and the court documents and had gotten the go-ahead. Says Baron: "I doubt he expected his new editor, as his first act—or ever, for that matter—to be confronting the Catholic Church in court." It was the start of many months of encouragement from the top.

Editors had reached a decision not to bring religion reporter Michael Paulson onto the team—at least not yet. Paulson and Robinson had discussed it, but historically beat reporters had been excluded from Spotlight investigations because it might interfere with their daily beat responsibility. Furthermore, says the Spotlight chief, "when the story breaks, we need to have an honest intermediate broker, the beat reporter who has credibility with the people he covers, because sometimes they won't talk to us."

On the Spotlight Team, Rezendes was "the Geoghan guy," which meant getting to know Mitchell Garabedian, who as attorney for the eighty-six victims had filed a total of eighty-four separate lawsuits. Rezendes's approach involved a lot of schmoozing with the lawyer, something he considered himself quite good at. "But mostly I got close to his clients," he says. He spent weeks interviewing victims, many of them lower-middle-class young adults who had been abused years before. Rezendes's experience in East Boston was valuable. "Some victim would be telling me his story, but be embarrassed and untrusting, and I'd say, 'Where do you live?' And he'd say over on Hyde Park Avenue. And I'd say, 'Oh, yeah, over by the Hi-Top Liquor Store.' Because I knew the neighborhoods, I could shoot the breeze."

The task of building a database of priests fell to Carroll, who had grown up in suburban Dedham and had started in journalism on the staff of the rival *Boston Herald*. Carroll had trained in CAR, as computer-assisted reporting is known, and had taught its techniques to other *Globe* staffers. Somewhere he had heard in class that CAR had played a critical role in every Pulitzer Prize for Public Service since 1980. In the early days investigating the Geoghan story, the database was kept on a simple, even primitive spreadsheet.

Thanks to Robinson, though, the database got its first big infusion. "Robby had this bright idea, which was to look at the annual reports issued by the diocese—their Yellow Pages for priests, basically," says Carroll.[9] Stacking two decades of directories in the office, and scanning them name by name, team members found some bland-looking yet suspicious notations. For a large number of priests, the directories used terms like "awaiting assignment," "sick leave," "clergy personnel office," or simply "unassigned"—this in a Church with a severe priest shortage. Sometimes, of course, the priest would really be sick, as checks by Spotlight would show. But in many cases the team's investigations turned up a background of sordid abuse allegations that correlated with the bland annotations. Eventually the team's file would expand to include nearly two hundred names of suspect priests.

Carroll, like the rest of the team, found Robinson to be an inspiring—and untiring—boss. "Nothing fazes him. He's done every job at the paper, and he is a madman for work," says Carroll. As the Geoghan story developed, Robinson's day in the office started at five-thirty in the morning, ninety minutes before his normal start time.

The team did not publish any stories based on its database or initial interviews, which were sometimes off the record. Instead it built a critical mass of material that the team expected would help Robinson and Bradlee determine the story theme. Even without writing, though, there was plenty to do in the office. Looking through the Church directories for "red flags"—those "sick leave" or "awaiting assignment" designations—led to a grueling but productive team ritual, says Sacha Pfeiffer. "One person would be typing, one person would be calling out information, and we would be divvying up this tedious task of typing and reading," she says.

Reporters contacted more attorneys who had filed cases against the Church. And Spotlight studied every lawsuit it could find that named the institution to see what was alleged and what documents might be available. "Obviously, a lot of cases were slip-and-fall cases," Pfeiffer says, "but there were plenty that weren't."[10]

Reporters as Counselors

When it came to interviewing victims of priests, Pfeiffer's skills were quickly noted by fellow team members in the confines of their small office area. She had a special gift for the delicate task of drawing people out and getting them to at least consider going public about their harrowing long-ago experiences. The early interviews "gave us a sense of the dimension and the scale and the volume of the complaints. It was very depressing and sad," she says. Pfeiffer developed her patient, compassionate interviewing style with people clearly in distress about terrible remembrances of things past. Even talking off the record, interviewees could be extremely sensitive. "We often had these victims who were so embarrassed, and in an embarrassed way were trying to explain how this happened—still wrestling with it themselves." Working through it with them, she says, "after a while you begin to understand yourself how it could happen."

For one thing, she attuned herself to the earlier eras in which much of the abuse had occurred. Beyond the sense of being betrayed by someone in a position of trust, she says, "people were afraid of being labeled as gay, with all the terrible consequences that came with that," she says. Sometimes Pfeiffer got dramatic results when she was able to get an interviewee to move past that fear. "This wall broke down, and people just told their stories. Before, there had been this stigma, and people were embarrassed and afraid and ashamed, with all the self-blame that comes with sexual abuse—multiplied, because it was priests who were doing it," she says. "Then all of a sudden the stigma was gone, and they had this waterfall of stories." Occasionally victims decided to tell her their stories of abuse before communicating with their own families. Pfeiffer wouldn't let them. "In some ways, we ended up protecting the victims from themselves," she says.

As they compared notes, discussing among themselves the terrors that young Catholics were being put through by Geoghan and others, the four reporters related to each other on a personal level—something unfamiliar to them from previous Spotlight work. It was then that they realized for the first time that each had been raised Catholic, although none was personally acquainted with victims of accused priests, at least as far as they knew. Each had a visceral reaction to the idea of priests violating the trust of families by preying on their children though. That Church officials would protect the priests rather than their young victims seemed almost inconceivable.

The image of what constituted a Spotlight story was about to change at the paper. In fact, a dramatic shift had already occurred in what other reporters thought of the team. "When I first went down there, someone said to me, 'Enjoy your early retirement,'" Pfeiffer laughs. Because only a few Spotlight projects saw print each year, the team had also offered what Robinson called "the lure of never having to write a lead that contains the word 'yesterday.'" And the work schedule? "Spotlight was a job you could do and still get home for dinner."[11] These were luxuries that would not last.

The decision to keep Paulson on the religion beat did allow him to pursue a personal mission he had committed himself to when he took it over after moving to Boston from the *Seattle Post-Intelligencer* in January 2000. The mission—soon to be severely tested—involved improving long-ailing relations with the archdiocese. In Paulson's mind, problems between the paper and the Church stretched back way before the Father Porter coverage that had angered Cardinal Law. The *Globe* editorial page had also supported positions that were anathema to the Church hierarchy such as birth control, abortion, and gay rights. In the reporter's studied opinion, the *Globe* had first disaffected many rank-and-file Catholics in the mid-1970s. They had turned against the paper, he reasoned, over what they perceived to be its support of school busing in all-white neighborhoods as a means of achieving racial integration.

Reporting on school busing had won the *Globe* its second Pulitzer Public Service Gold Medal in 1975. Back then, the Pulitzer board had cited the *Globe's* "massive and balanced coverage of the Boston school desegregation crisis." Robinson, who had been among the staffers covering the busing crisis, shared Paulson's view that many blue-collar conservative Catholics had soured on the paper during the controversy. For a quarter-century, the *Globe* had lived with it. Neither journalist had any idea how another challenge to the Church from the paper might affect the way these disaffected Catholics viewed the *Globe*. They did know, however, that if the Church story developed into a huge project, bringing Paulson onto Spotlight was an option that would help the *Globe* explain some of these deeper issues.

Robinson describes the early progress on the team's research as "chipping away at a thick wall with the dull edge of a knife." As August wound down, though, prospects for a good story, and maybe several, seemed better each day. Not only was progress being made on the Geoghan case, but the number of priests in the database was swelling.

Wait 'Til Next Year

The *Globe* was nearing a decision about whether to go forward with legally challenging the confidentiality order in the Geoghan case. It was a sensitive internal issue in the Boston newsroom because the New York Times Company policy calls for corporate lawyers in New York to review all legal actions by units, including the *Globe*.

Was there any danger that the existence of a full-fledged *Globe* investigative project about the Church might reach the ears of a *Times* reporter? "Of course I was worried that *New York Times* lawyers would tell *New York Times* journalists," Baron says. But he had to trust that the editorial "wall" between that publication and its sister paper would not be breached. (In retrospect, he says of the Times Company lawyers: "They were helpful—and entirely honorable.") In writing its motion seeking to unseal the documents, the *Globe* and Times Company attorneys focused on the public interest aspect, not prurient details or the names of victims. "What we were interested in was the Church, and whether it and the cardinal had fulfilled their responsibilities to protect children who were in their care," says Baron.

On September 6, with Rezendes the only reporter present, the *Globe* attorney Albano argued the case in the Springfield courtroom of Massachusetts Superior Court Judge Constance M. Sweeney, a graduate of Springfield's Cathedral High School and of Newton College of the Sacred Heart, since absorbed by Boston College. The parties prepared for a ruling that might take two months or so.

The next day, Robinson had a reporting breakthrough. He met in downtown Boston with two sources. They provided a list of priests who had been accused of sexual abuse but whose accusers had been paid so that they would not sue. There were about thirty-five names on the list—three times the number that Robinson had considered worthy of a major story just a month earlier.

How to proceed now seemed clear: with the Geoghan angle becoming more competitive—if court documents *were* unsealed, they would go to the *Herald* and the *Phoenix*, too, of course—Spotlight would attack the story on two fronts. It would explore the Geoghan case in depth, no matter what the decision was on court-imposed confidentiality. Meanwhile, it would capitalize on the team's exclusive information about the shockingly high number of priests accused of being child molesters—and information suggesting that Cardinal Law and others were allowing accused priests to keep working with children in parishes.

If reporting along that second front turned up strong material before the year's end, perhaps even before a decision was made on whether to unseal the court records, stories published before December 31 could have been entered for 2002 Pulitzer Prize consideration. And if the *Globe* attorneys somehow managed to get the Geoghan case unsealed, a public service in itself, Eileen McNamara's columns might have been packaged with the news stories to make a potent entry for the Pulitzer Public Service category.

The *Globe* will never know.

After departing from Boston's Logan Airport on a warm, sunny Tuesday morning, two Boeing 767 jetliners operated by American and United, loaded with fuel for their transcontinental flights, were hijacked by terrorists. Three hundred miles down the coast, they were flown into the upper stories of New York's World Trade Center. A third 767, originating that morning in Washington, D.C., smashed into the outer E- and D-Rings of the five-ringed Pentagon. A fourth jetliner crashed into a field in western Pennsylvania without hitting a target, likely after passengers overpowered the terrorists.

In the heart-stopping shock of September 11, 2001, only one thing was clear in the *Globe* newsroom as editors and reporters watched the Twin Towers collapse: the paper's best people needed to be thrown immediately into a story with such global, national, regional, and local impact. Work on the Church stories was stopped. "The whole paper was mobilized to work on the 9/11 attacks," says Marty Baron. "If that meant Church reporting was on hold, so be it." The four Spotlight members, the elite of the paper's investigators, were reassigned to the toughest of the endless stream of story ideas that emanated from the actions of the terrorists.

It wasn't until mid-October that team members would return to the Church project. Nothing of their work on the topic would be published by the end of 2001, and thus nothing would be eligible for the 2002 Pulitzer Prizes. Those prizes, awarded that April, would overwhelmingly recognize 9/11 coverage—including the work of the *New York Times* for public service.

He Knew!

With November approaching, the *Globe*'s work on the Church story could wait no longer. Robinson was burning to follow up on the meeting he had

had with two secret sources less than a week before 9/11, yielding more than thirty names of priests and suggesting that the Church had been making widespread use of private settlements to avoid the embarrassment of lawsuits filed by victims. After Robinson had a talk with Bradlee, the decision was made to resume, and Spotlight members Carroll, Rezendes, and Pfeiffer rejoined Robinson in picking up with interviews they had abruptly interrupted a month earlier.

Along the first of Spotlight's two tracks, the long list of priests hit with abuse allegations began development again as reporters explored how and why the Church allowed accused priests to stay in parish work—even as parents of victims were being paid so that they would not pursue lawsuits. The second track followed Geoghan.

Matt Carroll's database continued to provide good leads. A priest listed on sick leave in the Church directories "became a person of interest to us and we went through every directory for every year to chart his entire career," says Robinson. "We did it with every priest, and it was extremely time-consuming. It took us several weeks, and at the end of that we had a list of well over a hundred priests, including almost all of the thirty-some for whom we knew there had been secret settlements."

Bradlee was encouraged about the interviews and the backlog of data coming together along the two tracks. He had been Metro editor in 1992 when the last big Church sexual abuse case had broken involving Fall River's Father James Porter. Bradlee had felt that there was a lot more to the Porter story than the *Globe* had been able to report. He wanted the Geoghan story to say more about the prevalence of pedophilia in the Church, if possible, and how the hierarchy was dealing with it. The Porter story "hit the wall" because there was little evidence to support the claims of victims, Bradlee felt. In that case, too, the lawsuits had been sealed at the Church's request. "What was missing there was the paper," Bradlee says. "There were a bunch of plaintiffs who had gotten together and threatened to sue, but no suits."

Lack of documentation would not handicap the Geoghan story for long. While Judge Sweeney was considering the *Globe*'s request to unseal the Geoghan records, attorney Garabedian found a way to make public—seal or no seal—some damning information about how the Church had protected the priest. And Rezendes, once again absorbed in his self-described obsession with finding Church documents, quickly got a payoff for the close bond he had built with Garabedian and his clients.

The lawyer reminded the *Globe* reporter of the slovenly Paul Newman character in the movie *The Verdict*. "You would go into his crappy little office and there'd be no receptionist, and cardboard boxes overflowing with documents and empty Styrofoam coffee cups. The place was a mess," Rezendes says. He believed that Garabedian appreciated the sensitivity Rezendes showed when talking with clients who were abuse victims. But the reporter was working the lawyer, too. "I tried to romance him and be the best friend he ever had," Rezendes says. "It's kind of an art form, getting people to tell you things. And it's as important as finding documents."

It was working. To get Rezendes the critical documents that both men wanted public, the lawyer attached them to a formal response that he was making to a filing by Church lawyers. In a sealed case, attorneys are allowed to file unsealed attachments in specific instances. A document to support such a formal response is one such case.

As Rezendes sat in the Spotlight office looking through this windfall, one of Garabedian's attachments "just exploded in my mind." It was a 1984 letter from Bishop John d'Arcy to Archbishop Bernard Law—still a few months from being elevated to cardinal—warning him about Geoghan's "history of homosexual involvement with young boys" and noting that the parish to which he was being assigned was already "divided and troubled" by other matters. "If something happens," Bishop d'Arcy wrote, parishioners might be "convinced that the archdiocese has no concern for their welfare and simply sends them priests with problems."

Rezendes was stunned. "All Law's public statements to that date were that we didn't know that much about pedophilia. It was that kind of response." Sitting upright in the Spotlight office as he read the letter, "I said to myself—I think out loud—He knew!" Rezendes also noted in one of the Church directories that in 1984 Geoghan had been reassigned to a parish in Weston, where one of his duties was working with altar boys. "At that point I knew this was a monumental evil that we were dealing with," Rezendes says. "As a story, it was going to be huge."

Technically, the documents Garabedian had filed were just as available to the rival *Boston Herald*, the *Phoenix*, or others in the press. But Rezendes believed that the Geoghan case court file—covering the eighty-four separate lawsuits against the ex-priest—was so overwhelming that the competition would not be able to find the meaty unsealed material on their own, let alone make sense of their part in the overall case. And he was confident that the lawyer would not tell other reporters. So rather than prepare a spot story, Rezendes proposed that the documents become part of Spotlight's plan for publishing a major feature on the Geoghan case. Spotlight would run a feature no matter what happened in the final court ruling on the *Globe*'s challenge to the sealing of the documents. Rezendes guessed right: the paper would be first to use the d'Arcy letter.

Meanwhile, the effort by Albano to unseal the entire Geoghan file also was advancing without the competition taking much note. On November 20, Judge Sweeney delivered a bombshell to the archdiocese— she ruled in favor of the newspaper. The Church appealed, but a month later, on December 21, it lost the appeal as well. The release of ten thousand pages associated with all those Geoghan suits was scheduled for late January, roughly two weeks after the trial's projected start date. The next strategy of Church lawyers was to write a letter threatening the *Globe* with legal action if it published material taken from records that were still confidential. Indeed, the letter said, sanctions would be sought even for asking questions of the priests involved.

The Spotlight Team proceeded undeterred, following the pedophile priest story along its two tracks: the Geoghan path and the trail of the secret settlements. In mid-December, Bradlee aimed Spotlight's primary resources at preparing a curtain-raiser. The story would spell out what Spotlight knew about the Geoghan case and the role played by Cardinal Law in keeping the priest in circulation. Envisioned originally as a single 3,000-word piece, the Geoghan coverage soon took on a life of its own. Certainly there was too much powerful material for a single pre-trial story. The paper set January 6 and 7 as target dates for a two-part series. As Matt Carroll's database continued to burgeon, it was about to become a hot January for Spotlight.

A Clerk, a Court, and a Clicking Clock

Just after New Year's Day, Rezendes get another break thanks to Garabedian. While the actual court-ordered unsealing of the Geoghan court documents was still three weeks away—a delay to allow for the documents to be "redacted" for release, with victims' names removed, for example— Garabedian quietly told Rezendes about some *new* Church documents to be filed the next Friday, on January 4. Under the terms of the state court order lifting the seal, new filings were immediately to become public. The documents sounded most intriguing. They included psychiatric notes on Geoghan and statements the priest had made to doctors, and they contained material that the Church had weighed and rejected in deciding to reassign him to other parishes. In addition, some actual, detailed claims against Geoghan were in the files. If the *Globe* could get the documents before the competition did—and if Garabedian had not told the *Herald* and the *Phoenix* of his Friday filing plans—the *Globe* would have a pre-trial exclusive that would enhance the first Spotlight stories significantly. It would put much of the past several months' reporting in a meaningful context.

The timing seemed to work, though just barely. The Sunday story on January 6 would concentrate on the question of why it had taken thirty-four years and a succession of three cardinals and many bishops to place children out of Geoghan's reach. The Monday story would liberally use the documents that Garabedian was to file on Friday. It would offer a timeline of Geoghan's abuses and provide shocking details of just how he turned the children in his care into his victims.

Incorporating notes from his teammates, Rezendes started drafting the Sunday story in advance for Spotlight editor Robinson to edit. It would run with all four team members identified in a byline box and Rezendes listed as writer. "Our plan," Rezendes says, "was to get these documents, go over them, and work all weekend." Sacha Pfeiffer would write the Monday piece. To get the promised copies of the documents Garabedian filed on Friday, Rezendes and Carroll would show up at the court clerk's office at 4:15 p.m., forty-five minutes short of closing time. The reporters planned to get them from the clerk, quickly copy them, and head back to Morrissey Boulevard to help crash out the two-parter. These would be the first Spotlight stories to appear since the Church project was authorized five months earlier.

But suddenly, maddeningly, the courtroom clockwork took on the misshapen quality of a Salvador Dali painting. "What I didn't realize was that nobody knew we'd won our case," Rezendes recalls. The favorable ruling just before Christmas—and the effect it had of making all newly filed Geoghan documents instantly a matter of public record—seemed foreign to the court clerk. As the minute hand sped south, she refused to make them available.

"I believe in pampering clerks, so I very politely asked if there was someone else I could speak to," Rezendes recalls. "Yes there was, but it took a while to get her supervisor to the counter, and the clock was clicking very loudly here." The supervisor, also unaware that the filings should be open, had a suggestion: tell it to the judge.

Off the two Spotlight reporters went to the chambers of the Honorable Vierra Volterra—"whose name I will never forget," Rezendes says—cooling their heels briefly in the jury box of an adjacent courtroom while he became available. "It was getting close to 5 o'clock. Matt and I went in to talk to him, and he had the documents on his desk. He said, 'These are very sensitive documents.' And I said, Yes, judge, they are. And he said to me, 'Where is the editorial responsibility in publishing these documents?'"

Rezendes tried not to sigh too noticeably. "I didn't believe I was going to have to get into a philosophical conversation with this judge." But by then word had gotten to Robinson to rush a fax of the appeals court order to the courthouse. As Rezendes explained how responsible the *Globe* intended to be, the court clerk reappeared, fax in hand. "To his credit, the judge glanced at the appeals court ruling and just said, 'Yep, that's it. You can have it.'" Their long weekend was just beginning.

At the chancery, Cardinal Law had been asked weeks before to provide the Church's side of the Geoghan story to the *Globe*, beyond the position it had taken in court. The cardinal had been silent. Now, told that a story was within a day or two of running, he called Baron directly to tell him that there would be no comment. He didn't even care to see the questions the *Globe* offered to fax him.

Down in the Spotlight office, the focus was on writing and editing stories over a nonstop weekend. Drafts went from Robinson to Bradlee and then across the newsroom to Baron's office. Robinson was impressed with what Baron sent back down to Spotlight. "Marty is a very quick, astute editor," he says. "I have a memory on that first story that it was three or four thousand words, and Marty came back in about a half-hour's time with a dozen fairly critical questions, including things that had not been addressed."

Epiphany, Indeed

On Sunday, the Feast of the Epiphany in the Church calendar, *Globe* readers had an epiphany of their own. The story that morning ran on page one under the headline "Church Allowed Abuse by Priest for Years; Aware of Geoghan Record, Archdiocese Still Shuttled Him from Parish to Parish":

> Since the mid-1990s, more than 130 people have come forward with horrific childhood tales about how former priest John J. Geoghan allegedly fondled or raped them during a three-decade spree through a half-dozen Greater Boston parishes.
>
> Almost always, his victims were grammar school boys. One was just 4 years old.
>
> Then came last July's disclosure that Cardinal Bernard F. Law knew about Geoghan's problems in 1984, Law's first year in Boston, yet approved his transfer to St. Julia's parish in Weston. Wilson D. Rogers Jr., the cardinal's attorney, defended the move last summer, saying the archdiocese had medical assurances that each Geoghan reassignment was "appropriate and safe."
>
> But one of Law's bishops thought that the 1984 assignment of Geoghan to St. Julia's was so risky, he wrote the cardinal a letter in protest. And for good reason, the Spotlight Team found: the archdiocese already had substantial evidence of Geoghan's predatory sexual habits.[12]

The front-page article jumped to two pages inside the paper, quoting from Bishop D'Arcy's 1984 challenge to Law's decision to move Geoghan to another parish. There was also one woman's "poignant and prophetic" 1982 letter to Cardinal Law's predecessor "expressing incredulity that the church to which she was devoted would give Geoghan another chance" after he had molested seven children in her family. A powerful interview with a victim, twenty-six-year-old Patrick McSorley, vividly detailed Geoghan's abuse of him at twelve years old and said that to "find out later that the Catholic Church knew he was a child molester—every day it bothers me more and more."

Monday's story ran under the headline "Geoghan Preferred Preying on Poorer Children" and included descriptions in Geoghan's own words,

LOTTERY, PAGE A2

Volume 261
Number 6
$2.00

Boston Sunday Globe

BREAKFAST FLAKES

TODAY: *Cloudy with snow at night, highs 34-41*

TOMORROW: *Snow ending noon, breezy, highs 31-36*

FULL REPORT: PAGE B8

JANUARY 6, 2002

Church allowed abuse by priest for years

Spotlight

This article was prepared by the Globe Spotlight Team: reporters Matt Carroll, Sacha Pfeiffer, and Michael Rezendes; and editor Walter V. Robinson. It was written by Rezendes.

Aware of Geoghan record, archdiocese still shuttled him from parish to parish

First of two parts

Since the mid-1990s, more than 130 people have come forward with horrific childhood tales about how former priest John J. Geoghan allegedly fondled or raped them during a three-decade spree through a half-dozen Greater Boston parishes.

Almost always, his victims were grammar school boys. One was just 4 years old.

Then came last July's disclosure that Cardinal Bernard F. Law knew about Geoghan's problems in 1984, Law's first year in Boston, yet approved his transfer to St. Julia's parish in Weston. Wilson D. Rogers Jr., the cardinal's attorney, defended the move last summer, saying the archdiocese had medical assurances that each Geoghan reassignment was "appropriate and safe."

But one of Law's bishops thought that the 1984 assignment of Geoghan to St. Julia's was so risky, he wrote the cardinal a letter in protest. And for good reason, the Spotlight Team found: The archdiocese already had substantial evidence of Geoghan's predatory sexual habits. That included his assertion in 1980 that his repeated abuse of seven boys in one extended family was not a "serious" problem, according to an archdiocesan record.

The St. Julia's assignment proved disastrous. Geoghan was put in charge of three youth groups, including altar boys. In 1989, he was forced to go on sick leave after more complaints of sexual abuse, and spent months in two institutions that treat sexually abusive priests. Even so, the archdiocese returned him to St. Julia's, where Geoghan continued to abuse children for another three years.

Now, as Geoghan faces the first of two criminal trials next week, details about his sexual compulsion are likely to be overshadowed by a question that many Catholics find even more troubling: Why did it take a succession of three cardinals and many bishops 34 years to place children out of Geoghan's reach?

Donna Morrissey, a spokeswoman for Law, said the cardinal and other church officials would not respond to questions about Geoghan. Morrissey said the church had no interest in knowing what the Globe's questions would be.

SPOTLIGHT, Page A14

GLOBE STAFF PHOTO/BILL GREENE

Former priest John J. Geoghan leaving his family home in Scituate in November.

Antitrust exception shields baseball

Proviso may stymie Reilly probe of Sox

By Bob Hohler
GLOBE STAFF

America's last great monopoly, Major League Baseball, long has prevailed over the meek and mighty: players seeking legal relief from owners who controlled them like chattel, fans pleading with judges to keep their prized teams from skipping town, elected leaders trying to examine how an exclusive group of rich individuals and corporations privately governs the national pastime.

All those who have challenged the multibillion-dollar industry — as Massachusetts Attorney General Thomas F. Reilly has over the sale of the Red Sox — have encountered a nearly impenetrable shield: an exemption from antitrust laws that for 80 years has provided big league baseball protection unrivaled in professional sports.

Reilly has cried foul, like many others before him. Saying baseball's protected status fostered a climate in which the high bidder for the Red Sox lost to a group that was favored by a "club" of owners that controls the sport, he called on Congress to examine the deal and repeal the game's sweeping exemption from antitrust laws.

But even though the Senate Judiciary Committee may review the sale in March as part of a hearing on baseball's antitrust exemption,

BASEBALL, Page D13

REUTERS PHOTO

President Bush defended his tax cuts vigorously at a town-hall-style meeting yesterday in Ontario, Calif.

Bush joins fiscal fight, defends tax cut

Economy will share priority with terror war

By Anne E. Kornblut
GLOBE STAFF

ONTARIO, Calif. — President Bush, marking a shift toward domestic politics after three months of war, yesterday launched a spirited defense of his tax cuts and promised to block any attempt to revise them, declaring, "Not over my dead body will they raise your taxes."

Joining an escalating war of words over the economy, Bush used his first major appearance of 2002 to lambaste Senate Democrats who have blamed last year's $1.3 trillion, 10-year tax cut for the recent downturn. In a town-hall-style meeting sponsored by Hispanic business leaders here, Bush mocked "some in Washington saying the tax cut caused the recession."

"I don't know what economic textbook they're reading," Bush said. "The best way to come out of a recession is to say to a small-business person . . . it's your money."

Then, raising a specter that no one has actually proposed, Bush said, "Not over my dead body will they raise your taxes."

While the president is determined not to let Democrats use a weak economy against him as they did against his father in 1992, his words yesterday were reminiscent of George H.W. Bush's 1988 campaign pledge, "Read my lips: no new taxes." Amid a slumping economy, that broken promise later became an albatross for the elder Bush in his failed reelection bid.

Later yesterday, in an almost identical speech in Oregon, Bush did not repeat the

BUSH, Page A16

US comes up empty in search for Omar

Cleric reportedly rides off; two other Taliban detained

By Elizabeth Neuffer and Colin Nickerson
GLOBE STAFF

KABUL, Afghanistan — Mullah Mohammed Omar, the Muslim cleric who is No. 2 on the American target list, has evaded a manhunt and vanished from the mountainous area in which he was believed to be hiding, Afghan officials said yesterday.

They said Omar had fled the region around the hamlet of Baghran, in south-central Afghanistan, possibly roaring out on a motorcycle. The team of US Army Special Forces and anti-Taliban Afghan troops who had been searching for him gave up the hunt and left yesterday, too.

For the past week, the same Afghans have claimed that a noose was tightening around Omar and hundreds of diehard Taliban loyalists in the area, as mujahideen fighters closed on their suspected positions in the rugged mountains near Baghran.

"There aren't any Taliban or Al Qaeda in Baghran now," Haji Gallalai, intelligence chief for the Kandahar region, told reporters. "Mullah Omar is also not in Baghran."

Even as Omar seemingly eluded capture, US forces in Afghanistan yesterday took custody of the Taliban's former ambassador to Pakistan, Mullah Abdul Salam Zaeef. He was deported from Pakistan after being held by authorities there.

The American forces also have taken custody of Ibn Al-Shaykh al-Libi, who ran some of Osama bin

OMAR, Page A22

Bomb probe eyes Pakistan links

Extremist may have influenced Reid

By Farah Stockman
GLOBE STAFF

LAHORE, Pakistan — The investigation of Richard Colvin Reid, the British national arrested aboard an American Airlines flight with explosives in his shoes, has led authorities to one of Pakistan's most secretive and controversial spiritual leaders, a man who over the past 15 years has brought more than 100 US citizens, mostly African-Americans, to Pakistan for religious and military training.

US officials believe that Reid, like the American converts, was a follower of Sheik Mubarik Ali Gilani, according to a Pakistani government official who has been asked by the United States to search for traces of Reid's past in Pakistan.

"He was there," said the official, referring to Gilani's walled compound in Lahore.

A member of Gilani's large extended family also said that Reid had visited the home. Both the Pakistani official and the family member declined to be identified.

But a spokesman for Gilani's network of followers said that Reid, 28, is unknown to them and called the report that he was a follower of Gilani a conspiracy to discredit the group, which has been targeted by the United States since the 1993 World Trade Center bombing.

"He is not a follower, and he is not known to any of the people within our system," Khalid Khawaja, a close friend of Gilani, said of Reid. "If there was anything like that, we would have known it."

The Pakistani official said he is

REID, Page A23

AFP PHOTO

DREAMS OF FLIGHT — Women waiting outside the Ariana Afghan Airlines office yesterday in Kabul after applying for 40 flight attendant positions. The vacancies drew 140 applicants.

Inside Today

Celtics beat Knicks

The Celtics snatched a 90-81 victory over the New York Knicks last night. Paul Pierce and Antoine Walker showed poise leading Boston's offense. **Sports, D1.**

Teen crashes plane

A 15-year-old student pilot took off in a plane without permission yesterday and crashed into a skyscraper in Tampa. **Nation, A7.**

'60s interrupted

For James Taylor and other affluent young people, McLean psychiatric hospital was a rite of passage. **Boston Globe Magazine.**

News guide, index - Page A2

For breaking news, updated Globe stories, and more, visit:

Boston.com

01643

0 947725 4

Rappaport's party-crashing quest for No. 2

JAMES RAPPAPORT
"It is not divisive"

By Yvonne Abraham
GLOBE STAFF

CONCORD — Heady from his first day of battle, still wearing makeup from multiple camera calls, James Rappaport, GOP candidate for lieutenant governor, paced from enormous room to enormous room in his mansion, rallying his troops via conference call.

Acting Governor Jane Swift had just announced her running mate for this year's gubernatorial race. Not Rappaport, of course, despite his best efforts. Swift had made it abundantly clear that he was not and never had been her man, and Rappaport was spitting out counterspin at a frantic pace.

Snippets of his speech were audible as he passed through the yellow living room.

"We now know what our goals are," he said. "This is about us taking our case to the people. Look, I was running first . . . It is not divisive . . . We're going to have to hang tough . . . There are five people running for governor on the other side. Why isn't that seen as divisive? They're going to paint us as the fringe . . ."

Swift chose aide Patrick C. Guerriero after making her way down an embarrassingly long list of potential, but unwilling, running mates to avoid giving Rappaport the nod.

But Rappaport isn't going to let a little thing like being dismissed by Swift stop him from becoming her No. 2.

And if the state Republican Party won't rally behind him, he'll just run as an outsider.

And if the GOP faithful won't cough up donations to help him, he'll use his own money, of

RAPPAPORT, Page A17

FIGURE 4.1 The *Boston Globe* began its series with an article across the top of the front page on January 6, 2002. *Source*: Used by permission.

explaining why he was "affectionate" with certain children. It laid out the psychiatric debate about the priest, again all from Church records, for readers to evaluate.

Both stories carried a "Contact the *Globe*" box with the Spotlight telephone number, a separate confidential hotline, and an e-mail address. The hotline was to get a lot of use—and almost none of it the carping about an "anti-Catholic" bias that many staffers had expected.

Indeed, Mike Rezendes feared that he would come into work to a demonstration at the door. "This is, after all, the most Catholic city in America," he says. Instead he encountered "an eerie quiet—no protestors, nothing." Then all at once, it seemed, the lines clogged with calls of an unexpected kind: "People were incredibly angry, yes. But not at us. It was at this institution that they loved." Or they called to report new cases of abuse. Checking the names of priests the callers named, Spotlight found that nearly all were mentioned already in its now-bulging database.

"Looking back, I believe the reason for not blaming the messenger was that we had the goods," Rezendes says. "We did not use anonymous sources. It was irrefutable. It was completely locked tight. There wasn't a fact in it that was wrong." And the documents, either quoted in the article or put online in their entirety, "were riveting and appalling."

As the new editor who was ultimately responsible, Marty Baron breathed a sigh of relief. Another followed when the usually combative Cardinal Law held a press conference a few days later. Far from attacking the *Globe*, the cardinal actually apologized to his flock. "It was clear that our stories were uncontestable, because he didn't contest anything," the editor says. "There was no fact that he challenged. And that alone added enormous weight to our coverage." Other newspapers around the country, seeing the Church's apologetic response, not only carried stories of the Boston paper's disclosures but also slowly began launching investigations of their own local parishes.

The *Globe* stories had been written and edited to display what Baron calls "a highly dispassionate tone," even at times "deadpan." The intention was to unburden the stories of any language that even hinted at an agenda. "We knew as a fact that the story would be explosive enough," he says. "If we started characterizing it, and using highly descriptive terms and adjectives, then that itself was going to become a target. There was no purpose served in turning over ammunition to people." Spotlight reporters would eventually adopt that tone on their own.

Robinson later hinted that Baron had done at least his share of toning down the final drafts, though. "Somewhere within sight of this news-room," he was to joke the day the Pulitzer Prize was announced, "there has to be a closet-full of adjectives he excised from these stories."[13]

"This Is Different"

The *Globe* investigative specialist Steven Kurkjian, a former Spotlight Team member, had recently been more of a "lone wolf" engaged in one-man projects for projects editor Bradlee. In preparation for the flood of Geoghan documents, Robinson managed to get Kurkjian assigned as the first of four additional Spotlight reporters for the Church stories. Eventually, one of his specialties would become the serious financial threat to the Church posed by the tens of millions of dollars of suits and by the waning support for Cardinal Law among the wealthy Catholic laity—which was not unrelated to the money crisis. By next December 1, Robinson and Kurkjian would be writing a page-one story headlined "Archdiocese Weighs Bankruptcy Filing."

But first, there was the crunch on the Geoghan case. A January 24 front-page story, written by Robinson and Matt Carroll with Kurkjian joining the team names in the credit box, contained a penetrating analysis of the volumes of documents in the Geoghan case. The story was an exclusive; the paper had gotten documents a day ahead of the general release. Robinson says the team talked Garabedian into providing material early. That "beat" on its rivals reinforced the sense that the paper was invincible on the Church coverage.

The next *Globe* blockbuster—on Thursday, January 31—was the long-awaited piece on the secret settlements that the Church had signed, covering an estimated seventy or more priests. Headlined "Scores of Priests Involved in Sex Abuse Cases; Settlements Kept Scope of Issue Out of Public Eye," the article was accompanied by thumbnails on twenty-three accused priests. The paper described the database that the *Globe* had assembled and how the Church's own directories had tipped the paper to suspected molesters.

By then Pfeiffer was already toning down her prose to reflect the direction from above to be careful with inflammatory words. "We learned to do that ourselves," she says. "We were aware how delicate this situation was." Her reporting style drew out victims to tell their stories in intimate detail. It awed other Spotlight members, who all were facing extraordinary challenges in the victim interviews that were increasingly becoming vital to the coverage.

In a way, she helped make it harder for herself and her teammates, she acknowledges, by pushing for strong language to describe what had gone on between priests and their victims. "You couldn't just continually use the word molest, because this meant a world of things. And it was important for readers to understand in more detail what had happened," she says. That put Pfeiffer in the position of pressing victims to detail the sex acts that the priest forced on them—an uncomfortable position for interviewee and interviewer alike. "You're dealing with a very delicate issue with very fragile people, but sometimes you would need to be firm with them," she says. "You need very specific kinds of information about what happened to them sexually, because you need to figure out if this was a rape case, or touching—if you're talking about criminal allegations."

She took to spending extra time explaining why she was asking such detailed questions. "It's invasive," she says. "So I would be very open and say, I'm sorry to have to ask this; I know it's very personal, but I need to understand what exactly happened, because I need to understand if it's a criminal act. Sometimes you'd have to hold your breath a little bit as you asked the questions." The answers often knocked her over.

Pfeiffer also was worried that readers would simply disbelieve such sordid truths. "Some people were resistant to the idea that a kid could be repeatedly molested by a priest. They thought that if something happened repeatedly, that meant it was consensual," she says. "We needed to explain to them how it was possible, how the psychology works, how a friendship can be very carefully turned into a sexual relationship." A manipulative power figure could do it, and it was important for readers to understand how even a child who sensed that something was not right could be persuaded to keep doing it.

Pfeiffer and other Spotlight reporters take pride in the sensitivity that the team displayed toward all sides, and especially the concern that came through in the victims' stories. (It was concern that would continue long past the winning of the 2003 Pulitzer Prize. On August 23, 2003, Geoghan was murdered in his prison cell. And Patrick McSorley, the Geoghan victim identified early in the *Globe* coverage, later committed suicide.)

If Robinson had one complaint about the way the *Globe* dealt with this multidimensional story, he says, it was the slowness with which reporters were added to Spotlight. "We were working sixteen-hour days and weekends. The phone wouldn't stop ringing." And the newly public Geoghan papers were an avalanche. "We went through that first month, and certainly through the huge Geoghan 'document dump,' with just the four of us." Kurkjian had reported for duty on the day the ten thousand pages of records arrived. Reporters Kevin Cullen and Thomas Farragher joined at the end of January. They hit the ground running. Among Farragher's contributions was a February 3 study of the Church's "culture of silence" in dealing with sexual abuse among priests. Cullen's contributions included a May 12 analysis of how the scandal was eroding the traditional deference that many Catholics had for their Church.

As personal as the issue of priest abuse was for reporters on the Spotlight Team who had been raised Catholic, it was especially so for Farragher, a former altar boy. "My mother thinks priests walk on water," he says. One day he was at home with her when his sister brought news that their own family priest—the clergyman who had married Farragher and his wife—had been alleged to be an abuser. (The report first appeared in the *Herald*, as it scrambled to get at least a few news crumbs from the banquet being served up by its overpowering rival.) "You build up a hard exterior and become numb to it. Then, unexpectedly, it would affect you," says Farragher. In general, he adds, the scandals "upset me more as a father than as a Catholic."[14]

At times, pure pathos flowed from the *Globe*'s pages. Take the February 3 story by Robinson. It began:

> Like other victims of pedophile priests, Tom remembers vividly what happened just after he was molested in a dark corridor at Immaculate Conception School in Revere by the Rev. James R. Porter. It was 1960. He was 12. But he still recalls running.
>
> He ran, and then he hid. Under a desk in a second-floor classroom, frozen in terror as Porter called out for him. And then he ran again, out of the school and home.

Chris was victimized about 12 years ago. He remembers struggling as the Rev. John J. Geoghan groped him in the rectory at St. Julia's in Weston before he squirmed out of Geoghan's grasp. As Geoghan yelled after him, "No one will ever believe you," Chris ran from the room. He ran from the rectory. He ran behind the church—and cowered there until his father came for him. Geoghan was right; Chris never said a word.

Now Tom and Chris have stopped running. Thomas R. Fulchino, the father, and Christopher T. Fulchino, his son, are victims of Massachusetts' two most notorious priest pedophiles—three decades apart. For their family, lightning struck twice.[15]

"It was such a tragic story," the team leader says. "To sit with the father and listen to what happened to him, and how he had gradually come to trust the Church again. And then to hear what the mother had gone through when the family almost came apart again. It was a story you couldn't over-write."

Enter the Beat Reporter

The final addition to the Spotlight crew—and a vital one as the story expanded to require more analysis about the impact on the Church—was religion reporter Michael Paulson, who had been left out of the first wave of articles. Paulson, too, had been consumed with special projects after September 11. That had also been a major story for religion reporters.

Just after the first Spotlight Church stories ran, Paulson contributed occasional stories for the scandal coverage, although his chain of command remained through the Metro desk in the upstairs newsroom. But soon it became difficult answering to two masters, as he describes the arrangement. "I was trying to juggle regular religion reporting and my role in the unfolding crisis," he says. So he approached Bradlee about becoming Spotlight's eighth member and was added to the team.[16]

He quickly became a key participant. "One of the things that made our coverage so much more distinctive than just being investigative revelations was Mike's ability to step back and bring the whole Church into the context of the story," says Robinson. Paulson—who kept his desk upstairs in the newsroom, closer to Bradlee—soon found himself writing more scandal-related stories than anybody. He wrote about the world's view of the American Church scandal, the action of bishops against priest sexual abuse, and, on December 14, a story headlined "A Church Seeks Healing: Pope Accepts Law's Resignation in Rome." The continuing stream of Church stories remained a major part of his beat even after Spotlight was finally pulled off the Church story in 2003.

"Lots of other religious denominations have been forced to rethink the way they prevent and handle abuse, too," Paulson notes. The national price tag of abuse settlements in 2005 had passed $1 billion—most of that after the first *Globe* story was published. And deeper questions continued to develop for Catholicism. "I think it will be a century before we really know how it all plays out. Does the American Church become smaller? Do people simply leave? Or does the universal church change more readily than people expect? It's not on the American news cycle that the Catholic Church changes," says Paulson, who moved to the *New York Times* in 2011 and for a time covered religion there. "When you think about the impact

FIGURE 4.2 The *Globe's* Spotlight team on the deck of editor Martin Baron's home. From left, Thomas Farragher, Michael Rezendes, Kevin Cullen, Michael Paulson, Ben Bradlee Jr., Walter Robinson, Sacha Pfeiffer, Matt Carroll, Baron, and Stephen Kurkjian. In the background is the Cathedral of the Holy Cross, Cardinal Bernard Law's home church in the Boston diocese. Photo by Essdras M. Suarez, *Globe* staff. *Source*: Used by permission.

of this crisis, most of it couldn't have been known to the Pulitzer board" when it made the decision on the prize.

But much *was* known, as Marty Baron's nomination letter for the Public Service Pulitzer noted. "By year's end, the scandal had forced the removal of four-hundred-fifty accused priests nationwide," he wrote. What had emerged, Baron pointed out, was "a nationwide pattern within the Catholic Church of concealing abuse by priests and a practice of shuffling abusive priests from parish to parish."[17] The editor also quoted Father Andrew M. Greeley as writing that without the *Globe* accounts "the abuse would have gone right on. There would have been no crisis, no demand from the laity that the church cut out this cancer of irresponsibility, corruption, and sin, and no charter for the protection of children."[18]

For the Pulitzer board members who convened at Columbia, too, the Church scandal "was obviously the big news of the year," says the *Oregonian* editor Sandra Mims Rowe, who was on the board. "You knew the *Globe* was going to end up being a contender long before you got to the meeting." But under the board's analysis, it was anything but automatic. In her term as a board member from 1996 to 2004, Rowe says, coverage

FIGURES 4.3 AND 4.4 The *Globe*'s 2003 Pulitzer Gold Medal, front and reverse. Photos by Essdras M. Suarez, *Globe* staff. *Source*: Used by permission.

of major stories was often faulted for flaws that turned up under intense review. "You'd see things and say, Boy, in the right hands, this could be wonderful, but the quality of the work just is not there," she says. In the *Globe*'s case, though, "the caliber of the journalism and the execution were something rare."[19]

That opinion extended far beyond the board. "In some ways, the clerical abuse scandal has become a journalism textbook. Consider the elements: power, corruption, intrigue, tragedy, sex, betrayal, money—and an institution that dates back 2,000 years," the *Los Angeles Times* New England correspondent Elizabeth Mehren wrote in a study of the crisis for *Nieman Reports*. "The villains are despicable. Meanwhile, the proverbial quest for truth and justice—what brought us all into this line of endeavor, after all—is always at the forefront."[20]

The scandal, of course, continues to have national and global repercussions far beyond journalism—remaining a major issue in the Church since the March 2013 election of Pope Francis. The pope went as far as to initiate in June 2015 a tribunal aimed at bishops suspected of enabling abusive priests.[21] And it continues to be felt most deeply in Boston, considered the nation's most Catholic city.[22] *Spotlight*, a motion picture account of how the *Globe* covered the Church story, was being prepared for release in late 2015.[23]

"There's No Harder Target"

Just when did the *Globe* team members first sense that the story had the potential to be a blockbuster and perhaps a recipient of the Public Service Pulitzer? Matt Carroll admits to acknowledging the prospect of a prize during the April 2002 Pulitzer announcements when the *New York Times* and its staffers walked off with its seven awards, including the gold medal. "I remember thinking, Gee, I wonder if they'll be announcing our names next year," he says. "It's one of the things you dismiss, and then move ahead."

Ben Bradlee had a feeling after he observed the lack of negative reaction to the first *Globe* stories from among the Catholic community and from Cardinal Law himself. It was then that he had told Baron that the story had hit a home run. "We struck a nerve," the projects editor says. "You never know when a story is going to have that kind of Zeitgeist." He and his famous father at the *Washington Post* checked in regularly with each other as the Church story developed, although they each say that they never compared the unfolding Church scandal to Watergate.

Comparisons of the two scandals come naturally to others. In some ways, notes Steve Kurkjian—veteran of three Pulitzer-winning teams at the *Globe*—the Church stories may have hit harder than Watergate because there was little surprise that Washington politicians, even at the highest levels, would lie to protect themselves. With the Church story, "never have you had an institution with this vaunted an image taking such a blow."[24] The *Globe's* reporting and the *Post's* Watergate coverage both focused on cover-ups, Robinson adds. He believes the Church's deceit was far more troubling than the crime. "It facilitated further abuse over the years, by the same and other people," he says, "and it undermined the integrity of the institution in ways from which it will never recover."

From Bob Woodward comes high praise for the *Globe*, along with a warning for the media about how few other papers assume the same kinds of risks that the *Globe* and the *Post* did. "It takes a particular kind of energy and courage on the part of editors and publishers to support daily incremental coverage," Woodward says. Too many projects today involve "low-hanging fruit," subjects that reporters and readers already know are tinged with scandal. "I worry sometimes that we don't pick the really hard, important targets that have much broader implications," he adds. "That's where I take my hat off to the *Globe*, because there's no harder target than the Catholic Church."[25]

2003—The *Boston Globe* for its courageous, comprehensive coverage of sexual abuse by priests, an effort that pierced secrecy, stirred local, national and international reaction and produced changes in the Roman Catholic Church.[26]

CHAPTER 5

FROM *TIMES* TO *TIMES*

2004–2005: Rivals Win in New York and Los Angeles

It's not enough to be good at what you do. You want to be part of a team that's winning. And this was like the Red Sox beating the Yankees. Winning those Pulitzers gave them the sense that they themselves were being validated, as well as the paper.

—*LOS ANGELES TIMES* EDITOR JOHN CARROLL, ON EARNING FIVE 2004 PULITZERS TO THE ONE FOR THE *NEW YORK TIMES*

Some intrigue in the Pulitzer boardroom spiced up the 2004 public service selection—and brought the *New York Times* more gold. The *Times* had nominated the workplace safety reporting of David Barstow and Lowell Bergman in both the investigative reporting and public service categories. But the work—focusing both on company safety lapses and the government's inability to deal with fatal plant accidents—had not been among the jury's finalists in public service, Barstow learned through the usually reliable rumor mill. (Not until 2009 did the Pulitzer organization manage to plug the leaking of jury nominations, in part by having jurors sign a pledge of silence.) Barstow held out hope that the *Times*'s work could still win in investigative reporting, although his reading of one other supposed finalist—the Toledo *Blade*'s exposure of long-ago Vietnam atrocities committed by a unit called Tiger Force—seemed to suggest tough competition. Barstow was proud of the *Times*'s work but the *Blade*'s work had the look of a Pulitzer winner too. He held his breath.

In the days leading up to the Pulitzer announcement, Barstow got the classic bad news/good news treatment from the rumor mill. The Pulitzer board had picked the *Blade*'s Tiger Force stories for investigative reporting. But his and Bergman's stories had been moved by the board back to the public service category, where they had won. One finalist was the *Providence Journal* for its series focusing on the causes of the Station nightclub fire, which had killed one hundred rock concert attendees in West War-wick, Rhode Island. Another was the Louisville *Courier-Journal* for stories on the delays in Kentucky's criminal justice system.[1]

What had happened was this: during the jury deliberations, the inves-tigative reporting and public service panels had decided between the two of them to nominate the Barstow-Bergman *Times* entry in investigative reporting and not public service. But as the Pulitzer board pondered the six finalists spread across investigative reporting and public service, it saw the workplace safety story as a better fit for the gold medal than anything on the jury's public service list.[2]

Most board members had already read the *Times*'s workplace reports—a "familiarity" edge the *Times* gets in most years—and they had left a strong impression. The board then reviewed the investigative reporting jury's report. "Thanks to the indefatigable investigative reporting of the *New York Times*, the American public now knows that too many employ-ers force countless workers to toil in conditions so unsafe that many con-sider themselves fortunate to survive the workweek," the panel wrote. "The *Times* investigation has led to widespread cries for reform; a search-ing government investigation of its own conduct; and has already resulted directly in several criminal indictments."[3] That recommendation gave it the ring of a public service winner.

The joy was keen in Times Square. Without this prize, the newspaper would have been shut out of Pulitzers for the first time since 2000. And as a gold medal, it was special too. The *Times*'s fifth, it tied the paper with the *Post-Dispatch* for the most ever won by a single news organization. (The *Times*—which had won medals in 1918, 1944, 1972, and 2002—had collected by far the most overall Pulitzer awards: ninety through 2003.)

The *Times*'s first three-part project, a January report called "Dangerous Business," had begun with a tip received by investigative reporter Lowell Bergman. The tip had a 9/11 connection. Bergman, the former CBS *Sixty Minutes* producer/reporter who had joined the *Times* as an investigative reporter in 1999 and was jointly serving as a producer and correspondent for Public Broadcasting System's *Frontline* program, had been grounded on a flight just after the terrorist attacks on New York and Washington. While waiting for flights to resume, he got to talking with a federal Justice Department source who was looking into the death of a worker at a Texas company called Tyler Pipe. A question the source asked Bergman piqued his interest: "Did you know it's only a misdemeanor to kill a worker?" The Tyler worker, Rolan Hoskin, had been crushed to death on an unprotected conveyor belt. Eventually Bergman was teamed to do the three-part investigation of Tyler with Barstow, who also had come to the *Times* in 1999 and had joined its investigative desk in 2002.

At first Barstow saw the Tyler Pipe story, with the death of a single worker, as having small dimensions—at least relative to what he had been covering. "I'd spent months and months dealing with widows and widowers and confronting mass death," he says. Not only had he reported regularly from Ground Zero and reported and written a number of the "Portraits of Grief" vignettes, but he had also developed a specialty: investigating payments flowing to the 9/11 victims. "I was charting all kinds of screw-ups and inequities and other problems that plagued the entire messy process," he says.

One early interview about the workplace situation in Tyler with an old-timer who had forty years as an iron pourer changed everything. "It was a real lightbulb moment," says Barstow. The man, with his forearms covered with scars, told of the pressure Tyler had been under since Birmingham-based McWane Incorporated bought the plant in 1995. The company had laid off half the work force, including maintenance employees and, critically, extra "relief" workers for men on the line in the 130-degree summer heat in the plant.

"You have to have breaks if you're going to keep the line going," Barstow says. "You need to stay hydrated, with lots of fluid, and that means lots of bathroom breaks." But with new managers cutting back on replacement workers, there were fewer breaks. "Workers couldn't leave or they'd be disciplined," the reporter says. "Many workers had no choice but to pee in their pants." Such a predicament for the husky iron workers dramatized the situation for Barstow. Some employees would not be quoted for the record because talking about having to urinate while on the plant floor, for example, was humiliating. Still, the number of such off-the-record reports suggested this was happening with some frequency.

If that image drove his initial interest in the story, the broader implications of the McWane/Tyler case soon gripped him as well. Barstow and Bergman's reporting was backed by their computer-assisted analysis of the more than 200,000 on-the-job deaths reported over the twenty-nine years between 1972 and 2001. Only 151 of those deaths had been referred for prosecution of a company, and a mere eight cases had resulted in prison sentences over that long span. When a sentence was imposed, the longest was six months.

Barstow saw a strong international economic angle behind the numbers. American businesses were being pressured to adopt minimal safety levels as a cost-cutting technique to stay competitive in the new global environment. If they didn't cut costs enough, they lost out in the marketplace. If they trimmed safety measures, and workers died, the price was not as severe. Regulators at the Occupational Safety and Health Administration (OSHA) were soft, and companies had the upper hand. In the first series, McWane's safety violations were compared to those of other big pipe companies, showing it to have a significantly worse record.

One morning, "probably in the shower," Barstow says, he came up with a line to describe the scene that the series was painting: "part Dickens and part Darwin." Along with the story of Rolan Hoskin's death, that became the opening of the first story on January 8. "In writing that lead, I was trying to get at it as vividly and powerfully as I could," he says. He notes that the reporters and their editor, Paul Fishleder, agreed to start the series with an anecdotal account. In Barstow's experience writing multiparters, such an organizational approach seemed inverted. "An overview usually comes first, with the series then broken down into parts. But in this case I was worried about connecting with the readers," he says. "So Day One was just the story of what happened when McWane took over this plant. Day Two we stepped back and looked at who owns the plant. Day Three was what does the government do about it." It was not doing much, the third story maintained, with OSHA records supporting that conclusion. Fishleder, as the primary editor, became the sounding board as Barstow shaped the series and each story in it.

Along with Fishleder, Barstow credits executive editor Howell Raines and deputy managing editor Andrew Rosenthal for early support of the story idea. The editing—and self-editing—challenges were enormous. Barstow estimates his rough draft of the first article alone at 35,000 words. He cut it first to 15,000 and then whittled it into a more polished 7,000. "This means that an awful lot of great material ends up on the cutting room floor. Believe me, every word in the final piece was scrutinized for whether it absolutely had to be in the story." The old lesson still holds: "Make the point, make it with power and precision, and then move on. Don't make the reader read one word more than necessary."

A television documentary version of the three-part report was to appear on Public Broadcasting System's *Frontline* program. Barstow found some advantages to having the filming entourage around him for some of his interviews. "A big project is like running a small business, with the photographer and all the others on the team. These can be great for extending the reach of your eyes and ears," he says. "You grab resources from wherever you can." He had been apprehensive about the TV element at first because of bad earlier experiences. "But the partnership on 'Dangerous Business' worked really well. It did give more firepower, crucial on a story with so many tentacles," he says. Along with those additional staffers available for research, though, was a negative. Television's needs "slowed us down because we often had to 'redo' interviews for the benefit of the cameras—that is, go back with a camera crew after I had already interviewed someone for the newspaper," according to Barstow. "It also added greatly to the administrative burdens of the story: more meetings, more coordination required to sync up the stories." The TV–print connection reflects the future of investigative reporting, he says. "It will be multiplatform, multimedia, with TV, print and web integrated for the biggest possible bang." And this project showed how the two forms could actually benefit from each other. (The Pulitzer board says that only the print version was reviewed during the jury and board deliberations. Still, some board members suspect that such joint entries may one day earn their own category.)

Needed: A Second Series

When the three parts ran in the *Times* in January, and even later when reforms were proposed, and indictments were sought against some McWane managers, Barstow found his feelings were mixed. While very pleased with the series, he says, "I worried that some folks might walk away assuming McWane was some sort of anomaly." The question of why workplace deaths usually go uninvestigated—and how outrageous that is—needed more attention. That unanswered question paved the way for months more of work and eventually the second series in the Pulitzer package, "When Workers Die."

The regulators were at the center of the second series, which Barstow handled as the lone reporter, with research assistance from Robin Stein. One focus was on the paradox represented by the law that created OSHA. The law established that an employer's worst offense would be to cause a fatality by willfully violating safety rules. Yet the *Times*'s analysis of the data—"almost certainly the first systematic examination of these worst workplace deaths," the paper said in its Pulitzer nomination letter—found that OSHA doesn't even ask prosecutors to consider filing charges in 93 percent of cases.

This series began with a graphically portrayed accident too, following Barstow's sense that a strong connection with the reader was needed to tell the story. The first installment was headlined "A Trench Caves In; A Young Worker Is Dead. Is It a Crime?" It began:

> CINCINNATI—As the autopsy confirmed, death did not come right away for Patrick M. Walters. On June 14, 2002, while working on a sewer pipe in a trench 10 feet deep, he was buried alive under a rush of collapsing muck and mud. A husky plumber's apprentice, barely 22 years old, Mr. Walters clawed for the surface. Sludge filled his throat. Thousands of pounds of dirt pressed on his chest, squeezing and squeezing until he could not draw another breath.[4]

The story went on to point out that Walters had spoken often to his family about being buried alive. That was because his company, a small, family-owned outfit called Moeves Plumbing, frequently sent him into deep trenches without safety equipment. Local OSHA officials were upset too because Moeves had been implicated in a "nearly identical" worker death thirteen years earlier. The *Times* article compared those two cases and pointed out the lack of OSHA action to correct the unsafe conditions.

The second story, headlined "U.S. Rarely Seeks Charges for Deaths in Workplace," offered stark statistics showing how few prosecutions resulted from fatalities caused by workplace safety violations. Charts and graphs showed how the various states stacked up in enforcement, and one particular passage stood out: "For those 2,197 deaths [in U.S. workplaces between 1990 and 2002] employers faced $106 million in civil OSHA fines and jail sentences totaling less than 30 years, The Times found. Twenty of those years were from one case, a chicken-plant fire in North Carolina that killed 25 workers in 1991." By contrast, one company, WorldCom, recently paid $750 million in civil fines for misleading investors. The Environmental Protection Agency in 2001 alone obtained prison sentences totaling 256 years.

The third installment aimed for one bright spot in an otherwise bleak picture, as news organizations often seek to do. It involved the approach of one state that has taken on the duty of fighting for victims when workers are killed on the job. The headline: "California Leads Prosecution of Employers in Job Deaths."

The *Times*'s entry got the typical polish that the paper applies when it submits for the Pulitzers. The submission was a seventy-six-page, eleven-inch by fifteen-inch spiral-bound book. It presented not only the original articles and editorials supporting them but also readers' opinions and letters from officials heralding the two series, along with descriptions of the *Times*'s online multimedia presentation with Barstow's audio commentary and a description of the *Frontline/New York Times* report.

2004—The *New York Times* for the work of David Barstow and Lowell Bergman that relentlessly examined death and injury among American workers and exposed employers who break basic safety rules. (Moved by the Board from the Investigative Reporting category, where it was also entered.)[5]

A Medical Center's Maladies

While the *New York Times* won the 2004 gold medal, the *Los Angeles Times*'s overall performance that year was at least as noteworthy. Its staffers won a total of five Pulitzers, including prizes for teamwork in breaking news and national reporting. Remarkably, *Los Angeles Times* people had been finalists for four other prizes. Some staffers gloated about the "five-to-one" score over their New York rivals. And a rivalry it most certainly was. For years the West Coast paper had complained that it failed to receive the respect it deserved from the "Eastern press establishment"—particularly at Pulitzer time. Still, New York's Gray Lady *had* won that 2004 gold medal.

Even as editor John Carroll acknowledged the prior year's bounty, he had his eye on a developing story with public service possibilities for the next year's prizes: a complex analysis of operational troubles with racial complications at Martin Luther King Jr./Drew Medical Center on the edge of the Watts section of Los Angeles.[6] When they began studying the Los Angeles County hospital system in 2003 with a broader story in mind, *Times* health-care reporters Tracy Weber and Charles Ornstein did not think that a look at the King/Drew part of the system had much promise. Their impression was that the story had "been done." And it had been. Fourteen years before, in a Pulitzer Prize category then called specialized reporting, *Times* reporter Claire Spiegel had been a Pulitzer finalist with a powerful three-part series about King/Drew that concentrated on the lack of resources available to the hospital. By then, the medical center had already garnered the unfortunate nickname of Killer King. King/Drew had been created after the 1965 Watts riots with a largely black and Latino medical staff. There were problems, but the community was extremely defensive about King/Drew.

In 2003, John Carroll and managing editor Dean Baquet had backed Weber and Ornstein's vision of a far-reaching story highlighting patient care comparisons among all the county's medical facilities. The impetus for that story had been a front-page study the two reporters had done early in the year. It cited a lawsuit in which doctors had pointed to specific cases of patient deaths resulting from long waits for care. The delays in question had not been at King/Drew but at another facility.

Julie Marquis, the deputy Metro editor who had been assigned to manage Weber and Ornstein's work, says there was another reason to avoid focusing on King/Drew in their new examination of medical care. It was "like shooting fish in a barrel," she says. "We did not regard that as the most challenging investigative project we could do. One had a sense there was nothing you could do about it. And, of course, there were reasons not to try: a lot of political and racial associations with that hospital that the other county hospitals did not have."

In early May Weber and Ornstein started gathering data, including malpractice suits against each county hospital. "It became clear really early on that King/Drew's problems were much greater than those at the other county hospitals—even the ones that were two or three times larger— so both of us went back to John and said we need to focus on King/ Drew first," Ornstein says. At the same time, King/Drew found itself in the news independent of the two reporters' project. It was learned that two patients had died because nurses had overlooked the readings on the patients' heart-rate monitors. Then the hospital lost its accreditation to train surgeons because of its problems—"a huge deal for an urban hospital," adds Weber.

The "Grim March"

An internal hospital faculty meeting at King/Drew, attended by Ornstein and Weber, first brought home the depth of the hospital's story. As the expected complaints arose about how the medical center was underfunded, the director of the health department—who was white—countered that this was not true. Funding was sufficient, he said. The problem was the staff misspending what it received under the hospital director's leadership. The hospital director was black. "A faculty member got up in the back of the room and said, 'The black overseer always whips harder than the white master.' And everyone in the audience got up and started clapping," according to Weber. "Charlie and I said to each other, This is more than just about a bad hospital. It has all sorts of other overlay."

The more they compared King/Drew to the other medical centers, the more they saw how severely out of step it was. Slowly the case for taking a broader health-care approach eroded. King/Drew was just too important a story on its own. "It was initially perceived as a patient care story," says Marquis. "Strangely enough, after we decided that we began to accumulate a lot of data on how badly run the hospital was, and how it squandered money, and not so much about patient care." As the reporting continued, though, the theme of poor patient care resurfaced. The story would have a patient care dimension as well.

In October 2003—fourteen months before the series was eventually published—Marquis, Weber, and Ornstein wrote a memo outlining a project they envisioned. The project was between four and six parts and looked at the problems of King/Drew one by one. When Carroll read the memo, he saw the potential for something special. His vision would confront head-on the complexity and the racial sensitivity of the situation. "He wanted to meld together the political, medical, historical, and social aspects of this hospital," Marquis says. "He was trying to find a way to tell this story without making it seem the standard investigative story on a hospital's medical foul-ups."

The *Times* decided to add to the Weber-Ornstein team, a decision the two reporters supported because "we knew we couldn't do it all ourselves," Ornstein says. Marquis and those she reported to—Metro editor Miriam Pawel and managing editor Baquet—called on Mitchell Landsberg, who was fresh from having worked rewrite on the team that had covered the year's devastating California wildfires. (That coverage would win the 2004 Breaking News Pulitzer.) Steve Hymon, who had moved onto the health-care beat when Ornstein and Weber teamed up to investigate King/Drew in earnest, was also added, along with reporter Daren Briscoe. Briscoe, the lone black team member, was selected in part because of the racial insights he might be able to provide in such a sensitive story. "I'm not sure it was easier for him," says Weber. "He had a difficult time as an African-American reporter working on the story." (Briscoe was to leave the paper about midway through the project to go to *Newsweek* magazine, and the paper decided not to replace him.) Carroll, who checked in from time to time on the team's progress, was impressed with the team spirit among the reporters. In his experience with staffers pursuing such complex stories, he said, "often there is kind of a grim march to get them done."

Grim or otherwise, the marches he had helped supervise stretched back to the 1970s, where he honed his editing skills at the *Philadelphia Inquirer* with editor Gene Roberts. Carroll had first seen a Pulitzer gold medal project take shape as he worked on a police brutality investigation that won for the *Inquirer* in 1978. In a sense, though, he had even grown up with public service journalism. His father, Wallace Carroll, had been a Pulitzer board member in the 1960s and Wallace Carroll's North Carolina newspaper, the *Winston-Salem Journal and Sentinel,* had won a gold medal in 1971 for its environmental coverage.[7]

In the years before coming to the *Los Angeles Times*, John Carroll had served as an editor with the *Baltimore Sun* and with Kentucky's *Lexington Herald-Leader*, where he had become skilled not only at supervising projects but also at doing the final write-through of the stories. As a Pulitzer board member himself from 1994 to 2003, he also had an insider's sense of what the members might like in a public service candidate.

Working for him at the *Los Angeles Times* were a number of veteran editors, including managing editor Baquet, who had started his career in New Orleans working for a time at the *Times-Picayune*. Baquet had covered health-care issues himself for the *New York Times* and had previously served on a Pulitzer-winning investigative team at the *Chicago Tribune*. In June, longtime editorial page editor Janet Clayton succeeded Pawel as Metro editor. Both Clayton and Baquet are black. Clayton was particularly attuned to the community aspect of King/Drew from her editorial page experience. "She knows everything about the history of L.A. and all the players in our story," says Weber. It was not a simple history. The black community took great pride in having King/Drew there, even if, paradoxically, the facility was sometimes feared because of its care deficiencies.

While the reporting and editing teams did not include a physician, reporters constantly sought out doctors to review cases and the medical files, says Weber. To help reporters understand the case that was eventually to become their lead example—involving second-grader Dunia Tasejo, who had died after being hospitalized for injuries from a minor car accident— "we had not only the head of [the pediatric intensive care unit] from Stanford, we had a couple of other doctors look at it to make sure we understood our way through the file." The reporters' understanding was that Dunia had died from a mind-boggling progression of hospital mistakes.

The team often had trouble getting the data they needed for their analyses. While some difficulties stemmed from the federal privacy act, which allowed hospitals to deny certain information to reporters, there was a special problem in getting material from King/Drew administrators. "They hated our guts," says Weber. At the same time, though, the team found other records that it never thought it could get. "We learned there were a lot of public records that we didn't know were public records," Weber says. "Who knew that you could get a record of every surgery at the hospital that every doctor had done?" They tracked the records down. Further, workers' compensation cases became public records if the case had been appealed to the state appeals board. Within those cases, personal medical records and psychologist reports became public too. And even if reporters were not prepared to cite certain records in the series, the documents often corroborated strange accounts that the team's reporting was turning up—accounts about staff accidents and brawls that ran up costs at King/Drew.

Carroll loved such project management above all his many other *Times* duties. "I get a greater satisfaction from these gigantic things, and figuring out what they're trying to say," he said. "It's inevitable that people who are writing these stories and gathering vast amounts of information get awfully close to it. And I've never seen one of these stories come in a publishable form." He had learned the rewriting trade in his *Inquirer* days, working with gifted rewrite man Steve Lovelady, a veteran of page-one editing work at the *Wall Street Journal.* "Lovelady was unlike anything I'd ever seen in terms of what he understood about the possibilities of creative editing, and not just making sure everything was spelled right," said Carroll. "He opened my eyes." In fact, he described his work on the King/Drew series as "the Lovelady job."

True to the form that Carroll had observed over the years, he saw that even the excellent job of reporting on King/Drew was going to need serious organizational help. "Very often you need to think through fundamental questions like, What is this about?" he said. "You have to do a lot of work to get a reader through a long story." And the King/Drew epic was developing into a long story. Each of the eventual five parts would fill two or more inside pages, although much of the space reflected lavish use of photographs by Robert Gauthier. "We wanted to make sure the photographer was plugged in fairly early and was a full-fledged member of the team," says Carroll.

The first installment of "The Troubles at King/Drew" ran on December 5, 2004, under the headline "Deadly Errors and Politics Betray a Hospital's Promise." It began with a patient care horror story:

> On a warm July afternoon, an impish second-grader named Dunia Tasejo was running home after buying ice cream on her South Los Angeles street when a car sideswiped her. Knocked to the pavement, she screamed for help, blood pouring from her mouth.

Her father bolted from the house to her side. An ambulance rushed her to the nearest hospital: Martin Luther King Jr./Drew Medical Center.

For Elias and Sulma Tasejo, there was no greater terror than seeing their 9-year-old daughter strapped to a gurney that day in 2000. But once they arrived at King/Drew, fear gave way to relief.

Dunia's injuries were minor: some scrapes, some bruises and two broken baby teeth. The teeth would have to be pulled.

"They told me to relax," Sulma recalled. "Everything was fine."

At least it should have been.

What the Tasejos didn't know was that King/Drew, a 233-bed public hospital in Willowbrook, just south of Watts, had a long history of harming, or even killing, those it was meant to serve.[8]

What happened to Dunia, in brief, was a bewildering series of medical errors that eventually cost her her life. First she was accidentally oversedated; then hooked up to a ventilator to deal with the paralysis the oversedating caused; then starved for oxygen by incorrect ventilator settings; then taken off a breathing tube too early; then left unmonitored as her vital signs were worsening and she started calling "Mama." Eventually declared brain dead, she was removed from life support two days later.

As the *Los Angeles Times* team had planned through so many rewrites, the first story was used to outline much more than the issues of medical errors and neglect that made King/Drew the state's top payer per patient of medical malpractice. The piece noted that whole "departments are riddled with incompetence, internal strife and, in some cases, criminality." Finally the story promised that the series ahead would explain how for years the governing county board of supervisors had "shied away from decisive action in the face of community anger and accusations of racism."

The other four parts solidly backed up the outline. In an eyebrow-raising passage in the second part of the series published on December 6—a section headlined "Under-funding Is a Myth But the Squandering Is Real"—these paragraphs appeared on the first jump:

Vast sums at King/Drew go to workers injured in encounters with seemingly harmless objects.

Take, for instance, the chair.

Employees have been tumbling from their seats at King/Drew almost since it opened its doors. The hospital's oldest open workers' compensation claim involves Franza Zachary, now 71, who sprained her back falling from a chair in October 1975—costing the hospital more than $300,000 so far.

The bills for two other chair-fallers have topped $350,000 each, county records show.

Between April 1994 and April 2004, employees filed 122 chair-fall claims at King/Drew, more than double the number at Harbor-UCLA. And King/Drew has spent $3.2 million—and counting—to pay for them.

The final part "laid bare the racial dynamic between the community and the Board of Supervisors," according to the *Times*'s Pulitzer nomination letter. The supervisors, meanwhile, "were left with no choice but to face up to their own failure."

Editing from the Top

Several team members had been apprehensive at first at the thought of their top editor running the series through his computer. "Demanding is not an adequate word to describe his editing," says Mitchell Landsberg of John Carroll. Landsberg says others who had been rewritten by Carroll had told the team it was in for a torturous time. "You're going to have days when you'll wish you'd never gotten started with this," Landsberg was told. "But in the end he'll make sure it's the best story it could possibly be." Landsberg, the son of a veteran Associated Press Sacramento reporter and World War II correspondent, says that after reading the final version he realized that "everything they said was true." One thing that helped, adds Weber, was that the very final draft again became a collaboration. "Actually, he ended up being remarkably approachable about things you didn't like."

Based on what he had learned serving on the Pulitzer board, said Carroll, "I think King/Drew was a good candidate for the Public Service category because it not only involved very hard digging and investigative work and very careful accusations drawn against doctors and all sorts of people, but it also involved explaining a very sensitive racial dynamic in local politics that had caused the community to tiptoe around this issue for thirty years. We sort of broke the rules by discussing it very directly and pulling no punches. The political discussion in that story was nuanced, but very hard-hitting."

The board also had an appreciation for risk taking—something the *Times* was certainly doing in the King/Drew series. A hostile community of King/Drew supporters, said Carroll, would have objected strongly if they found "any chinks in the story or anything was untrue." There were risks simply in the writing style too. "Racial stories have to be written in the most precise terms. There's a tremendous potential for community anger, and picketing, and even community violence," he said. As he crafted the stories he tried to be aware of "the belief on the part of many that the white establishment is trying to take away this hospital, and has been for years."

When *Times* parent Times Mirror Company was acquired by Tribune Company in 2000, there were fears that the prize-winning level of its reporting might be hurt. The 123-year-old paper's 2004 and 2005 performance—including its fifth gold medal—seemed to illustrate that those fears were exaggerated. But just one year later John Carroll would feel forced to quit rather than comply with new Tribune-ordered staff cuts that the editor saw as damaging to the publication's journalistic capabilities. (Carroll died in June 2015.) The *Los Angeles Times* was far from finished in the arena of public service, however, as it would prove with yet another Public Service Gold Medal in 2011.

2005—*Los Angeles Times* for its courageous, exhaustively researched series exposing deadly medical problems and racial injustice at a major public hospital.[9]

CHAPTER 6

THE STORM BEFORE THE CALM

2006: The *Times-Picayune* and the *Sun Herald*'s Summer of Katrina

God plays a real part in many of the Public Service awards.

—MICHAEL GARTNER, PULITZER PRIZE BOARD MEMBER, 1981 TO 1991

August was fading fast along the Gulf Coast, but the 2005 hurricane season was at its peak. The *Times-Picayune* editor Jim Amoss had taken to watching storms like Tropical Depression Number 12 with equal parts awe and anticipation. His New Orleans newspaper was prepared for the worst. Or so he thought.

Amoss, who had led the paper to national acclaim during his fifteen years in charge, had put together a staff that was especially adept at pursuing projects. In 1992, 1996, 1997, and 1999, in fact, *Times-Picayune* entries had been finalists for Pulitzer Prizes. Stories making the Pulitzer short list had explored a range of environmental and social topics. And in one of those years, 1997, the paper had been selected for its first two Pulitzers ever. Cartoonist Walt Handelsman had won, and so had the *Times-Picayune* itself in the public service category.[1] That award had honored a series of articles titled "Oceans of Trouble," which analyzed the problems faced by fisheries along the Gulf Coast and around the world.

Building on the prize-winning work, Amoss had turned his staff's attention to another coastal problem: how poorly the below-sea-level city was protected against nature's inevitable onslaughts.[2] The work uncovered evidence of inadequate hurricane preparation in the community. Reporter Mark Schleifstein—working with John McQuaid, his partner from the "Oceans of Trouble" series—helped prepare a five-part series in 2002 that pointed out serious weaknesses in the area's system of levees. It was titled "Washing Away" and its second-day headline read "The Big One: A Major Hurricane Could Decimate the Region, but Flooding from Even a Moderate Storm Could Kill Thousands. It's Just a Matter of Time." That time would come during the early hours of Monday, August 29, 2005, with the arrival of Tropical Depression Number 12, renamed Hurricane Katrina by the National Weather Service. The Gulf Coast would remember it as Killer Katrina.

The newspaper had designed its building—located south of Lake Ponchartrain and north of the Mississippi River bend that gives the Crescent City its nickname—to be ready for a major hurricane. Beneath its conspicuous tower, the building was outfitted with a windowless "bunker" area operating as a generator-powered emergency newsroom. Still, it was sobering for the 140 staffers camping there overnight when the hum of the main, nonemergency power stopped at four o'clock in the morning that Monday. The sudden quiet within contrasted sharply with the howling wind without. Any who were dozing early that morning awoke abruptly. A large window in an executive office blew in, and then another and another. The storm was at full force: torrents of rain and increasing structural destruction, readily visible in the huge gashes appearing on the Superdome nearby. Much later, Amoss could wax poetic about the moment. "Standing in our building's lobby, you could hear the oddly peaceful melody of the wind whistling past the entrance cavity—three sad, flute-like notes played over and over," he wrote. "At times, the wind would shriek to a high-pitched wail before returning to the three-note dirge."[3]

Then the raging storm crested. It was time for the *Times-Picayune* to step up. "On Monday morning I told the staff that this was the biggest story of our lives, and that it was absolutely vital that we tell it as only we can tell it," said Amoss.[4] The telling would require resources unique to a newspaper, especially their newspaper he said, and it would flow from the accumulated, layered knowledge of the complex New Orleans community. From the centrally located headquarters the staff fanned out by any means possible, including boat and bicycle, to see what Katrina had wrought. With phones out and even cell phones dead, however, there would be none of the typical minute-to-minute reports flowing into headquarters during the day. The reporters' notes would have to be brought back to the newsroom in person.

From what Amoss could see and hear during the day, broadcast reporters and journalists from out of town clearly had too narrow a focus on what was happening across the city. Many were ensconced in the French Quarter and Garden District tourist areas along the river. But one thing the out-of-towners seemed to be getting right: as the fierce winds finally died down, with little apparent flooding, they declared that New Orleans had dodged a bullet. And that meant that so had the 137-year-old *Times-Picayune*. "I thought, this is great. We're okay," Amoss remembers thinking.[5]

At nine-thirty on Monday night, Amoss gathered his editors under the emergency lights of the bunker to plan the coverage for the next day. As he described it, "When we started the meeting, we were deciding how to best report the apparent duality of the situation: that the city had been saved, but that the Lower Ninth Ward and St. Bernard Parish had been devastated."[6] Then in an instant that duality vanished. Breathlessly, features editor James O'Byrne and art critic Doug MacCash dashed into the meeting with a report no one wanted to hear: on a six-hour bike ride, they had witnessed breaks in the levee along the 17th Street Canal that led into the lake. To the north, huge portions of the city were being flooded, and the lake waters were moving inexorably south. From a train bridge over Canal Boulevard they had seen a newly formed rushing river, seven feet deep, heading toward the city's business district. "Don't worry about spinning it," O'Byrne advised his editors. "We're going under water."[7]

As disbelief turned to horror, thoughts of winning another Pulitzer Prize were far from anyone's mind. Self-preservation was a more real concern. Most staffers had already evacuated their families, but they had no picture of what it would take to cover the destruction around them. Further, they worried about whether anyone would be reading their reports. The decision had been made on Monday not to publish a print version for the next day. The paper would appear instead online on the paper's affiliated website www.nola.com (for New Orleans, Louisiana). Still, the drive to get the news out had never been more critical. The headline they prepared for the online version of page one was "CATASTROPHIC."

"The Camille Standard"

In fact, there had been relatively little direct wind damage to New Orleans even at the height of Katrina. Seventy-five miles to the east, at the landfall of the swirling mass around her eye, though, the storm unmercifully hammered the Mississippi coast cities of Gulfport and Biloxi with a level of destruction never before seen on American shores. Right in its path was the *Sun Herald*. The 47,000-circulation Gulfport-based paper with fifty-five staffers was only one-fifth the size of the *Times-Picayune*. Like most small dailies, the *Sun Herald* itself had never won a Pulitzer. But its executive editor, Stan Tiner, was known for a supportive, instructive style. It is where he had gotten his nickname "the coach."

Like the *Times-Picayune*, the Mississippi paper had fortified its building and trained staffers to deal with storms. The 121-year-old *Sun Herald* had not missed a publication date since the hurricane of 1947, and the staff did not want to break that string. The newspaper had also created an emergency plan—one that involved drawing on outside help if necessary. Working through the chain that owned it, Knight Ridder Incorporated, the *Sun Herald* arranged for its sister publication farther inland, Columbus, Georgia's *Ledger-Enquirer*, to publish the Mississippi paper if a coastal catastrophe stopped its own presses. Knight Ridder tradition called for providing financial aid and lending journalistic support from its other papers during emergencies. "Stan rallied the troops and on the Friday before, he laid out our mission," says features editor Scott Hawkins. The rallying cry: "This is going to transform our coast forever, and will put us to the test as a newspaper."[8] On Saturday, Tiner's theme became personal safety for his team. He and publisher Ricky Mathews advised staffers to care for themselves and their families first and then get back to the newsroom as soon as possible. As the warnings about Katrina became direr, a disturbing thought occurred to Tiner: "We had no way of knowing how many of our staff we might have seen for the last time."

In the beginning, southern Mississippi used the "Camille standard" to measure the new storm. People still could see the old water lines marking how far inland the seas had reached during the area's previous record hurricane in 1969. That was the worst-case scenario in the minds of long-term residents. Many who were outside the area ravaged by Camille chose not to evacuate. "They had a sense of invulnerability," according to Tiner. "They thought they were immune from death."⁹

As the storm's power built on Monday, though, it was clear that Camille was no longer the worst case. Katrina was sending surges far higher—creating walls of water twenty-eight feet high—and causing destruction much farther inland.

A skeleton crew was able to keep the solid one-story headquarters building open even as two-thirds of the *Sun Herald*'s reporters, editors, and photographers remained largely scattered. The *Sun Herald*'s website (www.sunherald.com) continued to churn out information. For the many south Mississippians who had evacuated and those few in the area who had electricity, the site provided a valuable source of eyewitness news as Katrina drove inland west of Gulfport on Monday morning. Everywhere, staffers crossed their fingers that the arrangement with the Georgia paper would allow Tuesday's papers to be published and to make their way south to the *Sun Herald*'s battered coastal market.

In short, Monday at the *Sun Herald* was not a day for thinking about awards any more than it was at the *Times-Picayune*. Survival came first. Overcoming the many natural obstacles to getting essential information to beleaguered readers was, of necessity, secondary.

Waiting on the Levee

The *Times-Picayune* staffers, camped out in the newspaper's building as dawn broke on Tuesday, August 30, had only to look on their own doorstep for proof that the observations from James O'Byrne and Doug Mac-Cash's bike trip were accurate. The sky was cloudless and Katrina was being downgraded again to a tropical storm. Yet water was at the third stair of the *Times-Picayune* entryway, rising one inch every seven minutes. Cell phone communications in the city remained out. No signs of federal assistance were evident and, as far as reporters could detect, little effort was going into public safety—barring the SWAT team dispatched to quell disturbances at the Orleans Parish Prison just across the interstate. (Guards lost track of fourteen prisoners, some of whose orange prison overalls were later found just outside the *Times-Picayune* building.)

It was time to evacuate. "We had planned for wind, water and an extended period without electricity," Amoss wrote later. "But with almost an entire city going under for an indefinite period, with no civil authority functioning, with a communications blackout, with no federal presence and with no sign that order would be restored any time soon, we were facing an unprecedented challenge for an American newspaper."

Loaded in the back of a flotilla of newspaper delivery trucks, the staff took off for higher ground, unsure exactly where the next stop would be. "We left with the queasy fear that, for the first time since the Civil War, we might not produce a newspaper for tomorrow"—even an electronic version, according to the editor. "We already knew that New Orleans had become a dangerous and difficult place to practice journalism. It would get worse."[10] Only as the trucks rolled toward the city limits did staffers begin to see the big picture emerge. Eighty percent of New Orleans was

FIGURE 6.1 The *Times-Picayune* employees evacuate their New Orleans building in a newspaper delivery truck as water rises the morning after Hurricane Katrina hit. From left, A. J. Sisco, Kim Chatelain, editor Jim Amoss, page-one editor Terry Baquet, managing editor Dan Shea, Mark Schleifstein, and sports editor David Meeks. *Source*: The *Times-Picayune* staff photo by Kathy Anderson. Published courtesy of the *Times-Picayune*.

flooded. Gradually the staff began to make the first plans for forming teams for the complex dual job ahead: covering the scene and creating and managing a remote working newsroom that could sustain a full-fledged news operation.

Veteran reporter Mark Schleifstein had continued to follow the levee systems' weaknesses since his "Washing Away" series. (In fact, he had become not only a weather expert but something of a Cassandra, to the point of advising readers to keep an ax in their attic for emergency escape from floodwaters. For many, it would be life-saving advice.) Schleifstein recalls the tide of emotions as the staff split up during the evacuation that Tuesday. He was one of the majority of staffers choosing to relocate to a temporary newsroom to the west and inland, in the town of Houma. There the *Times-Picayune* planned to publish for a time using the presses of the New York Times Company-owned *Houma Courier*. Schleifstein's family had been evacuated and his home was under twelve feet of water. He was planning to serve in that temporary newsroom, where he could do broader stories that might not need to be written from within the city limits. "More important, I know how to take dictation and I know all the editors. I was the grunt, but I was enjoying it," he says. That is why he did not join the team of a dozen reporters, editors, and photographers who headed back south into the damaged city to set up a bureau and report from the scene. "Now," he adds, "I wish I'd been with them."[11]

The staffers who made the return trip to New Orleans ran into trouble almost immediately. Witnessing a Wal-Mart being looted on a mass scale and police officers participating in the rampage, reporters dove in until they began to feel threatened by the mob. Finally the editor in charge, David Meeks, pulled his *Times-Picayune* team back. The spot story describing the Wal-Mart melee—headlined "Looters Leave Nothing Behind in Storm's Wake"—was the first of many accounts of post-storm events in areas of the city that other news media had not reached. The *Times-Picayune* stories, for the most part written in a makeshift news bureau at the house of one of the team members, continued to have the feel of reports from the front lines of some strange domestic battlefield.

Meanwhile the newspaper operation created to get the paper out— electronically only for that first Tuesday, Wednesday, and Thursday— remained in exile. After Houma, it moved north along the Mississippi

River to Baton Rouge, where for six weeks the staff used the facilities of Louisiana State University's Manship School of Journalism. A fleet of thirty rental cars kept the staff mobile.

Work prepared under such conditions, both from the online and the print editions over a period of months, was compiled to become the *Times-Picayune*'s Public Service Pulitzer entry at the start of 2006. One story, on September 26, carried the provocative headline "Rape. Murder. Gunfights," although the deck line suggested something entirely different. It read: "For three anguished days the world's headlines blared that the Superdome and Convention Center had descended into anarchy. But the truth is that while conditions were squalid for the thousands stuck there, much of the violence NEVER HAPPENED." The debunking grew from the *Times-Picayune* reporters' failed efforts to confirm reports of mass criminality from the Superdome and Convention Center. Some false reports circulated widely through the Internet and ended up in many respected publications around the globe. Some aired on such popular broadcast outlets as Oprah Winfrey's television program. (Police Chief Eddie Compass told Winfrey on September 6 that "some of the little babies [are] getting raped" in the Dome. And Mayor Ray Nagin added more horrors: "They have people standing out there . . . in that frickin' Superdome for five days watching dead bodies, watching hooligans killing people, raping people." The *Times-Picayune* reporters, checking out every report, told a different story:

> As the fog of warlike conditions in Hurricane Katrina's aftermath has cleared, the vast majority of reported atrocities committed by evacuees have turned out to be false, or at least unsupported by any evidence, according to key military, law enforcement, medical and civilian officials in positions to know.
>
> "I think 99 percent of it is bulls———," said Sgt. 1st Class Jason Lachney, who played a key role in security and humanitarian work inside the Dome. "Don't get me wrong, bad things happened, but I didn't see any killing and raping and cutting of throats or anything. . . . Ninety-nine percent of the people in the Dome were very well behaved." Dr. Louis Cataldie, the state Health and Human Services Department administrator overseeing the body recovery operation, said his teams were inundated with false reports about the Dome and Convention Center.[12]

Michael Perlstein, a criminal justice beat reporter who worked on several debunking stories, recalls helping check out reports that a nine-year-old girl had been raped and had her throat slit at the Convention Center. "Once we heard that, obviously we scrambled to corroborate it," he says. But the closer they looked, the more the stories changed: "She was thirteen; she was six; she was nine. There were more than one. There was a freezer full of bodies. That's when we realized, we can't go with this. It was like that grade-school game of telephone: a person who died of natural causes, and was under a blanket, then it's that he got killed, then it's a murder, then it gets multiplied."[13] Amoss now writes off the worst of the crime stories as racist. "You see it again and again, even today," he says. "The urban legends that arise often have a basis in assumptions of racial primitivism. And there are stories going around New Orleans now about all sorts of incredible anarchy and crime being committed that have some racial basis and that turn out to be totally untrue."[14]

Managing editor Peter Kovacs quickly came to the conclusion that these news leads were wildly exaggerated. "Most journalists would be skeptical about these kinds of reports coming from their own hometown," he says. "If you looked at who was in the centers, it was families with their kids; it was old people; it was people you see in New Orleans every day. If what people were saying was true, why were people staying there like sitting ducks?" The answer was that the stories were not true. The tales were largely fabricated, as the reporters found out. "It was unfair to the victims of New Orleans to suggest that people were so lawless and that the victims put up with it. It disrespected what they really did suffer," Kovacs says, adding, "Now I understand how the Salem witch hunt happened."[15]

The newspaper was drawing more than thirty million daily visits to the www.nola.com site from around the world, but the printed *Times-Picayune* made a special impression when it began reappearing in free deliveries to homeless shelters and areas of the city where people congregated. It proved the city was alive, its life's blood—its news—still circulating. The *Times-Picayune*'s 2006 public service entry blended print- and online-published material as the Pulitzer rules allowed. It contained breaking news revelations and analytical pieces, including several intensive looks at why the levees built by the U.S. Army Corps of Engineers failed. (One headline, "Soft Soils Under Levee Sank City," ran on October 15.

Another, "Corps Never Pursued Design Doubts," ran on December 30.) Some analysis had a global slant: a November 13 article titled "Beating Back the Sea" examined the steps taken in the Netherlands to manage a similar flooding threat in the European country's below-sea-level lands.

A Pulitzer Surprise

In addition to the storm's human toll, the price tag for the damage was soaring—and would eventually exceed $80 billion nationally, making it the costliest U.S. storm ever. More than eighteen hundred people would die Katrina-related deaths.[16] And with the hurricane ranking as among the top American stories of the year, Jim Amoss and the *Times-Picayune*'s coverage quickly became the talk of journalists around the country. Beyond those thirty million website hits, dozens of articles focused on the excellence of the paper's coverage.

Not that the paper was cocky—far from it. The staff knew well that the paper faced enormous business challenges as 2006 began, with advertising and circulation both a shadow of their former levels. As a business, it had lost much of its market to the storm—readers and advertisers—without any idea when they might return.

Amoss himself is a low-key native New Orleanian who spreads credit around freely and does not much like to brag. "Any good newspaper has to have a staff that can spring into action as a team, and be deployed in a coordinated way and have a maestro, or several levels of maestros, directing it," he says. "But it would be disingenuous to suggest that I imagined this in some fashion. It is so unimaginable what happened to this community and what happened to this newspaper that it really couldn't have been planned for."[17] Still, when his staff's accomplishments were celebrated in the *Columbia Journalism Review* or in the article Amoss wrote for *Quill*, the magazine of the Society of Professional Journalists, other newspaper editors took note. And in February, *Editor and Publisher* named him editor of the year.

Thus, many journalists were shocked when premature word began to spread on March 8, the day the Pulitzer jurors ended their deliberations, that the *Times-Picayune* was not among the three finalists in public service. Instead, Mississippi's *Sun Herald* was on the list for its Katrina coverage, along with the *Washington Post* and the Toledo *Blade*. The second two choices had been expected. The *Post* had examined the split between national security and individual liberties during the nation's war on terrorism while the *Blade* had exposed illegal activity—involving Ohio's governor and others—in connection with a state investment fund in rare coins. With the New Orleans paper in the running, the *Sun Herald* had been considered a definite dark horse, if it was mentioned at all.

How the *Times-Picayune* failed to make the jury's cut yet nonetheless ended up with a gold medal is a classic study in the circuitous process by which winners are sometimes chosen. The board may start with the nominations presented to it by jurors, but it has full discretion to add, subtract, or draw from other categories for its final award determinations.

When the jurors congregated on Monday at Columbia, the seven members assigned to public service were led by the *Tampa Tribune* executive editor Janet Coates. Having worked just southeast along the Gulf Coast from where the storm hit the hardest, she was quite familiar with the work of the *Tribune*'s neighbor papers. She had also been a junior-level editor on the Knight Ridder *Miami Herald* during its Hurricane Andrew coverage fourteen years earlier.

While there were seventy-eight entries, the number was actually about 15 percent lower than in recent years. Coates believed the decrease reflected other papers withholding submissions in the category because the *Times-Picayune* seemed a shoo-in. But the jurors were committed to starting from scratch and not letting prejudgments affect their review.

Also on Coates's jury were journalists from Akron, Baltimore, Indianapolis, and Seattle, along with an *International Herald Tribune* editor and one journalism legend: the University of Maryland journalism professor Gene Roberts. As an editor, Roberts had turned the *Philadelphia Inquirer* into a virtual Pulitzer-winning machine in the 1970s. Before that he had been a *New York Times* reporter and had led its civil rights coverage in the 1960s. (Roberts, a former Pulitzer board member, was in the process of co-authoring a book that would win the 2007 Pulitzer Prize for History: *The Race Beat: The Press, the Civil Rights Struggle, and the Awakening of a Nation*.)[18]

On the first day of jury deliberations, individual jurors started reading copies of the submitted entries. (Submission of electronic files was still several years away.) Rejects were taken off the table, literally, and piled onto the floor. By the end of the first day, half the public service submissions remained in contention. The second day the jury cut the candidates down to twenty and then winnowed them down to about twelve.

At that point, the job got much tougher, Roberts remembers. "I thought as many as eight or ten of the entries in Public Service were extraordinary," he says. Indeed, in his mind there were five or six that legitimately could have earned the Public Service Pulitzer in another year. But in 2006, the public service panel was riveted by the storm and the two papers that had covered it so well. When only six entries remained on the table, they included the *Times-Picayune* and the *Sun Herald*. The jury was reluctant to give over two of its three finalist selections to coverage of one event, even an event like America's worst hurricane ever. The board members decided to nominate the *Post* and the *Blade* for certain. But for their third choice, they split between the *Times-Picayune* and the *Sun Herald*. So a query was sent to Pulitzer administrator Sig Gissler. Could the jury simply make a joint entry—nominating both Gulf Coast papers, along with the Toledo and Washington nominations?

"Basically, he said no, it wasn't possible," according to Roberts. "We should come up with a total of three, and if the board wanted to award two Gold Medals, then that was its prerogative but not ours."[19] A vote was taken, and the third pick became the paper whose hurricane coverage was a slight favorite: the *Sun Herald*. Jurors then prepared a note to the board elaborating on their thinking and listing the *Times-Picayune* among its three "alternates" for the Public Service Prize. "We knew there was going to be a buzz about our finalists," recalls Coates. But by including the New Orleans paper among the alternates she believes the jury sent a signal that both Gulf Coast papers were worthy.[20]

The buzz started early, thanks to the rumor mill that routinely spread advance word about the finalist selections in those days. (In recent years Pulitzer secrecy has prevailed.) Within weeks, the *New York Times*, having heard that the *Times-Picayune* was not a jury selection, published a comparison of the *Sun Herald*'s and the *Times-Picayune*'s hurricane coverage. The *Times* wrote, "The *Sun Herald* likes to emphasize that it did not miss a day of print publication, while the *Times-Picayune* points to the scope of the disaster in New Orleans and its near-impossible reporting conditions."

Overshadowed in Mississippi

Why had the public service jurors favored the *Sun Herald*? Most of those who died storm-related deaths had been southern Louisianans, and much of the damage had been in that state's Delta region. But Katrina killed more than 200 and displaced hundreds of thousands along the Mississippi coast as well, flattening whole communities that had been the Gulfport paper's market. And while the *Times-Picayune* had clearly distinguished itself, few denied that the Mississippi news organization had pulled off a near miracle of publishing.

"This was a smaller paper, with a newsroom that was a victim of the disaster as much as its community had been, and you saw the completeness of their voice," says Coates. "Its editorial message got stronger and stronger and stronger." The message? "We are a community and we are being forgotten here, and we need help in the face of disaster and the ineptitude of the relief effort. What we saw in the entry was a paper picking up everything it has and throwing it—and not in a helter-skelter way. It was trying to make order out of chaos."

Roberts, who was as high as any juror on the work of the *Times-Picayune*, notes the continuity with which the *Sun Herald* seemed to explore the story in every aspect of the storm with its spot-news, feature, and editorial writing. "It seemed to me that they must have had even the janitors writing," he says, "because they were everywhere for a staff that size." The website's public service "was just mind-boggling," adds Roberts. "They were responding to individual requests, putting out constant notice of where people could get relief. If you had been a victim of the storm it would have given you up-to-the-minute ideas about what to do."

And then there was the underdog factor. It was something that Stan Tiner alluded to in his Pulitzer nomination letter: "Much of the country was focused on New Orleans . . . meanwhile South Mississippi was struggling to survive, having taken the full force of Katrina's killer winds and deadly storm surge head-on," he wrote. "The *Sun Herald* provided hope to its community, giving authentic voice to their struggle, their anger and triumph." He recalled that on Monday, August 29, "thousands of South Mississippians, dazed and disoriented, living in improvised shelters or in the shells of their own homes were handed an eight-page *Sun Herald*

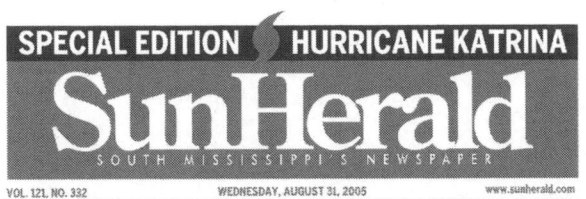

FIGURE 6.2 The *Sun Herald* front page two days after Hurricane Katrina hit. *Source*: Used by permission of the *Sun Herald*, South Mississippi News Leader.

detailing the full scope of the disaster and timely information on where to turn for help. Many actually cried in disbelief." One woman asked, looking through the pages from amid the rubble of East Biloxi's Main Street: "A paper? How did you do this?"

If the jurors *did* factor in the *Sun Herald*'s ability to put out a print edition without missing a day—thanks to its effective prearrangement with its Georgia sister paper—they were also awed by the journalism being produced. It was both artful and helpful, filled with hard news and sympathetic editorials geared to its stricken readership. And it contained some of the most remarkable color photography ever taken in a disaster. Stunning shots appeared each day during the storm, sometimes presented sideways on a full page to help capture the scope of the horror and the pathos.

Executive editor Tiner had dispatched a team of five copy editors and designers to Columbus—nearly 10 percent of his staff—and a Monday paper was distributed free at shelters where survivors were congregated. On Tuesday the page-one banner, "Our Tsunami: At Least 50 Die in a Storm as Fearsome as Camille," echoed remarks by Biloxi's mayor. Inside the eight-page paper, headlines included "How It Felt" and "After Landfall: What Mississippi—and the Nation—Can Expect as Katrina Moves North."

With two-thirds of the reporters still not heard from on Tuesday, the Wednesday paper was largely written by a handful of staffers in the *Sun Herald* building using the intermittent power from a generator and pulling together what technology they could to send their material to Columbus for publication. On Monday night, out-of-town reinforcements arrived, causing quite a stir. Working with Knight Ridder's vice president for news in San José, California, Bryan Monroe, Tiner had arranged for a team of journalists from the *Miami Herald*, the *Charlotte Observer*, and elsewhere to fly into Atlanta the day before the storm. The team had driven down through Montgomery, Alabama, finding ways to circumvent downed bridges and other obstacles and arriving late on Monday evening. There Tiner had been in the newsroom when hulking shadows began to move in the emergency lighting near the entry from the hall. "Bryan's a large guy, and with the lights so low there was an eerie feel to it when they showed up. We hugged in the hallway, and I said, 'The Marines are here,'" recalls Tiner, himself an ex-Marine. Along with them, Monroe's team members brought gasoline, water, chain saws—and at least $12,000 in cash. "There wasn't anything to buy," Tiner notes, "but it was a good feeling knowing you had some money, anyway."[21]

The banner on Wednesday encapsulated the message that Tiner saw developing from the disaster: "Hope Amid Ruin: Hundreds Now Feared Dead, but Survivors Emerge." It ran above a large photo of a mother and son reunited and embracing amid the destruction of their neighborhood and a smaller photo of three firemen removing a body from similar surroundings.[22] Both in print and online, the suffering readers saw their plight personalized and understood. Beyond a daily chart headlined "What You Need to Know," the paper ran a bulletin board of messages from family members and others seeking lost loved ones and trying to match needs with services being offered. The precedent for these two approaches, in fact, had been set at two other Knight Ridder papers that had won Public Service Prizes for their disaster coverage in the recent past. In covering Hurricane Andrew thirteen years earlier, the *Miami Herald* had pioneered the bulletin board approach. The *Grand Forks Herald*, winner in 1998, came up with the directory of services when the North Dakota paper covered a plague of flooding disasters. It had served readers with a bulletin board too.

The Mississippi paper added many touches of its own, launching the "I'm OK" phone line, for example. The 800 number and e-mail discussion board for readers was part of its extensive Web-based service. The paper registered 1.6 million "page views" online on its peak day Wednesday, compared with an average of about ninety thousand before the storm.

While his staff nearly doubled to around ninety eventually thanks to the temporary out-of-state Knight Ridder influx, the *Sun Herald* bylines were still prominent. Their editor's input was vital, staffers say. Tiner referred to his coverage strategy as "journalistic triage." The paper couldn't tell all the stories that were flowing in, so it took what editors considered the most important, emphasizing where possible that growing theme of hope. "We could have written stories for five years about how many people died and how the government screwed it up," he says. "But part of the plan was to try to organize the storytelling in a way that did not cause our people despair." Adds Tiner, "The moment a big story like this comes, you can't tell people what they've got to do. Their instincts as reporters and editors and photographers are to go where the information is and get it back to this nerve center. I learned during all this how good my staff was."

Tiner knew that small papers had a chance at the big prize. He was friends with Texas editor Joe Murray, whose *Lufkin News* had won the 1977 gold medal for exposing deceit in the Marine Corps's coverage of a local trainee's death. "I've thought for a long time that the prize has value for little guys like us, whether we ever win it or not," says Tiner. "It's probably not going to happen," with the *New York Times, Washington Post,* and other powerhouses on the job. "But if I work hard and do the best journalism that I and my little staff are capable of doing, the gods of journalism just might smile on us."[23]

If the gods didn't smile on the *Sun Herald,* the Pulitzer board certainly did. At the April meeting, it voted the *Sun Herald* a 2006 gold medal, with the *Washington Post* and the Toledo *Blade* as finalists. That move, of course, validated the jury's choices. Then, however, the board elected to give a second medal to the *Times-Picayune*—the first time since 1990 that two public service winners were named in a single year. It was only the seventh time in Pulitzer history and set the stage for the decision eight years later, when both the *Washington Post* and the *Guardian-U.S.* website were honored.[24]

2006—The *Sun Herald,* Biloxi-Gulfport, Miss., for its valorous and comprehensive coverage of Hurricane Katrina, providing a lifeline for devastated readers, in print and online, during their time of greatest need.

and

2006—The *Times-Picayune,* New Orleans, for its heroic, multi-faceted coverage of Hurricane Katrina and its aftermath, making exceptional use of the newspaper's resources to serve an inundated city even after evacuation of the newspaper plant. (Selected by the board from the Public Service category, where it was entered.)[25]

CHAPTER 7

STOCKS AND SOLDIERS

2007–2008: The *Journal* on Options,
the *Post* on Walter Reed

Journalism is still this mighty tool for good. You always think you know
this basic fact but seeing it unfold so viscerally is a powerful reminder.

—*WASHINGTON POST* REPORTER ANNE HULL

Returning in 2007 to the one-winner-per-year norm for public service, the
Pulitzer Prizes honored the *Wall Street Journal* with its first gold medal,
for reporting on the corporate abuse of executive stock-option incentives.
And in 2008 the *Washington Post* earned its fourth, for exposing shameful
conditions at Walter Reed Army Hospital, which housed injured veterans
home from the wars in Iraq and Afghanistan.

The work that led to the *Journal*'s award began to take shape late in 2005,
after Boston investigative team leader Mark Maremont had his attention
called to the strange games being played by some companies in setting the
options, "strike price"—the price at which executives are entitled to buy
shares when the terms of their grants allow it. In most cases, the strike
price is the quoted value of the stock on the day the company's board of
directors approves the options. Such a design provides a fair corporate
baseline to use in rating the performance of individual executives over
time. All within a week, reporter Maremont was tipped to some peculiar
legal disclosures being made by a handful of companies in Securities and
Exchange Commission (SEC) filings and also to the existence of academic
research focusing on unusual stock-option timing issues.

At first he had trouble understanding the filings. There was almost certainly hanky-panky in the corporate accounting for stock options at some
companies, but Maremont wasn't sure exactly what was being masked by

the bookkeeping. As for the academic research, the tipster had pointed the reporter to a study by University of Iowa professor Eric Lie, who thought that low-strike price patterns might reflect companies using hindsight to identify historical lows and then to set their strike prices after the fact. Maremont found other academic research, including an eight-year-old study by David Yermack at New York University's Stern School of Business, suggesting that companies may have manipulated strike prices by controlling the release of news to depress the quote on the day in question.

As October 2005 ended, the picture got clearer. "One of the companies I'd been looking at fired its top three executives and said they'd been doing funny things with stock-option dating," Maremont recalls. An article that he prepared with two other reporters appeared on November 3 on page seven, mainly discussing the problems at Mountain View, California, software maker Mercury Interactive Corporation. It was a typical *Journal* collaboration between reporters from its news bureaus. While two other staffers had closer contact with the company involved, Maremont brought his recent familiarity with the backdating issue to the story. A week later, he wrote his own article. It began: "Federal regulators and academics, scrutinizing a broad pattern of well-timed stock-option grants, are exploring the extent to which companies improperly backdated grants to provide insiders an extra pay windfall."[1] Maremont again focused on Mercury, which admitted to backdating in SEC filings and acknowledged that it had been improper. Noting the academic research at Iowa and NYU, his article mentioned several other companies that had disclosed that they were being investigated by the SEC. The story ran on page one as an "extra," a term the *Journal* used for a major news article each day that is elevated to run on the first page. (The *Journal*'s front page was dominated most days by three feature stories that were its signature attractions: two "leaders," its main magazine-style features, and the "A-head," so named because of the shape of the hood that appears above the italic headline type. Headlines of leaders were often topped with snappy, boldface "flash lines.") The decision to include the backdating story on the front page was made at the previous day's New York national news meeting, where the final call belonged to managing editor Paul Steiger.

With Maremont's story airing the academic work on backdating for the first time in the general press, he expected others in the media to pick up on the phenomenon. He was wrong. "I'm not sure why exactly," says the reporter, "but the story didn't really gain any traction." Indeed, he can't remember competitors publishing a single word about the backdating. Why did other papers not follow the *Journal*? Competitive pride may have played a part. Even among editors at the archrival *New York Times*, Maremont speculates, there may have been a hands-off attitude: "Somebody else had gotten it, and they weren't going to pay any attention." Journalists also might have thought the problem was limited to a few obscure technology companies. Finally, it was possible that—even after following the blatant criminality of the Enron Corporation scandal six years earlier—reporters found it hard to believe that corporate executives would secretly game the system to increase the haul for themselves and their compatriots.

As the competition ignored the story, Maremont and the *Journal* were only getting started. New York-based James Bandler, a reporter on Maremont's investigative team, joined him in studying the subject, as did fellow Boston staffer Charles Forelle. At twenty-five years old, Forelle was not long out of Yale, where he'd been a math student. (Eventually Boston reporter Steve Stecklow would become the fourth team member.) In addition to further developing the academic research, the team learned as much as it could about the SEC investigations that were under way. The reporters' main goal was to identify companies that issued options with low strike prices year after year to see if the trend was broad enough to suggest a wider page-one feature story.

While Professor Lie provided the reporters with data showing patterns of historically low strike prices at certain corporations, that by itself wasn't very compelling. The *Journal* needed solid evidence of companies misdating their options. "We figured it was unlikely that you'd call these companies up and they'd say, 'Yup, we did it; you caught us,'" says the team leader. "And it would take enormous effort to find a mole."

Charles Forelle had an idea. Talking with Maremont in the hallway one day, the young math graduate suggested that the paper do its own probability analysis to determine the odds of these historically low stock prices being accidentally chosen. Maremont liked the approach and asked Bandler and Forelle to work together on a formula that used data from daily electronic stock-trading charts, applying it to companies suspected of strike-price manipulation. Because the algorithm being used was the

Journal's own, the team members knew that extreme care had to be taken in their research. "Essentially, what we were doing was accusing these companies of improper or even illegal behavior on the basis of stock charts and our own mathematical analysis," Maremont notes. "There were no Deep Throats here," he says, referring to the famous anonymous source consulted by the *Washington Post*'s Bob Woodward in pursuing the Watergate stories in 1972. And no governmental or corporate leakers had offered accounts that could backstop them if they were wrong. The reporters were on their own.

They spent nearly four months trying to figure out which companies had the most egregious patterns of low strike prices between 1995 and 2002 and thus might qualify for a place on page one of the *Journal*. They then called independent, nonemployee directors serving on the compensation committees of those companies to learn what they recalled about how the grants were made. Meanwhile, Forelle continued to refine the methodology, consulting with an assistant professor of statistics at Yale.

"The Perfect Payday"

The first front-page feature story to result, on Saturday, March 18, 2006, was "The Perfect Payday"—the headline that Joe Barrett of the *Journal*'s page-one editing staff contributed. (Page-one flash lines typically emerged from brainstorming sessions among the page editors.) Forelle wrote in a sidebar that ran with the main article:

> To quantify how unusual a particular pattern of grants is, the *Journal* calculated how much each company's stock rose in the 20 trading days following each grant date. The analysis then ranked that appreciation against the stock performance in the 20 days following all other trading days of the year. It ranked all 252 or so trading days in a given year according to how much the stock rose or fell following them.[2]

In the *Journal*'s centralized national editing system, largely unchanged since legendary editor Bernard Kilgore designed it in the 1940s, bureau chiefs or team leaders were responsible for proposing front-page projects to the editing staff in New York and then for delivering the articles. When submitted, the stories went into a backlog of page-one candidates to be processed for publication. Managing editor Steiger and his deputies—for the backdating stories the key deputy was Pulitzer-winner Daniel Hertzberg—had overall authority for when and how the stories would be presented. The basic editing of feature articles after they flowed into New York, however, was in the hands of a special page-one staff headed by Michael Miller. Veteran editor Dan Kelly was assigned to work with the backdating story and successive feature articles on that theme.

The decision to run "Perfect Payday" on a weekend fit with the paper's deliberate goal of beefing up the Saturday edition, only a few months old at the time. But the placement gave Maremont pause at first because Saturday *Journal*s had become a showcase for softer features and lifestyle coverage, not major investigations like this one. Still, there was an upside: more space for graphics and display.

As the story—which carried the byline of Forelle and Bandler with a contributing line for George Anders—worked toward the top of the New York backlog, its seemingly glacial progress tested the nerves of Maremont's team. The *Journal* had asked the companies cited in the article to respond, and now they had time to go further than merely issuing a comment. One of them, Affiliated Computer Services Incorporated, announced that it had begun internally investigating possible stock-option improprieties. The *Journal*, its feature story still not ready, published a deliberately small news article on the announcement, buried in the back of the paper. "We wanted to get it on the record," says Maremont, "but we didn't want to call a lot of attention to it."

Affiliated Computer was the lead example on March 18. Ironically, the comments of its chief executive Jeffrey Rich provided nearly as much punch as the *Journal*'s stunning statistical calculation—that the chances of a company randomly picking Affiliated's historically low strike prices over seven years was "around one in 300 billion." For comparison, the article added: "The odds of winning the multistate Powerball lottery with a $1 ticket are one in 146 million." Rich, however, attributed the repeated choice of favorable option-grant dates to "blind luck." Indeed, he said, backdating would have been absolutely wrong. Maremont smiles at the blind luck comment provided to Bandler, who "was very happy when he finally got hold of that guy and got that great quote out of him."

The article finally put backdating on the national journalistic map, even if the *Journal* retained a huge head start in covering the topic. Staying out front, Maremont's investigative team wrote more feature articles, and the news stories were frequently positioned as page-one extras. Managing editor Steiger "was very much in favor of keeping up the drumbeat of coverage," says Maremont. Later stories showed how companies backdated options as a way of cutting executives' taxes and demonstrated that the stock market's post-9/11 plunge had provided corporate backdaters with cover for their schemes.

Maremont and editor Dan Kelly agreed that not much needed to be written about backdating's legal status. Whether criminal or not, the activity would clearly be seen as deceptive by readers, the two men believed. And the value of any stock that was not fairly earned should have belonged to all the shareholders.[3] The *Journal* focused more on explaining how companies had originally intended stock-option mechanisms to provide a more equitable, performance-based incentive system and how backdating distorted that design. (Later, when the federal government pursued cases of backdating-related securities fraud, tax fraud, and other offenses—many against companies that had been cited in *Journal* stories—officials detailed the lawbreaking involved. In its case against Mercury Interactive, for example, the SEC alleged that former senior officers "perpetrated a fraudulent and deceptive scheme from 1997 to 2005 to award themselves and other employees undisclosed, secret compensation by backdating stock option grants, failing to record hundreds of millions of dollars of compensation expense, and falsifying documents to further the scheme." The government was litigating cases against four former Mercury executives. But the $28 million corporate penalty that Mercury paid, according to SEC chairman Christopher Cox, "should send a clear signal that fraudulent stock option backdating and other financial fraud will be severely punished.")

A View from the Opinion Page

At most news organizations, which keep the reporting and opinion sections separate, there is strong support among columnists for the work of their fellow investigative journalists who dig up scoops. But on the laissez-faire *Journal* edit pages as Maremont and his team developed their story, columnist Holman W. Jenkins Jr. kept up his *own* drumbeat: ridiculing the news articles as a witch hunt and characterizing the practice of back-dating as "innocuous and even sensible."[4]

At first, the Jenkins columns infuriated Maremont, although the reporter eventually found them almost comical. A logical extension of Jenkins's argument seemed to be that executives should be free to ignore an accounting rule if they disagreed with it. "That strikes me as a recipe for chaos," says Maremont, "and something that the editorial page should have repudiated, not welcomed." Reflecting on the interoffice conflict, though, he soon saw the Jenkins columns as "a net positive, because being attacked by the paper's far-right editorial page was seen in most of the media world as a badge of honor and a sign that the scandal had really hit a nerve in the plutocratic class."

Jenkins's criticisms were the exception, and most *Journal* reporters and editors took pride in the groundbreaking coverage. In the spring, the Dow Jones board of directors asked Maremont to make a presentation and discuss the stock-option scandals. When one board member asked how many companies Maremont thought might eventually be tarred with the backdating brush, the reporter estimated thirty or forty. "Of course, I was wildly underestimating the scale of the scandal at that point," he says now. (Asked whether Dow Jones itself was ever suspected of such abuses, he laughs. "As a recipient of Dow Jones stock options, I can assure you there was never any backdating," says Maremont. Indeed, "they kept granting them at a high point.")

After being selected as a finalist by the Pulitzer public service jury, the *Journal*'s entry was forwarded to the full Pulitzer board, which happened to be chaired by *Journal* managing editor Steiger that year, his final one both on the board and as the newspaper's managing editor. That made the gold medal—voted while Steiger was out of the room—especially precious.

"I believe one of our highest callings as a news organization is to unearth the ills of business so that society can fix them," Steiger said in a memo to the staff. "The exposure of the pernicious disease of options backdating was a particularly dramatic example of just that." The *Journal*'s reports led to federal investigations targeting 140 companies and calls for regulatory reforms. More than seventy executives lost their jobs. And with a second

2007 Pulitzer, for international reporting, the 118-year-old *Journal* added to a winning tradition that included twenty-five Pulitzers since 1980—an average of nearly one per year.[5]

Since the winning of the prize, Maremont and Steiger agree, stock-option offenses faded as a target of regulators. "Enforcement petered out because there were lots of bigger fish to fry," says Steiger, including issues related to the nation's financial meltdown. But the stock-option stories carried a powerful message "that somebody's watching," he adds. "When you're privileged in society, as business executives are, it's even more incumbent upon you to play by the rules."[6] Indeed, one of Steiger's favorite tests of ethical behavior had played out, quite literally: "How would this look on the front page of the *Wall Street Journal*?"

2007—The *Wall Street Journal* for its creative and comprehensive probe into backdated stock options for business executives that triggered investigations, the ouster of top officials and widespread change in corporate America.[7]

"The Other Walter Reed"

At most papers, editors make the call on who will team with whom. But as the top *Washington Post* investigative reporter—who had won the 2006 Beat Reporting Pulitzer for detailing the secret prisons being maintained around the world—Dana Priest had more freedom. So when she got an astonishing tip that September about dreadful conditions at the Walter Reed Army Medical Center, where many of the injured from America's Iraq and Afghanistan campaigns were sent, she was able to find a teammate herself. She chose Anne Hull.

The requirement for a partner was clear to Priest after two weeks of visiting Walter Reed, as she saw the need to determine how widespread the patient abuse was. "My head was reeling from all these different problems, and I'm trying to find patterns and put them into a framework," says Priest. "But I'm also thinking, 'Maybe it's just this guy, or maybe this family's weird or something.'"[8]

Also, Priest knew that her own expertise was in digging out information from organizations, not making families comfortable in telling their stories. Meanwhile Hull had written in the past about the orthopedic ward there, largely with a patient focus. So even though Priest barely knew Hull—herself a five-time Pulitzer finalist—she approached Hull about teaming up and combining their separate interviewing strengths. As Hull summarizes it: "Dana has spent much of her life examining broken or negligent systems or institutions. I have focused on the people being crushed or forgotten by those institutions."[9]

Priest also saw the need for a symbol of Walter Reed's problems that could crystallize the situation for readers. Then she heard about Building 18—a rundown slum of mold and mice and misery that, the pair would learn, was almost beyond description. "For me, that was the clincher," she says. "We didn't get to Building 18 for another month, at least, after we heard about it. But I knew that *if* this building existed, it was going to be a symbol."[10]

Very clear to both Priest and Hull was that they had to report this story delicately. Any leak about their interest in Walter Reed could draw attention from medical center personnel, who would certainly try to thwart their reporting—and would likely provoke a storm of competition. With that attitude of extreme caution, Priest and Hull began a four-month process of finding families and patients they could feel safe interviewing, confident that they would not tell the authorities. "The net just kept growing, and we interviewed dozens and dozens of people," says Hull. "Each individual story was its own sad, heartbreaking scenario with its own complications."[11]

While not considering this an undercover assignment, because Walter Reed was a public facility visited by veterans' families, the reporters discussed ways to avoid arousing official suspicion that they were journalists. (At one small meeting of family members Priest attended, "I did my best to sit in the corner," she says, but had to excuse herself when "a colonel came into the room and started to acknowledge people" one by one.[12])

Worried that bringing in a staff photographer would attract too much attention, Priest took pictures of one room in Building 18 herself. "I was sure I'd gotten the goods," she remembers thinking as she raced back to the newsroom. But the grainy, dark walls that showed up in her shots provoked none of the disgust that the reporters had felt upon seeing the place. So Priest and Hull welcomed photographer Michel Du Cille, a master of discrete shooting, as a teammate.[13] Avoiding public halls with lots of people around, "he would scope out places where you wouldn't be easily seen," says Priest. "The best photos he took were of individual soldiers who had agreed to be photographed."[14] (Du Cille's work was so striking that he was eventually included in the Pulitzer board's citation for the *Post*, along with the two reporters.)

Writing together and working with a *Post* editor were the next enlightening experiences for Priest and Hull. "I wanted to pin down as many moving parts as possible, as quickly as possible, and she wanted to do the opposite—to let a thousand flowers bloom, slowly, at their own slow-as-molasses natural pace," according to Priest. "What she draws from this is a rare intimacy, and because she is such a great writer, she can then put that on the page for all to feel." For Hull's part, she learned from Priest "the value in casting something in black and white." In an interview with the Poynter Institute's Al Tompkins, Hull said that she is often "carried away by the gray." But instantly "Dana can figure out the mission statement or promise—'only the best of care for our nation's wounded'—and juxtapose it with the brokenness of something, such as Building 18." Added Hull, "It's hard to convey how strategic and steely she is. Those are things you can't really learn but can only hope might rub off a little."[15]

Priest wasn't always steely during the reporting. In fact she sometimes dissolved in tears. "The depth of the injuries and the road to repair seemed so overwhelming for some of these soldiers and their families," she told Tompkins. "Each story was the same, yet it was completely different; a different body part gone, a different, awful nightmare, a different set of burdensome family or financial problems."

Priest relishes her memories of watching Hull draft the stories with one of the *Post*'s top editors, David Maraniss, better known now as a nonfiction author. Maraniss and Hull were "like kids in a candy store; they just became so excited about every sentence," says Priest, a self-described deadline writer. "I was exhausted by it," she adds with a laugh. "But Anne and David seemed to get more alive with every single word they would study, and change, or not change. Like, really, every single word." And the editor's approach made him like a third reporter. "He came in with a fresh eye and a fresh mind," Priest says, "and so he was definitely key to getting the right tone."[16]

The two-part series on President's Day weekend began with an overview evoking disgust over Building 18, followed by the horrifying experiences of the patients and their families. The first article began:

> Behind the door of Army Spec. Jeremy Duncan's room, part of the wall is torn and hangs in the air, weighted down with black mold. When the wounded combat engineer stands in his shower and looks up, he can see the bathtub on the floor above through a rotted hole. The entire building, constructed between the world wars, often smells like greasy carry-out. Signs of neglect are everywhere: mouse droppings, belly-up cockroaches, stained carpets, cheap mattresses.[17]

The picture was contrasted with the common perception of Walter Reed as "a surgical hospital that shines as the crown jewel of military medicine"— and which often served as the backdrop for official pronouncements about the nation's commitment to veterans.

If there was a shortcoming in the presentation, it may have been the reporters' reluctance to insist on a bigger role for the *Post*'s website—a role that has lately become key to the news packaging process. Priest and Hull "actively avoided our editors" overseeing the online presentation of stories. "We were afraid that it would leak," Priest says, noting that only in the last few years has she become comfortable putting much of her work on the *Post*'s site in advance of print publication. Still, readers swarmed to view whatever graphic online portrayal of the Walter Reed scandal the *Post* did put up.

The stories hit with what Hull calls "a ferocious wallop."[18] Reading in the *Post* about the "administrative nightmare and squalid living conditions endured by wounded warriors," Defense Secretary Robert Gates held a staff meeting and the next day met with President George W. Bush. Gates then held a press conference where he said, "This is unacceptable, and it will not continue." Gates wrote in his book *Duty: Memoirs of a Secretary at War*: "In a departure for a senior government official, I also said, 'I am grateful to reporters for bringing this problem to our attention, but very disappointed we did not identify it ourselves.'"[19] As investigations began, the secretary of the army fired the major general commanding the medical center within ten days of the first article, and then Secretary Gates replaced the army secretary too.

2008—The *Washington Post* for the work of Dana Priest, Anne Hull, and photographer Michel du Cille in exposing mistreatment of wounded veterans at Walter Reed Hospital, evoking a national outcry and producing reforms by federal officials.[20]

CHAPTER 8

PRIZING YOUTH

2009–2010: The *Las Vegas Sun* and the
Bristol (Va.) *Herald Courier*

We've been very aggressive in hiring young talent. I wouldn't say we target
Pulitzer winners, but it doesn't hurt to be one, since we're looking for the
best people.

—REBECCA BLUMENSTEIN, *WALL STREET JOURNAL*
DEPUTY EDITOR IN CHIEF

Usually it is a team that propels a news organization's Pulitzer-winning
public service. Often a single seasoned reporter leads the way. How rare
then that both the 2009 and 2010 gold medals rewarded the drive of individual reporters not yet in their thirties on their first major investigative
projects. How inspiring, too, for the crowds of college students who still
see journalism as a way to change society for the better.

Alexandra Berzon was twenty-eight years old and not long out of the
University of California at Berkeley's Graduate School of Journalism when
the *Las Vegas Sun* managing editor Drex Heikes tempted her with a job
offer—and a story. Why, during the $32 billion building boom along the
Las Vegas Strip, Heikes wondered, did there seem to be a fatal construction worker accident about every six weeks? Berzon, who in late 2007 was
seeking reporting challenges after briefly working for a technology magazine, was not sure Las Vegas was the best place for her. "She took some
persuading," recalls Heikes. "Then I toss the story idea out there, and her
eyes get this big," he says, making binoculars with his hands.[1]

What soon intrigued Berzon almost as much as the quantity of accidents were the lame excuses for them that casinos, regulators, and even
union leaders gave. The most common responses were that construction
was "innately hazardous," and "the workers just make mistakes," she recalls.

Berzon innately knew óne thing: "It wasn't true that people had to die." To her it seemed "an attitude issue."[2]

So in January 2008, with nine workers dead in just over a year, the newly hired *Sun* reporter began exploring construction site conditions, union and casino supervision over the jobs, and the Nevada Occupational Safety and Health Administration (OSHA) bureaucracy. She got to know the families of accident victims. And by late March she produced (and Heikes edited) the two biggest of what would grow to be fifty stories on the subject that year—work that would win the 2009 Pulitzer Prize for Public Service for the 180,000-circulation *Sun*. A financially struggling paper with eighteen reporters, it was distributed inside its rival *Las Vegas Review-Journal* as part of a joint operating agreement between them.

Vertical and Horizontal Reporting

Outside the newsroom Berzon had few allies on the story: not among the powerful casino industry or the regulators, both of which bore some blame, nor among union leaders, who were slow to speak up about hazards that plagued their members. But at the *Sun* she was quickly identified as a star. "Oh my God, she's the fastest, smartest investigative type I've ever seen," says Heikes, who had been recruited from the *Los Angeles Times*, where he edited that paper's magazine.

Heikes was particularly amazed by the high energy level displayed by Berzon, known in the office as Ali, from the moment the assignment was hers. "She comes back to me in two weeks, and she says, 'You know what? I think it's there, Drex,'" he recalls. At that point, "We just cut her loose, and in about six weeks she's got her hands around most of the guts of the story, what I call the vertical reporting: the hard facts."

Heikes remembers how one day two boxes of OSHA accident case documents arrived for Berzon. "She takes them in the conference room, and she comes out in four hours and she says: there's this, and there's this, and there's this. All smoking guns. That was the minute I knew we had a great story."

Then there was the unique rhythm of her interviewing. "You would hear her on the phone with people, and she was like a prosecutor. Very sweet;

very respectful. And then, 'Well, but didn't you say a week ago—I have it in my notes . . .' And she's closing the circle around these public officials and oversight people." The editor suggests that Berzon likely came by that style naturally; both of her parents are attorneys and her mother is a judge of San Francisco's U.S. Ninth Circuit Court.

Getting the story "horizontally," as Heikes describes it, involved weeks of painstakingly scoping out the stories of victims and their families. By the first week of March, drafts of her first two stories were ready for the editor's touch in what developed as a one-on-one relationship. The lead of her March 30 story introduced Harold Billingsley, "walking in his brown ironworking boots on uneven temporary decking" fifty-nine feet up in the superstructure of the MGM Mirage CityCenter—one of the biggest construction projects on a Strip then teeming with towering cranes.

He was heading to pick up extra bolts for his crew, his family believes. He stumbled.

Ordinarily, he would simply have fallen onto the decking. But at this exact moment in that exact spot, the decking contained a 3-by-11-foot hole that state investigators later said should not have existed.

Ironworkers wear safety harnesses for times like this. An attached cable is supposed to stop a plunge. Billingsley's was not attached.

Safety regulations called for a temporary floor or netting no more than two stories down, a last chance to break his fall. None existed.

The man friends called "Rusty" for his fiery red hair fell to his death.

His was the fourth construction fatality at CityCenter, adding to what had already become a disturbing trend up and down the Strip. In the shadows of the cranes, steel and concrete upon which Las Vegas has pinned its addiction to growth, a body count has emerged.[3]

Among those at the *Sun* most impressed with the product Berzon and Heikes turned out was managing editor Michael J. Kelley. Over the years he had designed the *Sun* to be a magazine-style newspaper, free of "paper of record" responsibilities, and he sees Berzon's collaboration as a prime example. "I think Drex envisioned it would be a couple of big stories. . . . But the more Ali kept digging around, and kept digging, it got legs," Kelley says. He gives credit as well to editorial writers David Clayton and

Matt Hufman, whose work helped win related congressional hearings and worker safety reforms.[4] "In a way it's not something you want to celebrate and whoop and holler about, when workers have died," Clayton said on the day of the Pulitzer announcement. "But workers are safer today because of what [Berzon] did and what this newspaper did."[5] Kelley, who had hired Heikes, notes that after twelve construction fatalities, the *Sun*'s stories seemed to wake up the community, bring about reforms, and get the sites cleaned up. "Winning the Pulitzer is fabulous, but the fact that this series stopped people from dying on the Las Vegas Strip construction projects is the most important part of what we did."

As attuned as Berzon was to the construction story, the announcement of the paper's Pulitzer Prize took her completely by surprise. Unaware even that it was Pulitzer Day, she was returning from an assignment when a receptionist blindsided her with congratulations. "It seems like it came out of the blue," Berzon recalls. "I didn't think we had a chance" in a year

FIGURE 8.1 Reporter Alexandra Berzon calls her parents to share news of the *Las Vegas Sun*'s win of the Pulitzer Prize for Public Service for exposing a high death rate among construction workers on the Las Vegas Strip, at the *Las Vegas Sun* offices in Henderson, Nevada, on Monday, April 20, 2009. *Source*: Tiffany Brown/*Las Vegas Sun*.

when there were so many huge national stories, including a historic presidential election and a financial meltdown. Among the finalists the *Sun* beat out in winning its first Pulitzer was a *New York Times* entry "setting a standard for depth and sophistication" covering 2008's economic collapse, according to the Pulitzer board.

The board especially noted Berzon's "courageous reporting"—an adjective she calls an exaggeration. "I'm not going to say my life was at risk," she says, although "there were some threats from union officials." To which Drex Heikes replies: "She was naïve about the risk" in a town where tough guys rule in a tough gambling industry. (He remembers sending three people along with her as she covered one union meeting.)

The public service jury chairman, the *St. Petersburg Times* executive editor Neil Brown, thought "the degree of difficulty on the story for a small paper was high," although "small paper or no, we did not rate it on a curve. The work stood up well against all comers." Fellow juror David Boardman, then executive editor of the *Seattle Times*, praised the work for taking on "so many of the significant powers in the community: the casinos, labor unions, and both the state and local governments." In addition, Boardman considered it among the best-written works in the category that year.[6]

In the Pulitzer celebration at the *Sun* office, Berzon flashed on her time spent as a reporting intern at the *Anchorage Daily News*, a publication that prided itself on having won two Public Service Pulitzers, one in 1976 on the power of the Teamsters Union in the state and one in 1989 for its study of problems with alcoholism and suicide among Native Alaskans. Said Berzon of the journalists she remembers from the Alaskan paper, "I know what a big deal that was for them. It's amazing to think that this prize could do the same thing for the *Sun*."

Berzon would soon leave the *Sun* for the *Wall Street Journal*, which saw her as a plum of a young reporter and moved her west to Los Angeles, where the gaming industry became one of her beats. "Alexandra, in addition to covering Las Vegas, is now doing more of a corporate investigative beat," says Rebecca Blumenstein, the *Journal*'s deputy editor in chief. "She's a good dive-bomber, and we've employed her in a number of areas."

From Los Angeles, Berzon has watched sadly as the *Sun* has come close to folding in recent years. Publisher Brian Greenspun has experienced

what he calls a "family implosion" among the Greenspun family owners that has left the future in doubt. Poor financial results in part have
been tied to its joint operating agreement with the rival *Las Vegas Review-
Journal*, where the *Sun* was appearing as a supplement distributed inside
when its Pulitzer-winning stories appeared.

"Certainly, the prize is a high water mark that shows you've been doing
something great," he says, remembering that on the day of the Pulitzer
announcement it "meant at least as much to me as a son as it did as a
publisher." He was thinking of his father Hank Greenspun—who was
famous for opposing Wisconsin senator Joseph McCarthy's anti-Commu-
nist demagoguery, among other campaigns—even though this was the
paper's first Pulitzer win.[7]

2009—*Las Vegas Sun,* and notably the courageous reporting by
Alexandra Berzon, for the exposure of the high death rate among
construction workers on the Las Vegas Strip amid lax enforcement
of regulations, leading to changes in policy and improved
safety conditions.[8]

Turning Methane Into Gold

Daniel Gilbert did not start reading newspapers until he left home in
Manassas, Virginia, to attend the University of Chicago. He liked them—
so much, in fact, that he joined the student Maroon publication in his
junior year, eventually becoming the news editor. After his 2005 gradu-
ation he chose a newspaper career, eventually settling at the rural south
edge of his home state, near the Tennessee border.

The job for the *Bristol Herald Courier* involved covering courts, but editor J. Todd Foster had said it would come with an investigative mandate.
After "experiencing the isolation of the place, several hours away from
any major city," Gilbert remembers of his first visit, it struck him that
investigative journalism in such a locale could offer a test of his ability
to succeed "anywhere, including at a small paper in Appalachia." Thus
he thought the job "a pure test of my reporting and writing abilities."[9]
In April 2010 the Pulitzer board gave Gilbert and the 30,000-circulation

Bristol Herald Courier the highest grade possible. The Pulitzer for Public Service recognized his ability to penetrate the complex world of natural gas royalties: tens of millions of dollars owed to thousands of homeowners in an industry-dominated environment monitored only by a bungling state agency.

It took a while for Gilbert—twenty-six when he joined the *Herald Courier* in late 2007—to get used to a part of his home state so unfamiliar to him. With a median income less than half that of the rest of Virginia, and with a poverty rate that was twice the state's, there were "two Bristols," he says. "Rusted-out husks of manufacturing plants testify to an industrial economy that shriveled long ago, though there are pockets of opulence" tied to the rich seams of coal still lying buried under the Appalachians.

Reporting his court stories, Gilbert encountered angry citizens who were due mineral rights to oil and gas companies but had not been paid

FIGURE 8.2 The *Bristol* (Virginia) *Herald Courier* reporter Daniel Gilbert talks to the staff. The page announcing the paper's 2010 Pulitzer is behind him. *Source*: Photo provided by *Bristol Herald Courier*.

royalties for two decades. The reasons behind the nonpayment were so complicated that other reporters had given up trying to explain them. And Gilbert's pursuit of the mineral rights story took him away from the basic court stories Bristol readers needed to get from him, making time spent on it hard to justify. Esoteric rules determined how the amount of methane gas production from coal seams was being measured, and that was supposed to be part of the basis for the payments that were due rights holders. And following the regulatory issues, by traveling the thirty-five miles to the mountain town of Lebanon, was always unsatisfactory because he came away with numbers that did not add up.

Gilbert was good with databases, but what he found did not seem to help much. Some tables hinted at the actual production levels for gas, while other tables suggested that about $25 million in industry payments to the state were being bottled up and made unavailable for the citizens. Gilbert came to think of the system as a "money prison" that kept money from the rightful recipients. "I knew that I wanted to take a good, long, comprehensive look so readers wouldn't get lost and then forget about it," he says. But the complexity threatened to baffle him as well. "It honestly took months for me to understand what the controversies were," he says—including whether industry was being conscientious in making escrow payments.

Printing out the 1990 Gas and Oil Act in the Virginia Code, he "dissected whatever I didn't understand and started looking for answers." He read a law school text on mineral rights and boned up on legal opinions. He sensed a powerful story about state and industry obfuscation, but proving it would depend on whether the gas-production database could be cross-referenced with the monthly escrow royalty numbers.

Red Bull and Vodka

Because those kinds of calculations were beyond even his skills, in November 2008 Gilbert proposed to editor J. Todd Foster that the reporter be allowed to attend a computer-assisted-reporting seminar held by the Investigative Reporters and Editors organization, based at the University of Missouri in Columbia. (IRE had its origins in 1976, when a group of journalists led by *Newsday*'s Bob Greene—himself the leader of teams that won two Public Service Pulitzers—joined together to probe the murder of the *Arizona Republic* reporter Don Bolles.) At a seven-reporter enterprise like the *Herald Courier*, though, attending the IRE class was a tough sell. In addition to Gilbert's time away from reporting in Bristol, travel and registration costs would total about $1,200. Plus there was less of a Bristol angle than his editors usually liked. And, of course, there was no guarantee of success from the class, even though he did a great job of explaining the unfairness of the system if it turned out Gilbert was right.

"I became very excited, but I told him, 'We're going to have to take on a very complex issue and deal with people in the middle of it,'" says Foster, who knew that two previous managing editors had spiked escrow payment stories. Those earlier reporters had not been able to get to the bottom of the issue. "Gilbert is the smartest twenty-something person I've ever seen in a newsroom," adds Foster, who dearly wanted to see what the CAR course in Missouri could produce. So with the help of some liquid encouragement, Foster found a way to win over publisher Carl Esposito to the idea of paying for Gilbert's training. "I took some Red Bull and vodka over to the publisher, and I told him, I've okayed a week at the University of Missouri. He said sure. Then he called me the next day, when there was no vodka flowing, and he said, 'Please tell me it's worth it.'"[10]

It was. Gilbert learned that he could indeed cross-reference the two databases—for production and for escrow payments—creating a chart in which the *Herald Courier* would ultimately show readers precisely how much was bottled up in those individual accounts and not being paid.

"They gave me a lot of leeway in working out the story," Gilbert says of his time back at the paper after he took the IRE class. "But the leeway wasn't carte blanche. There was no 'freeing me up just to do this.' Part of the arrangement was that I would bring something else back"—other stories on his court beat, unrelated to the oil and gas issues at the heart of the methane project.

Gilbert's mineral rights stories, beginning on December 6 and running through the end of 2008, discussed the fund's "obscure, untidy legacy" but began to give a clearer picture of how individual payment amounts flowed into the escrow accounts. It shows the amount of disbursements that were made and the amount that remained bottled up. It put him in touch with individual Virginians in the mineral rights program and their frustration.

"I spent months searching for people who hadn't received royalties, many of whom were reluctant to talk about it or to share their personal records with me," Gilbert says. "These voices gave emotional resonance to what would otherwise have been a dry story about the vagaries of mineral law and inadequate government oversight."

What he came up with was a people story as much as a mineral rights story. And his writing showed an uncanny ability to let people express their reactions to being wronged. Told of the thousands she was due from gas rights, one woman simply exclaimed, "Oh, my goodness. Oh, my word." Gilbert worked especially hard to make sure he did not "just give people a whole lot of zeroes" in his stories. In one, he wrote that the 1.2-cubic-feet-per-second daily methane flow from one family's property is "enough gas to satisfy the heating and cooking needs of an average American family for more than a year."

The seven Pulitzer public service jurors especially liked the results the *Herald Courier* produced: the state legislature began to act; the Gas and Oil Board was audited; and royalty money began to flow to deserving landowners at last. "The wheels are turning," the *Cape Cod Times* editor Paul Provonost said after the board named the *Herald Courier* the winner. "Especially in public service, showing some sort of impact is vital.... I tried not to have a soft spot for a paper that is small, but small papers really do have a hard time" when they try to carry off a major project like Gilbert's, Provonost adds.[11]

"The gas industry is not a particular fan of mine," Gilbert said the day the Pulitzer was announced. "Some of them complained that the series was biased and didn't include all the good things the gas companies do and all the people who *are* getting royalties. My response was, Okay, but that's not what I was writing about." The gas industry had to learn to deal with Gilbert, though, in the job he later accepted—as a colleague of Alexandra Berzon's at the *Wall Street Journal*. There, stationed in the Houston bureau, says the *Journal*'s deputy editor in chief Rebecca Blumenstein, he was put "in the middle of one of the biggest stories around: the natural gas boom."[12]

The legacy of the gold medal lives on in Bristol, where the new owner, billionaire investor Warren Buffett's company, took over two years after the paper won the Pulitzer. In rural Virginia, the *Herald Courier* was one of sixty-three papers in the financially struggling Media General operation purchased by Buffett's Berkshire Hathaway Corporation. And since then, says new publisher James Maxwell, the *Herald Courier* has added ten members to the newsroom staff, an increase of more than 50 percent, and was building a new display case for its gold medal. Maxwell, while working at Oregon's *Medford Mail Tribune* twenty years ago, learned about the tradition of the Public Service Pulitzer when that newspaper put the prize that it won in 1934 on display. "That was a moment I'll never forget," he says. The publisher has plans to make this newer gold medal a Bristol resource. "The prize belongs to the newspaper, but to a certain extent also to the community. The opportunity to hold it is something everyone in town deserves," says Maxwell.[13]

2010—*Bristol* (Va.) *Herald Courier* for the work of Daniel Gilbert in illuminating the murky mismanagement of natural-gas royalties owed to thousands of land owners in southwest Virginia, spurring remedial action by state lawmakers.[14]

CHAPTER 9

THE TRADITION SURVIVES

2011–2012: Return of the *L.A. Times* and the *Philadelphia Inquirer*

It's given us our mojo back.

— SHELBY GRAD, *LOS ANGELES TIMES* CITY EDITOR

It is hardly the proudest memory from Ruben Vives's *Los Angeles Times* reporting on corruption in the city of Bell, California: when city manager Robert Rizzo, at their first meeting, told him that his annual salary was $700,000 a year, Vives let out an involuntary "Jesus Christ!"[1] Still, Vives and investigative partner Jeff Gottlieb relish recounting that very human reaction when they speak with journalism classes. Without fail, students are fascinated to hear how the celebrated reporting pair helped the *Times* win the 2011 Public Service Pulitzer Prize for exposing Bell's widespread abuses. (Rizzo's salary actually turned out to be closer to $800,000 and a later Gottlieb and Vives story eventually established that benefits pushed his total compensation to more than $1.5 million.)

The *Times*'s Bell reporting, like so many Pulitzer-winning efforts, involved extensive collaboration of editors and reporters, building the initial disclosures into a solid, clear platform for corrective action. But along with enlightening readers, the Bell coverage had major *internal* impact: giving an embattled newspaper—owned by a Tribune Company that since late 2008 had been operating under bankruptcy protection—a rare reason to celebrate. "We had just gone through three or four top editors, and a lot of layoffs. The newsroom morale was low," says Kimi Yoshino, who together with fellow assistant city editor Steve Marble and city editor Shelby Grad was instrumental in designing the paper's months of Bell coverage. "But this story really had an outrage factor that captivated people's attention, both the public's and the newsroom's."[2]

Across the country, the *Philadelphia Inquirer*—like the *Times*, a publication with a long tradition of public service but lately under the control of an owner in bankruptcy proceedings—felt a similar sense of staff renewal after winning the next year's gold medal. The *Inquirer*'s 2012 Pulitzer was for a deeply reported study of the culture of high school violence in Philadelphia, leading to better community understanding and corrective policies.

Indeed, the two cases illustrate a truth that increasingly applies in the struggling media businesses these days: there is nothing like a great story, well handled, to deliver a much-needed lift.

"Is a City Manager Really Worth $800,000?"

Ruben Vives and Jeff Gottlieb got their first real break on the Bell story in June 2010 as they explored the announced plan of a struggling neighbor city, Maywood, to outsource its municipal management to the ostensibly healthier Bell. Turning their focus from Maywood to Bell, the reporters dug up indications that part-time Bell city council members were making in the area of $100,000 a year—far above the stipend of $5,000 or so that one would expect in one of California's poorest cities with fewer than forty thousand people.

For more than a week, officials stonewalled the reporters before finally arranging a Friday meeting in a conference room at a Bell city park. It was there, surrounded by other administrators, that Rizzo mentioned his salary—getting the surprised response from Vives—and delivered some documents the reporters had requested. What they heard at the meeting and read later suggested a dozen new Bell story ideas to the pair.

Assistant city editor Marble called in Gottlieb to team with beat reporter Vives after Vives filed his first stories on Maywood. Marble saw the Maywood-Bell angle adding a complex element to the story that a seasoned reporter like Gottlieb could help Vives develop. Vives, only in his third year of reporting, was no stranger to *Times* investigations; he had served as a translator for the reporting team that led the *Times* to its 2005 gold medal for its King/Drew reports exposing medical problems and racial injustice at the hospital. Over the previous thirty years Gottlieb had done investigations for four California papers. (He left the *Times* early in 2015.)

Vives remembers being upset at first that he would be sharing a story like the Maywood-Bell relationship, which seemed to have juicy possibilities. But the two reporters hit it off and began producing stories together that got the notice of both readers and editors. As the possibility of a Bell scandal developed, the pair knew the way the *Times* would typically treat it. "I wondered if this was going to be a project: a five-part series," says Vives. That would be similar to the approach that John Carroll, the *Times* editor at the time of the King/Drew series, took six years before. But instead the editors chose to play the Bell story in "a very un-*L.A. Times* way," says Gottlieb—developing it one disclosure at a time. The result "was that it built momentum," Gottlieb says approvingly. "People would pick up their papers and say, 'Okay, what happened today in Bell?' It became very episodic, almost like a soap opera, with the Bell guys as the bad guys, and us as the good guys."[3] And the scandal built.

Marble, who devised the coverage plan with Yoshino and city editor Grad, says, "I don't think there was ever a point where we thought about slowing down and doing this as a multiple-part series." The editors wanted the salary element to run out right away, making a strong online splash and then perhaps winning a place on the front page. After several weeks of articles by Gottlieb and Vives, the editors would plan to call in other veteran *Times* reporters for other angles of the story, aiming many of those for the front page too.[4]

After seeing Gottlieb and Vives's first story on exorbitant Bell compensation, managing editor Davan Maharaj agreed not to approach developments in the city with a planned series. On July 15, the *Times* published a stand-alone story—under a front-page headline asking "Is a City Manager Worth $800,000?"—accompanied by a prominently displayed graphic showing the sky-high pay of Bell officials, starting with Rizzo. Maharaj had asked Michael Whitley, assistant managing editor for design, to create a graphic. Whitley did more than highlight Bell's range of high salaries and demographics; he also wrote the headline, which Maharaj loved. "This is a very effective headline," the managing editor told the copy desk. "If you can beat it, go for it."[5] They couldn't and the headline ran.

Especially in recession times, the story of overpaid officials in an impov-erished city resonated with readers. And on the merits of the online version, the story quickly spread around the country, prompting news organizations to dig up salary statistics for their own local officials. The *Times* top edi-tor, Russ Stanton, knew the story was resonating nationally when he was visiting Pittsburgh a few days after the first Vives-Gottlieb story and saw "a story on Bell on the front page of the *Post-Gazette*." Meanwhile, follow-up coverage by his paper "took its natural, rightful course; it wasn't a project we spent two years on," according to Stanton, who adds that "these are my favorite kinds of stories [because] they come off of beats."[6] Within weeks, other *Times* stories followed: about tricks the Bell city council and admin-istrators played to allow a jump in their pay, including secret approval of special benefits for officials. Rizzo, it turned out, had won vacation and sick leave benefits that totaled more than twenty-eight weeks a year.

Among the dozen or so reporters brought in to contribute *Times* sto-ries was Kim Christensen, veteran of a Pulitzer-winning project a decade earlier at Portland's *Oregonian* newspaper. "The first thing I was asked to do was make sure we'd gotten all the public records that were available," says Christensen. Then, working with reporter Paloma Esquivel, the two of them focused on the city's broader financial issues. "While those guys were raking in big bucks," he says, "they were cutting city services" and still boosting the property tax rate.[7]

One of the *Times*'s premier writers, Christopher Goffard, was also assigned to write a December 28 article on Rizzo's eighteen-year con-version from "an obscure civil servant into what a prosecutor called an 'unelected and unaccountable czar.'" The piece was designed to wrap up the Bell experience for readers—and, perhaps not incidentally, would cap the paper's Pulitzer entry of sixteen separate stories. It began:

> The new boss kept his office Spartan and impersonal, the wall stripped of photos, the desk conveying no hint of his life beyond the red-brick walls of City Hall.
>
> It was 1993, a bleak, recession-bit year, and Robert Rizzo arrived in Bell trailing the vague whiff of scandal. His last city administrator job, in the high desert city of Hesperia, had ended badly, with accusations that he'd steered city improvement funds toward salaries.

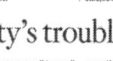

FIGURE 9.1 The *Los Angeles Times* front page from September 22, 2010. The photo by Robert Lachman shows former Bell City Manager Robert Rizzo being taken into custody, charged with misappropriating millions of dollars of city funds. *Source*: Copyright © 2010, *Los Angeles Times*. Reprinted with permission.

But the Bell officials who hired him did not dig deeply into his past. They needed someone fast, and Rizzo, then 39, came cheap. His starting salary was $78,000, which was $7,000 less than his predecessor had made. . . .

Now Rizzo and seven other Bell leaders past and present are charged with looting more than $5.5 million from one of the county's poorest municipalities. It is a hydra-headed scandal that has spawned several federal, state and county investigations and transformed a forgotten suburb into a synonym for rogue governance. It has resonated as a morality tale in which Rizzo is cast as a greed-crazed, cigar-chomping puppet master who cheated his way to an $800,000 salary and a 10-acre horse ranch.[8]

Times editors note that the Pulitzer Prize entry package they submitted contained both analytical pieces and reports from the beat with no fewer than fifteen names appearing in the bylines. "You had the greed of people taking big salaries. And then you had this second tier of reporters discovering that there was something more heinous going on: this wholesale bilking of some of the poorest people in California" over about a decade, says city editor Shelby Grad. "That's what made this a prizewinner."

In journalism circles, the lead writers who got the scoop made the Bell story particularly appealing. Jeff Gottlieb and Ruben Vives made numerous appearances discussing their work and when the Pulitzers were announced, the focus was on them, even if they were not individually acknowledged in the citation. In a *Los Angeles Times* column headlined "An Unlikely Duo Wins Pulitzer for Bell Coverage," media writer James Rainey called them "perfectly cinematic . . . a pair of mismatched bookends, both raised in Los Angeles but from worlds apart."[9] (The Guatemala-born Vives had to fight at an early age for a green card and then eventually won a translator's job at the paper, while Gottlieb attended Pitzer College and the Columbia University Graduate School of Journalism before beginning his career.)

The Bell stories were also popular among readers, Grad believes, because they served as a reminder of how hard it can be to find out information that politicians want to hide—especially when data like municipal pay is supposed to be readily available. The failure to catch the Bell abuses earlier in regular beat coverage weighed on some editors at the *Times*. "What

FIGURE 9.2 The *Los Angeles Times* Bell reporting and editing team in the *Times*'s lobby. Front row, left to right, Robert Lopez, Ruben Vives, Jeff Gottlieb, and Paloma Esquivel. Second row, Richard Winton, Steve Marble, Kim Christensen, and Hector Becerra. Third row, Kimi Yoshino, Christopher Goffard, Shelby Grad, and Corina Knoll. Not pictured: Paul Pringle. *Source*: Photo by Mark Boster, *Los Angeles Times*. Copyright © 2014, *Los Angeles Times*. Reprinted with permission.

happened in Bell is also an indictment of us," says Marble. "This is an area we used to cover; we'd go to all the meetings." But mainly because of staff cuts, "we just stopped doing that. . . . And the city became like a fortress."

While *Times* municipal coverage had indeed become far thinner in the years prior to the Bell investigation and both the staff and the actual newspaper had shrunk in size, Shelby Grad says that the paper's culture always remained focused on the kind of in-depth reporting represented by both King/Drew and Bell. And he ticks off several major stories—in between those two Pulitzers—that either won prizes or were in contention for them. "You see how much smaller [the newspaper] is, and the struggle that it's had," he says, "but I do think there remains very much a culture that's focused on that kind of work. That's the reason Bell happened."[10]

The 2011 Pulitzer gave the *Los Angeles Times* its sixth gold medal, one more than its longtime rival the *New York Times*.

2011—*Los Angeles Times* for its exposure of corruption in the small California city of Bell where officials tapped the treasury to pay themselves exorbitant salaries, resulting in arrests and reforms.[11]

"Assault on Learning"

Any newsroom fallout from the bankruptcy of the *Los Angeles Times*'s Chicago-based owner rates as minor compared to the chaos that faced the *Philadelphia Inquirer* on its path to the 2012 Public Service Pulitzer. In July 2010, the *Inquirer* editor Bill Marimow had green-lighted a major project proposed by investigative reporter John Sullivan studying widespread Philadelphia school violence in hopes of trying to reduce the plague of attacks. The deputy managing editor for special projects, Vernon Loeb, would edit. But in October Marimow was abruptly demoted by order of the publisher, making him a reporter again. While the *Inquirer* staffers felt bad for Marimow, they also wondered what would happen to the nascent school violence project for which Sullivan was teamed with higher education beat reporter Sue Snyder and school district reporter Kristen Graham. Executive editor Stan Wischnowski, named to succeed Marimow, made up his mind early; the project would continue with a five-reporter team. He added database reporter Dylan Purcell and general assignment reporter Jeff Gammage. The management turmoil continued when Loeb left for a job at the *Washington Post*. So Wischnowski pulled Mike Leary out of the *Inquirer* managing editor's slot to edit the project.[12]

Throwing those resources into such a difficult project "wasn't an easy call," says Wischnowski, noting that some day-to-day reporting had to be suspended for lack of staff. And keeping Snyder off her higher education beat, for example, meant someone else from the already-short staff had to fill in—in one of the top cities in the nation for universities. "But I just had a gut feeling it was the right decision" because the project seemed so important and the *Inquirer* had the right personnel for the job.[13] The reporting, he knew, would fly in the face of the widely accepted claim by

Philadelphia school administrators that schools were actually becoming safer—a claim Sullivan and his teammates believed to be a self-serving lie bolstered by bad data.

Wischnowski felt the passion that the team brought to the subject. Sullivan, who had a rough upbringing, had followed the gut-wrenching world of youth violence in the city for years, including spending a summer in an emergency room following gunshot victims. The reporter felt strongly that school disciplinary systems needed an overhaul, with more proactive treatment strategies getting a chance. In the past, school violence had been presented in largely racial terms. Readers still recalled the *Inquirer* reporting from 2009 that had studied the case of African American students attacking Asian Americans. But this story would focus on overall student violence, including blacks fighting blacks—who make up the majority in Philadelphia's public school universe. Sullivan felt that the project was an opportunity to meet broader needs of the community by looking at the educational benefits that would come with reducing violence. He had been able to persuade Marimow and now he persuaded Wischnowski.[14]

Snyder and Graham's preliminary reporting added evidence to the case that violent incidents in schools were worsening, not easing, and it also built a source list for use on the project. "That was crucial, because between the two of us we knew thousands of teachers," says Graham. The school district had claimed a 30 percent reduction in violence in recent years, but what teachers told the newspaper was that "*reported* violence was down thirty percent, but the level of under-reporting was just astonishing." Teachers were increasingly afraid in their classrooms, she adds, no matter what the school district's statistics said. And they told Snyder and Graham about their fears. Sullivan turned to Temple University to produce an independent survey for the newspaper's project and those results also challenged the school district's numbers.

Especially exciting for Snyder and Graham was their first shot at an *Inquirer*-style team investigation, part of the newsroom culture since the 1970s when legendary editor Gene Roberts built the paper into an investigative—and Pulitzer-winning—machine. (After his arrival the paper won its first Pulitzer Prize, then sixteen more over fifteen years, including two involving Marimow as a reporter. The paper had won for public service in 1978 and 1990.) "I loved being part of that *Inquirer* tradition," Snyder says. "A lot of it was casting this wide net to get everything we can" about school violence. Another element, often part of the beginnings of an investigation: "We didn't know where we were going."

The Holy Grail

The two reporters' net also turned up one dramatic case of violence that would become the project's lead example. "Very early on in the reporting, I was at a meeting at the city Human Relations Commission," recalls Graham. "This teacher was testifying, and weeping, about how she had been administering a test to a student, and a group of fifteen or twenty students were going from classroom to classroom, looking for this young girl, to attack this student." The teacher had testified, "This is what's going on. People are being attacked in our classrooms." Graham had heard lots of stories about school violence, but "this mental image was so strong" that she took the teacher's phone number, following up later and eventually finding the victim of the attack: student Teshada Herring.[15] Finally sitting for an interview with Sue Snyder, Teshada told in graphic detail about her beating by schoolmates at Audenried High School who, as part of a fighting ritual, had smeared Vaseline on their heads to protect their skin from scars and to keep their hair from being ripped out—the way Teshada's would be. Teshada's mother added significantly to the family drama.

Snyder told Sullivan about the interview. "As soon as she talked about the Vaseline on the faces, I knew instantaneously that this was the lead of the story," says John Sullivan. As editor of the project, Mike Leary agreed to design it around that opening. "We wanted to take readers inside schools, to show them what was really happening," Leary says. "This needed to be a series of strong narratives; this wasn't a numbers story."[16] Leary also knew there was a security tape from inside the school showing the attack, and he pressed the reporting team to find it—thinking it would be a huge benefit for the online presentation. As the reporters and editors planned for what would eventually become a seven-part series, creating other narratives to bolster the account of Teshada's beating in part one, Snyder and Graham saw the security video as "the holy grail."

Sullivan had a special attachment to the segment he had proposed for part five, turning the focus away from the victims of school violence and toward the perpetrators—students who had often been let down by a school disciplinary system offering little hope of ending the cycle of violence. Just as the narrative story approach created sympathy for those who were attacked, Sullivan's plan for part five was to help readers understand how the mentality of the assailant develops and the importance of effective intervention to help turn their lives around. A youth deciding to attack others is a "complicated, subtle, and elusive story," wrote Sullivan, who as a youth himself had had run-ins with official discipline, helping inform his reporting. Editor Leary saw part five as one of the project's best components, to be followed by part six's examples of success in other jurisdictions and part seven's prescriptions for change in Philadelphia. (The other editors were Rose Ciotta and Avery Rome with multimedia editor Frank Wiese leading the online team.)

But even as the story progressed, the *Inquirer* newsroom felt more and more like it was being torn apart in a battle for control by rival teams of owners. Union troubles pitted one set of staffers against another and reporters and editors worried about large-scale layoffs or perhaps even a closure of the paper. Marimow, having been demoted by a new publisher, decided to leave and take a teaching position at Arizona State University's Cronkite School of Journalism and Mass Communication. (He had stayed on as an *Inquirer* reporter for a time, even working on some school-related stories. And he confesses to being conflicted about it. "First of all I love reporting. And I knew from the time the company went bankrupt that if another group of owners came in I would be vulnerable," he says.) At the head of the investigative team, Sullivan—who was also facing family challenges—compared the interoffice strain to what he had experienced reporting for the *Inquirer* in Iraq, where one sometimes didn't know who was the enemy.

Snyder was worried about the story. And they both recall an emotional meeting in which Sullivan bared his concerns to her. This is Sullivan's account: "We went up to the cafeteria and she asked, 'What is going on with you?' I said, 'I'm distracted.' And she said, 'I need you now; this story can't happen without you.' We both cried at that table."[17] Sullivan suspects that some of that emotion carried through to the part-five story he was writing at the time.

For her part, Snyder says that his finishing that story added a key element to the series: "It was about how the school district was failing to help students who were in trouble, and who were acting out. He was able to bring that story to life." For the entire team, she adds, "There were times when we got dejected and down. But hearing the stories from the kids and their parents, it was so emotional. We knew how important it was to keep going. So we did."

It was Snyder who finally found the holy grail: the Teshada beating video. When the reporter was repeatedly told by her sources that they did not have access to the security tape, Snyder just pressed them for suggestions about who might—coming up with this list of possibilities. After many fruitless calls, finally one person blithely told her, "Yes, I have it. Come on over." Snyder took Sullivan with her to pick it up. "It was so exciting to be going out there," she says. They then gave the video to multimedia editor Wiese for inclusion with part one of the series.

Writing that first part was also a struggle, says Snyder, because she, Sullivan, and Graham all contributed. "We all had our writing styles, and we all knew that with that first story it was so important. But somehow we did coalesce." The three wrote for the top of the story paragraph-by-paragraph in an exercise that felt like a modular, Lego-style project until Mike Leary got into the editing. The story began:

> For Teshada Herring, the action was unmistakable: The girls smearing Vaseline on their faces and fitting scarves to their heads were preparing for a fight.
>
> The ritual—well-known in Philadelphia schools—is intended to keep skin from scarring and hair from getting ripped out.
>
> As Teshada passed the group on her way to class at Audenried High that morning, the events of the previous week flashed through her mind—a fight she had witnessed, Facebook posts warning that someone from her neighborhood would be attacked, a text blast to her phone that all but named her as the intended victim.
>
> She wondered: Would they come for her? . . .
>
> Suddenly, a band of more than a dozen girls and boys—captured on video roaming the halls and looking into classrooms—barged through the door.

FIGURE 9.3 The *Philadelphia Inquirer* front page, with a dramatic still from the video of a beating, opens its "Assault on Learning" series on school violence, March 27, 2011. *Source*: Used by permission of the *Philadelphia Inquirer*.

The group converged on Teshada and began to beat her.

In less than a minute, they vanished.

"It was like a tornado," her teacher would later say. "They went one way, then they went the other way."

In Philadelphia, schools are no sanctuary.[18]

Leary notes that the paper was careful about protecting student identities during the series, holding many discussions about what photos to hold back and what photos to run. But for the video of Teshada's beating, he says, "It was real life. And there was a news reason to show it." A still from the video also helped add to the first day's graphics on the front page. Because of staff cutbacks, Leary says, "the paper was stretched thin in a lot of ways, and some reporters ended up taking some photos for the series, adding to those that the regular staff photographers produced. A critical component of the series was a database that readers could search online to see the number and type of violent incidents at each school along with video narratives.

By the time the *Inquirer*'s Public Service Pulitzer was announced—for school violence narratives and videos that, according to the Pulitzer board, stirred "reforms to improve safety for teachers and students"—John Sullivan had left, taking a teaching position at Northwestern University's Medill School of Journalism soon after the series was written. (He returned to the newsroom to celebrate with teammates when they heard the announcement from Columbia University.)

Marimow by then was back as well—and again sitting in the editor's chair. He had been rehired just weeks before the Pulitzer announcement, after yet another ownership change in what seemed to be developing as a perpetually unstable situation.[19] His return created a peculiar job shift for Stan Wischnowski, who resumed his executive editor's role with Marimow's return. "It was a wild range of emotions," says Wischnowski. After getting a tip that the *Inquirer* might win the Public Service Pulitzer, "within a span of seven to ten days I was also getting the news that I would no longer be the editor. I don't know another situation when an editor is told he may win the Pulitzer, and days later hears he's out." Next came an institutional hit from owners: selling the downtown building that had been the paper's home for seventy-five years on top of another downsizing to accompany the office move.

In that strange confluence of announcements, however, the thrill of the prize still overwhelmed everything else. "For us to win our first Pulitzer in fifteen years, in this city," says Wischnowski, "was a true 'Rocky' story." Wischnowski and Marimow, as the two top editors, were working closely together through the first half of 2014 when yet another change in ownership control took place.

Marimow, in comments quoted in the *Inquirer*'s own story, added the perspective of an investigative reporter whose career spanned the paper's four glory decades: "To me, a Public Service Pulitzer also is a sign of sustained excellence over the ages. There are only two other newspapers in America—the *Washington Post* and the *Los Angeles Times*—that have had three Pulitzer Prizes for Public Service in the last thirty-five years. So we're up there where the air is rare."[20]

2012—The *Philadelphia Inquirer* for its exploration of pervasive violence in the city's schools, using powerful print narratives and videos to illuminate crimes committed by children against children and to stir reforms to improve safety for teachers and students.[21]

PART II

Coming of Age

CHAPTER 10

FIRST GOLD

1917–1919: The Great War, Brought Home

The medal is most artistic in design, and very precious, as it is an award
for distinguished public service by a high court of public opinion.

—*NEW YORK TIMES* PUBLISHER ARTHUR S. OCHS
TO THE PULITZER ADVISORY BOARD, JULY 8, 1920

With the Pulitzer Prizes now signifying the pinnacle of excellence in both
journalism and the arts—and celebrating their centennial in 2016—it is
hard to imagine Columbia University struggling to get the awards off the
ground. Yet unheralded and overshadowed by world war, the selection of
the first winners was barely noticed in 1917. Two months earlier, President
Woodrow Wilson had declared war on Germany. And even the Pulitzer
advisory board members did not seem much interested in the awarding
of the first prizes. Only four of the ten board members joined Columbia
president Butler in the school's Low Library for the May 24 selections.

Not that the jurors had given them many nominees to consider. The
jurors for the non-journalism categories, who had been chosen from the
American Academy of Arts and Letters and who included literary lights
from Yale and Harvard universities, made only a few recommendations.
And the board voted no award at all for a novel or a drama that first
year. For the American History Prize, the winner was not even an American but the French ambassador, Jean Jules Jusserand, for his book *With
Americans of Past and Present Days*. A Biography Prize was voted for *Julia
Ward Howe*, written by the daughters of the lyricist of "Battle Hymn of
the Republic."

In the journalism categories, small juries of Columbia faculty members had been set up, with Journalism Dean Talcott Williams serving on

each. It isn't clear whether jurors simply lacked energy for the job or just found the prior year's journalism unworthy. But they forwarded only two works for consideration—and none at all for public service. The two nominations that the jurors did send to the board reflected both the wartime environment and their own eastern backgrounds. From the *New York Tribune* there was an anti-German editorial published on the anniversary of the sinking of the *Lusitania*, and from the *New York World* there was a series of dispatches by Herbert Bayard Swope titled "Inside the German Empire."

As Pulitzer Prize historian John Hohenberg put it: "The Advisory Board, concluding that first rather desultory session on the prizes, quietly voted the recommendations of all the juries." That meant no recipient for the Public Service Prize that first year. For the few literature and journalism prizes that *were* awarded, Columbia adopted a deliberate policy of restraint and barely promoted them. For the most part, only newspapers that won them said anything about the prizes.

In a strange way, Columbia's early low-key approach to the Pulitzer Prizes may have helped establish them for the long term. The prizes provoked little criticism, and there was certainly no hint of their being cheapened by excessive touting. As Hohenberg wrote, "Outside the garish spotlight of public cynosure, and relatively free of critical inspection, the system for determining the awards was molded into a reasonably efficient operation." In later years, as word began to get out about quality journalism being recognized, the board's secrecy about the process added to the intrigue.

It would not be until the 1920s that the journalism prizes began to attract significant attention and draw larger numbers of nominations. By then they were benefiting from their association with great early literary winners like Eugene O'Neill, Booth Tarkington, Edith Wharton, Willa Cather, Edna Ferber, Sinclair Lewis, and Thornton Wilder.[1] It was just what Joseph Pulitzer had wanted.

The *Times* at War

By failing to select a public service winner in 1917, the advisory board had stumbled in the inaugural Pulitzer award process. But as the board left its infancy and stepped haltingly into its second year—another one clouded by the war in Europe—it made a choice for its first gold medal that could not have been more propitious, either for the recipient or for the Pulitzer Public Service Prize itself.

While there are no board minutes available to prove it, those first members must have engaged in serious debate about just what Joseph Pulitzer had meant by newspaper public service. Was the award intended to honor a series of stories? Or could a campaign of some sort—or perhaps even a philosophy expressed through a public-spirited style of coverage—qualify as a "disinterested and meritorious" contribution to society? After all, hadn't Pulitzer himself served the public by using his paper to allow Lady Liberty to raise her lamp over New York Harbor?

In 1918, the advisory board cast a vote for a winner that reflected both fine reporting *and* a new philosophy of coverage. In selecting the *New York Times*, the Pulitzers also happened to acknowledge one of the day's meteoric newspaper success stories. The award, in fact, may well have been meant to recognize the international reporting phenomenon that the *Times* had become since the war in Europe started, and even before. The paper had changed the nature of overseas newspaper reporting.

Joseph Pulitzer himself had been sharply at odds with Adolph S. Ochs in Ochs's first years after buying the struggling nine-thousand-circulation *Times* in 1896. Ochs rapidly remade it into a daily that would appeal to the thinking person, just as Pulitzer had successfully played to passions and to fascination with public crusades. Editorially the *World* called the *Times* a creature of the trusts and Ochs the "keeper of the deficit." Meanwhile the *Times* opposed both Pulitzer and Hearst for practicing "freak journalism" as they beat the drum for war with Spain.

Ochs had worked wonders with the *Times*, not only building circulation to more than one hundred thousand copies in eight years but also hiring extraordinary journalists who saw balanced, in-depth coverage of a range of topics as the desperate need of a growing class of sophisticated New Yorkers. Surreptitiously, Pulitzer joined them. In the thaw that Pulitzer initiated with some rival publishers after the yellow journalism period ended, Pulitzer invited Ochs for a visit to his Chatwold residence in Bar Harbor, writing: "You may not know that I have the *Times* sent to me abroad when the *World* is forbidden and that most of my news I really receive from your paper."[2]

With good reason. A 1951 corporate history by celebrated *Times* reporter Meyer Berger noted that "Ochs had a genius for picking men of stature as aides, and he gave their talents free rein, in the newsroom or in the counting room." One such choice was managing editor Carr Van Anda, an Ohioan who joined the *Times* in 1904 from the *Sun* and immediately began to give meaning to Ochs's new slogan, "All the News That's Fit to Print." Berger wrote: "There may have been somewhere in newspaper history a more perfect publisher-managing editor team than the Ochs-Van Anda set-up, but none comes to mind." Both loved science, especially new discoveries, and both believed a wide swath of New Yorkers hungered for their new approach. "There were many in the trade, and out of it, who preferred garnished fact and the literary touch—the journalistic cocktail—to the news that Van Anda served straight. They found the *Times* stuffy and elephantine in pace, even if it was complete, and honest." Those readers had plenty of alternatives at the *World*, the *Herald*, the *Sun*, the *American*, the *Press*, and others. "The years were to prove that the Ochs and Van Anda formula was best for the long haul, that an intelligent reading public bought newspapers—strange as it seemed to some—to read the news," according to Berger.[3]

When it came to covering science, the paper not only excelled but also used technology for its own purposes. A decade before the war, Ochs's *Times* had carried the "First Wireless Press Message Across the Atlantic," as the paper's own headline proclaimed on October 18, 1907. The technology gave the *Times* an edge over the competition for years, especially in wartime.

There were stumbles. But what history later exposed as one editorial blunder offers a fascinating insight into the *Times* and into the era before the war. A piece of *Times* lore has its roots in a June 1908 interview that correspondent William Bayard Hale conducted with Kaiser Wilhelm II on the imperial yacht *Hohenzollern* off the coast of Norway. It was six years before European hostilities were to begin and the German leader's thoughts were largely unknown. But in a two-hour diatribe, he told Hale that blond, Protestant Anglo-Teutons from northern Europe were destined to rule the world. "It is a mistaken idea that Christianity has no countenance for war. We are Christians by reason of forcible conversion," he said to Hale. "The Bible is full of good fighting—jolly good fights."

The reporter, who hadn't dared take notes, madly assembled a long memorandum. Afraid to send it by cablegram, Hale told his editors: "Result so startling that I hesitate to report it without censorship of Berlin." When they finally saw it, Ochs and a collection of *Times* editors that included Van Anda and Charles Miller considered it potentially world-shaking. For the sake of national interest, though, they decided that Hale should go to Washington and show it to President Theodore Roosevelt. Calling it "astonishing stuff," Roosevelt said it should not be run. "I don't believe the emperor wanted this stuff published," he told Hale. "If he did, he's a goose." Roosevelt had no power to block the *Times*. But Ochs, agreeing that this particular news was *not* fit to print, locked it in his private safe. There the memo stayed, incredibly, for thirty years, coming out only in an article appearing in the *Times* Magazine in 1939. There it was cited to compare the Kaiser's ranting to that of the German leader of the time, Adolf Hitler.[4]

If the *Times* ever regretted the decision not to give the world an early peek at the Kaiser's warmongering there wasn't much time for second-guessing. Soon it was telling readers of impending war in four-column headlines like this, from July of 1914:[5]

AUSTRIA BREAKS WITH SERVIA;
KING PETER MOVES HIS CAPITAL;
RUSSIA IS MOBILIZING HER ARMY;
BERLIN AND PARIS MOBS FOR WAR

Three years later, on April 3, 1917, above the full text of President Wilson's address to the nation in six columns, another headline appeared in the familiar eight-column banner format:

PRESIDENT CALLS FOR WAR DECLARATION,
STRONGER NAVY, NEW ARMY OF 500,000 MEN
FULL CO-OPERATION WITH GERMANY'S FOES

That headline was surely on the minds of the five advisory board members as they assembled at Columbia for the first Pulitzer Prize decision in May 1917. Meeting again the *next* May, though, that *Times* war declaration story and others that followed it were certainly part of the deliberations that led the board to awarding the 1918 gold medal to the New York newspaper.

One way Van Anda had made the *Times* unique was by using the paper's established edge in cable to saturate readers with dispatches, giving them the ability to judge for themselves what diplomats and leaders were saying in Europe even as *Times* reporters covered the same ground in their balanced way. Ochs freely bankrolled it. The *Times* figured that it spent $15,000 per week for cable use alone, for example, more than Ochs's predecessors had spent on foreign coverage altogether.

Did the coverage formula work for the *Times*, other than winning for it the first Pulitzer Public Service Prize? Its circulation skyrocketed during the war to 323,000 with annual advertising linage—2.2 million lines when Ochs bought the paper—surging to 23.4 million lines.

Van Anda's legend would continue to grow. In 1919, the *Times* copyrighted a story stemming from a meeting of astronomers in London, discussing findings from a May 29 solar eclipse that proved a little-known scientist's theory that starlight did not travel to earth in a straight line but instead curved around the sun. The *Times* thus introduced Americans to Albert Einstein.

A later Van Anda–Einstein story involved the editor's reading of one of the physicist's lectures at Princeton. "It came at a time when relativity was only understood by Dr. Einstein and by the Deity," according to a fellow professor who told the tale. "Dr. Einstein had already lost even the professorial mathematicians who were here to hear him, but the *Times* called me before going to press to ask whether there was not some mistake in the figures. . . . Mr. Van Anda thought one of the equations was wrong." The professor checked, found that the *Times* had accurately presented what Einstein had said, and decided to check back with Einstein himself. When Einstein was consulted he was astonished. He scanned the notes and nodded. He said, "Yes, Mr. Van Anda is right. I made a mistake in transcribing the equation on the blackboard."

It was also Van Anda who "went feverish over an Egyptian King who had slept some 3,500 years and restored him and his times with great fidelity and journalistic art." What had fascinated the editor, of course,

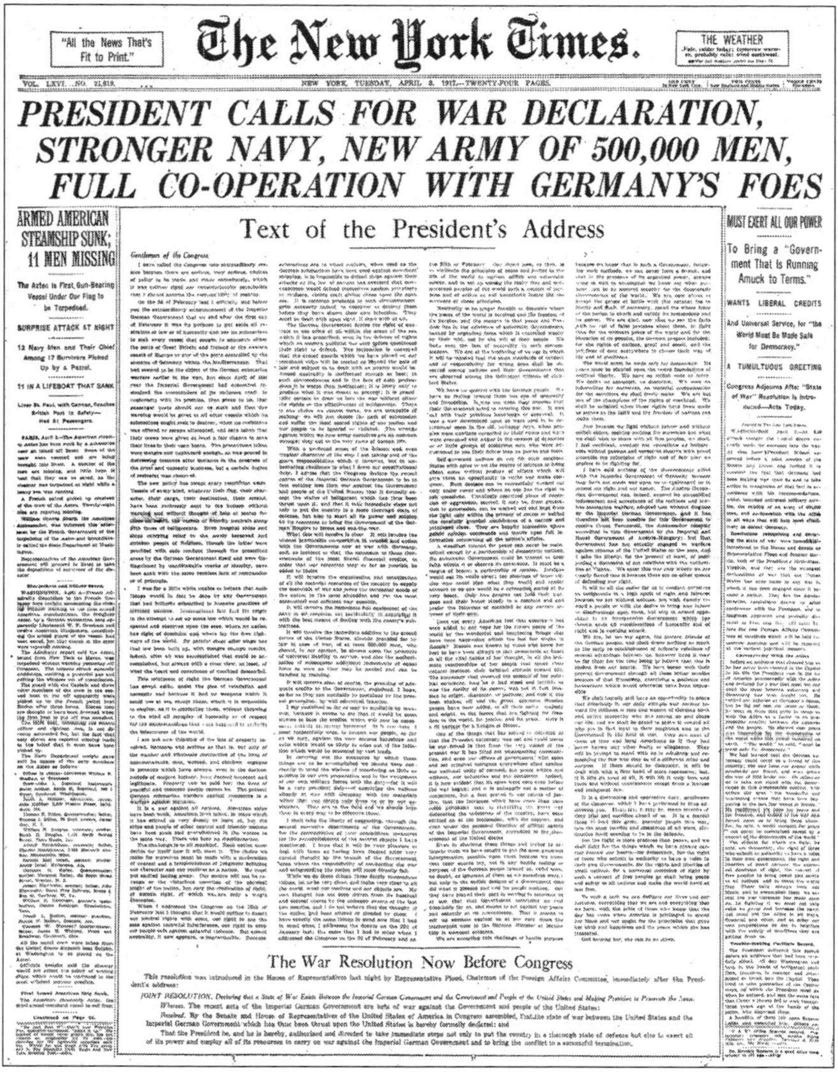

"All the News That's Fit to Print."

The New York Times.

THE WEATHER

VOL. LXVI...NO. 21,619. NEW YORK, TUESDAY, APRIL 3, 1917.—TWENTY-FOUR PAGES.

PRESIDENT CALLS FOR WAR DECLARATION, STRONGER NAVY, NEW ARMY OF 500,000 MEN, FULL CO-OPERATION WITH GERMANY'S FOES

ARMED AMERICAN STEAMSHIP SUNK; 11 MEN MISSING

The Aztec is First Gun-Bearing Vessel Under Our Flag to be Torpedoed.

SURPRISE ATTACK AT NIGHT

12 Navy Men and Their Chief Among 17 Survivors Picked Up by a Patrol.

11 IN A LIFEBOAT THAT SANK

Text of the President's Address

Gentlemen of the Congress:

MUST EXERT ALL OUR POWER

To Bring a "Government That Is Running Amuck to Terms."

WANTS LIBERAL CREDITS

And Universal Service, for "the World Must Be Made Safe for Democracy."

A TUMULTUOUS GREETING

The War Resolution Now Before Congress

JOINT RESOLUTION.

Resolved, By the Senate and House of Representatives of the United States of America in Congress assembled, That the state of war between the United States and the Imperial German Government which has thus been thrust upon the United States is hereby formally declared; and

That the President be, and he is hereby, authorized and directed to take immediate steps not only to put the country in a thorough state of defense but also to exert all of its power and employ all of its resources to carry on war against the Imperial German Government and to bring the conflict to a successful termination.

FIGURE 10.1 The *New York Times* of April 3, 1917, was already printing full texts of documents, such as President Wilson's declaration of war. *Source*: Copyright © 1917, The New York Times Company. Reprinted by permission.

FIGURE 10.2 Carr Van Anda, managing editor of the *New York Times* when it won the first Pulitzer Gold Medal. *Source*: From the *Times* photo archives. Copyright © 1912, The New York Times Company. Reprinted by permission.

was archaeologist Howard Carter's November 1922 discovery of King Tutankhamen's tomb. The original 250-word Associated Press story was all but ignored by the rest of the press. But Van Anda lined up an exclusive relationship through the *Times* of London to give his *New York Times* rights to the story. Its front-page article pointing out the "incomparably magnificent and wondrously beautiful" throne, among other things, helped start a national King Tut craze.[6]

A Precious Medal

The decision to forego that first gold medal in 1917 eliminated a potential problem for the Pulitzer board: no medal yet existed, nor had it even been designed. Columbia president Butler commissioned sculptor Daniel Chester French to design a Pulitzer medal in the fall of 1918, paying him $1,000. At the time, French was best known for his Minute Man statue in Lexington, Massachusetts, created in 1875 when the sculptor was twenty-five. (His statuary masterpiece, the seated Lincoln in the Lincoln Memorial on Washington's Mall, would not be dedicated until 1922.) But he had also designed a series of impressive commemorative medals. Today his nine medals are considered classics of the form, although by far the best known is the Joseph Pulitzer Medal. French worked with apprentice Augustus Lukeman on the medal, initialing it with DCF/AL just behind the left foot of the printer on the reverse.

Originally there was no printer. Butler had ordered the likeness of Benjamin Franklin on one side—French apparently chose to base his Franklin profile on a bust by Jean-Antoine Houdon—and a simple inscription on the other: "For the Most Disinterested and Meritorious Public Service Rendered By Any American Newspaper During the Year. . . ." But as they made their clay mock-ups, French and Lukeman thought the reverse too plain. French wrote to Butler that "interest would be increased by introducing an early press with a figure of a printer at work. I hope you may think so." The Columbia administrator called it "a little touch which is quite a stroke of genius."[7] (In early designs the printer wore a shirt and printer's cap, although the final medal has him bare-chested with his shirt draped across the far end of the press.)

The first medal, not minted until the year after the announcement of the *Times*'s Public Service Prize, took even longer to make the seventy-block trip from Columbia to Times Square. The *Times*'s files show that publisher Arthur Ochs acknowledged its receipt by hand delivery on July 8, 1920, with a two-paragraph letter that noted its "artistic design."[8]

An even more surprising delay may be the twenty-six years it took for a second gold medal to find its way to Times Square. The *Times* would not win another Public Service Prize until the *next* world war, in 1944. In other areas, though, the paper became a Pulitzer-winning machine—capturing thirteen prizes during that span.

1918—The *New York Times* for its public service in publishing in full so many official reports, documents and speeches by European statesmen relating to the progress and conduct of the war.[9]

In Defense of "Americanism"

If board members chose the *Times* in 1918 for its objective and thorough presentation of the combatants' original documents, their 1919 choice reflected quite a different approach to wartime coverage. Indeed, the board unanimously voted to give the gold medal to a newspaper that had engaged in a long struggle to oppose "Germanism in America." That effort had included blocking the teaching of German-language courses, opposing anti-war legislators like Senator Robert La Follette, and defending the reputation of its state, Wisconsin, against detractors who claimed that anti-war sentiment there emanated from its heavy German-American population.

The paper was the *Milwaukee Journal*, edited by Lucas Nieman, whose next seventeen years at the paper would be dedicated to keeping the news free of special interests—in an era when partisan advocacy was a feature of many other papers. Nieman would later become the benefactor of Harvard University's Nieman Foundation.

The jurors, again Columbia professors, made their nomination "tentatively" until they could conduct "investigations to confirm or disprove our present impression as to the risk and effectiveness of this service, pending the result of which we do not feel able to make a positive recommendation."[10] That is how the jury system was working back then.

A spokesman for the board, the AP's Melville Stone, explained why it honored the Milwaukee paper, remarking that "in a city where the German element has long prided itself on its preponderating influence, the *Journal* courageously attacked such members of that element as put Germany above America." President William Howard Taft was among those congratulating the paper on its award.

According to a 1982 history of the *Milwaukee Journal*: "Privately, Nieman and his staff were jubilant," creating a slogan for the paper: "First by Merit." More jubilation grew from the paper's achieving both record advertising linage and circulation after the prize. A *Journal* editorial said: "Wisconsin, which has been so misrepresented and so maligned and so misunderstood, is awarded the Pulitzer Medal for its patriotism in the Great War."[11]

1919—The *Milwaukee Journal* for its strong and courageous campaign for Americanism in a constituency where foreign elements made such a policy hazardous from a business point of view.[12]

CHAPTER II

REPORTING ON THE ROARING

1920–1929: Ponzi's Scam and an Ohio Editor's Murder

The Jazz Age had had a wild youth and a heady middle age . . . the most expensive orgy in history. . . . It was borrowed time anyhow—the whole upper tenth of a nation living with the insouciance of grand ducs and the casualness of chorus girls.

—F. SCOTT FITZGERALD, *THE CRACK-UP*

The Pulitzer Prizes for journalism entered the new decade like a child prodigy in that period of early, awkward adolescence. As an institution it had its brilliant moments—certainly one was the choice of the *New York Times* for the 1918 gold medal—but it was still quite immature.

Again, no award was voted in the public service category for 1920. (The board would skip the category in 1925 and 1930 too.) But the board took one step that was to have great long-term significance for the prize process, adding the thirty-five-year-old *St. Louis Post-Dispatch* editor Joseph Pulitzer II to its ranks. Together Ralph Pulitzer and his idealistic younger brother, Joseph, would infuse the prizes with their father's principles, as well as the benefactor's ambition for the prizes to become part of the national scene. Public service stories that displayed real courage in the telling would get extra attention on the board with these New York and St. Louis newspaper executives in the room. So would any coverage that brought about significant benefits to society. JP II especially launched a flurry of personal correspondence with other board members before each meeting, seeking their thoughts about how that year's awards were doing, encouraging nominations, and seeking their thoughts about how the Pulitzer Prizes were doing in general. He was frustrated by the lack of response from newspapers around the country and hated for the board to have to pass over a category for want of good candidates.[1]

The board started to take its job seriously. More members showed up to select prize winners, and they began strenuously debating the nominations that were forwarded from the Columbia journalism faculty members. Frequently the board reversed the jury recommendations.

Further, the board began to see that if it found a truly exemplary work to honor—particularly with a Public Service Medal—it could provide a much-needed model of excellence for the industry and could also boost the image of the Pulitzer Prizes themselves. This was an important development, coming at a time when the prizes still had almost no public image at all. The number of entries began to grow slowly, often because jurors and editors brought candidates to the table that they had seen during the prior year. The time when newspapers clamored to nominate their own best work was still in the future.[2]

Meanwhile, as the war began to fade as a dominant story, front pages reflected the emergence of disturbing social problems: the tenacity of racial hatred and the flourishing of political graft and corruption. Battling these evils would become central for Pulitzer board members selecting the gold medal winner.

A Story for the Jazz Age

The national mood was also undergoing a swift, if not altogether clear, transformation as the 1920s began to roar. For many people, the former idealism about the turn-of-the-century world veered toward cynicism. A strange, frantic self-indulgence took hold. After the horrors of the battle-fields of Europe, immediate gratification made more sense to some than did sacrifice. But it was also a time filled with paradox. Newspapers often saw themselves as standard-bearers for old national ideals, even as they began to reflect the new era's hedonism in their pages.

There could not have been a better newspaper story for the Jazz Age—or one that grew more powerfully from the anything-goes spirit in America—than the one that the Pulitzer board cited in its 1921 public service award. For once, the board had a real choice in the category. Meeting in early April, a jury of three Columbia journalism professors offered the board two possibilities. One nomination was for the *New York Evening Post*, which had brought attention to "the shortcomings of the

Government work for the relief and rehabilitation of the soldiers of the World War," according to John W. Cunliffe, the new director of Columbia's journalism school and the leader of each of the juries. It was, the jury had noted, a project benefiting "a great number of deserving men to whom the country owed a debt that was being neglected." The stories had been written by Harold Littledale, who had won a Reporting Pulitzer in 1918. Indeed, the jury helpfully suggested that when the board compared it with the other nominee, "in case of performances of equal intrinsic merit, it may perhaps be good policy to broaden the scope of the School's relations to the newspaper world and especially not to confine its awards too closely to metropolitan papers."[3]

The remark was something of a slight to Boston, home to the other nominated newspaper, the *Boston Post*. That city also thought of itself as metropolitan, and the *Post*, its largest paper at the time, actually sold more copies than even the *New York World*.[4] The *Post*'s nomination was "for the pricking of the Ponzi financial bubble, in investigating his claims to be operating in foreign exchange and throwing doubt on him at a time when the public officials were inactive and other newspapers were either ignoring him or treating him as a genuine financial wizard." The work was undertaken "at great risk of incurring heavy damages." If the jurors saw a negative in this story winning the Public Service Prize, it was that—unlike the veterans who were helped by the New York paper—"the persons chiefly benefited by the exposure of Ponzi were foolish persons who were seeking something for nothing and who were entitled to little sympathy."

The nomination did not have to identify the "Ponzi" involved. It was celebrated huckster Charles Ponzi. During an exhilarating summer the previous year, the bombastic Italian immigrant had devised a get-rich-quick scheme that had captivated the nation's attention—and made Ponzi a cult figure. In a Ponzi scheme, as such enterprises are now known, early investors receive hefty payouts from the funds provided by subsequent investors, although the schemer puts in place no fundamental profit-making machinery. The success of early investors builds publicity for the investment ruse, although it ultimately peters out when not enough later investors can be found to pay off earlier ones. Investors demanding their money back find that there is no cash.

The *Boston Post* work already had a powerful supporter on the board in Robert L. O'Brien, who called it "a piece of newspaper enterprise of the first importance." That opinion carried extra weight because O'Brien edited the rival *Boston Herald*—which had been thoroughly whipped on the story by the *Post*. And he was far from alone as a fan. Calvin Coolidge, then the Massachusetts governor, praised the stories, as did a host of local politicians, many of whom had been flat-footed in their enforcement role while the *Post* unmasked Ponzi's duplicity.

The jury wrote in its nomination letter that the jurors were "in doubt which of these enterprises was more deserving of the Prize"—the *New York Post* or the *Boston Post*—but the board saw a clearer choice. The Ponzi reporting was simply the perfect Joseph Pulitzer–style campaign: great reporting of hard-to-get information, helping protect the "common man" from scams, and taking the form of shocking front-page news that stirred terrific controversy. The investigation had also required editor Richard Grozier, son of publisher Edwin A. Grozier, to face serious financial risk from the brazenly litigious Ponzi and from legions of adoring followers who saw the *Post* as out to hang their innocent hero. These fans were ready to drop the *Post* as a result, especially as rival papers were proclaiming Ponzi a financial wizard well into the *Post*'s investigation.

The *Post*'s work also drew on the expertise of Clarence W. Barron, who had started the successful Boston News Bureau in the city's financial district. In 1902 he had spread his influence south to New York by buying a company called Dow Jones and its main product, the *Wall Street Journal*. Barron, whose name lives on in the weekly Dow Jones paper *Barron's* and whose descendents controlled Dow Jones for 105 years (until 2007), was to be both an expert source for the *Post* and something of a guest columnist as the paper broke the news in the Ponzi case.

Clipped by Coupons

Edwin Grozier, after working for a time under the *Boston Globe*'s Charles H. Taylor, had actually served the first Joseph Pulitzer at the *World* in the pre–yellow journalism years. Grozier loved Pulitzer, describing his mind as "like a flash of lightning, illuminating the dark places." But eventually Grozier left the editorship of the *Evening World* to return to Boston

FIGURE II.I After first disclosing Boston financial scam artist Charles Ponzi's criminal record in Canada under the name "Ponsi," the *Boston Post* on April 11, 1920, shows how Ponzi would look with a moustache painted on his mug shot. Below the clean-shaven Ponzi is another big news story for Boston, about a New York Yankees ball player familiar to locals. The headline says "Ruth Injures Knee Sliding." *Source*: Used by permission of the *Boston Globe*, courtesy Boston Public Library.

and buy the troubled *Post*, asking Taylor's permission in that age of gentlemanly exchanges. "If you have even the slightest objection," he told Taylor, "I won't consider purchasing the paper." Taylor responded that if Grozier "can gather up any of the crumbs that fall from the Globe's table, you're welcome to them"—to which Grozier retorted: "If I can, I shall go after the cake, too!"

Grozier saved the paper with a series of Pulitzer-like stunts and promotions, printing the names of every child that contributed to the *Post*'s campaign to buy elephants for the local zoo. Like Pulitzer, he played up crime stories, winning subscribers with the heavy coverage of Lizzy Borden and other grisly crime stories. He also promoted Irish causes, which stuffier Boston papers did not, and he cut the price to one cent from three. In time, the paper's circulation actually exceeded that of the *World*, with its much larger market. When Grozier took ill in 1920, though, it was his son Richard who proved himself by challenging the Ponzi phenomenon as it swept his city.

The thirty-eight-year-old, slight-of-build Charles Ponzi, nattily dressed in his trademark boater hat and cane, had a flair for selling and a wonderful head for business—as long as that business was crooked. Unbeknownst to Bostonians who first heard his get-rich-quick promises in early 1920, he had a past full of fraud and forgery, having served prison terms in Montreal and Georgia. Almost as ardent a stamp collector as he was a con artist, he had devised a plausible-sounding investment plan—with implausible returns of 50 percent in ninety days—based on foreign exchange rates in a post-war Europe of collapsing currency values.

To get those returns for investors, Ponzi pledged that he would put their dollars into humble-sounding instruments called "International Reply Coupons," or IRCs. These actually did exist; IRCs had been created by a global agreement before the war to help governments fix the values at which their nation's postage stamps would be redeemed. Countries designed coupons with floating redemption rates reflecting what currency was being used in the transaction to allow the international mailing of letters. Thus mail posted at a certain rate in, say, the United States would be delivered to Spain or Italy, no matter what happened to rates in those countries when the U.S. mail was sent.[5]

In 1919, Ponzi examined one of the IRC certificates that an associate in Spain had sent him and began to think. We know something of his thought process because of accounts he gave about his adventures later in life. As Boston journalist Mitchell Zuckoff writes in his 2005 book *Ponzi's Scheme*, "in a flash of insight, some might even say genius, Ponzi saw something more, a global currency whose value fluctuated wildly depending on where it was used."[6] Ponzi did some calculations: if one U.S. dollar could purchase five IRCs in Boston, it could buy sixty-six IRCs in Rome once the dollars were exchanged for the severely devalued Italian lira.

It was a moment reminiscent of *The Producers'* Max Bialystock plotting with Leo Bloom how they might make more money with a flop than with a Broadway hit. To make money with this kind of exchange himself, Ponzi would have to start with a hoard of original dollars to buy the IRCs in countries with devalued currencies—a hoard he did not have. Then he would have to buy and transport the huge bundles of coupons that would have to be involved if any meaningful profit was to be produced. That's if it was even legal. "But those critical details would wait for another day," Zuckoff writes. Ponzi decided instead to use his brainstorm to sell others on investing in Ponzi's own securities. That would get him his bankroll. He would then deliver the promised returns by paying them off with the investments of later investors.[7]

His international trade in IRCs never began. What did begin was a promotion based on persuading others that Ponzi could manipulate the system to turn a huge profit for them. For fifty cents he registered the name of a new company at the end of 1919: Securities Exchange Company, a name that existed over a decade before a federal government "Securities and Exchange Commission" was to appear to *protect* the investment community from scams like Ponzi's. Shamelessly Ponzi began building a foundation for his scheme that was designed to insulate him from the authorities. At the police commissioner's office, he made a point of putting money in the Boston Police Relief Association and promised more.

Just for fun, he put out feelers with postal officials about whether the exchange he had dreamed up for IRCs might actually be possible. Could he redeem IRCs for cash—a key part of his scheme—if he had them? No, he was told. But by that time the promotion was already going crazy, with ninety-day, 50 percent Securities Exchange Company notes flying out of his downtown Boston shop. The post office began examining his scheme. It would "begin" for many months without result. But Ponzi was bringing in $30,000 per week at the start. Then more and more, both in tiny investments and soon in $10,000 chunks.

He was also digging himself deeper into a hole each day, of course. Each coupon was a debt he had no hope of repaying without plundering later investment dollars. As his secretary kept doling out the company promissory notes, she wrote investors' names on index cards. The names multiplied quickly with the cash. From 1,525 investors he brought in $40,000 during May. Ponzi bought an expensive house in the suburbs and a fancy car for the commute. His lifestyle was lavish. New ways had to be found to keep drawing investors, but Ponzi's pitch kept working. He cut the payout time in half and touted that "a little dollar could start on a journey across the ocean and return home in six weeks, married and with a couple of kids."

"Can It Be Real?"

Enter the newspapers. On June 9, the *Boston Traveler* was the first to promote Ponzi in the news columns, with an all-capital headline saying: "WE GUARANTEE YOU 50 PERCENT PROFIT IN 45 DAYS." The postal inspector that a *Traveler* reporter questioned failed to signal any problem with the investment and added a tantalizingly mysterious note: "We haven't figured out how they make their enormous profit, but they seem confident of their ability to do so." That triggered more investor interest. But basically newspapers didn't pay much attention for a few more weeks. There was lots of news cramming the front pages: Prohibition had gone into effect nationally in January. States were also debating a constitutional amendment to give women the right to vote. In Massachusetts, a murder in a Boston suburb was being blamed on two Italians, Nicola Sacco and Bartolomeo Vanzetti. Governor Calvin Coolidge was considering a run for vice president. Further, notes journalist Zuckoff, sports pages were full of Babe Ruth "pounding home runs for the New York Yankees after his stunning sale the previous winter by the Boston Red Sox. The Babe's move fueled the question of whether New York City might eclipse Boston as the 'Hub of the Universe.' Most Bostonians doubted it."[8]

It was July 4 before the *Boston Post* got involved, beginning a two-month flurry of stories about Ponzi. It started with a courthouse reporter's piece about a million-dollar lawsuit that a Ponzi associate had filed against him. The plaintiff couldn't be found to comment but Ponzi, as usual, had plenty to say. It was just a case of someone wanting money from him because he was so wealthy, he said, and any legitimate claim would be "satisfied because I have got two million dollars over and above all claims of investors against me in this country." The article then went on to note that Ponzi "is today rated as worth $8,500,000—purchaser of business blocks, trust companies, estates and motor cars." To the question of "Can it be real?" posed by the story, federal, state, and city authorities were said to be answering "that they have been unable to find that he is doing anything illegal."[9]

Richard Grozier was incredulous at the 50 percent profit claim though. He asked the *Post* city editor Edward J. Dunn to have some reporters look into Ponzi and his company more closely. One worry on his mind was that a number of *Post* employees, mostly in the press room, were investors with Ponzi. Various other investigations had also started to go with the postal investigation and bank examiners were talking with Ponzi's bankers. Using investor money, Ponzi set up a $1.5 million short-term certificate of deposit at the bank to placate inspectors.

City editor Dunn had two reporters, "P. A." Santosuosso and Herbert L. Baldwin, on the case. They turned to Clarence Barron as a source. Barron, short, bearded, and weighing 330 pounds at age sixty-five, had established himself as quite a Boston character. He had a reserved suite at the Ritz Carlton across from the Boston Public Garden to go with his Beacon Hill home and an estate in the posh South Shore community of Cohasset. The page of news his Boston News Bureau provided was aimed for Boston's high-finance readers, who paid the princely sum of one dollar for it. Yet Barron had strong views about Ponzi and his popularity, and he was a great interview. It ran under the headline "QUESTIONS THE MOTIVE BEHIND PONZI SCHEME: Barron Says Reply Coupon Plan Can Be Worked Only In Small Way." Identified as being "recognized internationally as among the foremost financial authorities of the world," Barron was quoted as saying: "No man of wide financial or investment experience would look twice at a proposition to take his money upon a simple promise to pay it back with a 50% increase in three months." Barron further raised the question of whether there could possibly be enough supply of postage to soak up the millions that Ponzi said was being invested.

The public reaction to all this cold water on the hot investment? The biggest rush yet from people wanting to *buy*. When Edward Dunn walked around the corner from the *Post* to check on the scene, his observation was: "Pigs being led to the slaughter." The scenario was to play out for several more weeks, each new skeptical story seeming to stimulate business rather than stifle it. On July 30, New York's postmaster was quoted as saying that the small number of postal reply coupons in existence made it "impossible" that a multimillion-dollar fortune could be created from them. Barron sharpened his old charges about it being a case of "robbing Peter to pay Paul," adding some sarcasm about the possibility that Ponzi could apply his investment formula to solve all of Europe's woes. "Surely," he said, "the allies could spare him a million and within three years clean up that debt tangle." The *Post* cartoons pictured a worried-looking Ponzi trying to keep his "pot of gold" boiling. An editorial by Grozier said, "It Cannot Last."[10]

But the charming Ponzi, now identified as a man of the people, was past criticism to many. In fact, the heavier the attack, the more his cult-figure status seemed to grow. He milked it unmercifully. In one of his frequent impromptu speeches to crowds he said: "Now please don't think that I'm boasting, but I have forgotten more about foreign exchange than C. W. Barron ever knew." When someone in an audience suggested he was the greatest Italian in history he said: "No. I am the third greatest." He rated Columbus and Marconi higher. Finally, to shouts of "Ponzi for mayor" and "Ponzi for governor," he suggested in a comment sure to win him fans that he might throw his support to an anti-Prohibition candidate. The *Boston Traveler*, ever the Ponzi supporter, ran a sports column comparing him with Babe Ruth. The bankers are trying to retire Ponzi "with the banks full," the writer said. "Just like trying to retire you with the bases full, hey Babe?" The *New York Times* observed that in the city to the north, "public distrust seems to be shifting from Ponzi to his critics and assailants."

But the *Post* wasn't finished. Its reporters were still gathering information, and sources were starting to step forward in response to its stories. It delivered a one-two punch. First, when Ponzi's own public relations man, William McMasters, a former *Post* reporter, became suspicious of his boss, he did some snooping around the office and found incriminating information—offering it to Grozier. The *Post* editor paid $5,000 for it, something the ensuing article did not disclose. Under McMasters's own byline, the article said that Ponzi had earned nothing from investments outside the United States and was at least $2 million in debt. His article ran on Monday, August 2, under the page-one headline: "DECLARES PONZI IS NOW HOPELESSLY INSOLVENT: Publicity Expert Employed by 'Wizard' Says He Has Not Sufficient Funds to Meet His Notes—States He Has Sent No Money to Europe nor Received Money from Europe Recently." Why had McMasters chosen to speak up? "As a publicity man," he wrote, "my first duty is to the public." While that statement might have stopped a few readers in their tracks, more than a few believed the rest of his claims. At last investors lined up outside Ponzi's office with withdrawals in mind, pulling out $400,000 on Monday alone. But some Ponzi fans still weren't convinced.[11] That would take one more *Post* story.

On August 8, Ponzi was comfortable at home in his bathrobe as he settled in for two hours with *Post* reporter P. A. Santosuossa. The questions were about his life before coming to Boston. There were holes in the story—holes that Santosuossa was looking for because he had heard rumors that Ponzi had a criminal record in Canada. Still, the reporter didn't have enough to confront Ponzi about it. After the interview was over, though, the *Post*'s Montreal correspondent provided the tip the paper had been itching for: that someone named Charles Ponsi, spelled with an "s," had been imprisoned there a decade earlier for forgery. The charge had stemmed from his employment at Banco Zarossi. Santosuossa called Ponzi back at home with his follow-up. Ponzi laughed off the direct question of whether he was the same Ponsi, who also used the alias Bianchi. Had he been in Canada at that time? Yes. Had he worked at that bank? "I might have."

For the *Post*, the next step was to immediately dispatch a reporter to Montreal—it was Herbert Baldwin—to nail down the report once and for all. His interviews were successful, bringing numerous confirmations from the Ponzi photo Baldwin displayed. With the addition of a mustache, he was told, it was the same man: the forger Ponsi, alias Bianchi. Or, as one said, "Bianchi, the snake!"

Being Ponzi, the trader still made efforts to deny it even after a story bylined by Baldwin ran on August 11, with its headline—"Canadian 'Ponsi' Served Jail Term"—and with details of the forgery conviction.

When he was told what the story would say and was asked to comment, Ponzi told the *Post* reporter: "Then you are going to get the presses ripped out of your building." But the bravado didn't last. Just over a month had passed since the unquestioning July 4 story in the *Post*.[12] Now Ponzi's life unraveled fast.

"It was this revelation that finally burst the bubble," said the *Post* in its nomination letter to the Pulitzer board. "Practically the last doubts were swept away." From the arraignment on through trial, conviction, and sentence, any remaining doubts certainly vanished. As the authorities swarmed, Ponzi admitted to having served the Georgia prison term as well.

Ever chatty, Ponzi said to the *Post*'s Baldwin at a moment toward the end of the trial: "You did a fine job on me. If it hadn't been for that story in the *Post*, maybe things would have been a lot different for me today." Much later, Ponzi was to detail the entire scam. "My business was simple. It was the old game of robbing Peter to pay Paul," he said. "The whole thing was broken."[13]

The Public Service Pulitzer was to be the highlight of the next three decades for the *Post*. A long period of decline began. Edwin Grozier died in 1923 and Richard Grozier died in 1946. The next gold medal to a Boston publication would be the *Globe*'s Pulitzer, won in 1966. That was ten years after the *Globe* had bought the *Post*'s library and the rights to its name.

1921—The *Boston Post* for its exposure of the operations of Charles Ponzi by a series of articles which finally led to his arrest.[14]

Swope's World

If Charles Ponzi was the perfect charlatan for the Jazz Age, the *New York World*'s Herbert Bayard Swope may have been the perfect journalist to represent the forces of truth, justice, and the American way. The winner of the very first Pulitzer Prize—in 1917, for his reporting on the German empire from Europe in the early years of the war—Swope was thirty-eight when he returned to the United States in 1920 and became a key player for Ralph Pulitzer's paper. With all his gifts, Swope was in a good position to help keep the *World* competitive in the changing mix of New York City newspapers. In post-war America, the *World* occupied much the same place that the *New York Times* does today, attracting many of the best journalists from around the country. And Swope was one reason. The tall, red-haired reporter had moved to New York from St. Louis and the *Post-Dispatch* much earlier. But even as a young man he had approached the status of legend for his driving desire to get a story, solving crimes ahead of the police and putting his personal mark on every story he covered. In Europe, besides winning the first Pulitzer Prize, he was best known for having donned tails and top hat to crash the Versailles peace talks—to which no reporters were invited—getting crucial, exclusive details for the *World*. He brought that same outrageous flair to editing once he returned to New York.[15]

"What I try to do in my paper," Swope once said, "is to give the public part of what it wants to have and part of what it ought to have, whether it wants it or not."[16] One Joseph Pulitzer aphorism that Swope favored was "Every reporter is a hope, every editor a disappointment."[17] But Swope attacked editing with the eye of a reporter, albeit it one who knew how stories should be packaged for the front page. Under his guidance, the paper would win two public service awards for the *World* in three years. The first gold medal, however, was the greatest. When the board approved it in 1922, it started a pattern that would prevail for decades—honoring stories for the Public Service Prize that pointed out racial injustice. Swope had decided that the *World* would take on the Ku Klux Klan.

The Klan of that day had risen to a level of prominence very quickly. The groups of hooded vigilantes that fought Reconstruction in the South and border states after the Civil War, making the lynching of freed blacks and cross-burnings their symbols, had died out before the 1870s. But seemingly from out of nowhere, a national KKK revival had occurred just before World War I. Among racists, the rituals and mysteries of the organization made it attractive in an almost romantic way. It was estimated to have half a million members in both cities and rural areas around the country, spewing hate at Catholics, Jews, and other minorities, as well as blacks. Little had been written about the new rise of the Klan, however.

Swope himself tracked down the individuals who had created the new KKK. As it turned out, the Klan's twentieth-century origins were largely a money-raising scheme, although as World War I approached, it also grew by building its isolationist appeal. It was actually formed in Georgia in 1916 as a chartered secret fraternal organization. Swope began to strip the mystery away.[18] The first of the *World's* twenty-one straight days of articles began with an eight-column banner headline proclaiming: "SECRETS OF THE KU KLUX KLAN EXPOSED BY THE WORLD; MENACE OF THIS GROWING LAW-DEFYING ORGANIZATION PROVED BY ITS RITUAL AND THE RECORD OF ITS ACTIVITIES."[19] For the *World*, it was a phenomenal circulation booster, adding about 60,000 readers during the run of the series. New Yorkers stood in line to wait for copies that rolled off the presses just after midnight. Swope also arranged for wide syndication, reaching two million readers through eighteen papers, mostly in the North and West.[20] The Klan series was also the unanimous choice of the Pulitzer jury, again a group of three Columbia faculty members led by John Cunliffe. The board enthusiastically approved and chose the *World* for the 1922 gold medal.[21]

The next year, the *Memphis Commercial Appeal* won the Public Service Prize largely for its cartoons challenging the Klan in Tennessee. (And two more papers in the 1920s—Columbus, Georgia's *Enquirer Sun* in 1926 and the *Indianapolis Times* in 1928—would win wholly or in part for campaigns involving the Klan in their areas.) In 1924, the *World* won again for a Swope-led campaign to expose the evils of involuntary servitude through the case of a young North Dakota man who was cast into "peonage" in Florida.

Swope would leave the *World* in the late 1920s, frustrated with how poorly Ralph Pulitzer and his brother Herbert were managing the paper. The paper would fold in 1931.

1922—The *New York World* for articles exposing the operations of the Ku Klux Klan, published during September and October, 1921.[22]

A Martyr for the Truth

In 1926, the *Canton Daily News* editor Don R. Mellett had been doing the nitty-gritty work of dedicated editors everywhere. A newcomer to the eastern Ohio town, he decided to keep track of local underworld figures and to try to make their operations known. It was work in the tradition of watchdog journalism. For a criminal with a house to plunder, however, the first step is often to kill the watchdog.

Mellett, one of seven sons in an Indiana newsman's family, arrived in Canton in 1925 as the business manager and then moved on to become the publisher of the paper. Its owner, former Ohio governor (and 1920 Democratic presidential candidate) James M. Cox, had wanted Mellett, then thirty-four, to help the paper narrow the circulation gap with the leading *Canton Repository*.[23] Mellett proceeded to do just that with a series of promotional stunts like hiring the "Marvel Man," a lip-reader, to go from place to place and listen in on conversations. (One story reported that the words actually spoken by Douglas Fairbanks in a silent film were "What the hell is the matter with you?" and not the subtitled "Anyway, I love you.") In one story, though, the Marvel Man discovered an ugly truth about Canton. He lip-read a drug deal between an addict and a pusher. A headline appeared that said "Traffic in 'Dope' Uncovered."

Crime was no stranger to Canton, as Mellett found in pursuing stories about various unsavory characters in town. While not a crime center like Chicago, Cleveland, Detroit, and Pittsburgh, Canton was considered a "hideout" for criminals on the lam from those cities. And Canton had its own bootlegging, gambling, and prostitution underworld, managed by a character named Jumbo Crowley.[24] With the combination of visiting thugs hiding out and local crooks running their rackets, Canton was a nest of vipers.

On January 2, 1926, Don Mellett stepped right into that nest. His editorial started:

> It is the opinion of The News that Canton needs cleaning up. Bootlegging, gambling, and houses of prostitution are running wide open, in flagrant violation of the law. If [Police] Chief [Saranus] Lengel denies this, proof is available to him. If he states he cannot clean up these vice conditions upon proof of their existence he should step aside and permit someone who can to do so.

The final suggestion was, "Get busy or get out." He could have been tougher, but Mellett was still getting to know the town. But Chief Lengel was kicked out by the reform mayor the paper had supported. (He was later reinstated by the civil service commission.) And as the publisher's knowledge grew, so did the boldness of his editorials. The March 1 paper carried an editorial with the headline, "Vice Cleanup Only Started; Climax Coming." It began:

> Canton's clean-up of vice conditions has only just started. The dismissal of the chief of police was necessary, it appears, as the first step toward building a more militant aggressive police department. With a determined police department on the job organized liquor, and dope traffic cannot operate, nor can gambling. Without protection, directly or indirectly the underworld cannot exist. And already the slight changes made in the police department are beginning to bear fruit. The fear of God is beginning to creep into the hearts of the law violators and a break-up is on the horizon. . . .
>
> Jumbo Crowley must be put out of business. His every place must be stopped and kept dark. . . .

He went on, naming names—a dozen more in this editorial and in later ones—for four and a half months. While the *Daily News* did sell more papers, the attack on graft didn't make him popular in much of the town of 107,000. Mobsters were upset, of course, to see themselves identified by name, with their supposedly shadowy exploits spread across the front page for all to see. But town leaders were also displeased that their town was portrayed as crime-ridden. It was bad for business.

After he and his wife returned from a dance, Mellett was putting his car in the garage when he was shot three times, once in the head. He died instantly. Newspapers around the country ran the story of this new martyr to the cause of using the newspaper to speak out for the community. Under the page-one headline "We Carry On," the *Daily News* ran an editorial saying: "Like a captain in battle leading his forces Don R. Mellett, publisher of the Daily News, has fallen—a sacrifice to the cause he waged against vice, and what he believed [were] efforts to corrupt the city government. Wanton murder stalked at midnight into his home."[25] Wrote Cox in a tribute to Mellett: "How foolish were the assassins and those who goaded them on! The taking of a single life in the present circumstances is of no avail. When a general falls at the head of his army, the spectacle of sacrifice moves his followers onward to increased devotion in the cause."²⁶

The local police, not surprisingly, were lax in their investigation of the crime. Chief Lengel had been reinstated earlier and a local grand jury failed to bring any indictments. It took the intervention of a special investigator from Chicago to get five men arrested, tried, and convicted. One was Chief Lengel, and another was an out-of-town mobster named Patrick (Red) McDermott, both eventually convicted of first-degree murder. McDermott said that a plan to beat up the publisher had escalated into a shooting. Chief Lengel, however, was eventually granted a new trial and freed when a witness against him at the first trial refused to repeat his story. Even now, there is uncertainty about who fired the fatal shot and who else might have been involved in the killing.

Of course, there was no Don Mellett to hammer away at the need for results. And soon there was no *Daily News* either. While the gold medal was sealed in the cornerstone of a new building for the paper, Cox sold both the *Daily News* and the building three years later, and it was combined with the *Repository*, which took over the new building. To the nation's journalism community, though, the *Canton Daily News*'s Pulitzer will always be a stark reminder of the ultimate risk editors and reporters can take on behalf of the public.

1927—*Canton* (Ohio) *Daily News* for its brave, patriotic and effective fight for the ending of a vicious state of affairs brought about by collusion between city authorities and the criminal element, a fight which had a tragic result in the assassination of the editor of the paper, Mr. Don R. Mellett.²⁷

"Pulitzer Prizes for Pulitzer Papers"

When the *New York Evening World* won the gold medal in 1929 for a series of criminal justice–related campaigns, it was the third Public Service Prize awarded to Pulitzer-owned newspapers and their twelfth Pulitzer Prize overall. Only forty-one journalism prizes had been awarded,

FIGURE 11.2 The *Canton* (Ohio) *Daily News* front page on July 16, 1926, carries news of editor Don Mellett's murder. *Source*: Reprinted by permission of the *Canton Repository*. Page provided courtesy of the Stark County District Library.

making the Pulitzer papers in New York or St. Louis owners of more than a quarter of them. Beyond that, most of the prizes had gone to eastern newspapers.[28]

The board members—and especially the Pulitzer brothers—certainly had not intended for the prizes to favor the Pulitzer newspapers. Joseph and Ralph were very sensitive about the appearance of favoritism when the *World* and the *St. Louis Post-Dispatch* won. They also wanted the awards to be accepted more nationally.[29]

In November 1929, the Pulitzer advisory board's executive secretary took a thirty-two-city tour of newspapers outside the East and made a disturbing report. The "indifference and apathy encountered are too generally prevalent," he said. "Many frankly admitted that they had ceased making nominations because they had concluded that the awards were generally made to the metropolitan newspapers of the east. Frequently allusions were made to the regularity with which the prizes were given to the Pulitzer newspapers."[30] The Pulitzer brothers quietly agreed that their papers would withhold making any entries for the 1930 prizes. They then withheld entries again in 1931 and perhaps in later years as well.[31]

Another way to approach the problem was to encourage nominations from outside the East and then to make sure the board gave them due consideration. In the 1930s, many more midwestern and western papers would be honored as winners in public service and other categories as well. The Pulitzer Prizes benefited from the diversity.

For all the perceived questions about favoritism, the Public Service Prize had at least been defined in the 1920s. No longer did editors wonder what kinds of stories the Pulitzer board would recognize with gold medals. Unfocused collections of articles, no matter how good, went out of favor as Public Service Prize candidates as the 1930s approached. By its acknowledgment of the Canton murder case, the Ponzi exposé, and campaigns against the Ku Klux Klan, the board showed that physical courage and financial risk-taking were qualities it prized, along with success in bringing about positive changes in the community. And the board clearly liked a powerful investigative story.

CHAPTER 12

FROM DEPRESSION TO WARTIME

1930–1945: Corruption and the Dust Bowl

[In the 1930s] the Pulitzer Prizes in Journalism became an intrinsic part of the profession in the United States. If they were not perfect, they were at least respected. Their permanence was not questioned.

—JOHN HOHENBERG, PULITZER PRIZE ADMINISTRATOR
AND SECRETARY, 1954–1976

Almost on cue in October of 1929, the bubble burst for the Roaring Twenties. Still, it took Americans a while to shake the notion that Charles Ponzi might have been right—that maybe everybody *could* get rich quick, magically, and without effort. In the 1930s, the Great Depression and the graft and crime that accompanied it provided the backdrop for much of the newspaper public service that the Pulitzer Prizes honored.

While the Pulitzer advisory board was eager to name winners in all the journalism prize categories, it sent a signal in 1930 that only top-notch entries deserved the gold medal. The board turned down all five jury selections without explaining its reasons and voted to give no gold medal at all that year. The three Columbia faculty member jurors had considered nineteen entries before unanimously recommending Maine's *Portland Evening News* for "its successful campaign against the exploitation of hydroelectric power from the State of Maine"—coverage that showed "unusual courage and independence." The other four were the *Brooklyn Daily Eagle* and the *New York Telegram* for unearthing city scandals, the *Detroit News* for promoting a reforestation project, and the *Cleveland Press* for a war on machine politics.

The advisory board gave no Pulitzer for editorial writing either. It saved all its journalism plaudits for reporting, where it again acknowledged the global coverage of the *New York Times*. Technology was a factor, as it had been in the 1918 Public Service Prize. The reporting winner was Russell D. Owen for reports on Admiral Richard E. Byrd's Antarctic exploration. The reporter had submitted his reports by radio transmission.

The next year was a sad one for Ralph and Joseph Pulitzer. In February, the *New York World* folded after years of losses and was merged into what became Scripps-Howard's *World-Telegram*. Ralph continued on the Pulitzer board as chairman (JP II would take over after Ralph's death in 1939). With the disappearance of the New York paper, concerns about Pulitzer Prizes for Pulitzer papers diminished. In the 1930s through the early 1950s, however, the *Post-Dispatch* became an even greater Pulitzer-winning force than the *World* had been, especially in the public service category.

Standing Up to Mob Rule

After honoring three cases of local watchdog journalism from 1931 to 1933—the work of the *Atlanta Constitution*, the *Indianapolis News*, and the *New York World-Telegram*—the Pulitzer board faced a tough choice in 1934. The jury, considering twenty-three nominations for the gold medal, offered the board a mixed recommendation that proposed no single winner.[1] In what seemed a peculiar proposal, two jurors recommended that the gold medal recognize the press as a whole, while a third juror opined that no entry was worthy of the prize.

Board members, unmoved by both arguments, dug into the entries on their own and found a winner in Oregon's 4,440-circulation *Medford Mail Tribune*. The *Mail Tribune* had courageously challenged a local demagogue who had used mob tactics—and his own newspaper—to try to overturn the town's government. In the end, he had sought to protect his power base by killing a local constable.

Llewellyn A. Banks, a wealthy orchard owner and alleged bootlegger who had moved from California in the 1920s, formed around him a group of extremist supporters to help him control local officials, including the Jackson County sheriff. The miseries of the Depression created a fertile environment for Banks to incite rebellion against the town government. In 1929 he had bought a newspaper, the *Medford News*. In the next few years he published invented charges about a "gang" that had "fattened at the public purse for fifteen years." Starting an organization of local ruffians he called the Good Government Congress, Banks used his newspaper and meetings of the group to push the area toward martial law, threatening existing officials with horsewhipping or hanging.

As the community became more divided, the *Mail Tribune* publisher Robert W. Ruhl challenged Banks, warning that the Good Government Congress was aiming to spark a local revolt. After a February election in which a close vote threatened to unseat Banks's choice for sheriff, the ballot boxes were stolen and Banks was charged with the theft. While state police issued a warrant for his arrest, Banks boasted that he would kill any arresting officer. On March 16, he made good on the promise. As constable George Prescott stood outside their door with his warrant talking with Banks's wife, Banks shot him through the heart with a hunting rifle.

The day after the killing, Ruhl began his editorial titled "The Challenge Is Accepted!" this way:

> Do the people of Jackson County want more innocent officers shot down in cold blood behind the skirts of some woman?
>
> Do they want continued lawlessness, continued pillaging of court houses, and burning of ballots?
>
> Do they want this reign of terror followed by another, until this community is reduced to a shambles and advertised far and wide as a place where crime is encouraged, sedition lauded, and murder condoned?
>
> If they do, then that is precisely what they are going to have. All they need to do now is to lie down and take it.[2]

Banks was eventually sentenced to a life term for murder, and some of his associates went to jail. In nominating his paper for the gold medal, Ruhl wrote that "the show is over, the play is played out! But it was a close call!"[3]

Inside the Advisory Board

Why was the Pulitzer board left by jurors to identify this story on its own? The jurors—the *Philadelphia Public Ledger* editor Charles Munro Morrison, the *New York Times* Sunday editor Lester Markel, and Columbia dean

Carl Ackerman—became embroiled in a debate about President Franklin Roosevelt's National Recovery Administration, the New Deal effort to get business on track by setting wage and other standards for industry. Publishers across the United States sought a waiver from NRA guidelines, contending that applying government standards to newspapers violated the First Amendment. Of course, a waiver would also mean that publishers could pay workers less.

A group of editors and publishers had nominated America's newspaper publishers in general for the Public Service Prize for standing up to the president. Morrison and Ackerman agreed in their jury majority report, saying that "the 'most disinterested and meritorious public service' rendered in 1933 was not by any single newspaper, but by the press as a whole in safe-guarding the freedom of the press in a national emergency." The report suggested that "the Gold Medal be placed in the permanent custody of *Editor & Publisher*" and circulated among members of various press associations. Some journalists did not quite see the emergency that concerned the two jurors and the publishers. A strong dissent came from Markel, who questioned "the advisability—and, more, the propriety—of that award." He also opposed those who argued that no medal be awarded.[4]

Through a communication from Ralph Pulitzer to his brother Joseph, it is possible to enter the board's inner sanctum at Columbia that year. JP II, who was not able to attend the 1934 board meeting, insisted on a full accounting of the proceedings. He got it in a May 2 letter from his sibling, the board chairman. Ralph's reply detailed the reasoning of the board in rejecting the jury recommendation and in selecting the *Mail Tribune*. His letter sheds light on the selection process of that time and demonstrates the strong commitment the Pulitzer sons felt to the original goals their father had in establishing the prize, particularly the gold medal. It was clear that in their minds, giving the Public Service Prize to a group of publishers was not appropriate. Ralph wrote:

> At the meeting I first stated my personal objections (1) that it departed from J.P.'s terms in giving it not to a newspaper but to a group of newspapers; (2) that it departed from those terms since they stated it was to be for a disinterested service, and the fight of the papers could not be

called a disinterested service, whether one believed in it or not; (3) that although I was fully aware that many of the men who fought for the freedom of the press clause were actuated solely by patriotic or unselfish motives I was equally aware that many were actuated by motives the very reverse, and that I thought under these conditions if the press pinned a medal on itself it would become a laughing stock.

I then asked each of the members to state their own personal objections which they did, and without any discussion it was decided not to bestow the gold medal as recommended by the majority report of the sub-committee which was to leave the medal un-bestowed this year.[5]

However, the board also "overwhelmingly" voted to reject Markel's proposed withholding of the prize. As entries were then considered one by one, Ralph first favored the *New Orleans Picayune* for its fight against the crooked populist governor of Louisiana, Huey Long. Then another board member brought up the *Mail Tribune* "as having rendered a remarkably courageous public service in fighting a powerful and dangerous bootlegger who had come into that town from California and introduced criminal practices." Ralph Pulitzer's letter continued:

At the risk of his life, the editor made a fight against this man and his gang and finally succeeded in having him sent to prison and the gang dispersed.

The point was made that a service of this kind in such a small town as Medford involved much more danger and courage than in a city like New Orleans. I was won over to this point of view and the Board unanimously voted for the Medford Mail Tribune.

In many ways, newspaper readers may have understood the Depression best as a series of local stories about a national and global economic issue. In addition to the New Orleans and Medford papers, other journals nominated for the Public Service Prize helped settle strikes in New Jersey, fought labor union crime in Cleveland, exposed sweat shops in Pittsburgh and Scranton, showed up bankruptcy process irregularities in Wilkes-Barre, and described the life of the unemployed in California.

The Pulitzer advisory board was not happy with the 1934 jurors. It asked future jurors to list three to five examples in public service and the other classifications without making recommendations of their own. The board would do the selecting.[6]

1934—The *Medford* (Ore.) *Mail Tribune* for its campaign against unscrupulous politicians in Jackson County, Oregon. [7]

A Dust Bowl Primer

Public service jurors called it a tie in 1938. After looking at thirty-three public service entries, they picked two to forward to the board "because both campaigns deal with extremely important matters and because both newspapers used great versatility and tenaciousness over a long period of time." One nominee was the *San Francisco News* for fighting vice and police graft. The other was North Dakota's *Bismarck Tribune* for a series called "Self Help in the Dust Bowl." The advisory board, however, saw the Dust Bowl project as something special for the age.

It was the work of publisher and editor George D. Mann, who died before the paper entered it for the Pulitzer. Managing editor Kenneth W. Simons took over as editor. He described the entry as an attempt "to aid the people of the Great Plains to restore prosperity and to forever abandon dependence upon relief systems, public or private." It said the project was aimed at eight million farmers victimized by the Dust Bowl.

The *Tribune*'s Pulitzer entry summarized the agricultural history of the Dust Bowl, helping readers understand what had befallen them:

> The northern great plains have been semi-arid for untold centuries.
> Drouth cycles were known and prepared for by the Indians, long before the careless and avaricious white man settled here. The evidence of aridity was here for all to see. . . . White settlement commenced in 1870 despite warnings that agricultural practices of Iowa, Indiana, Ohio and Pennsylvania were not adaptable in the northwest. . . .
> Through all the years the few men who could see the cumulative effects of blind land management were ignored when they uttered

warnings of future disaster. The ground was fertile. The rains fell. Crop prices made more and more wheat farming profitable.

Then came 1929. A drouth cycle commenced. Sixty years of solid exhaustion, sixty years of unscientific farming, began to take their toll. Farmers failed. Business failed. The regional economy tottered on the brink of destruction.

The Dust Bowl forced 130,000 families to flee the region, the stories said. But the *Tribune*'s coverage told the story "of the courageous people who have remained there to fight out their battle, one of the greatest in the history of our country."

The program it promoted involved having farmers stop single-crop planting, restore grass in place of grain on the ranges, replenish natural water reservoirs, and reforest areas cut for crop planting and purposes. Overall the philosophy "substituted the doctrine of self-help for that of government bounty," a drive that the paper said had won "partial acceptance." The paper produced sixty-nine editorials to go with its news coverage.

The series also covered the success stories of farmers who had used enlightened cultivation techniques and it celebrated the strengths of the Midwestern farmers who chose to hold their ground in the Dust Bowl. On July 22, it began:

> If there is any dominant trait that marks the people of western North Dakota apart from their brothers in other regions it is tenacity.
>
> Here on the northern great plains the tenacious Indian made his last great stand against an overwhelming wave of whites who coveted the soil where the buffalo grew fat.
>
> Here the tenacious ranchers who first settled the country struggled to keep open a range against a flood of peoples with plows who yearned for the free soil that Uncle Sam unwisely opened to farming.
>
> Here the tenacious farmers have clung to their homesteads against implacable drouth and hordes of insects.
>
> All of them—Indian, rancher and farmer—allowed that tenacity to blind them to facts that might have kept them individually and as a class from the brink of destruction to which they were at last inexorably drawn.

Various community and government programs were adopted to support the *Tribune* recommendations.[8]

The *Tribune*, now owned by Lee Enterprises, keeps the gold medal in a vault but has its Pulitzer Prize certificate on display in the newsroom and in the publisher's office. The honor for the paper's Dust Bowl coverage was an early statement by the board about the major public service that environmental reporting can perform. Decades later, environmental journalism would be a staple of the Pulitzer Prizes.

1938—The *Bismarck* (N.D.) *Tribune* for its news reports and editorials entitled "Self Help in the Dust Bowl."[9]

Flunking History

While its war coverage was again superb in the 1940s, the *New York Times* won its second gold medal by focusing on a home front issue: deficiencies in the teaching of American history. The idea for the project came from publisher Arthur Hays Sulzberger's wife, Iphegene Ochs Sulzberger.[10] A former history student at Barnard College, she feared that a test of what American young people really knew about U.S. history would turn up a poor result. Her hope was that exposing the level of the problem would lead to a drive to improve teaching requirements.

The survey was planned by distinguished Columbia history professors Hugh Russell Fraser and Allan Nevins and coordinated by the *Times* education writer Benjamin Fine. Among its more shocking results was that 30 percent of the students questioned did not know that Woodrow Wilson was president of the United States during World War I. In the middle of another war, the story took on a new significance because of what it said about how little Americans knew about their country.

Fine's April 4, 1943, story was headlined "Ignorance of U.S. History Shown by College Freshmen: Survey of 7,000 Students in 36 Institutions Discloses Vast Fund of Misinformation On Many Basic Facts." The *Times*'s nomination letter for the 1944 prize noted that a number of colleges had introduced American history after the article ran and that the states of Illinois and Pennsylvania had passed the first requirements for U.S. history to be taught.

There had been plenty of controversy over the story. Four days after the series ran, the *Times* carried a story saying that the *Harvard Crimson* student newspaper had called the test "one of the greatest hoaxes in American history." According to the *Crimson*, many students answered the questions facetiously while the *Times* took their responses seriously. The *Times* stood by the story and so did the Pulitzer advisory board. The Pulitzers had received thirty-two nominations in public service and the jury had pointed out several favorites—with the *New York Times* history study not among them—but the board took its own course in selecting the *Times's* work.[11]

1944—The *New York Times* for its survey of the teaching of American History.[12]

Back to the "Society Page"

On the home front, World War II impacted American journalism in many ways. Men who left their newspapers during the war often came back to the newsroom battle-hardened. They had a new military model for getting journalism jobs done, with mission-oriented teams that answered to higher authority. In some newsrooms, that military model already existed. In others, reporters turned to team investigations for the first time.

In another major shift in newsroom demographics, the war's end displaced thousands of other qualified reporters: women. Many had finally gotten a chance in the 1940s to do serious newspaper journalism. Some were forced to go back to the "women's page" or the "society page." It would not be a long-term exit. Women would stream back into hard news reporting in the 1950s and 1960s and begin winning their share of Pulitzers, including gold medals for their papers.

CHAPTER 13

A HANDFUL OF GOLD

1936–1952: The *Post-Dispatch* Makes Its Mark

I know that my retirement will make no difference in its cardinal principles, that it will always fight for progress and reform, never tolerate injustice or corruption, always fight demagogues of all parties, never belong to any party, always oppose privileged classes and public plunderers, never lack sympathy with the poor, always remain devoted to the public welfare, never be satisfied with merely printing news, always be drastically independent, never be afraid to attack wrong, whether by predatory plutocracy or predatory poverty.

— JOSEPH PULITZER, "PLATFORM," *POST-DISPATCH*, APRIL 10, 1907

How would one go about identifying the finest local newspaper staff ever assembled? Because newsrooms do not have the "all-century-team" distinctions that are so popular in the sports world, Pulitzer Prizes might leap to mind as a good metric for the task.[1] If the yardstick was the winning of Pulitzer Gold Medals, though, the runaway choice would have to be the *St. Louis Post-Dispatch* from the mid-1930s to the early 1950s. The paper won five in the fifteen-year period from 1937 to 1952, a record total that stood for fifty-two years. (The *Los Angeles Times* won its sixth Public Service Prize in 2011 to stand alone as the most honored.) Making the *Post-Dispatch* performance even more remarkable, though, was that it bracketed World War II, when more than half the paper's staff was serving in the military. Not counting the four war years, it won the gold medal every other year during that fifteen-year stretch.

Its winning journalism was eclectic, ranging from the exposure of local voter fraud and federal government corruption to an environmental project that helped cleanse its hometown's filthy air. The repercussions of the journalism were significant too. The clean air drive provided a model for other blighted cities from Pittsburgh to London. The paper's revelation of federal tax-related payoffs sparked high-level government resignations in 1951 and led to civil service being installed at the agency formerly known as the Internal Revenue Bureau. Quite literally, then, taxpayers have the *Post-Dispatch* to thank for the Internal Revenue Service.

How did one Midwestern paper launch so many gold medal–winning crusades in so few years? For one thing, the paper's long investigative reporting tradition, dating back to the first Joseph Pulitzer, attracted great editors and reporters from around the country. Its record for impressive reporting had continued through the 1920s because of writers like Carlos F. Hurd, John T. Rogers, and Paul Y. Anderson. (In April 1912, Hurd had been the only reporter on the *Carpathia*, the *Titanic*'s rescue ship; Rogers and Anderson each won early Reporting Pulitzer Prizes—Anderson in 1929 for helping expose the Teapot Dome oil reserves scandal.) The *Post-Dispatch* was especially well known in the 1930s and 1940s for its managing editors, first Oliver Kirby Bovard and later Benjamin Harrison Reese. Both had an almost military approach for running a newsroom but also inspired reporters to perform to the best of their abilities.[2]

O. K. Bovard personified the newsroom "field general," who instilled both loyalty and fear in his troops. OKB, as he signed his memos, lived for a good scoop and insisted on reporters who could dig deep and pursue tenaciously. Failure to get a story was not an option. Because he liked to build reporting campaigns on the accumulation of seeming minutiae, he hated "minor errors." He was known to fire reporters for getting a middle initial wrong. His biographer, James Markham, called him a "one-man journalism school" and wrote that a reporter "had only to show that he had worked under Bovard on the *Post-Dispatch*, and he could get a job almost anywhere."[3]

Some of the paper's scrappiness reflected a deeply rooted institutional inferiority complex. The first owner of the *Post-Dispatch*, after all, had left what he called "provincial" St. Louis for the East and the *World*, recognizing New York as the center of national and international influence—and of big circulation. (Not coincidentally, it also offered huge journalistic targets as the seat of some of the worst corruption in America.) The first Joseph Pulitzer often shortchanged his St. Louis paper, especially by taking talent eastward.

To succeed Pulitzer as editor of his flagship *World* he designated his oldest son, Ralph, while his second son Joseph Pulitzer II was eventually relegated to the post of editor and publisher of the St. Louis paper. In no small measure, however, the designation of JP II to run the *Post-Dispatch* became a key ingredient in the paper's rise to greatness.

JP II has sometimes been pictured as the Pulitzer son least likely to succeed, at least in his father's eyes. (His third and youngest son, Herbert, also worked at the *World*.) And a disappointed Joseph Pulitzer did indeed pull the struggling young Joseph out of Harvard in 1906 and sent him to work in St. Louis almost as chastisement. But the patriarch's thoughts about his middle son were more complex and conflicted than that. JP II had trained for years at his father's side at the Chatwold estate in Bar Harbor and elsewhere and had worked both at the *Post-Dispatch* and the *World* before being sent to St. Louis with the idea of preparing to take over that business. Young Joseph's biographer, Daniel Pfaff, believes that he almost certainly "was in Pulitzer's opinion the most promising of his three sons." Unlike the quiet Ralph, "Joseph was robust and outgoing, and had his father's vigorous confidence—minus the piercing style of command." And indeed, young Joseph might eventually have taken over both the *World* and the *Post-Dispatch* had he not been scorched by his mercurial father's remarkable change of heart about him. The father's reversal is reflected in a 1909 revision of his will, which reduced JP II's stake in the earnings of both newspapers from 60 percent to 10 percent while boosting to 80 percent the share assigned to Herbert and Ralph. (The remaining 10 percent went to top editors and managers of the papers.) As Pfaff describes it:

> The precipitating episode occurred while [young] Joseph was working at the *World*. One evening during dinner at the family's New York mansion on East 73rd Street, Pulitzer—whose hearing was extremely sensitive—erupted at his daughter Edith for making too much noise carving her squab. Joseph came to her defense saying he'd seen enough of his father's bullying and was leaving home for good. He left, but returned about a week later after accepting a compromise his father had offered: He would stay at the *World* a while longer with the possibility . . . of being permanently assigned to St. Louis.

FIGURE 13.1 Joseph Pulitzer II and son Joseph Pulitzer Jr. in the late 1940s, with bust of Joseph Pulitzer. *Source*: Used by permission, *St. Louis Post-Dispatch*.

Joseph Pulitzer II unquestionably loved both St. Louis and the *Post-Dispatch*, and the paper thrived with JP II as editor and publisher. He saw the rivalry with the *World* as a challenge to make the Gateway City paper even better. The editor was a vital ingredient. Unlike his bombastic father, this Pulitzer had a management style combining relentlessness with gentle persuasion. One of American journalism's underrated figures—perhaps because he liked to work out of the spotlight—the younger Pulitzer clearly outshone his brother Ralph as a manager. By studying the *World's* problems closely as it slid toward its 1931 demise, Joseph learned how to build journalistic excellence without sacrificing profitability. In his view, intelligently investing in news coverage was the path to financial success. That meant paying editors and senior reporters well, handing out bonuses for good work, and gently but firmly prodding top editors.[4]

Such prodding usually came via his "yellow memos," typed on his own special tinted newsprint stock. Dubbed "the yellow peril" by editors who got them, the notes were actually written with extreme deference in most cases. A typical opening for a yellow memo in which Pulitzer disputed some decision might be, "You'll pardon my disagreeing, but. . . ." The modesty was genuine, built on respect for his editors. Yet it ran deeper; beneath the patrician exterior and wealth, Pulitzer was an insecure man.[5]

The extent of that insecurity emerges in the oral history interview he gave in 1954, a year before his death. His candor may be partly explained by the condition that the interview would not be released during his lifetime:

> This is probably a stupid thing to say—but I always felt as a kid that my lack of intellectual attainment might not prove to be a serious handicap after all, but might give me a sense of what is generally popular, what the people want to know about. I don't know whether that makes good sense or not. I always had confidence that I could do something in the way of getting out and selling a newspaper. . . . I'm not a flaming first-page editorial writer and I'm not a great reporter and all that. I have never uncovered a great crime and I'm not a genius of the business office or anything of the kind. As a friend of mine at home says, "I do the best I can with my shaped head."[6]

A Force Was with Them

The staff was also guided by an inspirational written force: the eighty-two-word statement of principle known as the *Post-Dispatch* platform that is printed at the beginning of this chapter. Originally written by the first Joseph Pulitzer on his sixtieth birthday in 1907, it marked his retirement from active management of the paper he had founded in December 1878.[7]

Editors and reporters identified certain projects as "platform stories." Staffers knew that they would get a warm reception for any crusade that aimed to right wrongs on behalf of people with no voice of their own. The platform's leading proponent was Pulitzer himself. "I'm afraid I'm not as religious as I would like to be but this platform is literally my Bible. As it is a Bible, I hasten to add, for every man on the *Post-Dispatch*," he told the oral history researcher.[8]

Pulitzer's humility kept all this high-mindedness from lapsing into arrogance. He may have been the leader of his newspaper—and of the vaunted Pulitzer Prize advisory board, which he chaired from 1940 until his death in 1955—but he did not see himself as particularly powerful. His own insecurity, along with his divided loyalties to the *Post-Dispatch* and to the prizes, help explain the dilemma that Pulitzer constantly faced. While he feared that a Pulitzer-owned newspaper winning too many Pulitzer Prizes would undercut the image of the broad national awards program that his father envisioned, he also wanted the *Post-Dispatch* to win them.

That conflict explains the running tabulation he kept of the *World* and the *Post-Dispatch* Pulitzers in the 1920s, which continued for the *Post-Dispatch* alone after the *World* was sold in 1931. He wanted to make sure his paper was not winning *too many* prizes. It also explains the continuing schizophrenia he had about Pulitzer Prizes. Entering the 1930s, JP II ached for his paper to win a gold medal, yet he worried how it would look in journalism circles if that happened.

Much later, after the *Post-Dispatch* had won its five gold medals, managing editor Ben Reese would describe the conflict he observed in his boss: "As a matter of fact, he really hates to see the paper win the public-service prize, but he insists that we make entries. He's very anxious for wide participation, wide nominations" among the nation's newspapers.[9] Pulitzer's agonizing over whether the *Post-Dispatch* was winning too much would reach a peak between 1937 and 1952—to the delight of the rest of the staff.

"Ghost Voters"

What Selwyn Pepper remembered most about the summer of 1936 is the sweltering heat—to this day, still one of the hottest St. Louis summers on record. But for Pepper, the summer also stood out because of a story he was assigned to help cover in his first year as a *Post-Dispatch* reporter.

In six days—starting on July 22 under the headline "Wholesale Frauds Found in Primary Registration in City," the paper presented evidence that precinct by precinct, and even building by building, thousands of names were listed fraudulently on the voter rolls for the August 4 primary. That first day, the accounts of the reporters who had canvassed the city ran alongside photographs of clearly unoccupied stores or flophouses where dozens of "ghost residents" were registered to vote. Together the page-one stories and pictures underscored the absurdity of the claims that voters lived at the locations.

The paper had been tipped to the impending fraud by the activist head of an organization called the Citizens' Non-Partisan Committee. He relayed evidence to Bovard of a 1935 fraud that had occurred during the approval process for a $7.5 million city bond issue to develop the riverfront. With the system gearing up to conceal fraudulent registrations again in 1936, Bovard established a separate task force under then–city editor Ben Reese to attempt to document this attempt at election stealing.

Pepper, then twenty-one, had been among those armed with registration lists and dispatched by Ben Reese and assistant Raymond Crowley to check various buildings and see who actually lived there. At one flophouse along the Mississippi riverfront Pepper encountered a man who had no problem confirming that everyone on the reporter's list was a resident. Pepper recalled: "He kept saying yes to everything. So I asked if Ben Reese lived there. And he said yes. Did Raymond Crowley live there? Yes." After sweating through the interviews, he came back to the office and fed his notes to a rewrite man.[10]

Pepper's technique caught on. One follow-up story mentioned that a reporter had used such a trick with a woman hotel manager who had suspiciously confirmed all the registered voters on the *Post-Dispatch* list. "Her glibness in replying," said the story, "led the reporter to recite a list of names of prominent St. Louis attorneys. She assured him that each one lived there, too." Pepper summarized the entire effort as he remembered it nearly seventy years later: "It was thrilling, and also exhausting."

As evidence piled up, the newspaper declared that there was "a vicious conflict between two factions of [Democrats] to carry a vital primary election by fraud." After first laughing off the investigation as

FIGURE 13.2 The *St. Louis Post-Dispatch* of July 22, 1936, exposes the scope of the city's election fraud. *Source:* Reprinted by permission, *St. Louis Post-Dispatch.*

mere "newspaper talk," the bipartisan board of election commissioners, sworn to conduct honest elections, eventually relented. The board members ordered an official recanvass at the behest of the governor who had appointed them. On July 31 the *Post-Dispatch* carried the results: 46,011 phony names, nearly 15 percent of the legitimate city registration—clear evidence that party hacks were getting set to throw the election with last-minute votes they already had in their hip pockets. Six weeks later, the governor fired the election board.

Another staffer put on canvassing duty, Wayne Leeman, remembered doing voter interviews with a notary in tow—and thinking how much that was costing the paper. Whatever the price, JP was paying it. Perhaps Reese was thinking of the fraud exposé when he later said of Pulitzer's management of the paper: "There's no story in the world too expensive for us if we really want it."[11]

As was typical of such campaigns at the *Post-Dispatch*, and at many other newspapers of the day, none of the stories carried bylines. (Even in the paper's own Pulitzer Prize entry, and its eventual coverage of the award it received, individual reporters and editors were rarely mentioned by name.)

The next question for JP was whether to enter for the gold medal, given his conflicting desires. A yellow memo to Bovard, dated January 19, 1937, indicates that the editor signed off on the entry—but cautiously:

> Memo for O.K.B.:
>
> This entry appears to be well worth making. Let me say, however, that I should really prefer to have nothing further to do with our entries so that I can go into the meeting and say that . . . I had nothing to do with Post-Dispatch entries and that all I did was to lift the ban against them in the belief that the paper and its staff were entitled to consideration. . . . J.P.[12]

Of the twenty-one entries received in public service, the Pulitzer jury ranked the *Post-Dispatch*'s first among its five finalists. The board, without JP's participation, voted the same way.[13] As usual, none but the winner was identified publicly by the advisory board.

1937—The *St. Louis Post-Dispatch* for its exposure of wholesale
fraudulent registration in St. Louis. By a coordinated news, editorial and
cartoon campaign this newspaper succeeded in invalidating upwards of
40,000 fraudulent ballots in November and brought about
the appointment of a new election board.[14]

St. Louis Quits Smoking

When Bovard left the *Post-Dispatch* in 1938 in a dispute over control
of the editorial page, it was a huge loss. But the new managing editor
Ben Reese had learned Bovard's ways, as had the new city editor, Ray
Crowley.[15]

Pulitzer himself inspired the campaign that won the second gold medal.
Awarded eight months before Pearl Harbor, this prize would recognize a
civic war against an enemy that faced cities across the country: smoke. The
plague had made St. Louis perhaps America's filthiest city.

In making the regular trip between St. Louis and his father's old
Chatwold estate in pristine Bar Harbor, Maine, Pulitzer was increasingly
shocked to return to a Mississippi River industrial town so clogged with
pollution. For decades clean-up plans had been ineffective. The *Post-
Dispatch* supported some well-meaning proposals, but these invariably
dissolved amid finger pointing by city leaders.

In 1939 a statistic appeared in the paper that shocked St. Louisans: for
the first time since 1764, St. Louis's population was falling. Some experts
blamed it on the city's abysmal air quality. The paper assigned reporter
Sam J. Shelton to study the problem, assemble information, and make a
recommendation. He worked closely with Reese, Crowley, editorial page
editor Ralph Coghlan, and cartoonist Fitzpatrick—who excelled in using
his charcoal to depict the smoke-plagued city. The research approach "followed the traditional Post-Dispatch method of thorough preparation,
clear exposition, [and] aggressive and intelligent advocacy."

On Sunday, November 26, 1939, a long editorial appeared, tamely
headlined "An Approach to the Smoke Problem." It began: "St. Louis has
been talking about smoke for 50 years. Now let's do something about it."

The accompanying Fitzpatrick cartoon showed the city literally in the grip of smokestack emissions. It was captioned "Can't Go On Forever." The *Post-Dispatch* plan called for the city to ask producers of smokeless fuels to bid for St. Louis's business. The city would acquire clean fuel and sell it to individuals and licensed dealers.[16]

There was nothing tame about the outflow of reporting work that followed, much of it directed by Shelton. The stories were read with urgency because of particularly bad atmospheric conditions that winter. On some days St. Louisans looking out their windows saw only soot and darkness.

On Monday a page-one headline proclaimed: "St. Louis Chokes in Smoke." A photograph of City Hall, taken at nine-thirty in the morning, appeared all black, except for the barely discernible outline of a statue of Ulysses S. Grant—looking like he was leading troops into some awful smoky battle. Stories focused on a phenomenon called "midnight at noon." At one point, a picture was published of Carl Milles's then-new "Meeting of the Waters" fountain, which had been criticized by prudish St. Louisans for a lack of drapery over its nude figures. The forms were no threat to decency in the thick smoke. The caption was "No Veil Needed."

The newspaper's coverage effectively combined the visceral and the visionary. But it also had to explain what smokeless fuels were; St. Louis was a slave to the cheap high-sulfur soft coal mined across the Mississippi in southern Illinois. St. Louisans who thought about energy at all considered cleaner gas, oil, coke, and new technology products an impossible luxury. Shelton scoped out the problem from numerous technological and financial angles, often disregarding conventional wisdom—and ignoring the city's many hopeless hand-wringers.

The city and its smoke regulation commissioner, Washington University mechanical engineer Raymond R. Tucker, welcomed the *Post-Dispatch's* plan to buy and sell smokeless fuels and used it to launch a campaign of cooperation with industry. Authorities named a new seven-member committee, and the paper kept it focused by continually publishing news stories, editorials, and cartoons. All the while, Shelton and other reporters added information about smokeless fuel research.

Articles paid special attention to technologies for making Illinois coal cleaner, recognizing the threat that alternative fuels posed to a major regional industry.

An ordinance was enacted to "rid the city of the smoke nuisance" in three years by phasing in clean fuel requirements. It met with vehement objections, first from coal-fired railroads. But the barrage of newspaper stories made the public impatient with industry delays. A Fitzpatrick cartoon showed the city "Going *Down* in Smoke." The *Post-Dispatch* also let industry play good guy for a change, creating an "Anti-Smoke Roll of Honor" that listed companies agreeing to comply. When victory was finally declared toward the end of 1940, 841 companies were listed.

In something of a one-year test in the winter of 1940, the paper used before-and-after pictures to help tell the story. Days with similar weather conditions a year apart were chosen. Pictures taken through the same lens showed a remarkably improved air quality that readers could see for themselves. In December, Fitzpatrick drew eerie ghost-shaped clouds hovering over other cities across the river and asking of the clear St. Louis skyline: "How Did You Manage to Quit Smoking?"

The city remembered Raymond Tucker's role in the cleanup. After becoming Washington University's engineering school dean, Tucker was elected mayor in 1953 and served twelve years, being twice reelected. The *Post-Dispatch* offices, formerly on Main, became located on the renamed Tucker Boulevard.

At Columbia, the choice of a 1941 gold medal winner was not easy. With both Pulitzer and the *New York Times* representative Arthur Krock out of the room, the board chose the *Post-Dispatch*'s smoke campaigns over finalists that included the *New York Times*'s "comprehensive coverage of news of the war and world events." Once again the board passed over an international story for public service, picking the paper that had helped clean a city's air.

1941—The *St. Louis Post-Dispatch* for its successful campaign against the city smoke nuisance.[17]

Disaster in Centralia

Twenty reporters returned to St. Louis from World War II still hankering for a fight. Ben Reese soon gave them some domestic enemies to attack. Across the river, the Illinois administration of Republican Governor Dwight H. Green was rife with graft and cronyism. On a March day in 1947 in a remote southern Illinois town, a catastrophe occurred that at first seemed unrelated to the governmental corruption. It wasn't.

Selwyn Pepper and Roy J. Harris (the author's father) had both served in the Pacific—Pepper on General Douglas MacArthur's staff and Harris as an Army major who had been through the kamikaze attacks of the Okinawa campaign. On the evening of March 25 both got urgent calls at home from city editor Ray Crowley. Pepper remembered:

> He said there'd been an explosion in a coal mine in Centralia, Illinois. Get over there as quickly as possible. At the time I wasn't feeling very well. I was coming down with a cold or something. But a word from the city editor was a word from God, and you didn't dare say, "I don't feel well, I don't think I ought to go." You went. It was [first] a matter of finding out where Centralia was. . . . And finding the mine. But once I got there, there was the whole tableau sitting right in front of me: All the wives of miners under the lights, trying to find out what was happening. And it quickly became apparent that the miners were trapped down below, and might not get out alive.[18]

By late in the day, the tableau also contained a half-dozen *Post-Dispatch* staffers, with Harry Wilensky as leader. Six days earlier Wilensky had written a front-page story out of the state capital, Springfield, about a "shakedown" of Illinois coal mine operators for political contributions. The state department of mines and minerals was raising funds for the Chicago Republican mayoral campaign, and mine inspectors were threatening to enforce safety regulations—unless operators contributed.

The *Post-Dispatch*, then, saw in the wrenching disaster an additional element of graft—an element that other journalists hardly touched.[19] On that first day, a Wilensky-bylined story started this way:

CENTRALIA, Ill., March 26—The Centralia Coal Co., operators of the mine in which 104 miners are trapped 540 feet below the surface near here . . . had been warned repeatedly by the Illinois State Mine Inspector to improve conditions which constituted an "explosion hazard." Warnings of the danger due to an excessive amount of dust in the mine were posted in inconspicuous corners of the mine washrooms.

Pepper wrote in his sidebar:

A closely grouped, strangely silent crowd stood in the sunshine near the mine entrance today. They were first-aid workers, mine officials, and relatives of the trapped miners, waiting for the appearance of any possible survivors of the disaster, and of the bodies known to be below ground. Wives of some of the miners standing behind the first row of men, were weeping after an earlier showing of restraint.

It set the stage. The next day Wilensky dropped a bombshell, although his story inexplicably carried no byline:

CENTRALIA, Ill., March 27—Workers in the Centralia Coal Co. mine from which bodies are now being removed begged Gov. Dwight H. Green of Illinois more than a year ago to "please save our lives" by making the State Department of Mines and Minerals enforce safety regulations in the mine. . . . The four signers of [the letter to the governor] all were in the mine when the explosion occurred. [One] was brought out alive a few minutes after the blast. [Another] was killed, his body having been brought out last night. The other two signers . . . are unaccounted for.

Pepper remembered that Wilensky had found the save-our-lives memo in the dark, under glass on a bulletin board near the entrance to the mine. The day that the story ran, a Fitzpatrick cartoon starkly depicted a giant skeleton with a mining helmet on his skull, somberly addressing a mine inspector and a coal company official: "You Gambled But I Paid."

This doubled-edged coverage—with compassion for the grieving and outrage over the corruption—captured the key elements of this tragedy. Pulitzer wanted the reporting to say more, though. He saw a moral obligation for the paper. One yellow memo to Reese said:

> The Post-Dispatch having so often had to damn the miners and their leader, John L. Lewis, I somehow feel it is our peculiar duty to turn ourselves inside out to get to the bottom of what clearly appears to have been faulty inspection of the Centralia mine, to the end that safe conditions can be assured for the future, those responsible . . . be brought to justice . . . and that we undertake to do whatever we can do to help the prospects of the bereaved families.[20]

Pulitzer proposed tying the whole story together with words and pictures in one section. "This may take a full page or for all I know a dozen full pages. It may take a staff of a dozen men," he wrote. Reese began making the assignments.

As the rescue workers finished their grim task—111 miners in all were eventually confirmed dead—the *Post-Dispatch* did some of its best work capturing the emotion. It located letters that dying miners had left in a corner of the pit: "Dear Wife and Sons: Well, hon, it looks like this is the end. Please tell mom and dad I still love them. Please get the baby baptized and send [name] to the Catholic school. . . . Love to all of you." Another said simply, "Dear Wife: Goodbye. Forgive me. Take care of all the children."

Stories from the scene by Wilensky and Pepper, Harris, Evarts Graham, and Robert Dunlap, and from George Hall in Washington and Spencer McCullough in Chicago, also took aim at the political conniving. In a midnight interview at his home, mine inspector Driscoll Scanlan, who had refused to participate in that earlier shakedown of mine operations, told Wilensky that the mine department had "played politics with the lives of the miners." Scanlan had begged the department's director, Robert M. Medill, to close the mine because of the explosion danger—drawing from Medill the callous rejoinder: "We'll have to take that chance." Scanlan's problem, said Medill, was that he was "too damned honest."

FIGURE 13.3 A Daniel Fitzpatrick cartoon for the *Post-Dispatch*, "You Gambled But I Paid," illustrates the role of the mining company and state inspectors in the 1947 Centralia mine disaster. *Source*: Reprinted by permission.

On April 30 the paper ran Pulitzer's special section, edited by pictures editor Julius Klyman, and distributed sixty thousand copies free through the Illinois coal country and to Illinois legislators and state and federal agencies.

The nomination letter for the Pulitzer Prize described "a long and hard-fought campaign to change existing conditions in mine fields with the view of saving the lives of other miners in the future." The campaign had sought "four necessary changes: 1) Take mine inspectors out of politics; 2) Outlaw political contributions by Illinois coal companies and all other corporations; 3) Make failure to comply with state safety laws a felony; 4) Bring the guilty to justice." There was little jury debate over its 1941 recommendation of the St. Louis paper and the board agreed, giving the *Post-Dispatch* its third gold medal.

1948—The *St. Louis Post-Dispatch* for the coverage of the Centralia, Illinois, mine disaster and the follow-up which resulted in impressive reforms in mine safety laws and regulations.[21]

"Gravy Train" Editors

In August 1948, Ben Reese assigned Roy Harris to become the Springfield, Illinois, correspondent. It was a critical time for the state just to Missouri's east, across the Mississippi River. Republican governor Green was coming up for reelection in November, and the paper felt a duty to keep exposing the corruption that it knew pervaded his administration. For Harris it was his first out-of-town duty station since returning from the Pacific.

Springfield was a busy state capital for reporters interested in administration scandals. Harris's stories were about how prison wardens got luxury furnishings in their quarters and thousands of Green cronies were rewarded with "special investigator" badges. As the reporter made a routine check of state payroll data at one point, he became suspicious as names of some Illinois editors cropped up, seemingly as state employees. A small story appeared in October. The number of such minor scandals multiplied by the November election. Green was trounced by

Democrat Adlai Stevenson, although President Harry Truman's margin over Republican Thomas E. Dewey was extremely narrow. Even without Green, much of the wrongdoing from his administration lingered in Illinois government.

George Thiem, a reporter for the *Chicago Daily News*, also took an interest in the editors-on-the-payroll story. As representatives of one-person bureaus for papers that did not directly compete against each other, Harris and Thiem decided that they would be able to get more accomplished if they pooled their resources on the story.[22]

"About the end of March, a Statehouse employe [*sic*], chatting with Thiem and me, recalled the mention of newspapermen in the October [*Post-Dispatch* story] and suggested that further investigation might be productive," Harris later told *Editor and Publisher* magazine. "The job would be a tedious one, as I had learned last fall, but we decided to make a stab at it."[23] Tedious indeed. The state tracked its thirty-five thousand employees by county, listing them in numerous volumes. It took the two men more than two weeks to root through them all, with one reporter handling card files that listed Illinois newspaper staffers and reading off names while the other checked the payroll.

Because they had other state house coverage responsibilities as well, the two found collaboration on the project a godsend. "I seriously doubt that either of us would have dug up the payroll story, working alone, because of the grueling detail and extra hours involved," said Thiem. "We knew we were handling delicate if not libelous information and we had to be accurate. By the time we discovered ten names, we realized we were on the way to a good story." Harris added, "Each of those names represented a million-dollar lawsuit"—if for some reason the information was incorrect.

While it was perhaps a rare reporting arrangement, Thiem saw the teaming of journalists from different papers with similar interests as a natural arrangement if it was done carefully. "I've been impressed by the need for newspapermen to work together more closely to accomplish something for good government and the welfare of the taxpayers generally," he told *Editor and Publisher*, "rather than to struggle for individualist scoops."[24]

For a time, the two were pulled away by a tragic hospital fire in the town of Effingham, in which scores of people died. When they returned, their list of editors who were possibly on the payroll began to grow—and then shrank, as the double-checking of names, through legislators and others, reduced the count.

When they finally had the story, the two men sat together at separate typewriters in Harris's room at the Leland Hotel, writing late into the evening of April 13. It was nearly midnight when they filed their dictated stories by phone for their afternoon newspapers. Harris's April 14 story began:

> SPRINGFIELD, Ill.—Editors and publishers of at least 32 downstate Illinois newspapers were carried on the state payroll during the administration of Gov. Dwight H. Green, collecting more than $300,000 in salaries, inquiry by the Post-Dispatch revealed today. Most of them held "gravy train" jobs like "field investigators" and "messenger clerk."

Some actually did work at their state jobs, but the chief function of many editors "was to print canned editorials and news stories lauding accomplishments of the Republican state administration."

Harris and Thiem built up the list of editors confirmed on the payroll to fifty-one, with the total of payments to them reaching $480,000. A strong editorial ran a day after the first story in the *Post-Dispatch*, along with a Fitzpatrick cartoon showing editors tracking sludge across the good name of the press.

At first, few other newspapers around the country paid much attention to the Illinois stories. Then a *Washington Post* editorial took the press to task:

> At best, this looks like crass indifference to a particularly juicy bit of news. At worst it looks like a cover-up of scandal within the family. The newspaper press claims special status as a pillar of free and honest government. By the same token it has special obligations. Among these is the duty not to keep its own dirty linen from public view.[25]

Uncharacteristically, Pulitzer personally nominated the work in both the reporting and public service categories. (It was perhaps easier for him because a second newspaper was involved in the project as well.) The public service jury picked six of the seventy entries, listing the *Daily News/ Post-Dispatch* stories first. The board kept them first, awarding each paper a gold medal and citing Harris and Thiem for the work, only the second time individuals had been noted in a public service citation.

1950—The *Chicago Daily News* and *St. Louis Post-Dispatch* for the work of George Thiem and Roy J. Harris, respectively, in exposing the presence of 37 Illinois newspapermen on an Illinois State payroll.[26]

The Tax Man Taketh

Theodore C. Link returned to the *Post-Dispatch* in 1945 with a wound received as a Marine sergeant at Bougainville and threw himself back into the job with war-like fervor. Long known for his shadowy underworld sources, Link began writing stories about Illinois gangs as well as abuses in the Green administration. Sometimes he toted a gun for his own protection.

In early 1951 Link was tipped about federal tax cases in Missouri being fixed at high levels of the federal Internal Revenue. Federal agents were open to letting companies and individuals off the hook by reaching under-the-table deals. After pitching the story to managing editor Ray Crowley, who took over when Reese retired, Link quickly expanded the story beyond his home state. Selwyn Pepper worked rewrite for Link, who rarely wrote his own stories throughout his career. Sam Armstrong, the new city editor, directed the campaign.[27]

The resulting articles disclosed that case fixing had become almost routine among influential lawyers with friendly ties to public officials in Washington, D.C., St. Louis, and elsewhere. In one year, 63 percent of the tax cases approved for federal prosecution had been killed by internal revenue regional counsels or by people inside President Truman's Justice Department.

A federal grand jury in St. Louis at one point received a U.S. report saying there was no evidence of tax fixing, although the judge did not believe it and told the grand jury so. Link was able to learn that the report to the grand jury had been written at the suggestion of Truman's attorney general, J. Howard McGrath. A national scandal erupted over how Washington had withheld evidence.

One major case involved American Lithofold Corporation, a St. Louis printer with government contracts. The *Post-Dispatch* reported that the company's federal tax collector was on the American Lithofold payroll. Further, William M. Boyle, the chairman of the Democratic National Committee, served on the company's board. Boyle had been instrumental in helping American Lithofold win government loans.

The paper's editorial page, under its editor, Irving Dilliard, backed the developing stories. One Fitzpatrick cartoon pictured bureaucrats falling like grains of salt from a dollhouse-like Internal Revenue building. The caption was "Shake 'Em All Out." The new Internal Revenue Service almost did just that. By year's end, eight revenue collectors were fired or forced to resign, and two ended up behind bars. In all, there were 380 discharges or resignations and more than a dozen employees were indicted. Truman also fired his attorney general.[28]

When the Public Service Prize was announced, the *Post-Dispatch* installed its fifth gold medal with the four others on the wall of the publisher's private office.

1952—The *St. Louis Post-Dispatch* for its investigation and disclosures
of wide spread corruption in the Internal Revenue Bureau
and other departments of the government.[29]

CHAPTER 14

A NEW STEW OF ISSUES

1953–1969: Little Rock, the Suburbs, and Firsts for Women

Somehow, some time, every Arkansan is going to have to be counted. We are going to have to decide what kind of people we are—whether we obey the law only when we approve of it, or whether we obey it no matter how distasteful we may find it. And this, finally, is the only issue before the people of Arkansas.

—*ARKANSAS GAZETTE* EDITOR HARRY S. ASHMORE, SEPTEMBER 9, 1957

As the Pulitzer board searched for its public service medalist each year, the goal was to find the very best story—not to go out of its way to achieve a broad mix of winning news organizations. Had variety been the aim, of course, the *St. Louis Post-Dispatch* likely wouldn't have been a five-time recipient in so short a span. Likewise, board members were not looking to honor a diversity of story types that might be viewed as ideal from the standpoint of posterity. With as many as a half-dozen suggestions placed before them by each jury, they had enough to do just selecting the year's strongest candidate.

But as the nation's editors continued to tackle the topics that gripped the communities around them in the postwar years, the Public Service Prize winners did indeed manage to touch on many of the major themes of the age. Papers that exposed the grit of corruption and graft got their share of honors, recognizing that important duty of the watchdog press. Other selections in the 1950s and 1960s, though, began to reveal a new stew of compelling social issues—from school integration to legislative reform to drugs, sex, and the environment.

By 1950 the number of journalism categories had increased to seven, with the old reporting award being broken by the Pulitzer board into local, national, and international divisions. Cartooning had its own prize, as did photography. During the next two decades, in an expansion to eleven prizes, the board chose some unwieldy category names, such as local investigative specialized reporting (later called investigative reporting). Photography was divided into spot news and feature photography.

In the enlarged deck of awards, the gold medal sometimes began to take on the look of a "wild card"—with the board seeming to use the designation to mark what it considered to be simply the best newspaper effort of the year. Increasingly, though, the members began to see the public service award as a way to honor the special case of a news organization that reached across the classic Pulitzer Prize divisions, or perhaps that said something totally new to benefit the community. As always, though, the role of the press in dealing with racial issues was kept in focus.

A Klan Reprise—and Finale

In 1953, the *Whiteville News Reporter* and the *Tabor City Tribune* got special attention because they were the first weeklies to win "the coveted Meritorious Public Service awards," as *Editor and Publisher* magazine called them. (It was another case of two newspapers winning in the same year for writing independently about similar topics.) But far more important was the evil that they successfully attacked: a North Carolina rejuvenation of the Ku Klux Klan.

Over the course of the papers' campaigns, more than a hundred Klan members, including Imperial Wizard Thomas L. Hamilton, had been convicted of various crimes because of what the Whiteville and Tabor City papers wrote. The newspapers, whose editors were personal friends, were only twenty miles from each other and were close to the boundary with South Carolina, the state where Klan activity was most vicious. KKK terrorism, including beatings of both blacks and whites by night riders, had spread in 1950 and 1951.[1]

The fears in the community were sometimes matched by fears in the newsroom. "I would be lying if I said I haven't been afraid," the *News*

Reporter editor Willard Cole said to *Editor and Publisher*, "but the mission of a newspaper editor is to voice convictions, not to exhibit his own misgivings." Cole, who earlier had worked at the *Winston-Salem Journal*, kept three guns because of threats he had received. As the two newspapers attacked the violence, county, state, and federal agents moved in. When the prizes were awarded in May 1953, Cole called the North Carolina Klan "as dead as a door nail."[2]

Cole's wife, a teacher, also got some credit for finding a way to break through the silence among frightened victims that had hampered investigators and reporters alike. "She listened to children gossiping at school and learned of three beatings," the Associated Press reported in its coverage of the Pulitzers. "The information was relayed via Cole to the authorities who pried the information out of the reluctant victims."

The *Tribune* editor W. Horace Carter also admitted being terrified for his wife and two young children as cars drove past his home at night. At one point, his four-year-old son asked him, "The Klan gonna come and get you, daddy?"

1953—The *Whiteville* (N.C.) *News Reporter* and *Tabor City* (N.C.) *Tribune* for their successful campaign against the Ku Klux Klan, waged on their own doorstep at the risk of economic loss and personal danger, culminating in the conviction of over one hundred Klansmen and an end to terrorism in their communities.[3]

"Alicia's Toy" No More

The New York suburbs gave rise to a new kind of journalism in the 1940s. Publisher Alicia Patterson had begun molding *Newsday* into both a community voice and an enemy of corruption, especially the labor rackets.

Being taken as a serious publisher had not been easy. She was the great-granddaughter of the *Chicago Tribune* owner Joseph Medill and the daughter of Joseph Medill Patterson, founder of the *New York Daily News* and benefactor of Northwestern University's Medill School of Journalism. But ever since buying Long Island's Garden City–based paper in 1940,

FIGURE 14.1 *Newsday* publisher Alicia Patterson, who bought the Long Island, New York, paper in 1940, examines her first press. *Source*: Photo courtesy of *Newsday*.

Alicia Patterson had had to live down the sexist notion that *Newsday* was just "Alicia's toy."[4]

The story that carried *Newsday* to its first Pulitzer Prize—and a new sense of pride—was inspired by managing editor Alan Hathway. He had assigned reporter Helen Dudar, among others, to investigate Nassau County construction trades labor czar William DeKoning Sr. While individual names are not generally associated with Public Service Prizes, Dudar may be the first woman journalist involved with winning one. But bylines did not show her role. The editors, feeling that by naming reporters they might expose them to retribution from the individuals they were writing about, kept her name off her stories.[5]

Dudar had started at *Newsday* as an advice columnist while she attended classes at Columbia. She displayed special skill in crafting complex stories, although her role in the DeKoning investigation was to follow Hathway's instructions closely. As early as 1950, Dudar and other staffers found a nest of wrongdoing involving an area trotting racetrack where DeKoning also was involved. The paper kept up the pressure. Along the way, a number of its news tips came from New York City Anti-Crime Commission investigator Bob Greene.[6] Eventually DeKoning went to prison for extortion—and Greene jumped to *Newsday* as a reporter. The state investigation turned the *Newsday* stories into convictions. It was the work of Governor Thomas E. Dewey, who had so narrowly lost the presidential election to Harry Truman in 1948.

Newsday's victory over the labor boss was all the sweeter because some New York City papers had knocked their new rival as a "soggy suburban"[7]—and largely ignored the DeKoning story. The *New York World-Telegram* played down the Pulitzer news that year, and for what it *did* run it ordered up an article "belittling Newsday and saying that the Pulitzer Prize committee was crazy for not giving it to the Telegram." That assessment came from a reliable source: Fred Cook, the unfortunate *World-Telegram* reporter who was ordered to write the derogatory story. "I had to do it. I sure did hate it," he said. "It was buried in the paper somewhere. It was a disgusting performance."[8]

In a statement after the prize was announced, Patterson credited Hathway, who "spent more hours, more effort, more energy on the story than any other Newsday member. It was he who was cited by David Holman, DeKoning's attorney, as the man most responsible for DeKoning's downfall."[9]

Newsday's greatest successes in the public service arena were ahead of it, however. The successes would be largely of Bob Greene's making. In ten years, Greene would become a legend in investigative team reporting.

1954—*Newsday*, Garden City, N.Y., for its exposé of New York State's race track scandals and labor racketeering, which led to the extortion indictment, guilty plea and imprisonment of William C. DeKoning, Sr., New York labor racketeer.[10]

Leadership in Little Rock

Despite the inspirational work of the *Arkansas Gazette* in leading its community through the Little Rock school desegregation crisis of 1957, there is still an aura of sadness in looking back at that time. The most dramatic element of its coverage sprang from the September 2 decision by Governor Orval E. Faubus to call out the National Guard and state police to surround Little Rock Central High School, preventing fifteen black students from registering for classes. The front page soon carried pictures of black students being turned away from the schoolhouse door with white students taunting them. Then came the violence.

Editor Harry S. Ashmore and the *Gazette* had spent more than a year trying to avert such a collision. They had worked closely with the governor, whom the paper had helped elect. The *Gazette* had promoted a "ten-year plan for desegregation"—one opposed by the National Association for the Advancement of Colored People as too slow. But that plan, the *Gazette* contended, was within the spirit of the "deliberate speed" that the Supreme Court had sought in its 1954 *Brown v. Board of Education* ruling. Days before September 2, Governor Faubus had said he would keep his word and would not intervene to prevent black children from enrolling. That had led the *Gazette*'s Ashmore to editorialize optimistically on September 1. Headlined "A Time of Testing," the editorial said the paper was confident "that the citizens of Little Rock will demonstrate on Tuesday for the world to see that we are a law-abiding people."[11] When Faubus called out the Guard, though, all bets were off.

"Little Rock was actually a progressive city whose citizens were headed off at the pass by the governor," says Gene Roberts, who covered civil rights for the *New York Times* and later took the *Philadelphia Inquirer* to greatness as the editor. There in Arkansas, "you had a civil rights conflagration at a time when there was progressive civil rights leadership at the paper. Other places, papers were mediocre, and part of the problem, rather than the solution."[12]

The *Gazette* had dutifully been publishing both pro-segregation and anti-segregation views in its news column. A story that was part of its Pulitzer Prize submission, for example, was headlined "Petition Adopted at 'Mothers League' Meeting Asks Faubus to Prevent Integration of School."

FIGURE 14.2 The *Arkansas Gazette* of September 4, 1957, showed Little Rock in crisis and featured an editorial by Harry Ashmore. *Source*: Reprinted by permission of the *Arkansas Democrat-Gazette*, © 1957.

FIGURE 14.3 The *Arkansas Gazette* editor Harry Ashmore in 1957. *Source*: Used by permission of *Arkansas Democrat-Gazette*, © 1957.

The unbylined story said: "The petition was approved by a standing vote of most of the 250 men and women present at the second meeting of the League. . . . It heard impassioned pleas from several segregationists, including one from Texas, to fight the integration of Little Rock Central High School."

But racist opinions could not stand up to the eloquence of Ashmore's reasoned editorials. On September 4 he wrote one headlined "The Crisis Mr. Faubus Made." It began:

> Little Rock arose yesterday to gaze upon the incredible spectacle of an empty high school surrounded by National Guard troops called out by Governor Faubus to protect life and property against a mob that never materialized.

Mr. Faubus says he based this extraordinary action on reports of impending violence. Dozens of local reporters and national correspondents worked through the day yesterday without verifying the few facts the governor offered to explain why his appraisal was so different from that of local officials—who have asked for no such action. . . . On Monday night he called out the National Guard and made it a national problem.

It is one he must now live with, and the rest of us must suffer under. If Mr. Faubus in fact has no intention of defying federal authority now is the time for him to call a halt to the resistance which is preventing the carrying out of a duly entered court order. And certainly he should do so before his own actions become the cause of the violence he so professes to fear.[13]

Public service jurors gave the board a choice among the *Gazette* coverage and a wide range of other entries, including several old-time political graft stories and the *New York Journal American*'s coverage of a "mad bomber" in the city.[14] The board recognized, though, what an extraordinary statement the *Gazette* had made in its reporting of the desegregation crisis.

Roberts observes that this was the only Pulitzer gold medal awarded to a southern newspaper during desegregation in the region, making the joint recognition for the newspaper and Ashmore—in public service and editorial writing—all the more significant in journalism history. "I personally think that the so-called southern liberal editors during this period collectively made it the brightest era for editorial writing ever in America," says Roberts, whose book *The Race Beat: The Press, the Civil Rights Struggle, and the Awakening of a Nation*, co-written with Hank Klibanoff, won the 2007 Pulitzer Prize for History.[15]

Some *Gazette* readers did what they could to dim the moment, however. Despite the paper's "fearless and completely objective news coverage"— and, in fact, because of it—the *Gazette* suffered a subscriber boycott and pressure from advertisers. During 1957, circulation fell to 83,000 from 100,000. Later it would be forced into a merger with its rival paper to become the *Arkansas Democrat-Gazette*.[16]

1958—The *Arkansas Gazette*, Little Rock, for demonstrating the highest qualities of civic leadership, journalistic responsibility and moral courage in the face of great public tension during the school integration crisis of 1957. The newspaper's fearless and completely objective news coverage, plus its reasoned and moderate policy, did much to restore calmness and order to an overwrought community, reflecting great credit on its editors and its management.[17]

Speaking Above a Whisper

Like many newly hired women reporters of the 1950s, Lois Wille had found herself on fluffy "women's page" or "society page" assignments after getting a journalism degree and joining the *Chicago Daily News* in 1956. Starting as assistant to the fashion editor, she eventually got her wish to move over to the city desk. But at first it wasn't much better. She was one of the "our girl" reporters—getting her picture in the paper "powdering my nose in a flight suit" after she flew with the Navy's Blue Angels, for example. Soon, however, she began making her own breaks. In 1959, she hid in a laundry truck to get close to Nikita Khrushchev on the Soviet premier's 1959 tour through the Midwest. She got her interview.[18]

By 1961 Wille was covering poverty and public aid issues and latched onto one issue that at first was a hard sell with city editor Maurice "Ritz" Fischer. The public health agencies in the area "all had a policy of not giving out any information about birth control to indigent women—much less services," she says. The need for birth control services was discussed often among public health workers, "but it was never written about"—especially in heavily Catholic, conservative Chicago. "Ritz had given me a free hand to explore the issues," but this one seemed to sit on his desk without a decision. Then Fischer went on leave for some surgery and his assistant, Robert Rose, took over. "Rose was fearless," Wille recalls, "and he thought it would just be a hoot anyway to work on this story while Ritz was gone."

The story she prepared was balanced, examining the economic and social reasons advanced by proponents who claimed that offering the services would "reduce the rolls of those who receive public aid and rely on

FIGURE 14.4 The *Chicago Daily News* reporter Lois Wille in 1962. *Source*: Used by permission of Lois Wille.

public funds for medical care." They also argued "that those Chicago families who can least afford to provide for children are reproducing at high rates, thus contributing to delinquency and other social ills," according to the Pulitzer Prize entry by the paper. On the other side, birth control was "considered immoral by a large number of taxpayers."

The *Daily News* said: "Behind closed doors of conference rooms, in private gatherings of social workers, among clergy of various denominations, these issues were debated and discussed over and over again. But in whispers." Wille did not whisper. After intensive research and interviewing in which people had to be persuaded to speak for the record, she pulled together the cases and the arguments she needed. At that point, the Pulitzer entry letter said, "a disheartening problem thrust itself into the picture. The Catholic laymen and clergy she talked with gave her little sermons on why The Daily News should forget the whole thing." Indeed, the Church would not even offer a comment on the controversy.

City editor Fischer, now back at his desk, took it seriously that the Church was not planning to participate in the series. He arranged several meetings with Catholic leaders. And at one point, without Wille's knowledge, he even passed her story to a Church leader of his acquaintance, Monsignor John J. Egan. "I figured, This could not be good," Wille recalls, although, "back then I wasn't as appalled as I might be today." Father Egan, though, was one of the most progressive of priests in Chicago. He suggested some changes but also made sure that the Church would offer a detailed statement of the Catholic position to appear in the articles.

The eloquence of her writing—and of the people she got to speak to her—gave the series special power. In one story, Wille began:

> On a hot Saturday morning in August, Mrs. Sandra Allmon, 26, walked into Newberry Settlement Houses just off Maxwell St., waited in line with about 100 other women and poured out her story:
> "I asked about it at County Hospital when my youngest was born, and everybody shut up like a clam.
> "'I've got seven now, I told the doctor. And he said, 'Well, you're healthy enough for seven more.'"

"I have to credit Ritz," says Wille. "When he came back from his surgery he pushed it forward."

Still, the reporter also found herself assigned to write her own Pulitzer Prize nomination letter early the next year, something she remembers dashing off before she and her husband left for a vacation in the Mediterranean. When someone asked her if she expected to win, Wille laughed, "Don't be silly; this is just something I have to do. It's routine." And she believed it.

After a day of touring Egypt she was told that several cables had arrived for her, "I thought someone had died," she recalls. "Why else would we be getting cables?" Her husband came running down from the cable office. "You've won!"

Wille was to champion the hiring of women reporters at the *Daily News* until the paper closed in 1978. She then became the editorial page editor of the *Chicago Sun-Times*, leaving that paper when Rupert Murdoch bought it in 1984 and moving to the *Tribune*. She won her own Pulitzer for editorial writing at the *Tribune* in 1989.

1963—*Chicago Daily News* for calling public attention to the issue of providing birth control services in the public health programs in its area.[19]

Highway Robbery

A February 1963 telephone tip to the *St. Petersburg Times* Tallahassee bureau chief Martin Waldron suggested that fiscal controls over turnpike-related spending were abysmal. Huge amounts of public monies were being wasted. The call kicked off a six-month investigation of fraud in the state turnpike authority.

The authority had been created during the 1950s to operate more than 100 miles of toll roads from Miami and Fort Pierce, and in 1960 Governor Farris Bryant supervised the sale of $157 million in new bonds for an extension that would make the whole road more than 260 miles long. But the system was rife with waste and abuse.

Waldron's team included reporters Jack Nease, Don Meiklejohn, and John Gardner, and they were supported by editorial writer Warren Pierce and photographer Johnnie Evans. The team leader was a fearless but somewhat happy-go-lucky character, as associates described him. And to the serious business of investigating, Waldron introduced lighter moments. One was his decision—with the help of Meiklejohn and the *Times* accountants—to test just how much two people would have to eat to run up one of the huge meal tabs that turnpike authority employees were submitting.

In the "time capsules" that many of these long-ago Pulitzer-winning efforts represent, today's inflated dollars sometimes make the amounts of money seem laughable. This case is a prime example. The outrageous-looking meal tabs for two ran to $30—at a time when half as much could buy an elegant two-person dinner, complete with drinks and generous tip. Waldron and Meiklejohn picked Pierre's Restaurant and Lounge in Miami for their experiment. As Waldron later told it, the job was grueling, requiring the two to start with several martinis and whisky sours, followed by a Caesar salad, double sirloin, and cherries jubilee, and topped off with two brandies. When they failed initially, managing only a $23.10 bill, they stepped up the effort.[20]

"Another glass of brandy will cost what?" Waldron asked the waiter, only to be told that it would add just $1.10 more. After figuring a $5 tip, they did not mange to hit $30 until they bought the glass that their beverages came in—for $1—proof positive that the turnpike officials had been taking advantage of the lax oversight.

As a result of the paper's stories, the state legislature created a bond review board to regulate bond issues and a state audit was ordered, where previously the authority's own auditors had been in charge. Turnpike authority chairman John Hammer resigned, there was a full investigation, and members of the authority were stripped of their unlimited expense account privileges. It was the first Pulitzer Prize for the paper, which became the *Tampa Bay Times* in 2012.[21]

1964—The *St. Petersburg* (Fla.) *Times* for its aggressive investigation
of the Florida Turnpike Authority which disclosed widespread
illegal acts and resulted in a major reorganization of the
State's road construction program.[22]

Zoned Out in California

Like many investigations that lead to gold medals, the *Los Angeles Times's* successful probe into the sleazy side of city government grew over several years. In 1966, Metro editor William F. Thomas had received a telephone tip about abuses by city officials. "It was a zoning story, and a hell of a good one," said Thomas, who died in 2014.[23] Officials were taking bribes to make zoning changes, especially for the corners where the city's many gas stations were located. Property owners paying the bribes were profiting from the increase in values that resulted.

"I didn't want to form an investigative team," recalled the editor, who had a low opinion of reporters who called themselves investigators rather than journalists. "So I gave the calls to George Reasons, who had been an education writer. I told him not to be a policeman, or I'd pull him off. He did become a policeman, but he listened to reason."[24]

At the same time, Thomas listened to Reasons. When the reporter said he needed help with the expanding assignment, the Metro editor created a team with reporters Art Berman, Gene Blake, Robert L. Jackson, and Ed Meagher.

A barrier had to be surmounted before any rooting out of corruption could be done, though: the *Times*'s lawyer. As Bill Thomas was rising in the editing ranks at the Metro section, he saw the attorney blocking good work time after time. "I refused to send my stories up to him because they'd get killed if they had any hint of possible legal action," Thomas said. "This was a very careful newspaper. It didn't take any chances." At one point, however, the *Times* named a new general counsel, and arrangements were made for the paper to be represented if necessary by a trial attorney with the big firm of Gibson, Dunn, and Krutcher.

Thomas recalled his apprehension when he first attempted to get one of the tough zoning stories past an attorney in this new system the *Times* had created. When the editor handed the piece over for a reading, the lawyer started chuckling. "And I'm thinking, He's going to shoot this down," according to Thomas. But then, going point by point down the pages, "he started saying, 'We can win that. . . . We can win that. . . .'"

While the relationship eased the way for the stories by Reasons and others to appear, Thomas was not sure what impact the work would have. "They really didn't seem to be blockbusters," he said, "but they were really hard-work stories." Many of the abuses were extremely small, with some officials taking bribes of as little as $2,000. "That always amazed me," he said. "Why in the hell would they risk it for that much? Why wouldn't they hold out for ten thousand dollars?" Eventually he figured it out. The local politicians thought it was something everyone was doing and that this protected them from exposure. "And for two thousand dollars, maybe you wouldn't have such a guilt feeling."

The guilt feelings would come, however, courtesy of the *Times* articles. Incrementally, the stories "just kept unfolding, and then you'd run into a roadblock," Thomas said. Then "finally you figured you had enough to do a series." Taken together, the small exclusive painted the picture of a corrupt administration.

Three harbor commissioners were convicted of bribery in 1968, a $12 million city contract for a world trade center was canceled, and in recreation and parks two commissioners resigned and a golf course contract was canceled. The *Times* editor Nick Williams wrote in his Pulitzer Prize entry letter, "There can be no doubt that without the disclosures made over the past two years by The Los Angeles Times none of the above reforms, indictments and changes in the Los Angeles City government would have taken place."[25]

Looking back, even Thomas sounded amazed at how rapidly the *Times* was able to create such a reporting powerhouse in the 1960s. "The *Times* came out of nowhere—one of the ten worst, as *Time* magazine supposedly said—and in a period of ten years it became among the top three and stayed there." Thomas largely credited publisher Otis Chandler and editor Nick Williams, who Thomas would soon replace. They in turn credited Thomas. By the time Thomas retired as editor in 1989 the *Times* had won twelve Pulitzers, including another gold medal in 1984.

1969—The *Los Angeles Times* for its exposé of wrongdoing within the Los Angeles City Government Commissions, resulting in resignations or criminal convictions of certain members, as well as widespread reforms.[26]

CHAPTER 15

SECRET PAPERS, SECRET REPORTING

1972: The Pentagon Papers and the *Times*

Somewhere there is a line where the old skeptical, combative, publish-
and-be-damned tradition of the past in our papers may converge with the
new intelligence and the new duties and responsibilities of this rising and
restless generation. I wish I knew how to find it, for it could help both
the newspapers and the nation in their present plight, and it could help
us believe again, which in this age of tricks and techniques may be our
greatest need.

—JAMES RESTON, *NEW YORK TIMES*, PULITZER PRIZE
FIFTIETH ANNIVERSARY DINNER, MAY 10, 1966

When the Pulitzer Prizes celebrated their fiftieth year in 1966, only thirty-
three newspapers—a diverse assortment of large and small journals from
across the country—could boast having a Pulitzer Gold Medal. A mere
handful owned more than one. The *New York Times* had two, one short
of the number earned by the *Chicago Daily News*, a paper that would not
survive the next decade. The *Washington Post* had none. Starting early in
the 1970s, so much would change.

Two of the greatest pure newspaper stories of the century broke, one
in June 1971 and the other in June 1972. As foreshadowed at the Pulitzer
ceremony by James "Scotty" Reston of the *New York Times*, each story
would expose Americans to "tricks and techniques" in the halls of government.[1] Each had its antagonists in the administration of President Richard
Nixon. (Indeed, some domestic spying authorized by the White House
during the Watergate period was a reaction to Daniel Ellsberg's leaking of
the Pentagon Papers to the *Times*.) And each story very possibly would
not have seen print at all without the vigilance and courage of the news
organization that took charge of the coverage. First the *New York Times*

acquired, analyzed, and published the secret Pentagon Papers, describing deceptions that several presidential administrations had employed to keep Americans ignorant of U.S. policy in South Vietnam. Then the *Washington Post*'s Bob Woodward and Carl Bernstein parlayed their early scoops about "a third-rate burglary"—as the Nixon administration portrayed the Watergate break-in—into an investigation that gradually exposed White House involvement in that crime and many others.

With their work, both the *Times* and the *Post* created invaluable models of public service. And more than four decades later, both still are considered classics of American media history. Yet shockingly, for different reasons, each came very close to being shut out of the Pulitzer Prizes altogether.

The *New York Times* associate editor Harrison Salisbury tried to capture the power of the Pentagon Papers coverage in his description of the newspaper's final decision, after weeks of debate, to publish them. (His book *Without Fear or Favor* contains one of the better remembrances that the *Times* editors have produced over the years.) Salisbury set the stage on "that limpid Sunday of June 13, 1971," when the first so-called Vietnam Archive installment appeared, just as the *Times* publisher Arthur O. "Punch" Sulzberger was preparing for a trip to London:

> As Sulzberger checked over his carefully packed bags he had not the slightest premonition that publication of the Pentagon Papers story that morning was triggering a sequence of events which would lead inexorably, step by step, to the greatest disaster ever to befall an American president, a disaster so profound, so far-reaching in implication that by the time it was over basic relationships in the American power apparatus would be changed; the very system would quiver; a President would fall; the balance of the tripartite American constitutional structure would shift; and the role of the press in America, the role of The New York Times, and even the function of the press in other great nations of the world would be transformed.[2]

A Newsroom at the Hilton

Fox Butterfield was hardly the typical second-year reporter for the *New York Times*. A summa cum laude Harvard graduate in 1961 specializing in Asian studies, he had lived abroad and served as the *Times*'s Taiwan stringer for nine months before the paper hired him full time to work back home. Still, he was in the position of most other cub reporters when he was called back to Times Square as the new decade began: he took the assignment given to him. It was covering Newark, a city still simmering from recent race riots.

In one of his early stories he had covered a stormy teacher strike with strong racial overtones. At a particularly contentious city hall meeting, a band of attendees roughed up Butterfield right in the meeting room and stole his notes, along with his wallet and wristwatch. He wrote a first-person account of the incident for the front page and the paper assigned him a bodyguard. The old newsroom adage—don't make the news; just report it—had been violated, even if it was necessary in this case. So Butterfield was uneasy when he got a call from the secretary of the *Times* managing editor A. M. "Abe" Rosenthal telling the reporter to stop by the office one afternoon. "I could only assume the worst: that they were dissatisfied with my performance," Butterfield says. But the meeting was not what he expected.

Rosenthal asked his reporter, "Do you have any problem working with classified documents?" recalls Butterfield. "I didn't know what he was talking about. I said, 'I assume you've got them. If *you* don't have a problem, I don't think I would, either.'"[3] It was the correct answer. Butterfield became one of the first reporters to join Pentagon correspondent Neil Sheehan—who had acquired the documents known as the Pentagon Papers—in a team writing project that was nearly as secret as the documents they would be describing.

Once again, the *Times* was about to make news, not merely report it. The news would open up government records that officials wanted to keep closed, but it would also reinforce an endangered legal principle at the highest level: that government cannot engage in "prior restraint" of news that it does not want the press to publish.

Why had Butterfield been picked to work on the Pentagon Papers team? He gives two possible reasons. "One was favorable to me: I'd been an undergraduate working on east Asian history, and I'd already been to Vietnam myself. I'd actually been to Hanoi," he says. "Then there was an unfavorable reason: that I was so junior and so unknown that I could disappear from my beat in Newark, and the *Washington Post* would not know that I was gone." That kind of secrecy played an enormous part in the decision making at the *Times*. A large team was being assembled in a group of suites on the eleventh and thirteen floors of the New York Hilton. Joining Sheehan and Butterfield were veteran *Times* reporters Hedrick Smith and E. W. Kenworthy, along with editors Allan M. Siegal, Samuel Abt, and Gerald Gold. The group grew to include five secretaries, a researcher, and a makeup editor, all watched over by *Times* security guards.

It was no secret in journalism circles that the *Times* was working on something special. In his autobiography, Ben Bradlee noted that the *Post* reporters were aware that a "blockbuster" was in the works at some offsite location, although "we never found out who was part of the task force, much less what they were tasking-forcing about."[4] Nat Hentoff wrote in a May 20 *Village Voice* piece about a "breakthrough unpublished story concerning the White House, Pentagon and Southeast Asia." He also noted that there was an internal debate at the paper and asked, "Is this story going to be published? Or are there still Times executives and editors who might hold back such a story 'in the national interest'?"[5]

The blockbuster taking shape at the Hilton involved an analysis by the reporters of forty-three volumes of an extraordinary government history of America's involvement in Vietnam from World War II to May 1968. The entire forty-seven-volume history—seven thousand pages and 2.5 million words—had been commissioned by President Lyndon Johnson's defense secretary, Robert S. McNamara, after he had become disillusioned about the war. It was classified top secret.

Sheehan's source was a thirty-nine-year-old former RAND Corporation researcher, Daniel Ellsberg, then at the Massachusetts Institute of Technology. Ellsberg, a former Marine who had helped write the history when he worked at the Pentagon, had studied at Harvard six years ahead of Sheehan and nine years ahead of Butterfield. Ellsberg felt driven to take the Vietnam history public, believing that Americans needed to understand the decades of deception underlying U.S. Vietnam policy. He had tried other channels inside and outside the government but was unsuccessful until Sheehan agreed to copy the documents and prepare them for publication in the *Times*. Sheehan's initial okay came from Scotty Reston, the Washington-based columnist and revered elder statesman and vice president of the *Times*.[6]

Ellsberg held back four volumes as too sensitive, especially with peace negotiations going on in Paris at the time. But on Friday, March 19, in Cambridge, Massachusetts, Sheehan and his wife received sixty pounds of pages from Ellsberg. They lugged them to all-night copying shops over three nights and spent $1,500 of the *Times*'s money to make copies before returning the papers to Ellsberg. Sheehan and editor Jerry Gold then spent two weeks sorting through the documents in Washington, discussing alternate approaches that might be taken for publication. Sheehan thought they should run in three parts; Gold in as many as twenty. Such decisions, of course, would be made higher up—if the Pentagon Papers were to be published at all.

Punch Tells a Joke

On April 20, at three o'clock in the afternoon—coincidentally just hours after New York Times Company's annual stockholders' meeting—the *Times* top editors met to decide what recommendation to make to publisher Punch Sulzberger. Abe Rosenthal held the session in Reston's cluttered New York office with senior staffers that included Washington bureau chief Max Frankel, foreign editor James Greenfield, columnist Tom Wicker, and assistant managing editor Seymour Topping. Also present were general counsel James Goodale and Sydney Gruson, Sulzberger's assistant. Sheehan told them what he had, although not the source of the documents. The editors asked how confident Sheehan was that the material was genuine and whether there was any question of national security being breached by its publication. The assembled journalists could see no potential security violations. This was history, after all. "Not an editor expressed doubt. If the materials were authentic . . . then of course *The Times* had to publish the story," Salisbury later wrote. He continued:

> Frankel then put the key question to his colleagues—journalistically, did the story warrant defying the government and possible government legal action; did the documents, in fact, betray a pattern of deception, of consistent and repeated deception by the American Government of the American people?

There was agreement in the room that this was precisely what the documents showed. Reston added, "These are the government's own conclusions. This is not only what our article is about—this is its basic concept." . . . It was the lies, the government's lies, continuing one administration after the other, which lay at the heart of the matter.

So, added Rosenthal, this would be the manner in which The Times would present the material—it would be history. The government's own version of history.[7]

General counsel Goodale felt that the historical approach could be defended legally. He was concerned, however, that too many people had attended the day's meeting, and information leaks about the *Times*'s story could give the government a head start on plans to oppose publication. "Everyone has to remember. Be quiet!" Goodale said as they prepared to leave. "Because everyone in this room may have participated in a felony."

More tough decisions—and intensive study and writing—lay ahead before the scheduled June 13 publication date for the first installment. The paper's longtime outside law firm, Lord, Day, and Lord, was firmly opposed to the publication of secret, stolen documents and told Sulzberger that he could be jailed for authorizing it. This was a time of soul searching for editors too. Rosenthal and Topping both considered resigning if the decision was made not to publish. Reston said he would publish the papers in his own small journal, the *Vineyard Gazette* in Martha's Vineyard, Massachusetts, if the *Times* decided not to run them.[8]

They discussed the closest apparent precedents at the *Times*, although the precedents were too old to be of much help. There were the newsroom actions taken before the American-supported 1961 invasion by Cuban exiles at Cuba's Bay of Pigs. The *Times* had toned down its story, citing national security as the reason. It had, however, still published in advance of the invasion. (Later President Kennedy was to suggest that had the *Times* published more detail, perhaps the ill-fated invasion would have been called off, and "you would have saved us from a colossal mistake.")

The editors also reviewed the 1908 case of the *Times* reporter William Bayard Hale's interview of Germany's Kaiser Wilhelm, in which the Kaiser had spewed angry words about England and Japan and supported world domination by white people. The paper had consulted President Theodore

Roosevelt first and then killed the story after he opposed its publication. (It was Punch Sulzberger's grandfather, publisher Arthur S. Ochs, who had locked that interview away in his safe, where it remained until it was finally published in 1939.[9])

Through May, Sheehan and the Pentagon Papers team kept working at the Hilton while general counsel Goodale debated the outside lawyers, who remained strongly opposed to publication. At a May 12 meeting with Sulzberger, the publisher was noncommittal but allowed work to proceed, planning to make a final call later. Still, Goodale was concerned that the publisher might follow Lord, Day's advice and pull the plug. Word of the internal debate trickled in to the Hilton. The team members worried as they wrote.

On June 10, the publisher reviewed a new opening that was being written for the proposed story. Washington chief Frankel and Sheehan had often been at odds in the *Times* newsroom over the years, but they had been thrown together into this rewrite—"improbable collaborators on what each now saw as *the* story of his time," Salisbury called them.

Editors made last-minute presentations to Sulzberger about how to balance the documents and the reporters' analysis in the series. Should they cut down the number of secret documents reprinted and run more explanations? That could reduce the risk of the government opposing publication. Their presentations done, they waited for the final ruling from the publisher. He had already made up his mind. But in announcing his decision, Sulzberger didn't make it easy for the editors.

"I've decided you can use the documents—but not the story," he told them. After a moment of stunned silence, it dawned on them that their publisher was joking. Sulzberger was ready to approve the June 13 start of a series with just the balance of documents and analysis that his editors proposed. His major suggestion was for a review procedure to make sure that no military secrets were being published.[10] According to Floyd Abrams, who became part of the legal team defending the *Times* after Lord, Day finally backed down: "In retrospect, the decision [to publish] may seem obvious, but it was by no means an easy one at the time, and it remains one for which Sulzberger deserves enormous credit."[11]

Back at the Hilton, Sheehan had gotten to drafting the third of the installments to run in the series now dubbed Vietnam Archive. The decision had been reached earlier to start the archive with the 1964 Tonkin Gulf incident, which President Lyndon Johnson had used to widen the war. When the series reverted to a chronology, the earliest chapters would be written by Fox Butterfield.

The first day's thirteen-paragraph introduction, being crafted by Frankel, caused problems for some on the team. "Usually we lead with the strongest thing, but you had to read to the jump to see what it was really about," Butterfield says. "Neil and Rick (Smith) were unhappy with the way it was toned down, too," he adds. "It was as if you'd thrown a grenade in the room and then tried to cover it up."[12] The first day's story ran with a Sheehan byline:

VIETNAM ARCHIVE: PENTAGON STUDY TRACES 3 DECADES OF GROWING U.S. INVOLVEMENT

A massive study of how the United States went to war in Indochina, conducted by the Pentagon three years ago, demonstrates that four Administrations progressively developed a sense of commitment to a non-Communist Vietnam, a readiness to fight the North to protect the South, and an ultimate frustration with this effort—to a much greater extent than their public statements acknowledged at the time.[13]

An accompanying page-one story by Smith was headed "Vast Study of War Took a Year." Even if the treatment was too low key for some of the writers, the Sunday blockbuster was in print.

Then came the reaction—or rather the lack of it. At first, other media did not seem to notice the *Times*'s monumental project. Sunday was the slowest day of the week. Still, even the wire services left it alone. Had the weak opening fooled readers into thinking this was just another war story?

An exception was the *Washington Post*, which played the story prominently. It soon became clear that editors there saw themselves as badly scooped. They scrambled to find a copy of the Pentagon Papers for themselves. Finally one television network did pick up the story on Monday night. Harry Reasoner started his CBS broadcast with: "The *New York Times* has begun publication of what is an extraordinary achievement in journalism."[14] The *Times* staffers at the Hilton watched intently and felt some relief.

I Am Not a Weakling

The Nixon administration had also seemed to ignore the Sunday exclusive in the *Times*. For one thing, the archive shared the Sunday front page with presidential daughter Tricia Nixon's wedding. For another, Democratic presidents bore the brunt of the blame for Vietnam deception because the archive stopped before Nixon took office. The Pentagon Papers story was pushed toward the back sheets of the White House daily news summary. With Monday's second installment in the *Times*, however, the administration's view began to change drastically.[15]

One account of President Nixon's Monday communications suggested that national security advisor Henry Kissinger, concerned about the Paris peace talks being compromised, created a "frenzy" by playing to his boss' fear of leaks. Kissinger told the president that permitting publication would "show you're a weakling." People in the Justice Department took a firm anti-*Times* stand too.[16]

On Monday evening, a message came to Sulzberger's office from Attorney General John N. Mitchell: publishing the Pentagon Papers was illegal and "will cause irreparable injury to the defense interests of the United States." Mitchell "respectfully" requested that no further information from the study appear.

With the Tuesday paper being readied for publication, the *Times* brain trust tried to reach Sulzberger in London. As Rosenthal waited, he considered calling the press room and saying "Stop the presses!" That was something he had never done. Instead, he asked the supervisor to "slow things down a bit." When Sulzberger was finally on the phone, the course of action was briefly discussed. General counsel Goodale was strongly in favor of continuing with publication, as were all the editors. When Sulzberger asked if publication would increase the *Times*'s liability, Goodale answered, "Not by five percent." The publisher gave the go-ahead. First Amendment authority Floyd Abrams and his former Yale constitutional law teacher, Alexander Bickel, were retained to lead the legal fight.[17]

On the day of the third installment, the *Times*'s lawyers lost their bid to block a temporary restraining order, which the Justice Department had based on claims of irreparable injury to the nation. Prior restraint in the past had been viewed as acceptable only in the case of clear danger to a war effort, such as a newspaper's decision to print troop-ship timetables. Judge Murray I. Gurfein's TRO, which happened to come on his second day on the federal bench, was the first peacetime application of prior restraint. Faced with another choice—whether to honor the court order—the *Times* chose to halt publication and prepare a legal fight for the right to publish.[18]

Meanwhile the *Washington Post* had managed to get four thousand pages of the Pentagon Papers from Ellsberg. An editor had hauled a cardboard box of them down from Boston on an empty first-class seat he bought next to his own. It was a monumental job of reading, sorting, and annotating—done for the most part at Bradlee's Georgetown house—but an installment was quickly prepared for publication. It was ready just as the *Times* interrupted its series. Still, the *Post* needed the go-ahead from its publisher, Katharine Graham. And that decision was every bit as risky as the *Times*'s. The paper's parent company was about to go public. A felony conviction for espionage would chill that prospect and could also threaten its ability to retain ownership of lucrative television stations. After clearing publication with the *Post* lawyers, Bradlee called Graham. Her answer: "Okay, I say let's go. Let's publish."[19]

Hurray for the *Post*, Darn 'Em

The *Times* reporters at the New York Hilton, still pounding out installments that now might not run at all, were torn by the developments. "We were very upset to be enjoined, and then when the *Washington Post* picked them up there were mixed emotions," says Fox Butterfield. "We were amazed that these people could produce stories in a couple of days, when it had taken us months. On the one hand we were cheering them on for continuing to publish. On the other, we felt sabotaged."[20]

Shortly, however, the *Post* was enjoined as well. And a series of court battles began, providing some of the most inspiring judicial language ever about the media. The first such ruling came when Judge Gurfein, a former Army intelligence officer, lifted his restraining order. He had found that when pressed the government was unable to identify specific portions of the Pentagon Papers that could injure the United States if revealed. He wrote:

> The security of the Nation is not at the ramparts alone. Security also lies in the value of our free institutions. A cantankerous press, an obstinate press, a ubiquitous press must be suffered by those in authority in order to preserve the even greater values of freedom of expression and the right of the people to know. . . .
>
> In the last analysis it is not merely the opinion of the editorial writer or of the columnist which is protected by the First Amendment. It is the free flow of information so that the public will be informed about the Government and its actions.[21]

The government appealed that decision, and the Supreme Court set an expedited hearing date. Each day, however, was another infringement of the long-held principle barring prior restraint.

As other papers began publishing parts of the Pentagon Papers, new injunctions were issued. (Among the papers obtaining their own copies were the *Boston Globe*, the *Los Angeles Times*, the *Chicago Sun-Times*, the *St. Louis Post-Dispatch*, and the Knight newspapers.) Attorney Alexander Bickel argued on behalf of the *New York Times*:

> Prior restraints fall on speech with a brutality and a finality all their own. Even if they are ultimately lifted, they cause irremediable loss, a loss in the immediacy, the impact of speech. They differ from the imposition of criminal liability in significant procedural respects as well, which in turn have their substantive consequences. The violator of a prior restraint may be assured of being held in contempt. The violator of a statute punishing speech criminally knows that he will go before a jury, and may be willing to take his chance, counting on a possible acquittal. A prior restraint therefore stops more speech, more effectively. A criminal statute chills. The prior restraint freezes.[22]

Even the government prosecutor, Solicitor General Erwin N. Griswold, was by then half-hearted in his argument. (Griswold was to write eighteen

FIGURE 15.1 The *New York Times* reporter Neil Sheehan in 1972. *Source*: Photo by Barton Silverman. Copyright © 1972, The New York Times Company. Reprinted by permission.

years later in a *Post* op-ed piece: "I have never seen any trace of a threat to the national security from the Pentagon Papers' publication. Indeed, I have never seen it even suggested that there was an actual threat.")

The Supreme Court ruled six-to-three in favor of the *Times* and the *Post*, with Justice Hugo L. Black writing:

> The press was protected so that it could bare the secrets of government. Only a free and unrestrained press can effectively expose deception in government. And paramount among the responsibilities of a free press is the duty to prevent any part of the government from deceiving

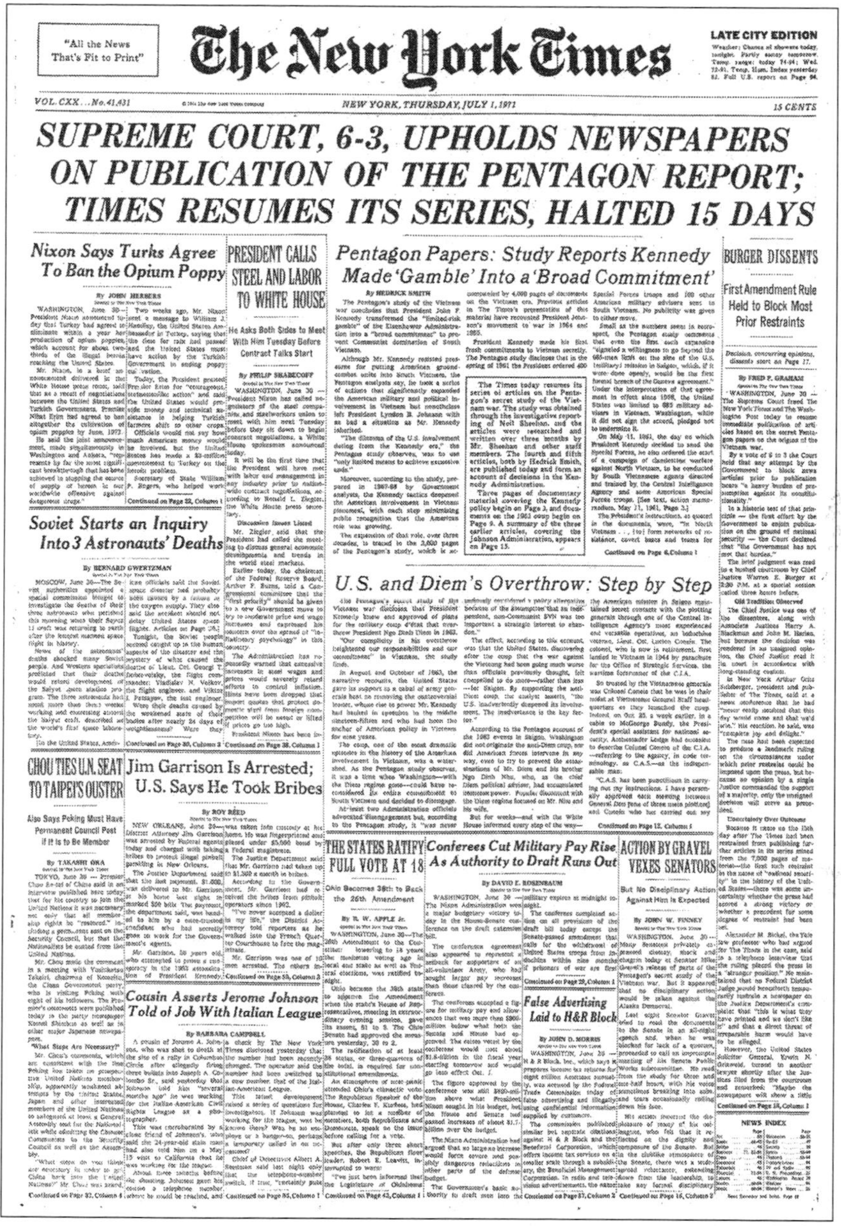

"All the News That's Fit to Print"

The New York Times

LATE CITY EDITION

VOL. CXX ... No. 41,431 — NEW YORK, THURSDAY, JULY 1, 1971 — 15 CENTS

SUPREME COURT, 6-3, UPHOLDS NEWSPAPERS ON PUBLICATION OF THE PENTAGON REPORT; TIMES RESUMES ITS SERIES, HALTED 15 DAYS

Nixon Says Turks Agree To Ban the Opium Poppy

PRESIDENT CALLS STEEL AND LABOR TO WHITE HOUSE

He Asks Both Sides to Meet With Him Tuesday Before Contract Talks Start

Pentagon Papers: Study Reports Kennedy Made 'Gamble' Into a 'Broad Commitment'

BURGER DISSENTS

First Amendment Rule Held to Block Most Prior Restraints

Soviet Starts an Inquiry Into 3 Astronauts' Deaths

U.S. and Diem's Overthrow: Step by Step

CHOU TIES U.N. SEAT TO TAIPEI'S OUSTER

Also Says Peking Must Have Permanent Council Post if It Is to Be Member

Jim Garrison Is Arrested; U.S. Says He Took Bribes

THE STATES RATIFY FULL VOTE AT 18

Ohio Becomes 38th to Back the 26th Amendment

Conferees Cut Military Pay Rise As Authority to Draft Runs Out

ACTION BY GRAVEL VEXES SENATORS

But No Disciplinary Action Against Him Is Expected

Cousin Asserts Jerome Johnson Told of Job With Italian League

False Advertising Laid to H&R Block

NEWS INDEX

FIGURE 15.2 The *New York Times* front page of July 1, 1971, leads with the Supreme Court decision and carries a new installment of the Pentagon Papers Vietnam Archive after an interruption. *Source*: Copyright © 1971, The New York Times Company. Reprinted by permission.

the people and sending them off to distant lands to die of foreign fevers and foreign shot and shell. In my view, far from deserving condemnation for their courageous reporting, the New York Times and the Washington Post and other newspapers should be commended for serving the purpose that the Founding Fathers saw so clearly. In revealing the workings of government, that led to the Vietnam War, the newspapers nobly did precisely that which the founders hoped and trusted they would do.[23]

Seventeen days after the first *Times* story, the *Times* and the *Post* resumed running the Pentagon Papers. Editors emerged from the experience awed by the Supreme Court's support—and relieved at the bullet the press had dodged. Looking back at the June 15 front page, which had carried the headline "Mitchell Seeks to Halt Series on Vietnam But Times Refuses," managing editor Rosenthal ruminated

> that if it had said, "The Times Agrees," the history of this paper and I believe of American journalism, would have been radically different. If we had surrendered to Mitchell, and had allowed the government, without a court battle, to dictate to us, I really believe that the heart would have gone out of the paper and American newspapering.[24]

After such a victory, one might expect a Pulitzer Public Service Medal for the *Times* to be nearly automatic. The public service jurors saw it that way, unanimously recommending a joint award for the newspaper and for Neil Sheehan. "It is fortuitous that the Pulitzer Prizes can recognize the accomplishments of both the newspaper and of a persistent, courageous reporter, and thus reaffirm to the American people that the press continues its devotion to their right to know, a basic bulwark in our democratic society," the jury wrote.[25]

But the board was divided. Before the session, Ben Bradlee lobbied board chairman Joseph Pulitzer Jr., editor and publisher of the *Post-Dispatch* (and JP II's son), arguing that the *Times* and the *Post* should both receive special citations. The *Times* should not win a prize for "anything hand-delivered by a single source to a newspaper," according to Bradlee. (He later relented, supporting the public service award for the *Times*.[26]) Leading the campaign for the *Times*, and the *Times* alone, to win the gold medal was chairman Pulitzer. On the other side was the *Wall Street Journal* editor Vermont Connecticut Royster, who had concerns "about the propriety of such an award," according to Pulitzer administrator John Hohenberg. "As the debate flagged, one of the board's members finally asked Royster with elaborate casualness, 'Vermont, if the Wall Street Journal had had the Pentagon papers, would you have published them?' Without a moment's hesitation, Royster answered, 'Yes.'"

At that point the board decided that its members could agree on the value of acknowledging the *Times*'s public service. The vote was unanimous, although the board worded the citation purely to honor the act of publishing the Pentagon Papers. From the beginning, the jury's proposal for Sheehan to receive his own prize was "set aside as a complicating factor."

Another barrier developed to the *Times* receiving the prize though: the twenty-two-member Columbia University Board of Trustees. Under the original terms of the Pulitzer Prizes, trustees could disapprove the decisions of the Pulitzer board, although they were not permitted to pick a substitute winner. The trustees had never before given such a disapproval. But on Sunday, April 30, they held a marathon closed session and twice informally voted down the award to the *Times*—along with a National Reporting Prize that the board had recommended for columnist Jack Anderson for work unrelated to the Pentagon Papers. After the voting, Columbia president William J. McGill asked them to reconsider. Finally the trustees agreed to let the awards stand. Without mentioning specific prizes, the trustees added a statement that had "the selections been those of the Trustees alone, certain of the recipients would not have been chosen."[27]

Awarding the prize to the *Times* in such a way—over the trustees' objection and without mentioning Sheehan—was an imperfect solution. Further, the citation itself said nothing of the journalism that had gone into interpreting the Pentagon Papers. And there was no recognition of other newspapers that had taken up the cause when the *Times* was enjoined, securing their own copies of the Pentagon Papers and publishing them under many of the same threats that the *Times* faced.

For many of those news organizations that was a defining moment too. Ben Bradlee later wrote that with the decision to publish, "the ethos of the paper changed, and . . . crystallized for editors and reporters everywhere how independent and determined and confident of its purpose the new *Washington Post* had become." The experience created "a sense of confidence within the *Post*, a sense of mission and agreement on new goals, and how to attain them. . . . After the Pentagon Papers, there would be no decision too difficult for us to overcome together."[28] It would only take a year to test that sense of confidence at the *Post*.

1972—The *New York Times* for the publication of the Pentagon Papers.[29]

CHAPTER 16

ALL THE EDITOR'S MEN

1973: Watergate and the *Post*

People don't win Pulitzer Prizes by being for; they usually win them by being against.

—PRESIDENT RICHARD M. NIXON, TO THE NATIONAL
ASSOCIATION OF BROADCASTERS, MARCH 19, 1974

Bob Woodward had not seen the movie *All the President's Men* for twenty-five years. Then one day in mid-2005 he sat down with his eight-year-old daughter Diana while she watched it for the first time. Noticing her squirming a bit, the *Washington Post* assistant managing editor asked what she was thinking. "The guy pretending to be you doesn't look like you at all," Diana told him. And what else? "Boring, boring, boring," she said. "And she's exactly right," Woodward agrees, chuckling—not just about the movie, but about the nature of the Watergate investigation itself. "Because it's about fitting little pieces together. You don't know what you have when you publish a little piece, but you publish it anyway."[1]

Any squirming of his own on the topic of Watergate may have more to do with how often he has been asked over the years to rehash the role of "Woodstein"—as the *Post* editors nicknamed the duo of Woodward and Carl Bernstein during their investigation—in the events that led to President Richard Nixon's August 1974 resignation. Just a few months before the father–daughter movie viewing, another flurry of national publicity erupted when Deep Throat chose to identify himself. Woodward's celebrated secret source turned out to be W. Mark Felt, the number two man at the Federal Bureau of Investigation during the time of the Watergate probe. (A smoke-wreathed Hal Holbrook, stepping from behind pillars in an eerie, dark garage, played him in the 1976 film.)

Alan Pakula's movie—with Robert Redford and Dustin Hoffman as Woodward and Bernstein and Jason Robards as the *Post* executive editor Ben Bradlee—actually holds up well today. For adults, at least, it now plays as a historical/political thriller. The mystery is not whether the president will fall but how two reporters and one cantankerous editor helped precipitate it, starting with the simple assignment to report on arrests after a break-in at the Watergate office building's Democratic National Committee offices.

Missing from the film, of course, is a historical perspective tying the Nixon administration's criminal activities to a greater political motive— something that four decades now permits. In recent years Woodward and Bernstein have offered an analysis positing the president's "five wars of Watergate." Starting with attempts to stem the anti–Vietnam War movement, the White House strategy expanded to interfering with perceived enemies in the news media and in the Democratic party, to undermining the legal system by paying hush money to witnesses, and lying to investigators. The final "war" was against history, in the reporters' view, and included the portrayal of spying, burglaries, and dirty tricks against administration targets as "capers" rather than episodes in a coordinated mission to subvert governmental processes.[2]

In one oft-quoted snippet from the White House tape recordings eventually released during the Watergate investigation, Nixon in July 1971—a year before the Watergate break-in—is heard telling chief of staff H. R. "Bob" Haldeman and Secretary of State Henry Kissinger: "We're up against an enemy, a conspiracy. They're using any means. We are going to use any means. Is that clear?"[3]

"Pure Opera Bouffe"

Years before Woodward joined the *Post* in 1971, the journalist believes, a skeptical spirit was growing in the media—a spirit that expanded during the Watergate scandal and to some extent continues today. It was "the back-to-back nature of Vietnam and Watergate" that gave it power. "If Watergate had been isolated, the impact wouldn't have been the same," he says.[4] In Southeast Asia, journalists had dealt with official deception on many levels. Seymour Hersh won the 1970 International Reporting

Pulitzer for his work uncovering the massacre of civilians by American troops in the village of My Lai. His stories had been carried by the small Washington-based Dispatch News Service but had been published by newspapers around the country.

At home, war protests created divisions in the media just as those protests widened the schism between Americans. During that time—marked by the tumultuous 1968 Democratic National Convention and the shootings of Kent State University students by Ohio National Guardsmen at a 1970 antiwar rally—many reporters developed a keen "question authority" mindset. And in Richard Nixon's White House, war protests fed his paranoia about the president's vulnerability, compounding his conviction that all opponents of his administration needed to be controlled.

The blue-bound Pulitzer Prize entry folders submitted by managing editor Howard Simons in late January 1973—months before the Nixon administration's role in the Watergate break-in was confirmed in any courtroom—offer one striking picture of the role of two young reporters and a courageous newspaper in exposing that insidious White House philosophy. Rather than any grand campaign, the folders present the matter-of-fact nature of the early *Post* coverage and how it built into a riveting drama mainly through accumulation. He filed two Pulitzer entries: one for public service for the paper and one for national reporting in the names of Woodward and Bernstein individually.[5]

The step-by-step nature of the *Post*'s Watergate reporting is what Bob Woodward still feels is not well understood. During a dinner he had with Al Gore during President George W. Bush's administration, for example, Woodward even challenged the former vice president's view of what the *Post* had done in 1972. Gore—briefly a visiting journalism professor at Columbia University after leaving office and a reporter with Nashville's *Tennessean* in the early 1970s—"talked about the purity of the Watergate stories." He said, 'Those were so wonderful, and now you write about Bush and you don't nail him,'" according to Woodward, then the *Post*'s associate editor. "And I said to him, 'You have consumed the Kool-Aid of the mythology of Watergate.' Because those stories were incremental, they were not perfect. They contained some mistakes, they contained some under-reaching, some over-reaching. It's what you would expect. It's daily reporting. We didn't say, 'In an outrageous violation of all constitutional principles. . . . ' We just said, 'This happened.' Very bland, bloodless, if you will. Not in the Pulitzer advocacy tradition." And, he adds, perhaps thinking back to his recent movie-viewing experience, "there was no music in the background."[6]

Here is how Howard Simons summarized that "bland, bloodless" work in the nomination letter that the managing editor hoped would fit the *Post* entry into the Pulitzer public-service tradition:

> It began as pure opera bouffe—four men, gloved and masked, breaking into Democratic National Committee headquarters in the dark of a summer night, armed with walkie-talkies and sophisticated electronic bugging devices. They even called it a caper.
>
> But this was the Watergate Case, the biggest political scandal of the decade.
>
> As this is written five men have pleaded guilty. Two more are on trial. A high White House official has been eased out of his job. The treasurer of the Committee to Re-Elect the President has resigned in protest. A Senate investigation is underway. The Administration has been politically embarrassed.
>
> The word "Watergate" has become a symbol for the deterioration of the American political ethic.
>
> All of this has happened as the result of the journalistic efforts of The Washington Post, its reporters—Carl Bernstein and Robert Woodward—editors, editorial writers and its cartoonist.[7]

It was a fine nomination letter, but the public service jurors were not persuaded. In March they made the *Post* only their third choice. It would take another month of confirming news to create media understanding of the *Post*'s real contributions. Only then was the full Pulitzer board able to find it worthy of the gold medal.

Tip of the Day: Choose the Front Row

The *Post* got onto the story fast that June 17 Saturday morning through a telephone tip to Simons within hours of the burglars' arrest. That call came from attorney Joseph Califano, who had been counsel to both the

Democratic Party and the *Post* in the past. Alerted by the managing editor, longtime police reporter Alfred E. Lewis accompanied the acting police chief to the crime scene and spent hours behind police lines. Other police reporters remained outside. Woodward—an ambitious first-year *Post* reporter not particularly enthused by having to cover a hearing related to a local break-in—went to the burglars' arraignment. He was in the front row to hear defendant James McCord tell the judge his last place of employment. It was the Central Intelligence Agency.

"No three letters in the English language, arranged in that particular order, and spoken in similar circumstances, can tighten a good reporter's sphincter faster than C-I-A," executive editor Ben Bradlee later wrote. (Carl Bernstein recalls Woodward's two-word reaction: "Holy shit."[8]) By the end of the day, ten reporters were working the story, including Bernstein, who explored the Miami connections that the burglars seemed to have. Both he and Woodward contributed to the main Sunday story, appearing under Lewis's byline. After that, Woodward and Bernstein were the natural choices to stay with it, at least in the early stages when it appeared to be the very "third-rate burglary" that President Nixon's press secretary described.[9]

"They got the story assigned to them because they were the first two reporters identifying themselves that Saturday morning," Bradlee said with a laugh. "The big shots don't work on Saturdays." The tougher assignment decision came later: keeping them on Watergate after they began turning up strong White House connections. "There were a few people on the national staff who wanted the story. You'd ask them, 'What fault do you find with Woodward and Bernstein, and what reason are you going to give for taking it away from them?' Then, opposition pretty much disappeared," according to Bradlee, who died in October 2014.[10]

They quickly made the most of the pairing. Professionally, they complemented each other well despite their many differences. Bernstein's reporting drive combined with a notoriously mercurial personality that often got him in trouble with editors. There was an office story, for example, about his forgetting a rental car he parked in a garage, running up a huge tab for the paper. For his part, the Yale-educated Woodward, though newer to journalism, had served as a naval officer and had chosen journalism over going to Harvard Law School. "Both are bright, but Woodward was

FIGURE 16.1 The *Washington Post* reporters Carl Bernstein (left) and Bob Woodward meet with publisher Katharine Graham during their 1972 Watergate reporting. *Source*: *Post* staff photo. Published by permission of the *Washington Post*.

conscientious, hardworking, and driven, and Bernstein messy and undisciplined. He was, however, the better writer, more imaginative and creative," the *Post* publisher Katharine Graham wrote in her 1997 autobiography. "In other ways the relationship was oil and water, but the end product came out right, despite—or perhaps because of—the strange mix."[11]

Woodward describes the imperfect art of newsroom teaming as "assembling the perfect journalistic brain, something no one person has that I know of." He notes, "Carl Bernstein and I never really look at things the same way, even to this day." But there was one big plus to their collaboration, Woodward points out: total-immersion coverage caused no problems at home. "We were young and unmarried, Carl and I."[12]

Their reporting encountered lots of dead ends, and some smaller threads of information led down curious alleys but turned up nothing definitive. Still, there were enough exclusives to keep Bradlee in their camp. "They got the White House involvement. They identified the money. They tied the money to the Committee to Re-Elect the President. And this was all Woodward and Bernstein, these nonentity reporters," according to Bradlee.[13]

The headline on their Monday, June 19, collaboration read: "GOP Security Aide Among 5 Arrested In Bugging Affair." Under the heat of a deadline, Bernstein literally snatched the final writing job away from Woodward, who had to concede that his new teammate had a gift for banging out clear, fast copy. The story started:

> One of the five men arrested early Saturday in the attempt to bug the Democratic National Committee headquarters here is the salaried security coordinator for President Nixon's re-election committee.
>
> The suspect, James W. McCord Jr., 53, also holds a separate contract to provide security services to the Republican National Committee, GOP national chairman Bob Dole said yesterday.

The news for Tuesday's paper did not develop until after midnight, when a night police reporter for the *Post*, Eugene Bachinski, called Woodward. A source at the station had told Bachinski of two interesting entries found in notebooks taken from the burglars. The story was another scoop, under E. J. Bachinski's and Woodward's names:

> A consultant to White House special counsel Charles W. Colson is listed in the address books of two of the five men arrested in an attempt to bug the Democratic National headquarters here early Saturday.
>
> Federal sources close to the investigation said the address books contain the name and home telephone number of Howard E. Hunt, with the notations, "W. House" and "W. H."

The world would learn one day that it was E. Howard Hunt, not Howard E. (He gained an infamous Watergate footnote for having performed some political dirty tricks while disguised in a cheap red wig.) To track down Hunt, Woodward first called the White House and got a number where he could be contacted. Finally reaching Hunt, the reporter asked him why his name was in the Watergate burglars' notebooks. Hunt said, "Good God!" He then mumbled "no comment" and hung up.

Now It Can Be Told

Helping link Hunt to the case was the man Howard Simons had dubbed Deep Throat after the pornographic movie with the same title—and because of the man's arrangement with Woodward that his information would be for "deep background," not publishable unless confirmed independently. His guidance was vital though. To Woodward, the appearance of Hunt's name in the notebooks was far from proof of complicity. "I called Felt twice that day," says Woodward of the long-secret contact he now can discuss freely. "Felt said to me, 'Don't worry, he's involved. He's at the center of things.'"[14] The high-level confirmation was what the *Post* needed to run with that story.

In the office, Bradlee was an editorial model of tough love, and he radiated aggressiveness. "It was 'go get 'em, kid; there aren't limits here,'" says Woodward, who had been at the *Post* only nine months the day he called the White House to find Howard Hunt. Amazingly, the cub reporter was not nervous for that first call. "And that's not because of me; that's because of the atmosphere of 'go get 'em, kid,'" says Woodward. Still, Jason Robards got Bradlee's demanding side right, Woodward says. "Those scenes of his slapping the copy and saying, 'You haven't got it, kid'—you want to strangle him, but that didn't mean 'I don't believe it.' That didn't mean 'We're not going to publish it.' It meant 'Work harder; get more sources; make sure it rings with me.'"[15]

The next major exclusive ran on August 1. In Miami, Bernstein tracked down an explanation for how a $25,000 cashier's check to the president's re-election campaign found its way into the Florida account of a Watergate burglar. Then on September 17 the reporters established that the fund paying the burglars was controlled by top aides to former Nixon campaign manager John Mitchell. (As attorney general, the same Mitchell had sought to enjoin the *Times* from publishing the Pentagon Papers in June 1971.)

Another *Post* blockbuster came on October 1. Mitchell, while still attorney general, had personally controlled a secret fund to spy on the Democrats. The story quoted Mitchell's response to Bernstein, who called him for comment at 11:30 p.m.: "All that crap, you're putting it in the paper? It's all been denied. Jesus. Katie Graham . . . is gonna get caught in a big fat wringer if that's published. Good Christ. That's the most sickening thing I've ever heard." It is well known now that Mitchell actually said that the publisher would get "her tit caught" in that wringer. "Leave everything in but 'her tit,' and tell the desk I said it's okay," the executive editor had said to Bernstein. (The publisher later wrote that Bradlee did not check with her before running the quote—and she added that it was "especially strange of [Mitchell] to call me Katie, which no one has ever called me.")

Nine days later, Howard Hunt's phone records led to another *Post* exclusive. He had made numerous calls to a California lawyer, Donald Segretti, who turned out to be involved in a broad network of campaign dirty tricks. The October 10 Woodward and Bernstein story began:

> FBI agents have established that the Watergate bugging incident stemmed from a massive campaign of political spying and sabotage conducted on behalf of President Nixon's re-election and directed by officials of the White House and the Committee for the Re-election of the President.
>
> The activities, according to information in FBI and Department of Justice files, were aimed at all the major Democratic presidential candidates and—since 1971—represented a basic strategy of the re-election effort.

Included was information tying the White House to a range of tricks, including some involving the Muskie presidential bid that had come apart in New Hampshire. Mark Felt had been a secret source on this story as well. The FBI was following the tricksters too. (Watergate burglars had also orchestrated a break-in at the Los Angeles office of Pentagon Papers leaker Daniel Ellsberg's psychiatrist.)

To get the demanding Bradlee to sign off on any story that the reporters' digging produced, the *Post* set a tougher-than-usual standard for getting information confirmed before publication. Bradlee required at least two solid, independent sources if the information was from individuals who would not allow their names to be used. "It grew out of paranoia," Woodward says of the rule. "Some source could be spinning you. And a second element was the seriousness of the charges. You're accusing someone of criminal, unethical behavior."[16]

Among perhaps two hundred Watergate stories the *Post* did in 1972, Anthony Marro lists only those of August 1, September 17, October 1, and October 10 as breaking "significant new ground." Still, following Woodward and Bernstein on their daily reports was exhausting, says Marro, whose *Newsday* was one of the few papers that tried hard to compete on the story. *Newsday* saw it as part of its investigative tradition and also felt a duty to follow up on previous investigations it had done into President Nixon's personal and business relationships. "You worked all day and all night, and everybody was under a tremendous amount of pressure, and we were still getting beat," Marro says.[17] Woodward does not disagree with Tony Marro that those few 1972 stories stood out. In between them, though, were dozens of smaller ones that would lead the reporters down the path, stone by stone, to the Oval Office.

"There'd be a little story on [page] B-38 about the expensive receiver that the Watergate burglars used to monitor the calls. A $3,000 receiver from a firm in Rockville called Watkins-Johnson—only I remember it," Woodward says. "Now $3,000 for a radio receiver was a lot of money. That story really didn't lead anywhere, except that it told you that this was a really well-financed operation. As you get these details and add them together, the facts created the momentum for understanding what was really happening."[18]

Avoiding the I-Word

As the pair worked on, Bradlee tried to insulate them from the heat of internal and external criticism—and from apathy from the rest of the media. "We knew at the time that people didn't believe what we'd written. Many of our colleagues on the *Washington Post* national staff didn't believe it," Woodward says, recalling how hard it was for a young reporter to accept that. Just as hard to accept were the daily Nixon administration denials and attacks on the *Post*. "The effort to discredit our reporting was staggering, unparalleled," says Woodward. "It gets your attention when you turn on the television and there you are, just roundly denounced. And you know what you wrote is right, and carefully done." But the interviewing and writing demands were so intense through the summer of 1972 that the two reporters had little time to worry about such things. Likewise, they gave little thought to how high in the administration the reporting might lead. "You kept your head down and stayed focused on the next story," Woodward says.

There was one moment, though, just before the October 1 story on Mitchell's control of the secret fund, when Woodward and Bernstein had a candid discussion in the *Post* cafeteria. "I put a dime in the coffee machine—that's what coffee cost then—and I felt a literal chill go down my neck," according to Bernstein. "I can still feel it today. And I turned to Woodward and I said, 'Oh my God, this president is going to be impeached.'" Woodward replied, "You're right. But we'll never be able to use that word."[19]

Even when things went wrong on a story the executive editor and managing editor stood up for "Woodstein." Bradlee and Simons had built up a strong editing crew to handle continuing Watergate-related news. "It takes a particular kind of energy and courage on the part of editors and publishers to support daily incremental coverage," says Woodward. At the time the *Post* did not have a standing investigative team with its own dedicated editors. Such editing—along with the extra time newspapers can give to special project reporting—sometimes makes catching potential errors easier.

The best known of Woodward and Bernstein's mistakes would probably have slipped through any editing processes. While he was interviewing Nixon re-election committee treasurer Hugh Sloan in late October, Woodward misunderstood what the official said about whether his grand jury testimony included mention of presidential chief of staff Bob Haldeman as one of the five officials controlling the secret fund that financed campaign dirty tricks. Flawed *Post* "confirmations" of what Woodward believed he had heard from Sloan led to an inaccuracy in an October 25 story. Sloan had not identified Haldeman before the grand jury. The error brought ringing denials from all over the administration and forced the *Post* to pull back to discover what had gone wrong.[20]

It would eventually come out that Haldeman *was* the fifth controlling person but that the grand jury had not asked Sloan about Haldeman, so Sloan had not mentioned his name. Still, the error gave ammunition to

Post critics. "You shouldn't make any mistakes, and the Haldeman story was a mistake," says Woodward.[21] Bradlee wrote of the error: "Mercifully for us, on the afternoon of October 26, Henry Kissinger gave a press conference at the White House to announce that 'peace was at hand in Vietnam,' and that gave us a little breathing room, since it occupied both the press and the Nixon administration."[22]

Soon Woodward and Bernstein returned to form. They would continue to lead the nation in coverage of Watergate-related stories through December 31 (the last day of eligibility for the next year's Pulitzers) and on into 1973 and 1974.

Along with the package of news stories in the 1973 Pulitzer Public Service entry, the *Post* submitted a dozen editorials by Phil Geyelin and Roger Wilkins. On the very first day after the break-in, one editorial appeared called "Mission Incredible," opening with the line: "As always, should you or any of your force be caught or killed, the Secretary will disavow any knowledge of your actions." Among the cartoons submitted in the package, one by Herblock, as Herbert Block signed his work, depicted a family on a guided White House tour. The mother had strayed down a stairway into a sludge-encrusted basement area filled with "taps," "bugs," "handguns," and "rubber gloves." The caption was "Sorry, Ma'm—The Lower Level Is Not Part of the White House Tour."[23]

"A Pimple on the Elephant's Ass"

Even with its string of exclusive stories, supporting commentary, and dramatic cover letter, the *Post's* bid for a Pulitzer Prize was a tough sell in early March of 1973—in part because of its timing. Many journalists still were suspicious of any stories under the Woodward and Bernstein byline. President Nixon had been inaugurated after his landslide re-election over South Dakota Senator George McGovern. Most Washington correspondents had made the *campaign*, not Watergate, the main story.

It had been such a strange contest, with one Democrat after another seemingly stumbling into some great gaffe. First Maine Senator Edmund Muskie withdrew after being embarrassed on the eve of the New Hampshire primary. The *Manchester Union-Leader* had received a mysterious letter suggesting that the senator condoned use of the slur word "Canuck" for French-Canadians. And later McGovern vice presidential choice Thomas Eagleton, a Missouri senator, withdrew after press reports that he had been treated for clinical depression in the past. A black cloud seemed to hang over the Democrats all the way to their flop at the polls. Surely this had been the real story, many journalists thought at the time—far bigger than a peculiar June 17 attempt to bug the Democrats, which had resulted in guilty pleas by men whose suspected ties to the Nixon campaign were all officially denied.[24]

None of the five public service jurors who convened on March 8 and 9 was from Washington, New York, or Los Angeles, where Watergate stories had been in the news more regularly. One juror was from Portland, Maine, and the others were from Chicago, Kansas City, Salt Lake City, and Riverside, California. Their overwhelming first choice was the *Chicago Tribune* for a probe of primary election violations that had led to indictments and convictions. Articles on police corruption by the *New York Times*, the previous year's winner for the Pentagon Papers, earned that paper a spot ahead of the *Post* as well.

In notes submitted to the Pulitzer board, the jury said that one juror had ranked it second and three ranked it third. "However, a fifth juror gave it a substantially lower rating on the ground that the Post had over-indulged professional restraints on unattributed information in order to make its point."[25] (Woodward laughs when first told of the argument from the work's detractor. "We weren't trying to make a point," he says.[26]) Beyond that, some jurors felt that office break-ins and campaign slush funds were relatively small potatoes, even if the reporting was correct. One unidentified juror told a Columbia official: "Watergate is only a pimple on the elephant's ass."[27]

The view of the *Post*'s coverage changed dramatically before the Pulitzer board met to choose their winners though. On April 5, Watergate break-in suspect James McCord, the former CIA man, told federal judge John J. Sirica that there had been White House pressure to keep the defendants silent. As more high-level figures then became implicated in the break-in and cover-up, others in the media began publishing stories that confirmed

CONFIDENTIAL · CATEGORY ONE

REPORT OF THE PUBLIC SERVICE JURY
PULITZER PRIZES FOR 1973

(1) For a distinguished example of meritorious public service by a newspaper through the use of its journalistic resources which may include editorials, cartoons, and photographs, as well as reporting, a gold medal.

To the Advisory Board on the Pulitzer Prizes

We, the members of the jury assigned to making recommendations in the Public Service category present for your consideration the following entries in order of our preference:

(1) Chicago Tribune, nominated by Clayton Kirkpatrick, editor: Expose of vote fraud in Chicago. 116.

The Chicago Tribune by persistent probing uncovered flagrant violations of voting procedures in the primary election which resulted in indictments and convictions of a number of persons. This entry was the first choice of four out of five jurors.

(2) New York Times, nominated by A. M. Rosenthal, managing editor: Investigation of municipal corruption and the erosion of criminal justice in New York City. 148.

The Times' articles on corruption in the Police Department, the construction trades and the courts were a courageous and imaginative application of the resources of a large and talented staff.

This entry was the second choice of three of the five jurors.

(3) Washington Post, nominated by Howard Simons, managing editor: Investigation of the Watergate case. 131.

The Washington Post, despite obstacles placed in its path by politicians and use of intimidation tactics, continued on a determined course to reveal the close ties of the Watergate bugging incident and White House personalities.

This entry was the third choice of three of the five jurors and the second choice of another. However, a fifth juror gave it a substantially lower rating on the ground that the Post had overindulged professional restraints on unattributed information in order to make its point.

-more-

CONFIDENTIAL · CATEGORY ONE

Report of the Public Service Jury -- P. 2

(4) Wilmington (Del.) Evening Journal, nominated by Leslie E. Jansler Jr., managing editor: Investigation of narcotics in Delaware. 133.

The Evening Journal did a courageous and thorough job in uncovering the numerous sources of narcotics in Wilmington and naming the pushers.

This was the first choice of one juror.

(5) Chicago Sun Times, nominated by James Hoge, editor: Series on Environment: Troubled Waters. 126.

(6) Buffalo Courier Express, nominated by Douglas L. Turner, executive editor. Investigation of malpractice in city affairs. 137.

Respectfully submitted:

/s/ Arthur C. Deck, executive editor, The Salt Lake Tribune (chairman)
George R. Burg, managing editor, The Kansas City Star
Ernest W. Chard, editor, Guy Gannett Publishing Co., Portland, Me.
Howard H. Hayes Jr., editor and co-publisher, Press-Enterprise Company, Riverside, California
Audrey T. Weaver, city editor, Chicago Daily Defender

March 8, 1973

FIGURE 16.2 The report forwarded to the Pulitzer board by public service jurors in 1973 made the *Washington Post*'s Watergate entry their third choice, after work by the *Chicago Tribune* and the *New York Times*. The board selected the *Post* as the winner. *Source*: Report provided courtesy of the Pulitzer Prizes.

much of what Woodward and Bernstein's hard-won anonymous sources had told them earlier. As Pulitzer Prize administrator John Hohenberg put it:

It was in this charged atmosphere that the Advisory Board met at Columbia on April 12. The same membership as in 1972 met around the black oval table in the World Room under the lighted Statue of Liberty stained glass window, only this time Messrs. Bradlee and Reston were out of the room. . . . Within a few minutes after Chairman [Joseph] Pulitzer [Jr.] had declared himself in favor of the Washington Post for the public service gold medal, all nine Board members in the room agreed to reverse the Public Service Jury.[28]

The Pulitzer board gave the *Tribune* the Spot News Pulitzer after its members had decided on the gold medal for the *Post*.

Bradlee had been prepared to resign from the board if the *Post* had not won for its Watergate coverage.[29] But even after the gold medal was won, he had a delicate job to do: explaining to Woodward and Bernstein that the Public Service Prize was for the newspaper, not for individuals. Officially, they would not be winning it themselves. In fact, the reporters were not listed in the Pulitzer citation. Woodward remembers Bradlee reassuring the reporters that they should not worry because they would forever be identified with Watergate.

"It was one of his all-time understatements," Woodward says.

"I don't consider myself as having ever won a Pulitzer Prize," he adds, "and that is factually correct." As he thinks about it, Woodward

FIGURE 16.3 The *Washington Post* executive editor Ben Bradlee ponders history in the making. The headline reads "Nixon Resigns." *Source*: *Post* staff photo by David R. Legge. Published by permission of the *Washington Post*.

believes it is wise for the Pulitzers to have an award acknowledging a paper and not individuals. "Anything that's a little humbling is a good thing," he says.[30]

"The Light Comes Out in Darkness"

The board never gave an explanation for why the two reporters' names were left off the citation. Reporters by then had been identified in Public Service Prize citations three times: in 1947, 1950, and 1960. Some board members who have served more recently have viewed the omission of Woodward and Bernstein—as well as Neil Sheehan's exclusion from the 1972 *New York Times* citation—as unfortunate mistakes. "It would seem to me to have been entirely appropriate to have named Woodward and Bernstein, and to have named Neil Sheehan. They were central figures and it was their initiatives that led to the Prizes," says Seymour Topping, the retired *New York Times* editor who served as administrator of the Pulitzer Prizes during most of the 1990s.[31]

Gene Roberts, editor of the *Philadelphia Inquirer* during the Watergate years, believes that the public service citation should have named Woodward and Bernstein, but adds that individual Pulitzers should have gone to them as well. In his nine years on the Pulitzer board in the late 1970s and early 1980s, Roberts found the board too reluctant to acknowledge individuals by name when it honored a paper with the gold medal. "I think it's wonderful that the paper would win an award," he says, "but it's even more important to the institution of the Pulitzers to take a step backward and always put the reporters first."[32]

Other board veterans don't think the exclusion of the names is a serious concern. "It's not as if either of them failed to get the accolades," says the retired *Chicago Tribune* editor Jack Fuller. Besides, "Woodward and Bernstein did terrific work, and it was the centerpiece, but the *Post* stuck its neck out big-time and deserved the Public Service award."[33]

Just how exposed it was became apparent when tapes of conversations in Richard Nixon's Oval Office were released. In one conversation on September 15, the day Hunt and the burglars were indicted, the president told some senior aides: "The main thing is that the Post is going to have damnable, damnable problems out of this one. They have a television station . . . and they're going to have to get it renewed. . . . And it's going to be God damn active here. . . . [T]he game has to be played awfully rough."[34] What would people have thought of the Pulitzers had the *Post* not won a prize for its Watergate coverage?

Some board members from later years believe the damage could have been severe. "If the Prize had been awarded two months earlier, it would have been extremely embarrassing for the *Post* not to get the Pulitzer," says Gene Roberts. Seymour Topping agrees and extends that sentiment to the case of the *New York Times*'s publication of the Pentagon Papers the previous year. "Those two achievements were so outstanding that to put them aside would have indicated that there were extraordinary political considerations behind the choices," he says.

For Woodward, some lessons growing out of Watergate were very personal and long lasting. In recent years he has resumed doing "night work," as he calls it—going to interview sources at home after hours as he and Bernstein had done regularly. It was a technique that Bernstein proposed but that Woodward described well by saying that "the light comes out in darkness," according to Bernstein.[35] "That's where you get people alone, away from the office," says Woodward. "Seeing them empty their pockets, as Howard Simons used to say."

Simons, who died in 1989, also gets credit for teaching Woodward a broader life lesson. Just after President Nixon resigned, Simons "called me into his office with these arm motions that only he could do," says Woodward. On the desk was a reporter's recent obituary. "It had a headline like 'Joe Smith, 80, won Pulitzer in 1947.' And Howard said, 'That's you. This guy won the Pulitzer and you never heard from him again. That's what happens. Always remember, you're never going to have a story that has the impact of Watergate. Never.' And then he said the most important thing: 'Now get your ass out of here and get back to work.'"[36]

1973—The *Washington Post* for its investigation
of the Watergate case.[37]

Watergate's Legacy

The *Post*'s coverage of Watergate has continued to be among the most studied cases in journalism schools and—thanks largely to the book and the movie—a topic of general conversation as well. It has been the subject of several academic books as well. When the University of Texas created a home for Woodward and Bernstein's Watergate papers in 2005, Tony Marro, by then the retired *Newsday* editor, led a seminar in Austin to reexamine many Watergate-related questions, including the *Post*'s broad use of anonymous sources and what impact that had on later journalism. His position was that anonymity "can be as addictive as heroin" as sources gradually learn to expect being shielded. And that makes on-the-record material harder to get.[38] (Woodward disagrees that there is an over-reliance on anonymous sources, arguing that granting anonymity remains necessary for reporters to get at hidden truths.)

Another question posed at the Austin seminar: Just how much credit did the press deserve for driving a president from office? Marro, recalling days when he was among the reporters competing with the *Post* for early Watergate stories, argued that the media got too much credit. "The fact is that Nixon was ousted by a constitutional process that involved all three branches of government—criminal investigators, the courts, and the Congress," he told the assembled journalism students. It is a position that Bernstein supports. Calling the press-brings-down-a-president theme "an overstatement," he has said that Nixon's resignation "was about the system working. The legislature, the judiciary: It worked."

Woodward believes, though, that the full impact of the *Post*'s reporting cannot be truly known. Without press exposure, the White House cover-up might well have succeeded in protecting the guilty and obstructing justice enough that the facts remained hidden. After the intricate web of criminality was exposed, about forty people went to jail, including former attorney general John Mitchell, Nixon chief of staff Haldeman, and chief domestic advisor John Ehrlichman. "The truth of the matter is that prosecutors had some of this information, but they didn't use it. And we made it public," Woodward says. The *Post* stories—vehemently attacked at the time as biased, shabby journalism by a White House anxious to isolate the *Post* from the rest of the press—may also have directly led federal judge

John J. Sirica to put pressure on a key defendant, James McCord. Only in April 1973, when McCord began talking about the burglars' ties to the White House, did the conspiracy of silence begin unraveling, eventually setting off the avalanche of confessions and convictions.[39]

The 2012 occasion of the Watergate break-in's fortieth anniversary gave the American Society of News Editors a chance to assemble a panel that included Woodward and Bernstein, who otherwise spend little time together. The topic, "The Digital Age and Investigative Journalism," was largely eclipsed by recollections by the famous pair who covered the original scandal. (The then–*Seattle Times* editor David Boardman set the tone in introducing Woodward and Bernstein by equating the place of their Watergate reporting in American journalism with that of *The Birth of a Nation* in film, *Origin of Species* in science, and The Beatles in rock 'n' roll. Welcome, he said, to "our D. W. Griffith, Charles Darwin, and John, Paul, George, and Ringo.")

Woodward told of Yale University students who had written short papers on how Watergate might be covered today, with one student suggesting that the Internet could have helped root out offenses in the Nixon White House. "I came as close as I [ever] have to having an aneurysm," Woodward told the audience with a laugh. When talking to reluctant sources in 1972 it was often not until "the eighth interview you started getting the real story of what's going on," he said. Bernstein recalled that in some of those interviews, "we encountered incredible fear, bordering on terror" among sources who worried they might be unmasked by the administration.

Amanda Bennett, the executive editor at Bloomberg News when she served on the "Digital Age" panel, garnered agreement when she noted, "despite the talk about the tweets, how little has actually changed" in reporting techniques since Watergate. It is still a process of "just kind of following the string" with diligence and support from editors that leads to success in investigative stories. The *Post*'s Walter Reed Army Hospital disclosures and the *Boston Globe*'s coverage of sex crimes by Catholic priests—Pulitzer Public Service winners in 2008 and 2003, respectively—both were mentioned.[40]

The *Post*'s extraordinary diligence back in 1972 remains unquestioned. As rival reporter Tony Marro has said, "Woodward and Bernstein just worked harder than everyone else." They spent "hundreds and hundreds of hours assembling and updating chronologies and files detailing just who had been accused of what, who had admitted to what, who had pointed the finger at others, and who was still out there—a superior or a subordinate or a partner of the accused—who could fill in what pieces of the puzzle."[41]

And Gene Roberts, then of the *Philadelphia Inquirer*, takes it a giant step further. "It was maybe the single greatest reporting effort of all time," he says.[42]

PART III

Challenges for a New Era

CHAPTER 17

IN WATERGATE'S SHADOW

1970–1978: *Newsday,* the *Inquirer,* and Davids vs. Goliaths

Most of the best journalism is bottom-up, rather than top-down.

—GENE ROBERTS

It may now be a journalistic article of faith that Bob Woodward and Carl Bernstein's work at the *Washington Post* pushed news organizations into making investigative reporting a priority and set American youth dreaming of journalism careers. In the five years leading up to Watergate, though, the number of undergraduate journalism degrees had doubled. And investigative reporting was already experiencing something of a boom, with all reporters having gotten a boost from the federal Freedom of Information Act passed in 1966.[1]

Within a decade of winning the 1954 Pulitzer Gold Medal, *Newsday* was using team techniques that would eventually help it capture the 1970 Public Service Prize and yet another in 1974. Papers like the *Boston Globe* often cited *Newsday* as a model for starting their own teams. And when the national group Investigative Reporters and Editors started up in 1975, *Newsday* was at the center of IRE's effort too.[2]

Truth be told, it was a seriously flawed *Newsday* that won that 1954 Pulitzer. The paper had been responsible for the significant public service of "dethroning DeKoning," as its own corporate history described the exposé that led to William DeKoning's imprisonment. But even that 1990 book by staffer Robert F. Keeler noted that personal conflicts of interest were a driving force as managing editor Alan Hathway launched investigations of the area's labor czar.

In the early years after Alicia Patterson's purchase of the paper in 1940, *Newsday* had treated DeKoning with kid gloves, often concentrating on what appeared to be his philanthropic side. But then Hathway became personally involved with a drive to build an arena for Long Island. It was a move that, "combined with his private ambition to make some money, overruled journalistic common sense," Keeler wrote. Eventually, Hathway's interests had come into conflict with those of DeKoning, who controlled the workforce that was to be involved in building the arena project. And later, when DeKoning also backed a Republican congressional candidate to oppose *Newsday*'s choice for office, that second conflict became a "triggering event that finally pushed Hathway over the edge, prompting him to convert his files on DeKoning into an aggressive series of stories." So much for the "disinterested" nature of the journalism that the gold medal was supposed to recognize. The Pulitzer board probably had no idea.

The 1954 vintage *Newsday* was a weak journalistic model in other ways too. "Seizing her newspaper's greatest moment of glory," wrote Keeler, "Alicia Patterson decided to use the Pulitzer Prize not as a crown of laurel, but as a whip." Sure, that was partly to discourage staffers at the young paper from becoming smug in their success. But more than that, she considered the paper still "minor league" in its editing and its appearance. The copy desk was almost nonexistent, for example, leading to amateurish-style snafus.[3] After she invested heavily in its improvement, the paper was in much better shape by 1963—the year Patterson suddenly died of a stomach ulcer at fifty-six, leaving her wealthy husband to take over. He was Harry Guggenheim, a mining family heir whose relatives had founded New York's Guggenheim Museum with some of the family riches.[4]

The Greene-ing of *Newsday*

Of all of *Newsday*'s investments after winning the 1954 prize, the best might have been the hiring of Robert W. Greene to run investigations for the paper. Bob Greene was a born snoop. He had been doing some kind of investigating since a high school job as a "sniffer" for a department store, checking out the underarms of fancy dresses that women bought and later returned. His olfactory test proved whether a woman had worn the garment to a party before bringing it back for a refund.

In his early newsroom years at another New Jersey paper, other sniffing around led him toward local corruption that warranted a closer study. But Greene left newspaper work for a succession of government crime-busting jobs, where he sharpened his organizational skills and elevated his promotional abilities. Groups like Tennessee Senator Estes Kefauver's subcommittee studying organized crime and the succession of regional crime commissions for which Greene worked were very publicity conscious. By parceling out information to reporters in the late 1950s, commissions taught the public about "a guy by the name of James Hoffa, who nobody really knew at the time," said Greene. At the New York City Anti-Crime Commission, Greene had also been a major source of scoops for *Newsday*, helping reporters bring down DeKoning when it won its 1954 Public Service Prize. After a falling out with New York commissioners in a change of leadership, Greene jumped in 1955 to the paper that he had come to admire for its tenacity and for its shiny gold medal. He quickly built a reputation as a unique newsroom character.[5]

At *Newsday*, he was far from the only one. Greene started out answering to managing editor Hathway, a boisterous, profane Chicago-style chief. In later years Greene laughed when he recalled the strange chemistry in the office during the elegant Mrs. Patterson's frequent visits to Hathway's realm. "He was the barnyard dog. She was the genteel lady," said Greene. "Whenever Hathway wanted something investigated, he'd come to me," according to Greene. The reporter was the classic lone wolf at first, working on his own and keeping his sources to himself. Soon he began to spot ethical problems not only among the people he was investigating but also within *Newsday* itself. He talked about it with other reporters who had observed the same thing. The concerned staffers saw some conflicts of interest involving Hathway. But their greatest concern was with Kirk Price, whose job as the Suffolk editor put him in charge of coverage from that graft-ridden Long Island county.

If Greene began to write stories about abuses by officials in Suffolk County, "it was always a dead-end. You had a feeling you were being pulled off and steered in another direction." He suspected that Price was personally invested in some of the deals that staffers sought to investigate. Later it became more than suspicion. Greene went to Hathway about the problem in the mid-1960s, suggesting that Price be removed from that key job. According to Greene, "Hathway says, 'Absolutely not. Who is telling you this?' " For a time it created a personal crisis for Greene, who wasn't sure whether to stay at the paper. "So now what do you do?" he asked himself. He felt that he couldn't quit. He had two children and had just left the crime commission because of unhappiness with management. He decided to stay. Maybe he could be a force for change at *Newsday*.[6]

From Loner to Wolf Pack Leader

Greene traveled the South in 1964 exposing a yet-again resurgent Ku Klux Klan in a four-part series the tabloid headlined "The Klan Rides Again." In 1967 he went to New Orleans to look into District Attorney Jim Garrison's examination of President Kennedy's assassination. A lover of good food who weighed in at more than three hundred pounds, Greene liked big expense accounts almost as much as he loved big stories. But because Greene turned up dirt in abundance wherever he went, managers tolerated the size of his invoices. He became like Eliot Ness: untouchable.

Then in 1967, Hathway retired, Kirk Price died, and the investigative environment at *Newsday* changed. Bill Moyers, who had served as press secretary during Lyndon Johnson's presidency, became the new publisher. Al Marlens, who like Moyers was known in the office for uncompromising ethics, took over as managing editor. The new Suffolk editor was Art Perfall, who had tried to work on corruption stories under Price and had complained that he "could never get any movement from Kirk."

With Greene on the job, stories came furiously, many of them from the town of Islip. But the investigations quickly spread, exploring corruption as well in a succession of towns across Suffolk and Nassau counties. Greene's own worries about the ethics of his editors were over. Instead he devoted time to selling them on story ideas. Given a few minutes of preparation before talking to an editor, Greene usually found a way. He employed what he called "the red-meat philosophy," a sure-fire way to win over editors who needed persuading about a story. It worked like this: "You get something really good, and you say, Here's what we have already. That's the red meat. Then you say, If you give me time, I can get more. Editors get comfortable if you've got something in your pocket already."

His Suffolk proposal started with the meat of what they knew already: a *Newsday* editor, now deceased, had been involved in suspect deals in the county. Greene promised that he could prove a bigger scandal. From that small start, the first "Greene Team" soon sprouted.[7] Working through the Suffolk office of the Nassau County, New York-based paper, Greene combed through deeds and mortgages, creating paper trails that appeared to lead to various dirty officials. Greene also had a secret source with the federal Internal Revenue Service. The source, whom he nicknamed Zip, steered him toward more irregularities. "I'm saying, This is coming along pretty good, but I need more people to help me," Greene recalled. "They gave me one, and then one more." News clerk Geraldine Shanahan was assigned to the team and became a Greene favorite.

Greene found that he liked leading a team—his own wolf pack—and had a knack for teaching his investigation techniques and interviewing styles, unorthodox though they often were. His information-getting lessons started with a piece of advice: do enough research so it appears to the interviewee that you already know the whole story. "I like to think I know about 80 percent of the answers before I sit down," he said. Then the subject on the hot seat would ask, "Who squealed?" Alternatively, according to Greene: "The minute you start asking questions like you don't know the answer, they lie to you."

Shanahan, who later became the assistant foreign editor at the *New York Times*, got her reporting education from the Greene Team. Reporter Kenneth Crowe showed her how to root through documents. "Sometimes you didn't even know what you were looking for, but you'd know it when you found it," she says. "These people had dummy corporations. There was so much land, and they were chipping in together and buying parcels, and then would rezone it so it would become much more valuable. Then they'd sell it."[8]

The Greene Team's first investigation turned up companies that were part of an Islip rezoning scam by officials. The team's stories implicated the late *Newsday* editor Price. The work was entered for a Pulitzer Prize in 1968. It lost. Later, in October 1968, two of the officials netted in the Islip investigation were convicted, and similar disclosures by the team were made involving the town of Brookhaven. In 1969, *Newsday* entered again. Again it lost.

Sayonara, Indeed

But the team—which occasionally used the name Greene's Berets, after the crack Army unit in Vietnam—was hardly finished. Greene and his crew found that the Islip and Brookhaven investigation formula could be applied in most other Long Island towns with the same result.

In 1969 they turned to reports of corruption involving three leading lights of Long Island: state Supreme Court Justice Arthur Cromarty, a major Republican Party leader; Nassau County state senator Edward Speno;

FIGURE 17.1 *Newsday* reporters behind investigative team leader Bob Greene in 1970 are (from left) Gerry Shanahan, Anthony Marro, Jim Klurfield, and Ken Crowe. *Newsday* won the 1970 gold medal for their work. *Source*: *Newsday* staff photo. Used by permission.

and Babylon Republican leader Fred Fellman. Tony Marro, a Vermonter who had joined the paper in 1968, was added to the team.

"I knew very little about the team," says Marro, who eventually became *Newsday*'s editor. "It was supposed to be an eight- or nine-week assignment. I was basically gone for three years." He learned fast, a requirement in any Greene-run shop. "It was total immersion. You were locked up with a small group of people. You got assignments every day. You had to report what you did every day, and you had to read everybody else's reports." The intense process often produced stunning findings because few details of the entire three years of investigation ever got totally lost.

Food was often at the center of the job for Greene. As Marro puts it, "Ken Crowe taught me the difference between a mortgager and a mortgagee; Greene taught me the difference between chicken Kiev and chicken cordon bleu." His reporters believed that Greene owed his considerable girth to his taste for eating only the best that restaurants had to offer. The story is told of the boss hosting one group lunch and interrupting a new reporter as he was ordering the Salisbury steak. "When you eat with the team," Greene scolded, "you don't eat chopped meat."[9]

Greene sometimes used reporters as foils during interviews, and he often bluffed. Shanahan remembers a Greene interview with a county judge whom a *Newsday* source had accused of taking bribes to fix zoning decisions. "Greene wrote on a manila folder, 'Tapes'—and had the subject's name on them—to let that guy think we had something." Greene remembered that he had actually made up a reconstruction of what the tape of a conversation about a bribe *might* have sounded like, complete with background sounds of babies crying and screen doors slamming. He then packaged those tapes up as if they were the real thing and laid the package on the interviewee's desk. "His hands were shaking," recalled Greene. "Then I said, 'Did you know this guy was very much into electronics?' Now he's in shock; he's reaching for his water glass." Shanahan says, "He got the truth out of that guy."

If he had 80 percent of what he needed before the interview, the remaining 20 percent was often crucial because that was the part that implicated others. Greene told the story of meeting Babylon Republican leader Fellman at a place named, appropriately enough, the Sayonara Motel. They caught Fellman off guard when Greene spread six folders out on the hotel room floor. Each contained incriminating documents. He then gave Fellman the choice of admitting his involvement in "three from Column A and three from Column B," in a way that might save him from paying the heaviest amount of back tax. "Bob, can I have it all?" Fellman asked.[10]

"Off the Droshky!"

The Fellman case illustrated an interview technique that Greene's Berets called "off the droshky." The term came from a Russian fairy tale. As Tony Marro described it:

> There are many different versions of this story, but they all have the same unhappy ending.
>
> It starts with a family—father, mother and several children—traveling through the woods on a cold winter's night. They're riding in a Russian sleigh, which is called a droshky. Suddenly, a pack of starving wolves comes rushing out of the woods and begins to give chase. The horses try to race away, but the wolves keep getting closer and closer. The family becomes frightened, panicked, and desperate. Finally, to save the others, the father throws the youngest child off the droshky, into the jaws of the wolves.[11]

When someone like Freddie Fellman admitted to fraud or implicated Judge Cromarty, the Greene Team saw it as a case of Fellman desperately feeding the pursuing journalistic wolves. "It was always a moment of celebration when a reporter would come back from an interview, give a thumbs up to the rest of the team, and announce: 'Off the droshky!'" according to Marro.

While the information from Fellman tarred Cromarty, prosecutors ended up hitting the judge far more gently than they hit Fellman, who eventually went to prison. "We didn't like it that way," said Greene, because Fellman had cooperated with the team. "But there was huge juice protecting Cromarty." The investigation had produced enough good graft stories and convictions, though, for another try at the Pulitzer.

The third time was a golden charm for *Newsday*. Bill Moyers, who had become handy at writing the publisher's cover letter by that time, was able to note in 1970 that the investigations had led Governor Nelson Rockefeller to form a special commission on ethics. The Pulitzer jurors ranked *Newsday* first "for exposing secret land deals and zoning manipulations by public and political party office holders."[12] The board agreed, adding to the citation the element that the paper's work followed two earlier years of investigations. *Newsday* saw the 1970 prize as honoring all three years of investigations, as the Pulitzer citation had noted. It partied three times in celebration. Even one of the crooks it had exposed, Freddie Fellman, showed up.

Greene said that Fellman probably had no idea then that the Republicans had "made a decision to dump him"—a toss from its own droshky—and to protect Cromarty instead. At the party, Greene said, Fellman lived up to his reputation as a big talker, taking the floor at one point to make a short speech to the assembled journalists. "Wait a second," he said to the surprised revelers. "You couldn't have done this without me!" Long Island was just that kind of place. Greene, who died in 2008, said: "He was a crook, but I liked him."[13]

1970—*Newsday*, Garden City, N.Y., for its three-year investigation and exposure of secret land deals in eastern Long Island, which led to a series of criminal convictions, discharges and resignations among public and political officeholders in the area.[14]

Greene Goes Global

Like many stories that involve Bob Greene, the tale of how he wound up in Turkey and France leading "The Heroin Trail" project for *Newsday* is rather convoluted. Greene himself saw the assignment as the simple product of an investigation that had been quashed by higher-ups at the paper. That had been a study of President Richard Nixon's Florida ties to his friend Bebe Rebozo. The reporter blamed the executives of Times Mirror, whose flagship *Los Angeles Times* was a Republican stalwart, for stopping the project. With the Nixon-Rebozo probe entering the 1972 election year, the parent company was afraid the series would seem to be a political vendetta, Greene was told.

Greene was upset, of course. But when new *Newsday* publisher William Attwood suggested that the next team-based story would require Greene to go to Paris and scout the international drug trade's French connection, the reporter decided it was worth a try. "I'd never been to Europe before," Greene recalled. "And he says, 'Fly first class.'" They were trying to placate him, Greene knew, but he willingly let them.[15]

Eventually the thirty-two-part series would run in February and March 1973, a year after the initial conversation with Attwood and after reporters Les Payne and Knut Royce served for more than six months overseas with Greene. The main idea was to test the Nixon administration's claim that paying Turkey to stop growing opium poppies—the U.S. government policy—was drying up the heroin trade. (The team concluded that the payments were not working.) But from the start, the series had strong local and national angles. On the first day readers were introduced to the drug-shortened lives of three Long Island residents in their early twenties. Other installments, reported by a U.S.-based team headed by Tony Marro, concentrated on the New York and Long Island connections in organized crime. Other reporting originated in Washington, Miami, and Mexico. Marro, who had been in the Washington bureau when he was called for the project, was unhappy with the assignment. For one thing, in 1972 he had been in the middle of another little story—one growing out of a bungled burglary at the Watergate complex. "I can't pretend I was breaking a lot of stories on Watergate—I wasn't—but I knew it was a good story," he says.[16]

As might be expected of an ambitious global project being run by an investigator who had never ventured east of Montauk Point, this one had its zany moments. Keeler noted that "the *Newsday* invasion of Europe began like the opening scenes of *The Marx Brothers Stalk the Poppy.*" Greene's proposal for a Land Rover was turned down, but he was allowed a cache of weapons to accompany team members overseas and got *Newsday* to pay for a three-week Turkish-language course for team members.[17] (Les Payne, a former Army officer who was among the first African Americans hired by *Newsday*, would later tell of Greene's careful attention to the

Turkish words for lamb, eggplant, sea bass, and other delicacies that would be on the menus in Ankara. Payne joked that for his own part, he wanted to learn the Turkish phrase for "Let's get the black guy."[18])

One story from abroad tells of Greene, Payne, and Royce at a European gambling casino the night that the team leader hit it big time. "He was walking majestically towards the cashier's cage with a large pile of chips in both hands when his pants fell down," says Marro, who heard the tale later. "He couldn't put down the chips without spilling them, so Payne and Royce had to pull his pants up from the rear."

But thanks to the time spent on thorough organization of the international, U.S., and local Long Island elements, the *Newsday* report was clear and detailed. It contributed to an understanding of how the Turkey-to-France-to-America trail was operating while focusing on its local New York and Long Island outlets. Some at the paper felt that the headlong plunge into the Turkish-French connection was ill-timed, though, missing the bigger news: Southeast Asia had become a heroin hotbed in the Vietnam era, possibly with the encouragement of Central Intelligence Agency agents who were reported in other journals to have been taking political sides among nations in the region. *Newsday* had "a good story, but not a complete story," says Marro.[19]

Still, it was the unanimous choice of the Pulitzer jurors, ahead of a *New York Times* report on art thefts and a *St. Louis Post-Dispatch* project that took an altogether different look at the drug trade: defending the constitutional rights of suspects against "high-handed government agents."[20]

Bob Greene, who died in 2008, also became known for leading the 1976 collaborative effort by the group Investigative Reporters and Editors to solve the murder of the *Arizona Republic* reporter Don Bolles. "The Arizona Project" of IRE brought together thirty-six journalists from twenty-three news organizations in a project that Greene considered his proudest moment professionally. While many stories were written, however, the case was never completely resolved.[21]

1974—*Newsday,* Garden City, N.Y., for its definitive report on
the illicit narcotic traffic in the United States and abroad, entitled,
"The Heroin Trail."[22]

Bringing Gold to Alaska

Howard Weaver was twenty-five when his editors at the *Anchorage Daily News* teamed him with relative veteran Bob Porterfield in pursuit of a story on the mightiest institution in Alaska: Teamsters Union Local 959. Unlike the kinds of team formation decisions being made at larger, investigation-minded papers, the choices were fairly simple for executive editor Stan Abbott and managing editor Tom Gibbony. There were only a dozen staffers. Compared to mainstream American newspapers there was also a sense of remoteness in the forty-ninth state, which was literally a place apart in 1975. "You could not watch Walter Cronkite live in Alaska," says Weaver. "They videotaped it in Seattle, flew it up, and showed it at 11 at night."

The Anchorage-born Weaver felt close to the latest trends in investigative journalism though. A year earlier he attended a ten-day American Press Institute reporting seminar at Columbia. Inspired, he did not see a story on the Teamsters as particularly daunting. After all, he had been exposed to the *New York Times* reporter David Burnham, whose stories had covered Frank Serpico, the cop who blew the whistle on widespread payoffs in the New York Police Department.[23] Weaver had read the *Newsday* stories of Bob Greene from just across Long Island Sound, rating the paper "a well-oiled machine that could get to the bottom of things." And Watergate stories, reflecting the best of recent investigative journalism, were still in the news.[24]

Looking back now, he sees that he probably should have been a bit daunted. The *Daily News* was the number-two paper in Anchorage. Its thirteen thousand subscribers gave it less than one-third of the circulation of the *Anchorage Times*, which owned the building and leased its smaller rival space under a joint operating agreement. As for Teamsters in Alaska, there were twenty-three thousand of them—more than the number of registered Republicans in the state. The *Daily News* had one special thing going for it: publisher Kay Fanning, whose idea it had been to throw the paper's resources into finding out what made the Teamsters tick. She had also authorized Weaver to attend the Columbia investigative seminar. To her, Weaver was a logical choice for the Teamster assignment.

Fanning, in the mold of fellow publishers Katharine Graham and Alicia Patterson, had newspaper lineage, credentials, and instincts. After divorcing her first husband, Marshall Field IV, publisher of the *Chicago Sun-Times*, she married newspaperman Larry Fanning and persuaded him to buy the *Anchorage Daily News*. She took over after he died. "Kay simply couldn't see any reason why Anchorage ought to be backward," according to Weaver. "The phrases 'good enough for Anchorage' or 'just as nice as Seattle' didn't figure in her landscape."

So when she targeted the Teamsters for coverage, it seemed natural enough. Now, Weaver reflects, "It was a very brave thing for her to do. Remember that the head of the union was also on the board of the largest bank in town. There was no real labor-management distinction; it was all about power. And the Teamsters had a lot of it, and Kay Fanning didn't have much of it." Of the project with so much potential to damage her little paper, he notes, "it would have been easy to duck."

A Bubble of Dues Money

Fanning had not ordered up a Teamster story because of a tip about wrongdoing or fallout from some breaking news event. Instead she believed readers needed to know more about the state's most powerful institution. Weaver, for one, had been on good terms with the union and had even been a dues-paying Teamster at one time. "I had no animosity," says Weaver. "Au contraire, I saw unions as a social benefit." In fact, Weaver used his union history as an icebreaker in interviews.

The reporters did not feel they needed to turn up a scandal in order to give readers a fascinating story. In a mere eighteen years, through Alaska's meteoric oil boom, Jesse Carr's Local 959 had swelled up like a balloon over the Macy's Thanksgiving Day Parade—maybe menacing, maybe just big, but clearly hovering above everything else in the state. Teamsters in Alaska had the best health club in town, prepaid legal benefits, and other advantages. They had every benefit known to man. And it was all fueled by this enormous infusion of pipeline workers paying dues. The Teamsters Union was also big news nationally, and not only because of the specter of former convict/leader Jimmy Hoffa, who was to disappear in mid-1975. Labor reporters like the *New York Times*'s Wallace Turner had been following the Teamsters and their pension funds for years. Hoffa's predecessor, Dave Beck, was also mentor to Jesse Carr.

Alaska's Local 959 leadership knew that few of its strapping young members would ever retire as Teamsters—not in their state, anyway. They would move on, leaving behind much of the money they had pumped into the benefit pool. "It created this huge bubble," says Weaver—a bubble of dues money. The *Anchorage Times* wrote of the union providing cradle-to-grave coverage. "We were a little racier, and referred to it as womb-to-tomb. But the Teamsters referred to it as erection to resurrection."

As Weaver and Porterfield began their investigation, they found Local 959 entwined in the overheated Alaskan economy through a web of investments, often through complex trusts. It was easy to find individual Teamster investments, but it seemed impossible to grasp the whole picture of what they controlled.

The reporters immediately noticed the role of property. They discovered real estate investments in California especially. But they also found that few were willing to discuss the Teamsters' investments or to be identified with any story that might be seen as negative to the powerful organization—especially if it was written by a news outlet that was roundly perceived as weak.

Even while the reporting was unfocused, the reporters adopted a system and applied it relentlessly. "I was single, and Bob was married but soon to be single. We worked constantly on this story," says Weaver. "We developed these voluminous files, and had to make up filing systems to keep up with all this, because of course there were no computers. We'd make index cards, and we had big charts with four-colored pencils tying things together. This guy's on this board, and that guy's on another board." Jim Babb was added to the team and was assigned to work on sidebars on the operation of the pension fund and the legal structure of the investments. Were the Teamsters breaking the law? Nowhere that they could see clearly. Yet their money and power were everywhere in the state. It was still a big story.

Another Goliath, Big and Gray

If the Teamsters Union was Goliath, the *Daily News* was about to face a second giant as well. The *Los Angeles Times* was coming to Alaska to write about the union. "That really panicked us. It was shadowy," says Weaver, who learned that three or four reporters from Los Angeles had come to town and also interviewed people in Juneau about the union. The *Daily News* investigators, whose material was still unfocused, worried that they might have to rush something into print prematurely to beat or to match the *Times*. "In the end, we decided that we had to do our thing as best we could, and that we couldn't do what the *Times* did," Weaver says.

Then came the shock of seeing the *Times*'s story in November, a couple of weeks before the *Daily News*'s projected first installment. The headline read "Crime Wave Strangles Alaska." The *Times* led with: "Widespread lawlessness, a helpless government and the stranglehold of a single Teamsters Union chief severely threaten a state crucial to the nation's future energy independence."

Weaver recalls, "We just about freaked out. We hadn't found anything like that." He and Porterfield read below the strong language of the opening paragraphs, though, and determined that the paper had fallen back on generalizations, failing to make the case. "I don't want to 'dis' the *L.A. Times*, particularly because we won the prize and they didn't," says Weaver, "but we thought, 'That's the way you write it if you're from out of town.' We live here, and that's not the story we're going to write." While other Alaskans conceded that the *Times* was correct in its conclusion that the oil pipeline boom had increased crime, there was a wide sense that the paper had overstated the case. (Governor Jay S. Hammond wrote that "most Alaskans [don't] believe a midnight stroll down Cushman in Fairbanks [is] fraught with half the hazards faced on L.A.'s Sunset Strip at high noon.") Weaver says, "I suppose it's easier to be bold when your newsroom is 2,300 miles away."

The Alaskan reporters found suspicious information about the North Star Terminals on the south edge of Fairbanks, an operation led by a man who had been sentenced to a year's probation in California in the 1950s. On the one-hundred-person payroll under him were about forty individuals who had been convicted of murder, burglary, robbery, drug crimes, and other offenses. Three of the top six Teamster officials listed on the terminal roster had criminal records. The *Daily News* also concentrated on potential conflicts of interest involving union lobbyist Lewis M. Dischner. But the reporters found little direct lawbreaking. Instead their work concentrated on how the Teamsters were amassing enormous clout for a sparsely populated state, with a power structure that could exercise power far beyond the normal checks and balances of the union-versus-management environment.

The series moved toward a powerful conclusion too: that the inflated organization the Teamsters had set up in Alaska could not last. At his McClatchy office in Sacramento, Weaver years later kept a page of notes from the reporting tacked to his wall. "IMPLOSION" was written across the top. The Teamsters union would indeed see much of its power collapse in the years after the story ran. "But they were still in their muscle period then," says Weaver. The series, "Empire: The Alaska Teamster Story," ran through December, with organizational charts on trusts and funds and investments spread across pages.

Compared to the *Los Angeles Times*'s Crime-Wave-Strangles-Alaska take, this series was characterized by a low-key approach. The first-day story by Weaver and Porterfield was headlined "Teamsters: How Much Power?" It started:

> Teamsters Union Local 959 is fashioning an empire in Alaska, stretching across an ever-widening slice of life from the infant oil frontier to the heart of the state's major city.
>
> Secure under the unquestioned leadership of Secretary-Treasurer Jesse L. Carr, the empire has evolved in just 18 years into a complex maze of political, economic and social power which towers above the rest of Alaska's labor movement—and challenges at times both mighty industry and state government itself.[25]

A Standing-O in Juneau

While the *Daily News* was proud of the project, a Pulitzer Prize was hardly something it expected. For one thing, no Alaskan paper had ever won one. For another, the project was mainly explanatory, with no laws passed and no one convicted as a result. There had been some wrongdoing noted, but its real service was in giving shape and dimension to something that was previously unknown. "The union was big and powerful, but it existed only in myth," says Weaver. "How big? Once you gave it an actual shape, by describing the extent of its investments, the cross-directorships that they occupied, the techniques they used for negotiations, then it became real."

But the Pulitzer jury said in its report that the *Anchorage Daily News* "drove its way into the operations of the powerful Teamsters Union in Alaska to show the union's impact and influence on the whole spectrum of the economy and the politics of the state at a critical time of booming growth. The presentation was made fairly and dispassionately and without sensationalism, well conceived, well written and well presented. It is a remarkable performance by a small but vigorous daily newspaper."

Had the jury report been made public, the next sentence would have particularly cheered the Anchorage staff. "Our jury for Category 1 [Public Service] also had an entry by the Los Angeles Times covering essentially the same subject—the Teamsters in Alaska. However, it was our conclusion that the Anchorage Daily News's performance and product was the more meritorious and did qualify more fully for the Prize that we are recommending."

After the Pulitzer board announced that the *Anchorage Daily News* was its gold medal winner, champagne in the newsroom began a three-day celebration. Then came a standing ovation in the House of Representatives in Juneau when the award was announced. "For Alaska to win a Pulitzer was a big deal. The other paper even wrote a very generous editorial congratulating us," Weaver says. "I bet even Jesse Carr loved the idea that he was a big enough dude to lead to a Pulitzer."

Kay Fanning's courage in taking on the project and the Teamsters became clear only later. At Pulitzer time she was actually a few months away from an announcement that the paper was nearly broke. "Still, instead of kissing up to the power structure in Anchorage, she gave us a flashlight and sent us looking in the shadows," according to Weaver. He believes that the prize "probably saved the *Anchorage Daily News*, because I'm not sure McClatchy would have bought it if it hadn't noticed it for its Pulitzer-winning." (Fanning later became editor of the *Christian Science Monitor* and the first woman president of the American Society of Newspaper Editors.)

Soon the paper would pass the *Times* to become the state's largest paper. "And the *Daily News* staff would learn, by winning another Pulitzer, that lightning really can strike twice," he says. The second prize, also a public service award, would come in 1989 for a very different kind of story—a sensitive and powerful account of the anguish of alcoholism and suicides suffered by native Alaskans.

1976—The *Anchorage Daily News* for its disclosures of the impact and influence of the Teamsters Union on Alaska's economy and politics.[26]

A Trainee Dies, the Marine Corps Lies

Editor Joe Murray was in a grumpy mood when walked into his office at the *Lufkin News* early on Monday morning, March 15. It was supposed to be his day off, but work beckoned. And there in the waiting room outside his office was an old advertiser, probably with a gripe. "I'm thinking, 'Oh, man, whatever goes on in the paper, they come to the editor.' We'd probably run his ad upside down or something," Murray recalls. But it was not about an ad at all.[27]

J. A. "Bo" Bryan was related to a Lufkin, Texas, marine recruit who was the subject of an obituary about to be published in the *News*. Bryan believed that the truth of his relative's death was being covered up by the Marines.

The official word was that twenty-year-old Private Lynn "Bubba" McClure had died from head injuries suffered during close-combat training at the U.S. Marine Corps recruit depot in San Diego. "But Bo Bryan starts telling me this story, and it's a horror story," says Murray. It started with the description of his grand nephew, who had never succeeded in anything and was quite possibly retarded, but who had inexplicably been accepted by the Marines. Family members, told that it was a simple training accident, didn't believe it—in part because of the extent of the injuries that had killed young Bubba. And the injuries that Bubba's stepfather had observed when he visited McClure in San Diego before he died didn't seem consistent with a simple training accident.

"I was sitting there listening to him, and thinking, 'What am I going to be able to do about this? I'm just one person. We're just one little paper. How long is this guy going to keep talking? I'm a busy editor,'" says Murray. But then Bryan paused and looked right at him. "I'll never forget that moment, and what he said: 'They beat that boy's brains out—literally.' It sent a cold chill down my spine."

Bryan had been selected to represent Bubba's extended family because he was one of the few relatives with an education and had gotten results from Murray before. Years before, when Bryan's home-building enterprise had run into some environmental problems, the *Lufkin News* had run an item recounting the state's complaint. An unhappy Bryan had come to the office to tell his side and had gotten satisfaction. He trusted Murray to do the right thing again. Maybe there was something the *News* could do. The editor assigned reporter Ken Herman to look into the situation.

"We used to joke about how there were only two people there—me and Dwight Bailey—and they don't usually let the janitor write stories. So it was me," says Herman. Murray made a joke of it too, remarking that he only had three reporters, so he had assigned one-third of his staff to the case.[28]

Oft-Told Tales

Murray and Herman have recounted the tale many times. Pulitzer Prize projects quickly become the stuff of legend at a newspaper—and especially at a small one like the *News*, then part of the Cox newspaper chain. Still, each telling can bring out powerful emotions about events that moved people long ago.

Herman vividly remembers standing beside Bubba McClure's open casket as he was reporting on the funeral. "He was a slight young man, and he looked very un-Marine-like," says the reporter, who was only a year older. "The feeling was of this child in the proud uniform of the United States Marines." His first story, that Tuesday, was fifty-four short, hard-hitting paragraphs appearing under the headline "Marine McClure buried: He died trying to prove he was one of those 'few good men.'" It began:

> Lynn (Bubba) McClure, 20, joined the Marines to become a man and make his family proud of him.
>
> "I can't wait to show you my uniform," he had written his mother.
>
> Today, wearing that dress blue uniform, he was buried in a flag-draped casket.

As he was lowered into his grave, two questions puzzled his family and those who knew him.

—How did the tenth-grade dropout, considered "slow" by those who recall him, pass the Marine Corps entrance exam?

—What drew this slightly built youth into the rigors of Marine Corps boot camp where he was fatally injured in a training exercise?

Those who knew him said his brief life was scarred by failure and frustration.

Apparently he saw the Marines as the end of that failure. But three weeks after arriving at the San Diego Recruit Depot his hopes ended.[29]

Based on interviews with family and friends, the story examined the strange circumstances of the enlistment of the five-foot-six, 125-pound youth who seemed to have significant disabilities. It quoted Bo Bryan: "When I first heard he was in the Marines, I thought they meant the Merchant Marine." McClure had also been in trouble with the law, with a police record for reckless damage and public intoxication. They should have turned up on a Marine Corps background check and kept him out of the service, Herman and Murray knew, even if he had somehow managed to pass an entrance exam.

McClure had failed both Army and Marines exams eighteen months earlier. Details of his enlistment and the test that he apparently passed were not available. The Marines would not comment except to provide bare details of the training accident. In another section, the story offered heart-wrenching snippets of four letters home that McClure had "scrawled in a childlike penmanship." The first announced his enlistment to his unsuspecting mother. The last arrived the same day they were notified of his injury. He had written, "I been in boot camp about two weeks and it's making a man out of me quick."

A Cover-Up Unfolds

The *News* kept its focus local and sensitive to the family. The unbylined piece the next day said that the prior article had been "authorized by the young man's mother"—a notation, says Murray, reflecting some readers' concerns that the paper appeared to be playing up McClure's disabilities.

The story also quoted local congressman Charles Wilson, an Annapolis graduate who took a deep interest in the case. In talking with Representative Wilson, Herman got the feeling that McClure's death reflected what Wilson saw as weaknesses in the all-volunteer military.

The next Herman byline quoted a private investigator retained by the family who said McClure had been beaten to death with "continued blows." In pugil-stick fighting, recruits wear protective gear, including a football helmet and a face mask, although they are no guarantee against injury. The circumstances of McClure's enlistment, which involved his passing a second recruitment test in Austin, remained a mystery, although the story did note that a General Accounting Office study just released had raised questions of "recruiter malpractice and fraudulent enlistment."

The next *News* story, reported and written by Murray, sprouted from a moment of competitive exasperation. It also added a dramatic national angle. Herman was off for the weekend when his editor saw an Associated Press story come across saying that Marine investigators were blaming the town of Lufkin's law enforcement community for withholding information that could have invalidated McClure's enlistment.

"You cannot imagine how the ground was cut out from under me when that story came out of the AP from Washington," Murray says. The *Lufkin News*'s treatment of the McClure case and the congressional studies by then had attracted some national press. But the *News* had not expected to lose its edge like this. Murray's obvious next step was that "We had to find out who the Marines had been talking to here." The answer astounded him. He reached a Marine public affairs officer in New Orleans. "It was a Saturday," says Murray. "I got him at home, and he came in from his yard. By then I was real disgusted, but his job was to make the media happy." And in a convoluted way, he did that with the *News*.

Going into the office and checking the records to show who in Lufkin had been contacted about McClure, the public affairs man called Murray back with the information. A "Johnson" in the sheriff's department and a "Ms. Walker" at the Lufkin police station had provided the confirmation that McClure had no police record. Murray called the local police and sheriff himself to ask these Johnson and Walker characters how they could have gotten it wrong. "There wasn't anybody by those names," he says. Someone in the marine recruiting office had made Johnson and Walker up to cover the fact that no call had ever been placed to check on McClure's record. When it turned out the Marines had lied on the report, Murray says, "you can imagine how I felt. . . . I thought, I had 'em."

It is a cautionary tale for journalists seeking the truth, as well as for bureaucrats trying to cover their tracks. "Had the Marines taken that one more step and called to check themselves, they would have found out," Murray says. "But they stopped asking questions when they heard what they wanted to hear."

The headline on his story read "Fake Names Found in Marine Reports." It began: "The use of fake names has opened up the possibility of a cover-up in the investigation, and U.S. Rep. Charles Wilson said Saturday he would seek to find out if the recruitment records were deliberately falsified to protect those responsible for McClure's recruitment."[30] The story delivered another detail: not only had McClure passed a second recruitment test in a second city—after dismally failing the first in Lufkin—his score on the second test had been so high that McClure "was put in charge of the recruit detachment sent from San Antonio to San Diego." The *News* never figured out how the high score occurred, but clearly, says Murray, either someone took the test for him, gave him the answers, or changed his score. "We know his IQ didn't increase."

As the reporters did further interviews and private and government investigations, a complex picture of malfeasance began to take shape. The young marine with the learning disability had found himself placed in a "motivational platoon" in San Diego, where punishment was meted out through heavy menial labor and pugil-stick fighting sessions. On the day Bubba McClure was injured, he had been forced to fight seven men. No officer was present despite U.S. Marine Corps requirements. Eyewitnesses said that McClure had refused to fight while a drill instructor goaded the other recruits to pound him from all directions until he curled up in the dirt screaming, "God, make them stop." Knocked unconscious, he had a five-gallon bucket of water poured on him in an attempt to revive him. He remained in a coma until he died more than three months later.

Murray wrote editorials that conveyed a personal, small-town feel in siding with the family in its search for the truth beyond the lies. Ken Herman resumed his coverage on the news side. It was to have a bitter ending. While Congress launched hearings on recruitment techniques—and eventually tightened standards for the military—a marine court-martialed in McClure's death was eventually acquitted on charges of "involuntary manslaughter, assault, maltreatment of a recruit and violating an order to conduct close combat drills only with supervisory officers present." Murray says, "Maybe it was the biggest lesson in life I ever had." No matter how well you do in your job, the results in a courtroom can turn everything around.

Murray entered the McClure series in a statewide competition and got a good result: second place. (The editor of the winning Texas paper later jokingly told him, "We should have entered for the Pulitzers, too.") But the Lufkin stories had attracted the attention of Pulitzer Prize administrator John Hohenberg, who wrote to the *News* suggesting that it enter. The letter amazed the newsroom. "You simply don't ignore that kind of letter. In fact, we have it framed in the newsroom," Murray wrote in submitting the entry before the February 1 deadline. The submission was barely postmarked on time. The paper did not have a copier, and Murray had to poke a pocketful of dimes into the machine at the library.

The public service jurors unanimously picked the *Lufkin News* over the *Philadelphia Inquirer*, which was number two for its reporting on a state hospital for the mentally ill. "A small newspaper, with limited resources, chose not to settle for the official explanation of a local marine's training camp death," jurors said of the *News*. "What might have been a routine obituary became instead a search for better answers and, in time, because of the newspaper's efforts and determination, the cause of fundamental reform in the recruiting and training practices of the United States Marine Corps." The board agreed with the jury's first choice.

By the time of the Pulitzer announcement, Herman had taken a job at the Dallas office of the Associated Press and was home with his parents. The timing is now meaningful to him because he was to lose his father not long after the prize was announced. "It was a grand moment," Herman says. On top of that, the job offers began to come in from other news organizations, including the *Philadelphia Inquirer*. Ultimately he decided to stay at the AP.

The Brooklyn-born Herman, who had only been in journalism for six months when he started working for Joe Murray, credits his old boss with bringing out the best elements of his youth yet teaching him to temper his emotions for the sake of the story. "This is what Joe did," Herman recalls. "He kept me thinking that there is another side, or two or three, to this. Maybe I went a little far in drawing this emotional picture. It was a matter of not piling it on. You don't have to keep hitting people with it." He would have been happy with any Pulitzer, "but I happened to know that this was the Pulitzer of Pulitzers," says Herman. "It's the same one that Woodward and Bernstein got."

1977—The *Lufkin* (Tex.) *News* for an obituary of a local man who died in Marine training camp, which grew into an investigation of that death and a fundamental reform in the recruiting and training practices of the United States Marine Corps.[31]

From "Terrible" to Great

The *Philadelphia Inquirer* was a grand experiment for Eugene L. Roberts Jr., the North Carolina-born editor once called by the *New York Times*'s Harrison Salisbury "the best journalist living and breathing in the U.S.A. and probably the world."[32] Roberts had moved north to Knight Ridder's *Detroit News* as a labor reporter and later as the Metro editor. He then jumped to the *Times* in 1965, where he covered the civil rights movement with insight and intelligence, served as a Vietnam correspondent, and was promoted to national editor. Knight Ridder executive Lee Hills had tried to woo Roberts back since he left Detroit. In 1972, Hills made Roberts an offer he couldn't refuse: take over the *Inquirer*. It was a job most sane editors would have refused in a heartbeat. Roberts had half-jokingly told Hills over the years that he would leave the *Times* only to run some newspaper that the world thought was beyond rescue. At lunch one day, Roberts remembers, Hills said to him: "I have the very newspaper for you."[33]

Steve Lovelady, a *Wall Street Journal* page-one rewrite specialist who was among Roberts's first Philadelphia hires, recalled that the new editor used a variation of Hills's same improbable "lure" to get him to move from the *Journal* to the *Inquirer*. "It was a terrible paper, just an awful paper. It was so bad that after he talked me into going to work there, and then sent me a week's worth of papers, I was appalled and called him up to renege. I told him, Nobody, not even you, can salvage this dog." Roberts responded breathlessly, "Yeah, isn't it great!"

Then he turned up the heat on Lovelady. "You've already worked on a great newspaper; anybody can do that," Roberts told him. "This is the only chance you'll ever get to take a piece of shit and turn it into a great newspaper." The *Journal* rewrite man sat with those slowly drawled Roberts words for a minute. "It was a pretty compelling argument, if you bought the premise that he was going to succeed," said Lovelady. "But the

FIGURE 17.2 The *Philadelphia Inquirer* executive editor Eugene Roberts in 1977.
Source: *Inquirer* staff photo. Used by permission of the *Philadelphia Inquirer*.

first year I was there, there wasn't a day that went by that I didn't think, 'What have I done?'"[34]

During the eighteen Roberts years, the *Inquirer* did plenty. The paper or its journalists won seventeen Pulitzers between 1975 and 1990—including two gold medals, one in 1978 and one in 1990.

Inside the "Roundhouse"

Bill Marimow still recalls the strain of climbing to the common pleas courts building's ninth floor—and smelling the clerk's foul cigar—even though it has been nearly thirty years now. There in the fetid haze of Room 951, Marimow and fellow *Inquirer* reporter Jonathan Neumann slogged through records of "suppression hearings" showing how many confessions had been thrown out against defendants on trial for murder.

A source had given them a computer printout—a somewhat novel document for reporters in 1977—listing instances of judges approving defense motions because they believed the cops had beaten confessions out of the suspects. Mostly the beatings were administered in small interrogation rooms of "the Roundhouse," as police headquarters is known.

While that is how the *Inquirer* story started, underlying the investigation was Gene Roberts's newsroom management approach. Roberts encouraged and supported reporters who came up with enterprise stories that could make a difference in the community.

Marimow had been hired by Roberts's predecessor, John McMullen, a good editor who for two years was in the unenviable position of "shrinking the paper to greatness" through cutbacks ordered by Knight Ridder, as the reporter puts it. (The technique would be tried again in the years before Knight Ridder sold out to McClatchy in 2005.) Roberts, though, was unique. As a newsroom presence "he was an unadulterated pleasure," Marimow says. "I always used to wonder why he wasted so much time talking with me, one of the least-experienced reporters at the *Inquirer*." When Marimow was on the labor beat, Roberts once spent forty-five minutes explaining how, in his Detroit days, he used to carry four separate notebooks into meetings with the United Auto Workers leader. The notebooks helped him prepare for various profiles or analyses he had in the works. "I remember thinking, 'This guy is crazy; I'm never going to be able to do that,'" says Marimow. "The fact that I can remember the talk with such specificity, though, tells you about the influence he had."[35]

Any reporter bringing a good story idea to Roberts or Metro editor John Carroll would get time to pursue it, says Marimow, who was later to become the *Inquirer*'s editor. (After his first *Inquirer* stint, Marimow and Carroll would later work together at the *Baltimore Sun*, where Carroll was the editor before his move to the *Los Angeles Times*.) Younger reporters like Marimow and Neumann, then in their twenties, also had no fear of their story being assigned to others with more experience.

The police brutality story came up from the beat—a perfect expression of Gene Roberts's philosophy about the best journalism not being top-down. "That means that, as an editor, you have to have a sense for listening, as opposed to simply giving assignments," Roberts says. Keeping the original reporter on the story simply follows—as it did for Ben Bradlee in letting two young *Washington Post* reporters keep plugging on Watergate. "If you steal that story, and give it to a senior reporter, you could imagine what's going to happen," says Roberts. "People aren't going to come up with ideas."[36]

Neumann and Marimow had each been involved with earlier stories analyzing court issues and police problems, and Marimow had recently covered a murder trial during which the defendant confessed and was convicted—before someone else admitted to the killing. Police, it seemed, had beaten a confession out of the defendant and had also beaten various witnesses to make the case stick. (A federal grand jury eventually began looking at the wrongful conviction.)

Marimow had moved to city hall from the courts during the trial, with Neumann taking over. So they both had that bizarre case in their minds—along with lots of other ideas about the dysfunctional Philadelphia police force. "Toward the end of 1976 Jonathan and I put our heads together. What he had seen covering the courts, and what I had seen, suggested a closer look." And in January 1977 they began reporting what became known as the "Homicide Files."

They knew that records could help them document the cases being thrown out because suspects were beaten into confessing. Marimow visited a common pleas court source to see if such records might be available. "Presto, bingo, ala kazam, my source gave me a computer print-out." It was something new to him.

The printout showed that 17 percent of cases involved an illegal interrogation. So Marimow and Neumann began their climbs up to the ninth floor to that smoky records room to read transcripts of the actual suppression hearings. Beatings, threats, medical records, eyewitness testimony—all of it was revealed in the files. "Interestingly, most of the judges never ruled on whether there had been abuse," Marimow says. Instead they ruled out the confessions as the inadmissible "fruit of the poisoned tree" without disciplining the abusive police. Marimow then began interviewing judges to establish why.

The two reporters also realized the need to understand the pressures that homicide detectives faced on the street and in the station house. Some abhorred the brutal police tactics but lived with them anyway. Selecting three interviews from a number they conducted, the reporters assembled a sidebar for the first "Homicide Files" installment on April 24. Under the headline, "At the Roundhouse: How Detectives Compel Murder 'Confessions,'" the article began:

> It can be said with certainty that two things happened in the 22 hours between Carlton Coleman's arrest and his arraignment last October.
>
> One is that he was interrogated by homicide detectives. The other is that his health went from good to poor. When it was all over, he spent the next 28 days hospitalized for injuries of the abdomen, arms, shoulders, chest, calf, spine and back.
>
> Medical problems are not rare among those interrogated by the Philadelphia Police Department's 84-member homicide division. In fact, a four-month investigation by The Inquirer has found a pattern of beatings, threats of violence, intimidation, coercion and knowing disregard for constitutional rights in the interrogation of homicide suspects and witnesses.[37]

Two paragraphs later came a statistical hook: "From 1974 through this month, judges of the Common Pleas Court have been asked to rule in pretrial hearings on the legality of police investigations in 433 homicide cases," the story said. "In 80 of those cases, however, judges have ruled that the police acted illegally during homicide interrogations" with documentary evidence of coercion ranging from X-rays to photographs.

A Powerful Image

Gene Roberts had been struck from the beginning by an anecdote he heard from the reporters about a case in which "the interrogating officers had an old ornamental sword, and stabbed a person in the testicles with it," he says. "It sounded so outrageous and bizarre that you know that if we could definitively prove it, it would certainly get people's attention." The sword incident appeared in the thirty-ninth paragraph but jumped out at readers. It was explained that a twenty-three-year-old black suspect had been "stabbed in the groin with a sword-like instrument and blackjacked on his feet, ankles and legs until the blackjack broke in two." The four detectives doing the interrogation, as well as the suspect, were all named in the article.

The sidebar containing the detective interviews, which like all the stories carried the Neumann and Marimow bylines, presented mixed reactions from detectives. All had agreed to talk only if their names were *not* used. One said:

> I'm not going to defend the Police Department now. No way. I work on my own. There're people there [in the homicide division] I'd refuse to work with.
>
> We've got a new breed of guy now. Years ago we'd sit there [in the interrogation room] and talk with the defendants. The detectives used to think with their heads, not their hands. They were good, damned good, and they got the evidence clean.
>
> Now, all they care about is statements [from suspects]. I think statements are bull———.

Part two was headlined "How Police Harassed a Family." It started with the case of a home invasion—conducted by law officers—and it was accompanied by pictures that a family member had taken of a storm-trooper-like entry by armed police. Parts three and four examined the reasons police were not being charged with beating suspects even when the evidence was overwhelming.

Neumann and Marimow weren't finished. Reader response to the first series assured that. "We were deluged with calls about police in Philadelphia just beating people up on the street," Carroll remembered.

Marimow adds, "People were saying, You guys missed the boat. You ought to take a look at what's happening on the street." As the second series showed, what was happening was as severe as the Roundhouse beatings. Yet a federal prosecution against three police officers, which grew from that second series and was supported by numerous witnesses, resulted in the police officers' acquittal.

"Jonathan and I were devastated, because we believed the citizens were telling the truth." In yet another measure of Roberts's commitment to supporting his reporters, he and Carroll took the two staffers to a consolation dinner. "Gene was talking to us about how during the civil rights movement in the South juries were returning verdicts that had nothing to do with reality."

Other things were competing for Roberts's attention. Mayor Frank L. Rizzo (a former police chief) "virtually declared war on the paper," Roberts says. Further, a union sympathetic to the mayor and the police was jamming truck bays to keep the paper from getting out. These became supporting arguments to be included in Roberts's Pulitzer Prize entry—as were the columns in the rival *Philadelphia Bulletin* that had ridiculed the *Inquirer* reporting and sided with the police.

For Roberts, the *Inquirer*'s first gold medal was particularly sweet because it recognized the entire staff's work turning around the paper. Individuals had won three Pulitzers by then, but the paper had missed out on public service—the category that Roberts associates with the courage displayed by Southern editors who opposed the Ku Klux Klan and who supported the law during school desegregation.

The irony, he says with a laugh, is that the *Inquirer*'s accomplishments, in a way, sprouted from the depths that the publication reached in the 1960s. He never would have had a free hand to test his managerial vision at a successful paper, Roberts says, because "success breeds conservative thinking and non-risk-taking. Nobody wants to screw up a good thing." In Philadelphia, "they were willing to try anything," he says. "It's wonderful when newspapers are desperate enough to try good journalism."

1978—The *Philadelphia Inquirer* for a series of articles showing abuses of power by the police in its home city.[38]

CHAPTER 18

MIGHTIER THAN THE SNAKE

1979: The *Point Reyes Light* on Synanon

God, I thought, wouldn't it be amazing to win? If the miracle should happen, I don't want to be photographed looking like I just came off a ski slope. You're a country editor—dress like one, I thought, and took off the turtleneck and tucked a favorite red-plaid shirt into my blue jeans.

—DAVE MITCHELL, FROM *THE LIGHT ON SYNANON*, 1980

"Today is the first day of the rest of your life" hardly seems a sentiment to strike terror in the heart. Coined by Synanon founder Charles Dederich, the aphorism expressed the healing, New Age image he wanted for his commune of rehabilitated drug addicts.[1] Behind its guarded gates in California's bucolic west Marin County, though, Synanon was changing in the 1970s. It was becoming a brutal armed camp.

In 1977—two years after Dave and Cathy Mitchell paid what was then a princely $45,000 for the tabloid weekly *Point Reyes Light*—the young owner-editors did not know that. Synanon had owned property in their county north of San Francisco since the mid-1960s, they knew, and had been around for twenty years since its founding in the Los Angeles–area beach community of Santa Monica. It planned to move its headquarters to Marshall, just a short drive up Route 1 from Point Reyes Station, a charming but ramshackle town of 425. The Mitchells expected it would be a small news story for them.

Dave Mitchell had visited the Synanon property just after buying the *Light* and not thought much about it. A commune was hardly strange for northern California, home to all sorts of alternative lifestyles by the 1970s. Mitchell described his readers at the time, and the community in general, as "fairly evenly divided between longhairs and cowboy hats."

But he had come away from his tour with an itchy feeling that he couldn't quite describe. In his first stories, he tried. It had something to do with Synanon's size. "Above all it is big—much bigger than most people imagine," he wrote. "Synanon boasts a fleet of about 400 vehicles, not including scores of motorcycles. It also has three large boats moored in Tomales Bay, with more on the way, and six airplanes tied down at Gnoss Field in Novato." And its computer center was "appropriate for a large corporation." Mitchell also took note of how Synanon residents—nine hundred of them on three properties—worked the phones from cubicles, promoting various gift items and offering premiums to raise money. The overall impression, he said, was of "happy, articulate people seemingly living productive lives. Many of those I talked to told of drug and criminal problems before joining Synanon."[2]

In retrospect, Mitchell calls his early visit "the Potemkin Village tour of Synanon," masking dark secrets behind the false front of industriousness on behalf of charity. The real story was deeper. Dederich led the public into believing he ran a nonprofit, in Mitchell's view, "but it was really a corporation in the greediest sense of the word." Mitchell's skepticism showed through in his story. "They weren't happy with the story I wrote," he says.[3] In 1978 they were to get a lot unhappier.

The Mitchells had met as communications graduate students at Stanford in 1967 and gotten married. After several journalism and teaching jobs in the Midwest—and one unhappy reporting gig in central Florida, where the paper refused to examine the community's racial strife—they returned to northern California. They bought the *Light*, "convinced we would make it *The New York Times* of West Marin," they said in their 1980 book *The Light on Synanon*, written with psychology professor Richard Ofshe of the University of California, Berkeley. It was far from the *Times*. The Mitchells had one full-time employee, four part-timers, and twenty-six hundred readers. But the paper won numerous state and regional journalism awards in those early years.

Toward the end of 1977, rumors circulated about strange events at Synanon. At a dinner party at Dave and Cathy Mitchell's isolated hillside cabin off Route 1, just north of Point Reyes Station and a few miles south of Synanon's new headquarters, one guest suggested that Dederich was "going crazy" as he neared his sixty-fifth birthday. She did not want to talk much about Synanon, but she had heard that some members were frightened. Others at the party has seen Synanon criticized in *Time* magazine and the *Los Angeles Times*. The next day, Cathy suggested that it was time for an in-depth Synanon story in the *Light*.

The *Light* reporter Keith Ervin learned something from covering an altercation involving a group of Synanon members. The police filed no charges but noted in the report an ominous uttering from one Synanon member: "People cannot hassle Synanon residents and get away with it." His February 2 story included news of the weapons cache, along with a Synanon no-comment. During his reporting, Ervin had heard about a disgruntled Synanon neighbor, Alvin Gambonini, who was assisting Synanon youngsters running away from the property in an attempt to reunite with relatives. Gambonini said he had been roughed up by Synanon members two years earlier for his efforts.

A Grand Jury Speaks

A Marin County grand jury had checked out Synanon in 1976—actually criticizing the county's probation department for not sending young delinquents there for rehabilitation. And while note was taken of runaways from its compounds, Synanon's explanation satisfied the grand jurors: children ran away because the program was so rigorous.

Since then, however, Los Angeles attorney Paul Morantz had been representing parents who believed their children, Marshall-based Synanon members, were being mistreated. Morantz was friendly with many reporters in southern California and had worked in the past with *Los Angeles Times* reporter Narda Zacchino. Morantz wanted to go public about the abusive group that he believed was evolving into a dangerous cult. "I instituted warrant proceedings to get the children brought back to Santa Monica court," the lawyer says, and then, though he considered it to be "borderline unscrupulous," he called reporter Zacchino to alert her to the filings.[4] The resulting *Times* stories on runaways and alleged abuses created an unflattering picture of Synanon, and the Associated Press picked them up. *Time* magazine coverage in December 1977 referred to "a once respected drug program" that had become "a kooky cult."

The next year, a Marin County civil grand jury took a tougher look at Synanon. Its report on March 3, 1978, criticized public officials for failing to regulate it and noted that "the runaway problem, the lawsuits against Synanon to obtain the release of children and others, intemperate statements by Mr. Dederich, the arming of Synanon people, the altercations with neighbors at Marshall, [and] the reports of child abuse have placed Synanon in the public limelight."

In a *Light* story headlined "Grand Jurors Blast Synanon," Dave Mitchell balanced juror claims against a retort from Sheriff Louis Mountanos, who said he had found no abuse, only encounter sessions and other "games" at Synanon. Encounter sessions "have long been the organization's primary way of shaping members' behavior," the sheriff said. In a Keith Ervins sidebar headed "Underground Railroad for Synanon Runaways," Gambonini was quoted telling how the arming of Synanon had made him "scared to plow his fields near his border with the rehabilitation center."

Mitchell's next editorial was headed "A County/Synanon Alliance?" It pointed out how defensive county agencies were after the grand jury criticized them for supporting Synanon or even merely ignoring it. The strongest alliance seemed to be with Sheriff Mountanos, who actually employed two Synanon members as "reserve deputy sheriffs."

Mitchell was friends with a member of the sheriff's top brass, Art Disterheft, who ran the sheriff's substation, and they often chatted on Tuesday nights when the Mitchells were "pasting up" pages. (Dave had page negatives made on Wednesday for a press run and distribution the next day.) Disterheft was unhappy both with Synanon and with the sheriff who played down the organization's violent side. And on one March evening, he let slip to Dave that there was an assault case he might look into—one that Disterheft had been told not to discuss with the press. Mitchell found a report on file about a "split-ee," as Synanon members called those who left the organization, being beaten because he was suspected of spying for *Time* magazine.

A New Source of Income

Synanon went after *Time* in court as well, with a $76 million lawsuit over the story that called it a kooky cult. KGO-TV's owner, ABC, had been hit with a $42 million suit, and Hearst Corporation faced a $40 million action stemming from a long-running dispute over 1972 coverage calling Synanon a "racket." The *Los Angeles Times* and the *Light* had not been sued, although the Mitchells half-expected it at any time. It wasn't something they looked forward to; without a staff lawyer of their own, they would have had to arrange for outside legal coverage.

Despite the exposure, the paper's reporting toughened and broadened. On April 6 it ran financial details researched from state records. Synanon's assets were about $20 million, and Dederich had been granted a $500,000 "pre-retirement bonus." The organization could afford it, and it was soon to get even richer. Hearst settled its Synanon suit out of court for $2 million. (Apparently Synanon had found out that two hired men had stolen tape recordings from the organization for the Hearst defense, and that negative information had led Hearst to settle with its accuser.) News of the $2 million deal spread quickly in the media.

The strength of community weeklies, as Mitchell sees it, involves persistence: keeping tabs on subjects continually rather than doing an entire issue on them. Such coverage often brings out sources who might not otherwise talk. That is what happened with the *Light*'s weekly Synanon stories, which drew the interest of UC-Berkeley's Richard Ofshe. He had done a year's worth of research on Synanon several years before, and former members were telling him about growing violence that echoed what was in the *Light*. Ofshe agreed to serve as an unpaid consultant for the Mitchells.

Attorney Paul Morantz, whose Synanon-related cases had multiplied, remembers talking to Mitchell nearly every day as the *Light*'s coverage intensified. "Dave and I are similar kinds of personalities," he says. "We're knowledge-driven. Once he knew about Synanon, he couldn't go back." As the *Light* kept up the weekly drumbeat about Synanon's abuses, the Mitchells felt increasingly isolated. Not only were the police laying off, but the northern California press had also become uninterested. Those multimillion-dollar lawsuits were having a chilling effect, the Mitchells worried.

Then in late September they learned of another beating. The organization was reportedly ordering members to get vasectomies as a means of controlling their sexual lives, and one who disagreed with the policy had been attacked and was treated for a skull fracture. Dave's editorial was headed "Is Anyone Listening?" It ended by asking:

> Each case of violence by Synanon members is treated as unrelated to every other case. Marshall residents say they are intimidated; the county tries to solve the problem with better zoning.
>
> West Marin residents have a significant problem with Synanon. But like rancher Gambonini we wonder: is anyone out there listening?[5]

Opponents of Synanon were making some gains. Paul Morantz won a $300,000 September court victory in Los Angeles on behalf of a woman whom Los Angeles County had referred to Synanon's Santa Monica facility for counseling. Synanon had not allowed her to leave, shaved her head, and psychologically abused her.

One day as Mitchell was reporting on Synanon, the *Light*'s receptionist alerted him that Morantz had called with an urgent message. Synanon members were being urged to attack Morantz, he said, and the lawyer's address was being aired over the organization's closed-circuit radio station, called "the wire." The broadcast used terms like "break his legs." The attorney had called the police, bought a gun, and called the *Light*. The same day, as Mitchell was discussing this with one of the friendlier sheriff's department officials, the officer told the editor: "I don't want to alarm you, but you ought to let somebody besides your wife know where [your notes] are. If any harm should come to you, those notes will at least give us an idea about where to start looking."[6]

That evening, Ofshe gave the Mitchells his reading on what this all might mean. "Dederich usually telegraphs his punches. He has to because he almost never gives a direct order if he can avoid it," the psychology professor said. "It's a device to put distance between him and the act, so that afterward he can deny responsibility if he wants to." Mitchell then asked Disterheft whether a "goon squad" was being formed at Synanon, as he had heard. Disterheft called an acquaintance with the state attorney general's Organized Crime Bureau, and soon they had an answer. Synanon had started an internal group called "the Imperial Marines." The Crime Bureau had also opened an investigation of the Synanon beatings reported in the *Light*.

"They Got Morantz!"

On Wednesday, October 11, Mitchell had driven the week's *Light* negatives to the printer and was heading back to the office. Under the page-one headline, "State Probe of Synanon Widens," the paper carried this line: "Among the allegations being investigated is a threat against attorney Paul Morantz, who has represented a number of Southern California clients in disputes with Synanon." Half-listening to the car radio, "a sudden excitement in the announcer's voice caught my attention," Mitchell recalls. L.A. attorney Paul Morantz had been bitten by a four-and-a-half-foot rattlesnake hidden in his mailbox.

Mitchell concedes that—for the moment at least—he reacted "with unmixed joy," stopping to call his wife from a payphone and shouting "They got Morantz!" At last, the world would start paying attention to the *Light*'s story. Cathy was more terrified than elated. She was going to have to drive past Synanon to get to her teaching job. But if she stayed home, she worried that she might be attacked there. After paranoia, she later recalled, "my second reaction was, How stupid! There's no way Synanon can get out of it this time."[7]

What had Morantz himself gone through? For days he had been on guard because of warnings from the state crime bureau about the dangers of Synanon—examining his car before getting in and checking out his house whenever he got home. "I got into my house by opening the door, letting it swing back, and looking both ways. If my dogs didn't bark when I came home, I didn't go in the house."

On the fateful evening he had arrived at his front door after another crime bureau meeting, looking forward to watching the Dodgers playing a home World Series game. He carefully opened the door. Still, he says, "not in my wildest imagination was I thinking of the possibility of a rattlesnake being in my mailbox." Letting his border collies out, he took some groceries into the kitchen. "I remember thinking something odd was stuffed in my mailbox," according to Morantz. The box was built into the front wall, accessible inside through a grille. He wasn't wearing his contact lenses as he approached the flap from the side and he reached in thinking he was retrieving a package or perhaps a mass like some kind of scarf that had been stuffed in. When he had the mass in his grasp, he unthinkingly pulled it out. The snake's rattles had been cut off. "I actually saw the head strike out and bite me. As it happened my left hand swung into the air, and the snake went into the air and landed on my floor." He screamed, then thought of his dogs outside and slammed the door as the snake recoiled. Running out the back door, he yelled to neighbors, "Call an ambulance! I've been bitten by a rattlesnake. It's Synanon." Paramedics and firemen arrived together. The firemen killed the snake with a shovel, while the medics treated Morantz's painfully swollen and blistered left arm. Neighbors reported a suspicious car that had been spotted in the area. Some had written down a license number. The plates were registered to Synanon in Marshall.[8]

The *Light* story—which seemed prescient the Thursday it hit the street—was very old by the weekend. Two Synanon members were arrested, one of them the son of band leader Stan Kenton. The news was everywhere. Walter Cronkite intoned that the crime was "bizarre, even by cult standards."

The Mitchells planned five stories for the October 19 issue, harboring little illusion that their weekly could have anything fresh. Dave had interviewed Jack Hurst, a former Synanon president now out of the organization. While shocked by its gradual turn toward violence, Hurst had declined to be interviewed in the past. Now he was ready. His dog, purchased for self-protection, had been mysteriously hanged. "They're heavily armed and very dangerous—and specifically trained in terrorist activities," he told Mitchell. "I think I'm next."

During the interview, the editor learned that Hurst lived with a recent Synanon split-ee named Mary Inskip, who had told Los Angeles police that Dederich had personally urged members to attack Morantz. When Mitchell called her, she confirmed it, providing specific language that the leader had used. The *Light* could quote her by name.

It would be the paper's lead piece, although he wanted to run it by a lawyer first. "When I wrote the story, I knew that potentially someone might go ahead with a libel case," he says. For pro bono advice he called an attorney friend from Stanford, Ladd Bedford. (His "pay" was a couple of pizzas Mitchell brought for munching during their consultation.) Bedford suggested one critical word change in his lead. "The lawyer said, 'You've written here that Dederich called for the attack on

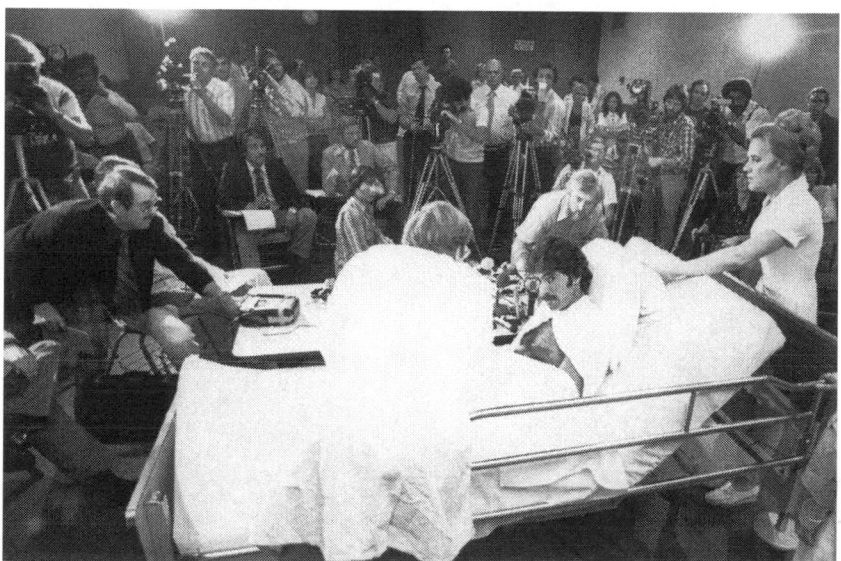

FIGURE 18.1 Los Angeles attorney Paul Morantz surrounded by the press in a Los Angeles hospital as he recovers from his 1978 snake bite. *Source*: Used by permission. United Press International photo provided by Corbis.

Morantz. You need to write that he called for *an* attack on Morantz. We don't know he specifically called for this one. And that would be hard to prove." (They even discussed the veiled order England's twelfth-century King Henry II gave for the killing of Thomas Becket: "Who will rid me of this meddlesome priest?"[9]) Once Mitchell cleared the wording he slapped a "Special Synanon Issue" on page one, printing four hundred extra copies. The story was an exclusive. Mitchell later learned that other papers had trouble getting reports of Dederich's attack order confirmed.

Different Spouses, Different Fears

The *Light* became a primary source for the nation's newly interested press. The Mitchells continued to have original information each week. As the rattler attack spread fear among other Synanon enemies, Dave Mitchell was strangely unworried. "If anyone physically attacked us, everyone would know," he says now. "That's the difference between being a small-town

FIGURE 18.2 Los Angeles police officer Richad Grotsley holds the four-and-a-half-foot snake placed in Morantz's mailbox by members of the Synanon cult. *Source*: United Press International photo provided by Corbis.

editor, where everybody in town knows the guy and what his battles are, and being someone like Paul Morantz, who's in a large metropolitan area where few people know what he's doing." Still, Art Disterheft ran extra patrols at the Mitchell house. And the night Dederich was arrested on a conspiracy charge, Disterheft spent the night there.

The moves were wise. Cathy believed that their hillside cabin, on a long driveway far from neighbors, made the couple vulnerable. "Dave was more macho than I was," she recalls. Disterheft's patrols only added to her panic level. "Coming up the long winding driveway, you'd hear this car and think, 'Oh my god, they've come,'" she remembers. The couple called off the patrols "because they were doing more harm than good."[10]

The Mitchells' aggressive coverage continued through the end of the year, with one late October editorial blasting Sheriff Mountanos and another story analyzing the legal case against Morantz's attackers. On December 28 the *Light* proclaimed Dederich its "Man of the Year," recounting his rise and fall.

Like Joe Murray at the *Lufkin News*, Dave Mitchell had problems getting his Pulitzer entry in the mail. The *Light* had left the task to the last minute, and with the deadline bearing down, Mitchell found himself "driving a million miles an hour" to get to San Rafael, the only Marin station that could postmark an envelope late.

The public service jury had the *Light* tied with the *Chicago Sun-Times* and its series on profiteering from abortions. The board went with the California weekly. When a Washington reporter called the Mitchells early on Pulitzer Monday to say he had heard a rumor that the *Light* might have won a Pulitzer, the initial shock quickly gave way to fear—that the weekly's onerous deadlines might make it miss its own award announcement. "We picked up the production schedule," says Mitchell. "If by chance we did win, it wouldn't screw up production." The story made it into the paper.

Later, after Dave and Cathy Mitchell's marriage broke up, he continued to run the *Light* for a time, selling it in 2005, but keeping its gold medal as a condition of the sale. Something of a California journalism guru, he remains an acolyte for weekly community newspapering while writing a blog called "Sparsely Sage and Timely." Cathy has retired as a professor at the University of North Carolina, Asheville, where she specialized in journalism history. Looking back on her time in Point Reyes, she says that "while the newspaper industry as a whole is in trouble, it is my view that the little guys like the *Light* have a larger possibility of survival."

In more recent years, the *Light* has been run by editor Tess Elliott and a small staff that sometimes attracts Ivy League graduates to its brand of "village journalism," as Elliott calls it. "Having that Pulitzer is invaluable," she says. "We put a mention of it at the top of our paper every week.

FIGURE 18.3 The front page of the April 29, 1979, *Light* announces its Pulitzer Prize. Pictured at the top are owner-editors Dave Mitchell (left) and Cathy Mitchell, with Synanon expert Richard Ofshe. *Source*: Used by permission of *Point Reyes Light*, © 1979.

It's what helps draw ambitious young people to be interns, and to be hired as staff."[11]

After recovering from the rattlesnake attack, meanwhile, attorney Morantz continued to battle cults and other Synanon-like organizations in the courtroom and later through writing books. His most recent is titled *Escape: My Lifelong War Against Cults.*[12]

1979—The *Point Reyes Light*, a California weekly, for its investigation of Synanon.[13]

CHAPTER 19

EVERYBODY'S BUSINESS

1980–1989: Considering the Company View

How shameful it is for the Knight family and its organ, The [Charlotte] Observer, to take the side of OSHA and the oppressive bureaucrats against the magnificent Southern textile industry. It is sickening to see the gutless minions of the news media siding with a few crybaby Americans who obviously are looking for a handout from the very hand that fed and clothed their families.

—W. B. PITTS, PRESIDENT, HERMITAGE INCORPORATED,
CAMDEN, SOUTH CAROLINA

Business and technology were on the mind of every reporter and editor in the 1980s, if only because computers were starting to take over their newsrooms. The machines on their desks started carrying names like IBM or Apple rather than Remington, Royal, or Underwood. The once-incessant clacking of typewriter keys—a background noise used in the movie of *All the President's Men* to suggest the machine gun–like media firepower—did, in fact, cease. The muted tapping that replaced it reminded journalists of the sound of calculators. Overnight, it seemed, the newsroom turned as quiet as an insurance office.

The lack of clamor was deceptive. Reporters were still inspired to pursue investigations in the spirit of Watergate. The best news organizations remained both vigilant and aggressive, and increasingly they created either formal or informal teams to pursue major projects. Reporters also added computer-assisted reporting to their arsenal. By 1989, when the *Anchorage Daily News* won a second gold medal, Howard Weaver—by then the managing editor—was using a Macintosh to crunch statistical data that illustrated the plight of native Alaskans. The computer also helped coordinate assignments and deadlines for his far-flung staffers. Compare that to the system used to plot out its 1976 series on the Teamsters. "We drew flow charts with colored pencils to show inter-relationships amongst people," says Weaver.[1]

The topics of Public Service Prize-winning stories ranged widely in the decade. Two were religion stories. Two looked closely at ethnic groups. And two involved the military. Reporters especially dug into what they called the business angle of the stories. But these were not the classic General Motors, Xerox, or Microsoft articles from the financial pages. Instead news organizations explored the role of companies in environmental affairs, the finances of churches, and the military-industrial complex.

The classic government corruption stories of city hall graft or malfeasance in the state house all but disappeared from the list of winners. But federal agencies and the military came in for plenty of questioning, as did various jurisdictions implicated in damaging the health and welfare of Americans.

Two Cheers for Charlotte

Knight Ridder's *Charlotte Observer* had a pair of winners in the 1980s. In 1980 the *Observer's* staff became intrigued with health issues in the giant Carolina textile industry. Factory workers intimately knew the plague of nearly invisible cotton dust that led to an asthma-like condition known as byssinosis, or "brown lung." But government, industry, and even medical professionals seemed to ignore the problem. The idea for the *Observer's* stories actually originated with the textile workers' union, a source that editor Richard Oppel viewed suspiciously. "In a way this was the wine from poisonous fruit, because the union had an ax to grind," he says. "But I'm a believer that you don't discount information as long as it's verified. A fact is a fact, wherever you get it from."[2]

Over months of investigation, a team of reporters, led by veterans Howard Covington and Marion Ellis, studied the potential dangers of cotton dust. Medical reporter Bob Conn and Robert L. Drogin also participated, along with Washington correspondent Robert Hodierne. Deep into the research, they remained stumped because of the lack of a proven link between the dust and various established ailments. But state government regulations were designed to limit exposure to the dust, and inspections were not being performed as required. That much was clear.

The paper was able to document obvious cases of workers handicapped by exposure to cotton dust, and the *Observer* used photographs extensively. "The pictures showed men who looked like they were ninety years old, but who were forty-five years old," Oppel says. Sometimes these victims had to rely on oxygen tanks. The *Observer's* eight-part series started on February 3, 1980, and was called "Brown Lung: A Case of Deadly Neglect." It contained twenty-two articles and eight editorials.

The outcry from industry was loud and long. The letter from a textile company president quoted at the beginning of this chapter and submitted by "gutless minion" Rich Oppel as part of the paper's Pulitzer Prize entry suggests the level of outrage the series provoked within certain segments of the community.[3] The first story began, "Cotton dust—an invisible product of the most important industry in the Carolinas—is killing people."

After the series, the North Carolina labor commissioner received funding to hire and equip staff members for inspections, and the state industrial commission added deputy commissioners to speed compensation decisions. The governor also ordered changes in the way compensation was granted. By the end of 1980, $4 million in workers compensation for byssinosis was paid out, more than the total paid in the previous nine-year history of the program. Impressed, the Pulitzer board awarded the *Observer* the 1981 gold medal.

1981—The *Charlotte* (N.C.) *Observer* for its series on "Brown Lung: A Case of Deadly Neglect."[4]

When "Enough Isn't Enough"

The *Observer* had been exploring another local business: Jim and Tammy Faye Bakker's PTL television ministry. (The name was an acronym for both Praise the Lord and People That Love.) Tipsters were plentiful, but as a private company PTL yielded few documentary trails for the paper to follow. The *Observer* stories stretching back to 1976 had raised more questions than they answered. Still, the coverage stirred the anger of the Bakkers and their PTL supporters. Already PTL was claiming, sometimes on the air, that the paper had a "vendetta" against it. As more unconfirmed reports of abuses at PTL streamed in to reporters, however, the *Observer* kept a close eye on the situation. The hard, verifiable evidence of malfeasance that the paper needed did not come its way for years.

In December 1984, the *Observer's* suspicions about Jim Bakker and PTL intensified when former church secretary Jessica Hahn called reporter Charles E. Shepard to talk about having been sexually assaulted by Bakker four years earlier in a Florida hotel room. Shepard, hired by editor Oppel in 1980, was not so interested in the report of a possible sex offense, which would be very difficult to prove. Instead he wanted to pursue the possibility that church money was used to hush her up. And he was especially driven to find that out after Hahn called him three weeks later and retracted everything that she had told him. "She threatened to sue [the paper] if anything was printed," Shepard wrote later. He later learned why. After one of Hahn's representatives had threatened PTL with a lawsuit, the organization had offered her money to keep quiet.[5]

Shepard got information in late 1985 that confirmed that Hahn was paid off with church funds. "What had seemed merely an episode in the private life of a public figure had become a story about misuse of donors' dollars—the very kind of news the *Observer* had pursued at PTL since the late 1970s," according to Shepard. The paper, however, set strict standards for sourcing any stories that alleged improper sexual conduct. "The sex lives of public people are not necessarily news unless and until we can establish that it affects their institutions," says Oppel.[6] Any story about PTL would have to show solid evidence of payoffs. And Shepard's information did not qualify yet. His source for the payoff allegation had demanded confidentiality, and Shepard could not corroborate the information. Shepard's later account of the reporting noted that Oppel insisted on for-the-record confirmation and documentary proof of any payoff before it could be mentioned in an article. "That seemed impossible," wrote Shepard. "PTL had structured the Hahn settlement to avoid a paper trail and seal the lips of those involved."

In January 1986, the *Observer* got a good lead about a separate problem facing PTL. Based on documents obtained through a Freedom of

Information Act request, the paper was able to write stories describing a Federal Communications Commission investigation into PTL's over-the-air fundraising.

Bakker's war with the paper escalated. The televangelist launched a crusade against the *Observer* on his nationally syndicated weekday program with the theme: "Enough Is Enough." According to Shepard, "He sought to intimidate the newspaper and its parent chain, Knight Ridder, with appeals to his supporters to cancel subscriptions, pull ads and deluge his adversary with letters and phone calls. He hired private detectives to investigate the newspaper's publisher, editor and reporters and former coworkers he suspected were aiding the newspaper." Reports of subscription cancellations came to Oppel from as far away as the *San Jose Mercury News*.

By the spring of 1986, Bakker had reason to think his intimidation strategy was working. Even the *Observer's* publisher, Rolfe Neill, felt the paper was being unfair to the Bakkers. "He felt we were picking the institution apart in a slow death," says Oppel. Shepard knew better, but proof remained elusive. Oppel allowed him one more chance to try getting corroboration for the information that Hahn had been paid off to keep quiet. "I went back to the phone," according to Shepard's account. By March 13 he had gotten a copy of a February 1985 check for $115,000 written by PTL's lawyer and an on-the-record confirmation from a Hahn representative. Soon even publisher Neill had to agree that the reporting had reached a critical mass. "He was behind us at that point," says Oppel.

As Shepard prepared his *Observer* story, managing editor Mark Ethridge III got a call from a lawyer for PTL threatening legal action if the paper published and demanding that Bakker and his number two, Richard Dortch, be interviewed. Of course, the *Observer's* past requests for interviews had been rejected. But now the story had to be delayed until the interviews could take place. In the meantime, Shepard learned that the church itself had begun an investigation based on the *Observer's* inquiries. Before the paper could run its story on the payoff or the sexual encounter that had precipitated it, Bakker resigned in what the paper called "a preemptive strike."

Then Shepard's exclusives started: about a $265,000 payoff to Hahn with church funds laundered through a building contractor; about Dortch being the one who negotiated the Hahn settlement; and about how Jim and Tammy Bakker had been paid more than $1.6 million for 1986. Dortch was fired by a new PTL board. Televangelist Jerry Falwell, who took over as board chairman, complimented the *Observer*'s coverage and spoke of PTL's "fiscal sins" of the past. And the 1988 gold medal—the paper's second of the decade—was awarded to the *Observer*. The medals were installed in a glass enclosure on a pedestal that visitors pass when they walk through the paper's lobby.

1988—The *Charlotte* (N.C.) *Observer* for revealing misuse of funds by the PTL television ministry through persistent coverage conducted in the face of a massive campaign by PTL to discredit the newspaper.[7]

A Survivor Seals the Story

The military correspondent for the *Fort Worth Star-Telegram*, Washington-based Mark J. Thompson, was doing his basic "beat reading" when he first came upon a piece in the trade newsletter *Helicopter News*. A problem called mast bumping, it said, had caused some accidents involving Huey troop-carrying and Cobra attack helicopters, then the backbone of Bell Helicopter's business.[8] Even from the short story, it was clear that this was a pilot's nightmare. Under certain operating situations the rotor could tilt too far and strike the mast that attaches the blades to the aircraft, usually causing the mast to snap "and turning the chopper into a coffin for all aboard," as Thompson puts it. But the position of Bell, which built the aircraft in Fort Worth, was clear. It was blameless. "If this bizarre snafu occurred, it would be either weather, pilot error, or something else that had already gone wrong that had doomed the flight," he heard from the Bell representatives. "Their basic line was so long as the pilot was smart, it wouldn't happen."

Having covered aircraft accidents before for the "Startle-Gram," as staffers called the then-Capital Cities publication, he was familiar with the pilot error explanation. F-16 fighter planes, also built in Fort Worth, had gone down a number of times, and the reporter had written about how pilots often put themselves in untenable positions in the Pentagon's hot fighters. As Bell suggested, the helicopter cases were probably the same thing, he thought. Still, the report was worth a check.

While the newsletter had mentioned that a single pilot had survived a mast-bumping crash, he wasn't identified. Thompson wanted to find out what he might say about the Cobra's safety. "I remember spending some period of time tracking him down," says Thompson, who tapped his Pentagon sources for the search, finally locating him at Patuxent River Naval Air Station in Maryland. "I said to myself, Gosh, if he concedes that he did something wrong, that wouldn't be much of a story."

Instead the interview would become seared in Mark Thompson's memory. Larry Higgins was flying with his co-pilot, who had been killed instantly when the rotor blade sliced through the cockpit. "He spoke very levelly. It wasn't quite a monotone," according to the reporter. "He knew what he wanted to say. He wanted me to understand that there was nothing goofy that day. They were test pilots, wearing parachutes and ready for any eventuality, they thought." Describing the accident, though, he hesitated with his answers. "It wasn't until I got to the third or fourth order of questions, where I showed him that I knew what was going on there—and that Bell had said that he must have flown outside the envelope—that he began to get angry," says Thompson. Higgins shot back at him: "You're damn right the helicopter ended up outside the envelope. The rotor isn't supposed to come through the cockpit." Thompson was stunned. For the story, which would take several months to report completely, "that was, to my mind, really the starting gun." Next came Freedom of Information Act requests and a raft of accident reports and other documents to show him the scope of the problem.

One other interview, with engineer Tom White at Fort Belvoir in Virginia, had an unpromising start. "Can you tell me about these accidents?" Thompson asked. "No, I can't," White responded. "Well, what if I sent a FOIA?" the reporter followed up. White hesitated. "I've been waiting years for somebody to ask that," he said. Suddenly Thompson knew he was about to get a wealth of valuable new documents. "White, it turned out, was an early and ardent advocate of the hub spring, a $5,000 modification that would have corrected the helicopter's problems."

The first of Thompson's five parts, with the rubric "Deadly Blades," ran on Sunday, March 25, 1984, headlined "Design Flaw Mars Bell Military Helicopters." It began:

WASHINGTON—Nearly 250 U.S. servicemen have been killed since 1967 aboard Bell helicopters that crashed because of a design flaw that remains largely uncorrected even though the Army discovered it in 1973, according to military documents and former Pentagon safety experts.

A top lawyer at Bell Helicopter of Fort Worth acknowledged the seriousness of the matter in 1979 when he urged the company to fix the problem even if it had to spend its own money to do so.

"I consider this matter very serious and, if we do nothing about it, very likely to be the subject of attempts at punitive damages," George Galerstein, Bell's chief legal counsel, told company management in a 1979 internal memo.

Galerstein's prediction has since come true families of five pilots killed since 1980 in crashes attributed to the design problem have filed suits seeking nearly a quarter of a billion dollars from Bell.

The death toll from the mast-bumping problem might be even higher, the article said: "It could not be determined how many helicopter accidents during the Vietnam War, during which Cobras and Hueys were extensively used, may have been caused by mast bumping." Bell did try to get the military to make changes but at the military's own expense.

Executive editor Jack B. Tinsley's Pulitzer nomination letter noted that "the Army assembled a blue-ribbon panel to investigate the questions raised by the series," finding that the paper's account had been accurate. The Army then took steps to correct the problem. "The reaction by Bell and its almost 6,000 area employees has been less positive," Tinsley wrote. "While the series was running, Bell sent a letter to Star-Telegram publisher Phil Meek demanding that the newspaper remove its news racks from Bell property and apologize for the black eye it had given the company." The company asked retail outlets around its plant to refuse to do business with Star-Telegram employees, and union representatives launched a drive that resulted in the paper losing about 1,300 subscribers.

Thompson, who later moved to Knight Ridder Newspapers and then to *Time* magazine, continued to cover defense-related scandals after the Bell reports and after his paper won the 1985 gold medal. "The military," he says, "is the gift that keeps on giving for reporters."

1985—The *Fort Worth* (Tex.) *Star-Telegram* for reporting by Mark J. Thompson which revealed that nearly 250 U.S. servicemen had lost their lives as a result of a design problem in helicopters built by Bell Helicopter—a revelation which ultimately led the Army to ground almost 600 Huey helicopters pending their modification.[9]

Flying High

An aviation story of another kind led to the 1987 Public Service Prize. The *Pittsburgh Press* public health reporter Andrew Schneider had been teamed with Mary Pat Flaherty the previous year on a project exploring the nation's organ transplantation system, which had earned them the 1986 Pulitzer in Specialized Reporting. In early September 1986, Schneider got a tip that set him on a new course with new teammates.

On a reporting trip in Florida, he received a call from a physician friend with an almost unbelievable tale: a seriously drug-overdosed patient had arrived at Pittsburgh's Mercy Hospital, near death, but had been whisked out of intensive care prematurely. Schneider's friend suspected that the individual removing the patient might have been a pusher. But whoever it was had argued that this patient had to leave the hospital immediately so that he could get back to work—flying for US Airways. Confidentiality rules prevented the hospital from notifying the airline or the Federal Aviation Administration about the pilot's drug problem. So this doctor called his reporter friend instead, hoping somehow to publicize the situation.

Once back in Pittsburgh, Schneider began looking into the pilot's past, including his medical record. "He had track marks every conceivable place he could have them. So this had to go back years," says the reporter, who later moved to the *Baltimore Sun*. "It raised the question, 'How could he pass his medical exams?'" The FAA requires six-month examinations of pilots.[10]

Schneider's first story, on September 21, examined the USAir pilot's case. Follow-up articles looked at the rules preventing airlines and the FAA from getting reports about impaired pilots and flaws in the system of physicals. He interviewed the examiner for the overdosed pilot and was told an unconvincing story. The doctor had not suspected any drug use, he told Schneider. The reporter found that in many cases pilot physicals were a troubling joke in the aviation business. "The so-called $50 exam meant that you held the 50-dollar bill out, and if you could see it, the doctor took the fifty from you and you passed," he says. That cleared the pilot to continue flying. The national press began picking up Schneider's stories.

Later that month the reporter got a call from a federal government source who had been reading the articles. "He said, 'You have to come meet some friends of mine.'" It sounded urgent, so Schneider flew to Washington, where a group had congregated with the source in the back room of a Japanese restaurant in Georgetown. Schneider did not know them or what to expect. "They looked as uncomfortable as whores in church. They were just very, very nervous," he says. His government friend introduced them—top officials from most of the country's largest airlines, each of whom had serious concerns about pilot medical reporting. They could talk to him only off the record, but what they said was chilling. Each had a number of pilots at his airline who were too sick to fly—heart problems were typical, along with drug dependency—and who could become incapacitated while flying to create a serious hazard to the public. But for various reasons, mostly union agreements, pilots could not be grounded if the FAA said they could fly, the reporter was told. Schneider responded to the airline representatives that there was no way he could do an investigation without pilots' names. But he assured them that any names provided would be kept in confidence. With their help, Schneider compiled a list of nearly three hundred allegedly impaired pilots.

In spot stories that ran through December 21, Schneider and his teammate on a number of stories, general assignment reporter Matt Brelis, followed leads that presented a picture of a dangerously faulty system. The FAA was created to protect the flying public, not to make life easy for addicted or medically impaired pilots. In an arrangement that reflected the power of the pilots' lobby in Washington, the FAA refused to compare names of licensed pilots with easily available registry lists showing motorists with license revocations for substance abuse, for example. Even when the FAA did learn of criminal abuse–related behavior by pilots, the agency "closed its eyes," according to the *Pittsburgh Press* reports.

The federal air surgeon, Dr. Frank Austin, frequently overruled those few warnings about pilot ailments that made it on the record. That kept impaired pilots flying as well. In an interview with the *Press*, Austin, a former Navy carrier pilot, defended the pilots' right to fly and said that in many cases that right had overridden medical information he had been given about individual pilots.

The *Press* also investigated a catch-22 in the FAA medical regulations. The rules required pilots who *were* found using drugs to be permanently grounded, without any provision for rehabilitation. With their careers at stake, those pilots who sought treatment in good faith were forced to visit clinics secretly, without reporting it. Some of the private clinics were not medically sound.

Among the reforms that resulted from the *Press* articles were the removal of Dr. Austin from his post, the installation of provisions for cross-checking pilots and drivers' registry lists, and a tightening of FAA medical exam requirements.

One other public service finalist, the *Fort Lauderdale News and Sun-Sentinel*, also had a medical theme, examining serious mishaps in the system of Veterans Hospitals.

1987—The *Pittsburgh Press* for reporting by Andrew Schneider and Matthew Brelis which revealed the inadequacy of the FAA's medical screening of airline pilots and led to significant reforms.[11]

Pulitzer, Reform Thyself

As chairman of the Pulitzer Prize advisory board from 1955 until his retirement in 1986, Joseph Pulitzer Jr. (as the third JP was known) built a reputation as a fair-minded moderator. He rarely tried to dominate a discussion or divert a debate among strong-willed board members. John Hohenberg, the Pulitzer Prize administrator for ten of those years, noted "that he, like his father and grandfather, was an articulate and devoted liberal Democrat of the old school." In fact the chairman's only short-coming, in Hohenberg's view, may have been "a distinct form of ances-tor worship that caused him to oppose any major change" that could lead the Pulitzer Prizes to deviate from what the first Joseph Pulitzer had intended.[12] The *St. Louis Post-Dispatch* editor also presided over a period of transformation that changed the Pulitzer Prize selection process signifi-cantly in the 1970s and early 1980s. He supported reforms vigorously and occasionally took the lead in creating them.

Smaller changes had been made in the early decades, of course: using working journalists in the juries rather than Columbia professors, for example. In the early 1950s, to reduce the domination by the same board members year after year, a maximum term of service was set. (JP Jr., like his father, was specifically exempted from the term limit, which is now nine years.) The board also stopped describing Pulitzers as being for "the best" work, calling the winner "a distinguished example" instead. In the case of gold medal winners, the citation for "the most disinterested and meritorious public service"—the wording of the benefactor's will—became "a distinguished example of meritorious public service." (After changing the description on the medal for a time, the original inscription has been restored.)

Larger concerns about the Pulitzer Prizes being tightly controlled by a handful of men remained valid through the 1960s, however. During his board term from 1940 to 1954, the *New York Times*'s Arthur Krock had been one such powerful board member, according to David Shaw, a *Los Angeles Times* media reporter who became a student of the prizes. Krock met with board friends for dinner the evening before formal voting on the prizes, where the group prepared their choices for consideration by the full group. Too many prizes for one paper was a Krock no-no. Fellow board member John S. Knight told Shaw about Krock's message to him when Knight's paper, the *Chicago Daily News*, found itself nominated by jurors for prizes in three categories. "Krock just took me out for a little walk and said I might want to be 'more restrained.' I got the message," according to Knight. With other editors in Chicago, they decided which single prize they preferred.[13]

The reforms that chairman Pulitzer championed in the 1970s bubbled up from news organizations, reflecting their growing awareness that all-white,

CHALLENGES FOR A NEW ERA

all-male newsrooms were unacceptable and that diversity in press leadership was something to be sought. By the year JP Jr. retired, the board not only contained both women and minority members but had also established a jury system emphasizing ethnic and gender balance.

Just as dramatic was a major alteration in the relationship of the Pulitzer Prizes to Columbia University—a relationship that his grandfather had designed into his plan for the awards before JP Jr. was born. When the time came to revise that relationship, JP Jr. took charge of the sensitive negotiations that separated the Columbia Board of Trustees from the prize-awarding process.

At Odds Over the Pentagon Papers

The chairman and other board members had begun questioning the role of the trustees during the tumult surrounding the 1972 awarding of the gold medal to the *New York Times* for its analysis of the Pentagon Papers. Trustees had twice voted down the board's proposed selection of the *Times*—objecting that the Pentagon Papers were stolen documents—before Columbia president William McGill talked them out of any decision to veto the prize. In the end, the trustees noted that terms of the Pulitzers allowed the trustees to accept or reject an advisory board recommendation but not to submit an alternate winner. Had the trustees been charged with making awards, they noted, "certain of the recipients would not have been chosen." Still, they conceded that the Pulitzer advisory board's "judgments are to be accorded great weight by the Trustees," and they eventually voted to accept the recommendations.[14]

There were similar worries about trustees potentially overruling the board the next year when the *Washington Post* was named the gold medal winner for its Watergate coverage after having been vilified by the Nixon administration. But on April 30, a week before the trustees met, key White House aides to President Nixon resigned and the president's press secretary issued a remarkable apology to the *Post* for having accused it of "shabby journalism." With little discussion, the trustees approved the *Post*'s prize.

Chairman Pulitzer had fought strenuously for the *Times* to win in 1972 and for the *Post* to win in 1973. But in 1975 he began to press for a change in the trustee–Pulitzer Prize connection. Columbia backed out of its oversight process, instead arranging to have the university's president represent the school on the board. By 1979 "advisory" was dropped from the board's title because it was no longer advising anyone on the prizes. The board had the final say.[15]

Finally, the Finalists

The reforms that Pulitzer championed and achieved *within* the board had a huge impact too. Gene Patterson, a board member from 1973 to 1984, was instrumental in this modernization—diversifying the board's membership and increasing disclosure about the selection process. At the same time, the role of the jurors was clarified. They became "nominating jurors" and the board emphasized in its instructions that the panels were not the final decision makers. Jurors were instructed to list their nominations in alphabetical order rather than ranking their top choices. Choosing the top entry was the board's job.

"There was no particular reformer-in-chief that I remember. We sat around this long table and kicked these things around," according to Patterson, who died in January 2013. "There was just stuff that needed to be done." That included increasing the board's size and geographic representation sharply and adding women, black, and Latino members.

For the first time, a system for publicly naming finalists also was approved. "There was some ancient feeling that it diminishes the Pulitzer Prizes to say there were people who didn't win. But everybody knew there were. And as editors we stand for the free flow of information," Patterson said. By identifying finalists, the board also acknowledged the honor that went with being in the running for a prize while giving the jury some credit for its choices. "And the public got a better look at how the Pulitzer works," he noted. The board meetings remained secret, and board members were told not to discuss the decisions afterward. "Like in a jury, you have to go into a room and talk quite frankly about the entries you have before you. In public, that dries up the spontaneity of the deliberations," said Patterson.[16]

In 1985 the Pulitzer board expanded the number of journalism categories from thirteen to fourteen, essentially creating the award lineup that would take the Pulitzers into the twenty-first century. (Explanatory journalism had been added the prior year. Specialized reporting gave way to beat reporting in 1991 and in 2006 was changed to local reporting.) Editorial writing and public service remained the granddaddies of the Pulitzer journalism awards.

More recent Pulitzer board members uniformly praise today's prize-selection process for its candor and fairness, saying that any vestiges of the past old-boy network are now completely gone. Gene Roberts, who was the executive editor of the *Philadelphia Inquirer* when he joined the board in the early 1980s, remembers that "there were one or two little things that I thought could have been interpreted as efforts to back-scratch. But the attempts were noticeably unsuccessful. In that group, the idea of back-scratching was very repellent."[17]

The former *Chicago Tribune* editor Jack Fuller, who was president of Tribune Publishing when his nine board years ended in 2000, says, "One of the great things when I joined the board was to find that some of the folklore was just absolutely wrong. The model was mutual respect, where you could disagree sharply without being wounded, or wounding."[18] Michael Gartner, a board member for nine years ending in 1991, agrees. "Integrity oozed out of the process," and there were very few predictable winners, because the discussion often swayed opinions. "There were never any lay-downs. You'd go into the meeting thinking, This one's going to be easy. And Jesus, the vote would be five to five to five," says Gartner, whose past positions include the editor of the *Des Moines Register* and the Ames, Iowa, *Daily Tribune*, the editor of the front page of the *Wall Street Journal*, and president of NBC News.[19]

Jurors and board members concede that their peers sometimes seem overly cautious about cutting-edge types of stories, tending to favor familiar formats in selecting the Pulitzers. "Journalism is exceedingly conservative about itself as a profession, and when the prize selection process is done by people who are at the top of the profession, it isn't surprising that they are also conservative about the winners they pick," says the former *Tribune* editor Fuller. And yet the board is extremely sensitive to the emergence of themes that reflect what readers find newsworthy. Increasingly one such ascendant theme was the environment.

CHAPTER 20

THE NATURE OF THINGS

1990–1998: The Scientific and the Sordid

"The Environment Story" is bigger and more important than ever, and it will only grow more so in years to come. [Journalists] recognize professional challenges in cracking the complexity of environmental issues, overcoming the pitfalls of fragmented reporting, and making important concerns more audience friendly.

—FROM THE STRATEGIC PLAN OF THE SOCIETY
OF ENVIRONMENTAL JOURNALISTS, FOUNDED IN 1990

Stories dealing with environmental issues and the natural sciences—or in two cases nature's fury and how Americans cope with it—dominated Public Service Prize-winners in the 1990s. Still, the business story was here to stay, and much of the coverage that was honored continued to have a corporate flavor. For one thing, reporters examined more closely the changing environmental attitudes within industry and governmental agencies.

On a smaller scale, news organizations were facing up to a serious environmental and health problem *internally*. As regulations spread from state to state, publishers gradually banned that ancient crutch of deadline writers and editors everywhere: smoking. Suddenly newsrooms were not only quiet, they were cigarette-, cigar-, and pipe-free—an amazing contrast for anyone who had known the noisy, smoky newspaper offices of the 1960s or 1970s. Of course, the same anti-smoking rules applied to every business, not just journalism. But the change particularly shocked reporters, many of whom were convinced that nicotine and caffeine were every bit as important as newsprint and ink to getting the news out each day. (It will be left, perhaps, to the next generation to witness ink and paper vanish as necessary elements of the daily press.) Somehow, though, reporters and editors managed to continue turning out great journalism in the twentieth century's last decade, even if the newsroom tab for coffee skyrocketed.

Blood and Water

The 1990 Pulitzer board picked both the mighty *Philadelphia Inquirer* and North Carolina's tiny *Washington Daily News* as gold medal winners, the first time in twenty-three years that more than a single Public Service Prize was awarded. One winning story involved the business of water, the other the business of blood. But both had the simplest of origins. For the family-owned *Washington Daily News*, which claimed its first Pulitzer Prize, it started with the editor puzzling over the small print on his home water bill. For the *Philadelphia Inquirer*, continuing its long string of Pulitzers under Gene Roberts, the genesis was a reporter's pensive moment during a Red Cross blood drive in the office.[1]

In Washington, North Carolina, Bill Coughlin noted a new statement on his water bill. It said that the city was testing for chemicals in the water system. As editor of the 10,500-circulation *Daily News*, he asked one of the paper's four reporters, Betty Gray, to look into it. Her digging turned up forty-two chemicals in the water, each of which she discussed with state and private toxicologists. One chemical, she was told, was a carcinogen far in excess of the Environmental Protection Agency's safe level. She then obtained memos showing that the state environmental agency knew the city's water was contaminated.[2]

Gray built her knowledge to prepare for an interview with the city manager, which came on the morning of Wednesday, September 13. (An afternoon paper, the *Daily News* had a noon deadline.) She learned that the federal act eliminating unsafe drinking water did not cover communities with less than ten thousand residents, like the *Daily News*'s city of Washington. Actually, it turned out, there were fifty-six thousand water treatment plans in the United States that were unprotected by the EPA.

After a few minutes with the reporter the city manager interrupted the interview, promising to get back to her in time for deadline. He then rushed to the newspaper with a legal notice that described the town's water as having "levels of certain chemicals which exceeded EPA recommendations." The notice was too late to run, but it became part of Gray's front-page story for the next day. Gray later confirmed that the city's knowledge of carcinogens in the water went back eight years but that there had been no regulations requiring a mayor, city manager, the state, or the EPA to inform the public.

Next Wednesday, the paper ran a report on a second cancer-causing chemical that was combining with the first to increase hazards so severely that the water plant might have to close. As the coverage continued, the mayor complained that the city was in "turmoil" because of the reports and said that the "citizens are ready to hang us." Though he protested to the paper's owner, the stories kept running—and the situation got worse. Within ten days, in fact, the state told residents not to drink the water, wash dishes with it, or even shower in it. Soon the U.S. Marines had set up a water distribution network for the city. "The scene was like conditions in some third world country," the editors of the *Daily News* wrote.

Repercussions started locally but spread nationally. In the next month's election, the mayor and most of the city council were defeated by others who made clean water their issue. Stories of other North Carolina communities with tainted water began appearing, and state and federal regulations were changed to prevent a recurrence of the North Carolina situation. The EPA also moved to extend safe water assurances to small communities. Publisher Ashley Futrell Jr. took special pride in the small paper's ability to prompt changes in federal standards. But it had been a mixed triumph. "When our town suffers, we suffer as well," Futrell said. "We live here." Editor Coughlin died in 2014.[3]

1990—The *Washington* (N.C.) *Daily News* for revealing that the city's
water supply was contaminated with carcinogens, a problem that
the local government had neither disclosed nor corrected over
a period of eight years.[4]

"We Don't Have to Tell You That"

The *Inquirer* business reporter Gilbert M. Gaul was donating blood when he had the idea for what he thought might be a "fun little business story" about what happens with the blood after it goes to the Red Cross. "I was lying there as the blood was running out of my arm, and it dawned on me that I didn't know a damn thing about what happened to my blood after they took it," says Gaul, now a *Washington Post* reporter in Philadelphia. He suggested a story to business editor Craig Stock, another loyal blood donor, and he liked the idea. Gaul started a file.

Gaul, a five-year *Inquirer* veteran at the time, had made a name for himself at a small but feisty Pennsylvania journal, the *Pottsville Republican*. There he had been on a team that uncovered the looting by organized crime of the locally based Blue Coal Company. Gaul and reporter Elliot G. Jaspin won the Local Investigative Specialized Reporting Pulitzer in 1979, and Gaul then won a Nieman Fellowship at Harvard. He found himself in great demand among metropolitan dailies and chose Gene Roberts's *Inquirer*. "It was everything you could possibly want in terms of journalism," he said of his new surroundings. "If you found something promising, you were encouraged to pursue it. It didn't matter where you were or what desk you were on. It didn't matter if you were 23 years old or 55 years old. You would get the time to see whether there was a great story there."[5]

Gaul started as a beat reporter covering medical economics for the *Inquirer*'s business desk. His early stories looked at hospitals, doctors, Medicare, and Medicaid. He also wrote some stories about how nonprofit medical corporations worked, which first put him in touch with the not-for-profit American Red Cross; although he didn't think much about it at the time. Then came blood drive day in 1988 at the *Inquirer* offices and the origin of his "little story." The first step seemed like it should be an interview with the local Red Cross head. Gaul's interview brought him up short. He had just started through his list of routine questions—How much blood is in the bank? What dollar value do you place on the blood?—when the director stopped him. "Why are you asking these questions? We don't have to tell you that," he said.

"I was taken aback, and my journalistic antennae went up," Gaul recalls. "I came back saying, 'You know, Craig, this is weird. They don't want to cooperate. They say we don't have a right to know anything. They won't even talk about the basic cost of a unit.' And so I began to poke around. I knew a lot of hospital people, and I asked them if I could talk to the blood banks in their hospitals. The lab people told me, 'this is what we have to pay for a unit of red cells, or for platelets.'" As he pieced together a reporting structure, he says, "I approached the story with my framework in business, which is something I still do today. I put together some spreadsheets—this was pre-Excel—and I began to see there were things that you just couldn't answer from the data that was available."

During his early research the Philadelphia area had an emergency blood appeal, which put Gaul on several new trails. He began to look at the ties between blood shortages and supply management, including widespread trading of blood stocks and the ethics of blood bank administrators. Basic questions sometimes led to deceptive answers. When Gaul asked a local Red Cross doctor to explain the shortage that led to the appeal, he blamed it "on donors not showing up in sufficient numbers. It happened every year following the Christmas-New Year's holiday. . . . Donors just didn't keep their appointments."

According to Gaul, "The answer didn't sit too well with me. I was ready and willing to give blood. Yet no one from the Red Cross had bothered to call or send me a postcard. When I pressed, the doctor acknowledged he didn't know why donors weren't coming. Management had never fully investigated the issue. It occurred to me that were this any other business, the blood bank would be down in the federal bankruptcy court. Instead, management turned to the media and declared an 'Emergency Appeal' for blood, which cost them nothing."

He built his database to include about a hundred blood banks around the United States. He interviewed administrators, noting which centers bought and which sold. Eventually he was able to track a half-million pints of blood around the country, watching them change hands several times. For additional information he turned to Internal Revenue Service Form 990s, tax returns for nonprofit corporations like the Red Cross. He remembers thinking it was particularly interesting that 61 percent of their business was blood when Gaul had thought its big business was disaster relief.

As a business beat reporter he kept working on other things, he says, but soon he was making both regional and national calls. Some of his findings about this blood business were startling. "Red cells are really a commodity and they're sold that way," he says. "And there's this whole secret black market for brokering blood, which on its face was not illegal.

But it raised a lot of questions, like what happens to the cost of blood as it moves along, and what happens to the safety of blood as it moves along." While he had not started out thinking about AIDS—still a relatively unexplained phenomenon when he started—it emerged as a huge element as the reporting continued.

Gaul had promised himself that he would only allow on-the-record sources in the story, although he would listen to sources who insisted that they be interviewed confidentially. "Due to the sensitivity of the subject, it absolutely had to be this way," the reporter says.

Eventually it was time to test the Gene Roberts system that was supposed to free reporters for big projects. "When I needed to be detached, I was detached," he says, noting that he was taken off the beat to pursue the blood story. Not that everything went that smoothly. At one point, Gaul was unhappy about the initial editing of his drafts, which he calculates had been cut in half. He asked his colleague, investigative reporter Don Barlett, to take a look. Barlett backed Gaul's longer version and showed the originals and the edited drafts to Roberts. A new editor was assigned, former national editor Lois Wark, who continued on the job through the end of the series.

Well into what would eventually become forty separate Freedom of Information Act requests—a total of about twenty thousand pages' worth of documents—Gaul produced a March 1989 story on one particularly woeful blood bank in St. Louis. The five-part series that made up the bulk of the Pulitzer entry ran in September. That series started with a piece on blood brokering, the overarching theme of the story. Subsequent pieces studied such elements as the role of the FDA. "It had been basically co-opted by the blood industry," says Gaul. "Their oversight was just abysmal." He also tackled the AIDS question in the blood distribution system. "As the reporting had begun, I knew AIDS was getting into the blood supply," he says. "I didn't even want to go there, because I was viewing it as purely a financial story." Soon it became clear that AIDS was too important to be played down, especially with Food and Drug Administration oversight so weak in the area.

Gaul used a number of editors as sounding boards along the way. He remembers flying the series past editor James Naughton for a comment. The reporter had been agonizing over a simple way to express the

FIGURE 20.1 Atop a desk, the *Philadelphia Inquirer* reporter Gil Gaul responds to staff acknowledgment as the paper learns it has won the 1990 Pulitzer Prize for Public Service. Photo by the *Inquirer* photographer Sharon Wohlmuth. *Source*: Used by permission of the *Philadelphia Inquirer*.

complexity of the transporting of blood supplies from station to station as it was being sold and resold. Naughton took one look at the story and said, "Oh, a chain of blood." The image stuck through the series.

Roberts contributed an organizational eye after Gaul and Wark laid the stories before him in the order they proposed. "Roberts looked at them and said, 'Why wouldn't you want your stories to go from the strongest to the weakest?'" according to Gaul, affecting his best North Carolina drawl. The FDA material was strong enough to carry the second day, they agreed, with the AIDS element moved up to third. "You get fixed ideas early on," says Gaul. "That's why you need editors."

As a result of the series, new certifications were proposed by a congressional committee and more inspectors were authorized, among other reforms—some of them related to the increasing threat of AIDS to blood supplies. The FDA also changed its monitoring system for foreign blood.

And donors can get more information today about what happens with the blood they donate.

After all he learned, is Gaul still a blood donor? Absolutely, he says. "The point of this series wasn't to harm blood donations, but to explore an area of medicine that is at best little understood."

1990—The *Philadelphia Inquirer* for reporting by Gilbert M. Gaul that disclosed how the American blood industry operates with little government regulation or supervision.

Rape and the Media

The story of Nancy Ziegenmeyer's brutal November 1988 rape—by an assailant who jumped into her car as she waited in a Des Moines parking lot—became the center of national debate in February 1990. That was because the *Des Moines Register*, with Ziegenmeyer's full support, ran a five-day series that named her as the victim and detailed all that had happened to her before and after. Among journalists, the series generated discussion about why newspapers generally do not identify rape victims. More broadly, it focused attention on how underreported the crime of rape is in the first place. "The fundamental issue was, Do we have a crime that is way under-covered, compared to its prevalence in society?" says Geneva Overholser, the editor of the *Register* at the time. "And that raises the question of whether it is under-covered *because* it is so faceless."[6]

Overholser had sparked the entire issue with a column she wrote reflecting on a recent Supreme Court decision supporting a Florida weekly that had published a rape victim's name without her permission, in violation of state law. Overholser weighed on one side the unfair stigma of rape against the journalist's commitment "to come as close as possible to printing the facts as we know them." She asked, "Does not our very delicacy in dealing with rape victims subscribe to the idea that rape is a crime of sex rather than the crime of brutal violence that it really is?" While she supported newspapers in withholding victims' names, Overholser wrote, "I believe that we will not break down the stigma until more and more women take public stands."

The column was read by Ziegenmeyer and her husband, who lived just east of Des Moines in Grinnell. For three weeks she considered whether to take up the column writer on what Ziegenmeyer saw as an invitation to identify herself as a rape victim and to use the newspaper in a good cause.

With the debate about naming rape victims unresolved even now, the series that eventually ran in the *Register* is still a useful journalism tool. Yet the story *behind* the paper's handling of the series is almost as intriguing. Indeed, decades after the gold medal was awarded, reporter Jane Schorer was still feeling that there was too little acknowledgment for her contributions when the *Register* claimed its Pulitzer.

A Teary Phone Call

Overholser distinctly remembers how close this Pulitzer came to never happening. "I'm sitting at my desk one lunchtime and my secretary is gone. The phone rings, and I pick it up," she says. "On any other given day I would not have picked up the phone." And had her secretary been there, "she wouldn't have passed it along, probably, because it was this teary woman saying, 'I just want to come in to talk.'" But with Overholser on the line, the caller continued: "I'm Nancy Ziegenmeyer and I've been raped, and I want you to use my name and use my picture, because your argument is exactly right." Ziegenmeyer wanted readers to understand, too, the harm that the legal system causes victims. Perhaps with one unvarnished case—her own—things could change, she said. Overholser decided to give the story to her feature department for assignment, to run when the assailant's trial ended. It would use Ziegenmeyer's name.

Jane Schorer, who would later write for the *Register*'s custom publications with the byline Jane Schorer Meisner, was a gifted but relatively new reporter who was formerly a secretary on the editorial page. She began interviewing Ziegenmeyer on August 2, 1989, the first of more than fifty meetings and telephone conversations the two would have over seven months. From the start, Schorer felt uneasy with how some editors treated her—debating whether "we need to have a real reporter do this," for example. But when she dove in, it was for good. Schorer did other assignments

while staying in close contact with Ziegenmeyer. For her editors, still waiting for a verdict, "it was pretty much forgotten and on the back burner,"
she says. But the story preoccupied her as the months passed. "The only
way I could do it was make a diary of it," she says. It seemed to work.

"When I finished the first one or two parts, I took it to Geneva and I
asked if she remembered this project. I laid it down on her desk," Schorer
recalls.[7] Alone in her office, Overholser read. "First of all, my jaw dropped
because it was so compelling. But second, I thought this is a very non-
traditional piece for us," says the editor. It would take special handling in
the newsroom. Overholser went to the small writing room where Schorer
was working. "Do you have any idea what you have here?" Overholser
asked, leaving the writer speechless for a moment—until she realized that
her boss loved the story. "From that minute on," says Schorer, "Geneva
took charge." A top editor at the *Register*, Mike Wegner, was assigned
to handle the series. Schorer was impressed with the five-part draft that
emerged starting on February 25, 1990.

Part one began:

> She would have to allow extra driving time because of the fog.
>
> A heavy gray veil had enveloped Grinnell overnight, and Nancy
> Ziegenmeyer—always methodical, always in control—decided to leave
> home early for her 7:30 a.m. appointment at Grand View College in
> Des Moines.
>
> It was Nov. 19, 1988, a day Ziegenmeyer had awaited eagerly, because
> she knew that whatever happened during those morning hours in Des
> Moines would determine her future. If she passed the state real-estate
> licensing exam that Saturday morning, she would begin a new career.
> If she failed the test, she would continue the child-care service she pro-
> vided in her home.
>
> At 6 a.m., Ziegenmeyer unlocked the door of her 1988 Pontiac Grand
> Am and tossed her long denim jacket in the back seat. The weather was
> mild for mid-November, and her Gloria Vanderbilt denim jumper and
> turtleneck sweater and red wool tights would keep her warm enough
> without a coat. . . .
>
> The fog lifted as Ziegenmeyer drove west on Interstate Highway 80,
> and she made good time after all. The digital clock on the dashboard

read 7:05 as she pulled into a parking lot near Grand View's Science Building. She had 25 minutes to sit in the car and review her notes before test time.

Suddenly the driver's door opened. She turned to see a man, probably in his late 20s, wearing a navy pin-striped suit. He smelled of alcohol.

"Move over," the man ordered, grabbing her neck.[8]

"What Kind of Weird Journalism Is This?"

"When I picked up the paper on the first day, I said, Wow!" recalls Schorer. Together with the story, spread across page one, were two columns headed "How this story came to be" and a reference to another article by Overholser. Getting to "Wow" had not been easy. "The *Des Moines Register* was a very traditional paper," says Overholser. "It was big on sports, big on agriculture, big on politics, big on agribusiness. It was certainly not a very soft and squishy paper." Schorer had assembled her account from Ziegenmeyer's own story, from her friends, from police officers, from prosecutors, and from the defense attorney. It contained emotional details unusual for a newspaper story of the time. And for some editors at the *Register*, it crossed the line of reporter familiarity with a source. "The cardinal rule is that a reporter never gets emotionally involved. I got emotionally involved, and I make no bones about it," Schorer says.

But the 1990s were becoming a time of experimenting with new forms, even at the *Register*. And Overholser felt that the paper's approach needed to accommodate the close relationship that Ziegenmeyer and Schorer had formed. It took two weeks for a final decision on whether to run it and in what form. Some editors, says Overholser, were uncomfortable not because of the sexual frankness—although it graphically described Ziegenmeyer's rape—"but because it was so edgy." The editors asked, "What kind of weird journalism was this?" she recalls. Telling a story about what the victim was thinking, some argued, was not serious journalism. But Overholser and other editors persisted. It was, she adds, "a piece of narrative journalism before we really knew the name."

The decision was to stay with the five-part story and to keep its descriptiveness intact. "If Nancy Ziegenmeyer is coming to me and saying,

'Tell my story,' then we were going to tell it with honesty," says Overholser. She remembers looking over the copy editor's shoulder and noticing that the term "after he had ejaculated" had been changed to "when he had finished." Overholser stopped him. "This is a crime of sex," she told him. "And if she's willing to say 'after he had ejaculated,' then we should say it. 'After he had finished' sounded like he'd had lunch or something."

Another element required careful treatment: the assailant was black and the victim white. That was rare considering rape statistics, says Overholser. Most attacks are intra-racial and involve people who know each other. The *Register*'s managing editor, David Westphal, proposed that an editor's note explain some of the unusual features of the series, including "how loath we were to contribute to that stereotype of interracial rape," Overholser says. "I felt then, and I believe now, that the extraordinary opportunity to be able to focus on rape was worth it. You just don't get that opportunity. It's impossible for young women to realize how little rape was written about back then." The editor, who later built a career in journalism education, believes the series' greatest success was putting the crime of rape on the national agenda.

That happened instantly and with deep controversy. Invitations arrived in Des Moines for national interviews, for Ziegenmeyer and Overholser mostly but also for the novice feature writer. "It totally caught us off-guard by getting so much publicity," says Schorer. "At the time it began we had no idea it would be a big story." Overholser also found the attention unsettling. She turned down several appearances but accepted others. Media attention grew, though, when the William Kennedy Smith case made the national news. Smith, Senator Edward Kennedy's nephew, was accused of rape by an alleged victim who was named by the media. (The case against Smith was dismissed.) In October, the *Register* editor was on the cover of *Working Woman* magazine.

"Geneva was being watched as one of the first female editors of a major newspaper. People were waiting to see what she would accomplish," Schorer says. The writer thought that some acclaim for the *Register* series was misdirected though. "There was plenty of credit to go around," she says. "Nancy deserves all the credit in the world for coming forward, and Geneva deserves all the credit in the world for having the idea in the first

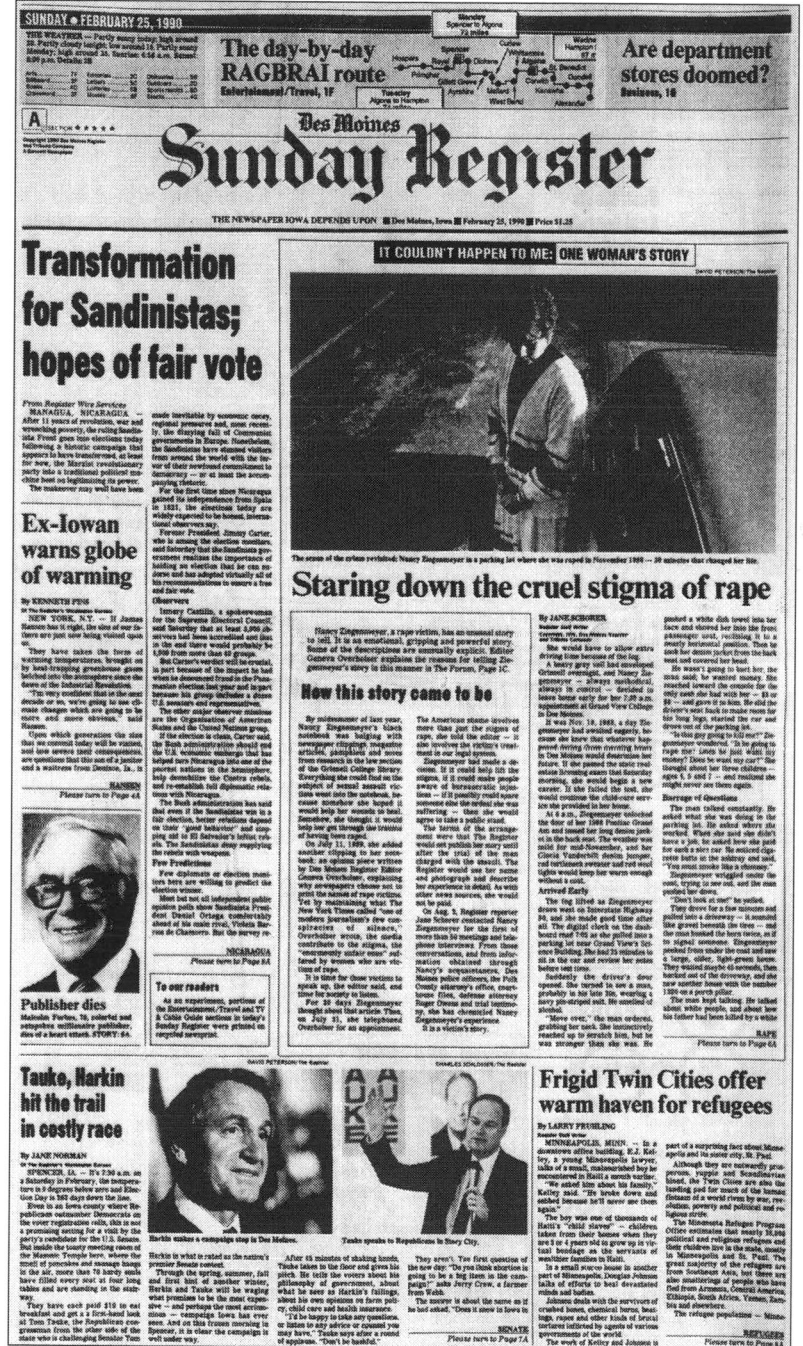

FIGURE 20.2 A dramatic photograph helped Jane Schorer's first story on rape victim Nancy Ziegenmeyer come alive in the *Des Moines Register* series that began on February 26, 1990. The story grew from a column about rape victims written by editor Geneva Overholser. *Source*: Used by permission.

place, and for making the finished product so outstanding." But, says Schorer, "it would have been fair for me to have the credit for presenting it the way I did."

The nature of the gold medal—going to the *Register* and not to the reporter—rubbed a raw nerve, even on the joyous day when the Pulitzer Prize was announced. Schorer says she wishes that the work had won for feature writing, where the *Register* had also nominated it. In that case the prize would have been in her name. "Public Service is more noble," she says, "but I would have liked to get the personal recognition."

Overholser understands her irritation. As a reporter, Schorer "absolutely took this story and made a miracle out of it," she says. Michael Gartner, who preceded Overholser as the *Register* editor, adds, "What made it work was that it was a compelling story. She was really a good writer." Gartner, then the president of NBC News, was also on the Pulitzer board that year, although he was out of the room for the discussion.[9]

Overholser was also out of the room when the gold medal was decided, of course. But she did have something to say when she re-entered the room and learned that the board was preparing a citation that excluded Schorer's name. "They said the paper was winning, and I said, 'That's great, but you've got to name Jane,'" says Overholser. Schorer's name was inserted.

1991—The *Des Moines Register* for reporting by Jane Schorer that, with the victim's consent, named a woman who had been raped—which prompted widespread reconsideration of the traditional media practice of concealing the identity of rape victims.[10]

Covering the Sierra Without a Parachute

The *Sacramento Bee* reporter Tom Knudson had once worked at the *Des Moines Register* as well and in 1985 had won a Pulitzer Prize for National Reporting there for a series on the dangers of farming. "It was a neat place to start out as a young reporter," says the reporter, who credits editors like Geneva Overholser and Mike Gartner for helping him. He later moved to the *New York Times* but eventually became frustrated with the style of reporting there. "I found myself visiting many places, but not knowing hardly any," he says. "They call it parachute journalism."

Switching to McClatchy's *Sacramento Bee*, he was chosen to open a Sierra news bureau, based in the town of Truckee. "The idea was to cover this part of the Sierra as a beat, with the forests, the watersheds and what have you," Knudson says. "I jumped at the opportunity and threw a kayak on top of my Jeep and just took a little bit of a road trip. Of course, I fell in love with the geography, as everybody does. But then I began to stop in community after community, talking with people about what are the issues, what are the concerns." Knudson recalls that there was some resistance in the newsroom to his covering the Sierra. It could have been jealousy, or a feeling that the paper was being too lenient with him. Fifteen years and a Pulitzer Prize later, he says, "I guess it's been laid to rest."[11]

When journalists cover the environment, they do well to look past the jurisdictions that governments create. "Water, air, wildlife—all these resources and individual components—they don't pay attention to boundaries," Knudson says. "Everybody was looking at their own backyard, but nobody was looking at the gem that is the Sierra Nevada." Stretching for 450 miles across dozens of counties, national forests, irrigation districts, and other divisions, he says, "this region has been 'piecemealed' to death." It was that observation that prompted a project on the plight of the Sierra. "The magic of the series," says Knudson, "was that I was able to go out and look at this huge region as a beat, and write about it as a single mountain range."

Knudson brought a fresh set of eyes to the Sierra. He traveled across the range looking for issues that arose over and over again in different settings. "If livestock raising is causing problems in one part of the range, and you find that it is in another part of the range as well, you can put two and two together," he notes. Many interviewees didn't quite know what to make of his mountain range focus. When a reporter is on an important story, the reporter says, "sometimes people know that, and they clam up faster, or they speak up more than they might." But to most people the Sierra seemed a nonstory. Knudson knew that it was anything but. "To see that there were all these forces leading to a general state of deterioration struck me as a pretty compelling story."

Air, Forests, Water, Wildlife, Soil, and Mankind

After eight months of investigation and two hundred interviews, the series was ready to run on June 9, with the headline "Majesty and Tragedy: The Sierra in Peril. From mining to malls, onslaught takes toll." Part one began:

> John Muir said it best.
>
> The Sierra Nevada, the naturalist wrote a century ago, "seems to me above all others the Range of Light, the most divinely beautiful of all the mountain chains I have ever seen."
>
> Remember those words. Savor them like old wine. Share them with young children.
>
> For Muir's words no longer hold true.
>
> Today, California's Sierra Nevada—one of the world's great mountain ranges—is suffering a slow death.
>
> Almost everywhere there are problems: polluted air, dying forests, poisoned rivers, vanishing wildlife, eroding soil and rapid-fire development. Even Muir's holy ground, Yosemite National Park, is hurting: Much of its forest has been damaged by ozone.
>
> Remarkably, the problems have drawn little attention, masked in part by the enormity of the range.

That sixth paragraph served almost as a table of contents. Part two focused on air pollution, part three on forests and wildlife, part four on streams and mining damage, and part five on the plague of growth. The last part also contained a prognosis and suggestions for how to turn things around.

Because of the project's size and scope, other reporters helped Knudson with basic research. But *Bee* editor Gregory Favre preferred that it be largely a one-man effort. Collecting data had been hard because much of the information was broken down by county or by district, requiring extensive travel among county seats. Computer-assisted reporting was still a few years in the future, the reporter notes. The editor working over the stories with Knudson directly was Terry Jackson. The photography ranged from breathtaking to disturbing. It showed the ravages of development.

"There was pressure to cut stories," Knudson recalls, "but I don't remember too many knock-down-drag-out disputes with editors."

By creating the feel that time was running out for corrective measures, Knudson's series got the immediate attention of legislators. A "Sierra summit" was convened to address some of the problems the *Bee* cited. Congress also took an interest. On its own, the U.S. Forest Service, whose policies were treated harshly in the series, conceded that the new perspective was valuable. Said a forest service spokesman: "I think there may be some initial hard feelings or concern. There were a lot of vested interests that were obviously challenged. But that's the name of the game. What matters is what happens to the Sierra. This could be a real vector for change."

Other finalists for the public service award were the *Washington Post* for a study of gun violence in its city and the *Dayton Daily News*, which examined national workplace safety issues—variations of themes that would recur in public service competitions ten years later.[12]

1992—The *Sacramento* (Calif.) *Bee* for "The Sierra in Peril," reporting by Tom Knudson that examined environmental threats and damage to the Sierra Nevada mountain range in California.[13]

The Big One

There was no question mark on the headline. On Monday, August 24, 1992, a banner with "THE BIG ONE" across the top of the *Miami Herald* told readers that Andrew was sure to be no ordinary storm; marked "Special Hurricane Edition," the day's paper was a public service in itself. But—far more than the *Herald* staff suspected—it was only setting the scene for what was to come over the rest of the year.[14]

"Hurricane Andrew, the biggest story ever to hit this newsroom, was the one story none of us wanted to see," wrote managing editor Pete Weitzel in the paper's cover letter for its Pulitzer entry in public service. "A stunned and dislocated population, much of it deprived of shelter, water and electricity, with little or no access to sources of information, needed the news, needed help, needed guidance."[15] Five years later, that description would apply as well to a second disaster-related gold medal awarded to another Knight Ridder paper, the *Grand Forks Herald* in North Dakota.

For the *Miami Herald*, planning to get staffers into the right place made a huge difference, says Weitzel, who after retiring from the *Herald* took over leadership of the Coalition of Journalists for Open Government. "It's very difficult to get around after a hurricane, so you needed to have some critical people positioned before the storm hit." In a way it was like preparing for an invasion in wartime. The *Herald* sent some reporters to the Homestead area, where they stayed in a motel the night before the full fury of the storm hit. It hit in Homestead.

"DESTRUCTION AT DAWN," read the Tuesday paper's banner. To allow for more organized placement of hurricane reports, the paper eliminated the Local section and concentrated Andrew-related news in section one, an approach it would use for weeks. Some 110,000 copies of the Tuesday paper were distributed free to shelters, hotels, and the few distribution boxes still in operation. The hardest-hit areas got forty thousand free copies for three weeks. "It built an enormous goodwill toward the paper," says Weitzel. The *Herald* published neighborhood-by-neighborhood damage surveys, along with daily updates on the basics: food, water, power and telephones, and street clearing.

As it provided vital information, the staff learned from its readers too. "Almost from the first day we began to realize that some of the traditional stories you begin to file in the wake of a big disaster—a fire or anything like that—didn't really serve the need here. Survey stories of the damage didn't serve concrete needs for people to know, What happened on my block? What happened in my neighborhood?" says Weitzel. "That created a tremendous challenge." The overview reporting, even if it was beautifully handled, lacked the specifics that readers needed. That problem could only be solved by sending the reporters back with orders, as Weitzel put it, "to get more nitty-gritty."

One surprising twist was what happened when the *Herald* created a phone bank to take incoming calls. "We asked clerks and secretaries to staff the phones to handle an unexpectedly heavy volume of calls from people seeking storm-related information, and also to take notes," he says. In this pre-Internet time, the *Herald* news staff found it was getting fast feedback about the real problems in the community and where they existed. "My secretary was helping run the phone bank," says Weitzel, "and she said that we were getting all these tremendously poignant calls from people. Can we help them locate a friend, or locate a relative?" The secretary, Bert Alberti, had the idea of putting together a "bulletin board" feature in the newspaper to help them connect. It would eventually take up several full pages each day.

Comparing the 1992 *Herald* feature to the *New York Times*'s "Portraits of Grief," which had its genesis in handbills passed around Ground Zero after 9/11, Weitzel says: "The Portraits, those little anecdotes, were one of the most brilliant things I'd ever seen. And this bulletin board feature had been the same kind of thing for us. It just mushroomed."

The *Herald* itself was working wounded. Three distribution warehouses were destroyed and the roof of its main building sustained heavy damage. Sixty newsroom employees had severely damaged homes. "All of us were going through the same experiences of the people we're writing about," says Weitzel. "We really were on the same page. And that's not always the case."

On Sunday, August 30, the paper had the beginnings of a scandal to report. Its headline read "Shoddy Construction Left Homes Vulnerable to Storm, Engineers Say." The next Sunday another headline proclaimed "Older Is Often Better for Dade Homes, Experts Say." The *Herald* stories reported that local building codes were either insufficient or were not being enforced. There were also signs that much construction was shoddy under any code structure.

The *Herald*'s analysis of why Andrew damaged certain buildings more than others answered a key question. Readers wanted to know why a community that had prepared so well for a storm could still be so devastated. In a story that same Sunday headlined "Why Help Took So Long," reporters Jeff Leen and Sydney Freedberg wrote:

> It was as if the emergency disaster planners wrote a super Act I—the evacuation—then forgot to script Act II—the recovery.
>
> What went wrong?

A lot.

Mobile hospitals and bulldozers arrived late. Vital phones and radios jammed. Food deliveries and National Guard units got snarled in traffic. Roadblocks turned away volunteers. Police didn't control intersections. City managers pleaded for help. Nobody activated the Army.

To be sure, thousands of good people labored heroically, monumentally, to establish order from a type of chaos that no one had ever seen before.

But for 100 critical hours after Andrew struck, governments reeled, and no one was in command. No hurricane czar, no Norman Schwarzkopf.

Sydney Freedberg had helped win a public service award for the *Detroit News* nine years earlier. Jeff Leen would later become a *Washington Post* investigative reporter and editor, helping it win gold medals in 1999, 2000, and 2014. Hurricane Andrew "was probably Jeff's statistical baptism," says Weitzel, allowing Leen to develop skills for detecting patterns that teams could use in their investigations.

The paper hammered the building construction theme. One story noted that the devastating 1960s hurricane Donna had prompted a major storm study that had specifically warned that building codes needed to be properly enforced or storms would continue to cause far more destruction than necessary.

The Pulitzer Public Service jury commented on the *Herald*'s "awesome commitment of resources." Specifically, the jury noted the *Herald*'s successes identifying "the economic & political decisions of the past in the form of lax zoning, inspection and building codes that had made them so vulnerable."[16]

1993—The *Miami Herald* for coverage that not only helped readers cope with Hurricane Andrew's devastation but also showed how lax zoning, inspection and building codes had contributed to the destruction.[17]

Wrestling with "Boss Hog"

For Raleigh, North Carolina's *News and Observer* in 1995, discovering how heavily pork producers had become concentrated in North Carolina had been the first revelation. It had happened almost out of the public eye and so had the pollution problem that came with it. "Actually, the story got started when two reporters, Pat Stith and Joby Warrick, worked together on stories about malfeasance connected with the State Fair," says Melanie Sill, who was just back from a Nieman Fellowship at Harvard and had become the editor of the Sunday paper while also running special projects. Eventually the two reporters uncovered the case of the state veterinarian taking gifts from pork producers.

"Nothing had been reported about this industry," Sill says. "It had been growing quietly in the state, and they're not huge employers." But the deeper the reporters looked, "more and more the questions developed." Soon enough, water-quality issues caught the reporters' notice. "By the time the series got into print, the veterinarian story went by the wayside," according to Sill, now the paper's editor.

The reporters and their editor met once a week and read each other's notes, she says, but three months into the project the focus still was unclear. "We were down in our humble office canteen, and I said, 'What is the story really about?' And Pat said, 'It's about who's in charge here.' The industry was writing its own ticket."[18] The journalists agreed and with the basic line of the series finally established, the story came together more easily in the remaining two months of investigation.

The reporters documented evidence that waste pits were leaking into ground water and creeks. One story analyzed how Wendell Murphy, a former state senator and a major hog farmer, had thwarted government regulation. A sidebar was prepared on the most noticeable issue for any readers who came close to a hog farm: the odor. "We thought about doing a scratch and sniff to run with the series," says Sill with a laugh, noting that they gave up on that idea quickly.

Metro editor Marion Gregory came up with the Boss Hog rubric that would run with the series. As often happens late in the editing process, the five parts were juggled fairly close to the late February days when they were to run. At first the story on Murphy was to lead the series.

(The headline "Murphy's Laws" seemed to fit.) But as they refined the drafts, the environmental impact story seemed a better opener. Editor Sill had Warrick root through a stack of discarded story openings to find one that she recalled and loved from an early draft. Opening the first day's story under the headline "Boss Hog: New Studies Show That Lagoons Are Leaking," the story by Stith and Warrick began:

> Imagine a city as big as New York suddenly grafted onto North Carolina's Coastal Plain. Double it.
>
> Now imagine that this city has no sewage treatment plants. All the wastes from 15 million inhabitants are simply flushed into open pits and sprayed onto fields.
>
> Turn those humans into hogs, and you don't have to imagine at all. It's already here.
>
> A vast city of swine has risen practically overnight in the counties east of Interstate 95. It's a megalopolis of 7 million animals that live in metal confinement barns and produce two to four times as much waste, per hog, as the average human.[19]

The two then examined the critical debate between industry and environmentalists over how much damage is done to the environment by letting hog manure decompose and then spraying or spreading it on crop lands, as was the approach of the existing agricultural system. The *News and Observer* cited studies to show that contaminants are getting into groundwater in unacceptable amounts, both through lagoon leakage and through rainwater that carries ammonia gas that the farms produce.

Sill says that when the Pulitzer entry was being prepared, Stith and Warrick told her she should include her name. "I thought, That's nice, but it's unlikely that we'll win."

1996—The *News & Observer*, Raleigh, N.C., for the work of
Melanie Sill, Pat Stith and Joby Warrick on the environmental and
health risks of waste disposal systems used in North Carolina's
growing hog industry.[20]

"Oceans of Trouble"

The series that won for the *Times-Picayune* in 1997—its study of the world's fishing industry—was a rare case of a gold medal-winner tackling global issues. But it did not start that way. The environmental writer Mark Schleifstein had originally thought about a much humbler fishing-and-the-environment feature aimed at the Gulf Coast alone. In the time-honored tradition of papers everywhere, the *Times-Picayune* editors had in 1995 launched a process encouraging story ideas from the staff. Their charge: "If you've got ideas for a story you want to work on for a week or two, tell us what it is," he says. Of course, the reporters knew that the two-week guideline was meaningless. It would be longer if the project turned out to be significant. Scrolling through a list of stories he kept on his computer, Schleifstein came across a fishing industry proposal he had dropped earlier. When he had checked to see who covered fishing for the paper and might be able to team with him, he was told that the *Times-Picayune* did not cover fishing anymore. Upset, he gave up on the story, which would be too big to do alone. It was to have examined the connection between coastal erosion and poor recent fishing results in the Gulf. Too bad.

But with this new mandate, he brought it up again. Editors liked the idea of a look at the problems of Gulf fisheries. There was still no fishing reporter, but he was put on a team with Washington environmental writer John McQuaid and outdoors writer Bob Marshall, with political editor Tim Morris in charge. They were shocked when environmental scientists told them how bad things had gotten in the Gulf—with estimates that all of Louisiana's wetlands would be gone in fifty years, eliminating the habitat for numerous Gulf species. Further, runoff from America's heartland down the Mississippi, having been permanently channeled, was creating a "dead zone" for sea life farther and farther out from the mouth of the great river.

At the same time, the Gulf was being overfished, following the pattern in other troubled fisheries like New England and Alaska. But after the team had continued for about five months along that line, it reached a realization: "What was driving overfishing in the Gulf of Mexico was Japan," the leader of an expanding worldwide fish market. Further, the shrimp industry so critical to Louisiana "was being flooded by aquaculture," much of it Asian.[21] Editors were asked to let the team redesign the series as a look at a global crisis. And the team made its case persuasively. "There was an utter connectedness," according to editor Jim Amoss, who approved the expansion. "To do it justice, we had to take a global look at it." Because the story would be much more expensive to report, the *Times-Picayune* went to the Newhouse organization, which approved adding budget.

The first day's story, by McQuaid, noted how fishermen must deal with changing environments in pursuit of a catch. "It comes with the job," he wrote. But lately they have been "helpless before the man-made changes tearing across the Gulf of Mexico, leaving a swath of wrecked lives and ecological havoc in their wake. . . . Part of a global sea change in fishing, the forces include disappearing fish and marshlands, a flood of cheap seafood imports and gill net bans. They threaten millions of livelihoods and the Gulf's unique fishing culture." A second McQuaid story that day highlighted the worldwide scope of the series. Headlined "Are the World's Fisheries Doomed?" it opened with a tale from another gulf, the Gulf of Thailand, where shrimp farming had caused coastal erosion and hurt other fishing industries.

The next day, Schleifstein targeted perils that existed for the oceans themselves. Headlined "The Dead Sea," the story was accompanied by a chart dramatizing how severely fertilizer runoff through the Mississippi deprives the Gulf of oxygen. Stories ran from March 24 to March 31, with the last headlined "The Big Fix," offering options, none of them easy.

The *Times-Picayune* long-timers often date its coming-of-age to the 1988 Republican National Convention in New Orleans, when the Newhouse chain decided to use the city's national spotlight to make a mark for the paper. "We spent a year getting ready for a week," says managing editor Peter Kovacs. Amoss says of the convention's impact: "It challenged some key people, and it had a residual effect of raising the bar journalistically in the news operation and making us more ambitious."[22]

The 1997 gold medal was something of a surprise to Schleifstein because he had sensed that there was a bias in that particular prize against global stories. Still, he says, "This really was one of those strange times when the morning we went to press, I looked at John and I said, Can you believe what we've done? We really thought we had a good chance."

Amoss, who joined the Pulitzer board several years later, believes that "Oceans of Trouble" benefited by being seen as a regional rather than a global story. "There's a natural inclination in the American press to reward strong local journalism, and the Public Service award certainly plays to that," he says. If the series "were just the *Times-Picayune* setting out to write about the world's fisheries, I think it would have been a totally different project, and probably wouldn't have won."[23]

But win it did. The *Philadelphia Inquirer* was a finalist again, this time for a project on the widening gap between America's rich and poor prepared by its team of Don Barlett and Jim Steele. The *Los Angeles Times* was back as well for the probe of a murder case that led to revelations of inefficiency and mismanagement in the justice system.[24]

1997—The *Times-Picayune*, New Orleans, for its comprehensive series analyzing the conditions that threaten the world's supply of fish.[25]

Blizzard, Fire, and Flood; What Next: Locusts?

In 1997, April was the cruelest month for the Red River town of Grand Forks, North Dakota. Indeed, a series of plagues bordering on the biblical swept the area. As editor Mike Jacobs and publisher Mike Maidenberg wrote to readers in an April 20 page-one editorial comment:

> Grand Forks has sustained deep wounds, and there will be scars. On Saturday evening, as we write, the river continues its historic rise and fire is tearing at the heart of downtown. Thousands of buildings are immersed. Several of the town's most historic structures are alight. There is no apparent power that can save them. These buildings were part of our past. . . .
>
> We must have wondered, all of us, whether any community anywhere had ever suffered so much, and yet we know that others have. Miraculously, we have been spared loss of life. Marvelously, we have found friendships we didn't know about, as strangers came to offer labor, called to offer shelter, reached out to offer strength. Could it have

been so in any other town? Yes, perhaps. But never on such a scale in our hometown. And it is in that spirit, from that indomitable strength, that our hometown will go forward. It is going to be a difficult time. Let us begin this morning.[26]

"We wanted to sound the theme of hope—not to say Woe is me, or Help us, but to look over the horizon and find the opportunity that could come from this disaster," says Maidenberg. It would set the tone for the news coverage as well. Under extreme deadline pressure, the small staff produced well-crafted news stories that gave readers the information they needed for coping, while being consistently reassuring.[27]

From time to time staffers had to reassure themselves. The paper had been driven out of its building, first taking up quarters at the nearby University of North Dakota campus and later—when the university was flooded—moving to a public elementary school ten miles from town. For seventy-one days the *Herald* put out the paper from the elementary school.

In the past the paper had an almost neighborly relationship with storms, naming the state's blizzards each year the way the National Weather Service names Atlantic hurricanes. It picked women's and men's names working up the alphabet. The paper had dubbed this 1997 storm Hannah. It had no idea how hard-hearted she would be. The same April 20 paper—the first published on presses at its Knight Ridder sister paper, the *St. Paul Pioneer-Press*—carried a lead story by Randy Bradbury under the headline "Downtown Fires Intensify Crisis." It began:

> Water continued to drive residents of Grand Forks and East Grand Forks from their homes Saturday. Too much water, and too little.
>
> In Grand Forks, those who weren't flooded out by the spreading waters of the Red River of the North were put on notice that the city soon would be unable to provide that most essential of services: safe drinking water.[28]

By the second day, the hopeful tone returned. Under the headline "A heart destroyed; Officials take a first look at the destroyed downtown," *Herald* contributor Monte Paulson wrote: "Clouds of steam rose lazily from the mounds of twisted metal and blackened brick lining Third and Fourth streets on Sunday afternoon as Grand Forks leaders struggled to figure out how their city will rise from the worst disaster it has ever faced."[29]

Jacobs and Maidenberg learned one benefit of being part of a chain. Knight Ridder sent people from other papers and contributed $1 million from its corporate fund. The storm-hardened *Miami Herald* staffers, particularly, provided ideas to help the Grand Forks paper plan coverage. The bulletin board approach for reaching victims in print—a technique pioneered during Hurricane Andrew—was also used in Grand Forks. Having Miami staffers around "saved us a lot of trial and error," says Maidenberg.[30]

Jacobs reviewed the 1997 coverage years later:

I'm a small-town guy. I've always worked in small cities. And I had a fairly well-developed notion of the newspaper's role in a small town. But nothing could have fused those points of view like this crisis did.

I always had thought of the newspaper as the "town nag." Now I describe it as a friend that's in a position to make helpful suggestions.

I think we're a humbler institution after the disaster. We used to be haughty.[31]

Some lessons were less romantic—like how the honeymoon doesn't last, even if a newspaper wins immediate public support for its disaster coverage.

Maidenberg calls it the golden time. "During a time of disaster, you and your readers are in sync. Everybody is really happy to get any scrap of news. But as time goes by, the newspaper has to write more critical kinds of things. It has to be a newspaper. When that happens, the golden time begins to ebb."

It ebbed in a big way during what became known as the Angel Flap, when the *Herald* published a story identifying the donor of $15 million in flood relief. The donor, McDonald's heiress Joan Kroc, had sought anonymity. But the *Herald* editors believed that so many people knew her identity already that it would be wrong to leave its readers out of the "secret." Jacobs felt it was a simple matter: "Never hold the news." A reporter tracked down the registration from the tail of an unmarked private jet that had flown into the area—the so-called N-number—and identified the visiting plane as Kroc's. An article was prepared.

"When people found out we were going to run the story we got frantic calls from the mayors of both Grand Forks and East Grand Forks saying, You can't run that story; she will be offended and we might not get any more assistance from her. I listened to them, and I made the decision that this was news," Maidenberg says. Talk radio hosts turned against the paper and so did many readers. "People were jarred back to the understanding that newspapers are going to be newspapers," he says. "Still, some people will always stay with you. They'll say, 'I'm angry with this, but I'll never forget what you did after the flood.'"[32]

Jurors and Pulitzer board members liked that the *Herald* remained scrappy as well as eloquent. From the perspective of James Naughton, then the president of the Poynter Institute and a public service juror that year, there was "an unspoken yet clear understanding that it would have to take something truly extraordinary to deflect us from picking Grand Forks."[33]

1998—The *Grand Forks* (N.D.) *Herald* for its sustained and informative coverage, vividly illustrated with photographs, that helped hold its community together in the wake of flooding, a blizzard and a fire that devastated much of the city, including the newspaper plant itself.[34]

CHAPTER 21

THE *POST* RINGS TWICE

1999–2000: Police Shootings and Shameful Homes

It is a capital mistake to theorize before one has data. Insensibly one begins
to twist facts to suit theories instead of theories to fit facts.

—SHERLOCK HOLMES, FROM "A SCANDAL IN BOHEMIA,"
QUOTED ON JEFF LEEN'S OFFICE WALL

Imagine attending this story meeting held by *Washington Post* editors and
reporters in the fall of 1998. Jeff Leen notes his investigative team's probe of
the high toll of shootings by District of Columbia police, a dark footnote
in the city that had become the murder capital of the nation. Taking turns
going around the room, the *Post* "poverty beat" reporter Katherine Boo is
pursuing a story about D.C. homes for the mentally retarded, where she's
uncovered horrid conditions. Both sound like winners. Were they ever.

In 1999 and 2000, a newspaper won consecutive Pulitzer Prizes for
Public Service for the first time—for reporting on projects that had over-
lapped in their newsroom. "You could have a thousand of these meetings and not have that occur," says Leen, who had moved to the *Post* in
1997 from the *Miami Herald* as a forty-year-old investigative specialist. He
remembers thinking, "I've got a good story, but she's got a good story, too.
I wonder if all the stories around here are like that."

The two projects were very different. The intensive nine-month investigation of police shootings was driven by computer-assisted reporting
and involved three main reporters, several editors, and a raft of staffers in
supporting roles. Kate Boo's was essentially a one-woman operation built
on a combination of interviews, old-fashioned data mining, and prose that
filled her editors with awe. "She writes like a poet, but she's got the skill
of an investigative reporter," says Leen, who served as one of her editors

during what evolved as two connected series in 1999. "She wrote with a lyrical sensitivity without becoming purple, and without getting in the way of the facts."[1]

Although the two projects might seem a reflection of the same investigative tradition that flowed from Watergate in the 1970s, this newer coverage was in the form of planned projects rather than the day-to-day incremental approach of Bob Woodward and Carl Bernstein's reporting. Woodward, now known more as an author of books on Washington politics than as a *Post* assistant managing editor, represents both traditions. After Watergate, he became Metro editor—"I was not good at it," he says with a laugh[2]—and was involved with the creation of the *Post* investigative unit, which he led for more than a decade.

A Job for Teamcop

The 1999 gold medal started with a simple statistic. Jo Craven McGinty, a computer-assisted reporting specialist who was being considered for a job at the *Post*, noted a high number of "Category 81s"—justifiable shootings by city police, charted by the FBI. D.C. officers had killed fifteen citizens in 1995. The memo wrote, just before Christmas in 1997: "When measured against the average population for the five-year period, District police racked up 8.7 homicides per 100,000 residents—the highest rate in the country among cities of at least 100,000. It is almost twice the rate of Atlanta, at 4.9, nearly three times the rate of Los Angeles, at 3.4, and more than four times the rate of New York City, which measured 2.1"[3]

The spike the numbers formed over Washington raised eyebrows in the newsroom. "Based on that information, though, you could write about eight paragraphs," says Jeff Leen, who was assigned by investigative editor Rick Atkinson to work with McGinty. Leen would decide what to do next with the computer pattern.

Such work was familiar to him from his time at the *Miami Herald*. He had worked on investigative stories during the Hurricane Andrew coverage in 1992. Other projects had included one on lawyers who billed for more than twenty-four hours a day and, with partner Guy Gugliotta, work that first identified Colombia's Medellin and Cali cartels and their role in the U.S. cocaine trade.

For the *Post* police gunplay story, he started with basic updating. "I spent two weeks reading ten years of *Washington Post* clips on shootings and I discovered a number of bad shootings, and a number involving cars," he says. Usually the driver had been struck with a bullet. Another element: the introduction of the controversial Glock 9-millimeter sidearm, which tended to fire too easily. Next came a stroll to the police department's public relations office, where McGinty and Leen were told the department did not keep statistics on police shootings. Leen laughs at the wave of embarrassment that came over him as he sat next to the *Post* job applicant. "I'm thinking, boy, I look like an idiot here. She's looking to me thinking, What do we do now? And I'm thinking I can't just walk out of here and say, Thank you very much. So I say, 'You do a press release, right?'" Yeah, the P.R. officer replies, there's a stack of them over there. "So I say, 'We want that stack.'"

The releases became one of several streams of information the *Post* created, together with news clippings, to reveal the large number of related lawsuits that had been filed. "I expected to get five or six, and there were seventy on the final list," Leen says. The clippings, releases, and lawsuits led to interviews with lawyers and other sources. In talking with attorneys, Leen and McGinty obtained a powerful new data stream: a paper copy of the very police list of shootings that the department had said did not exist. (Not long after the reporting began, the *Post* made a full-time hire of McGinty—a former University of Missouri journalism school employee. She later worked at *Newsday* and the *New York Times* before moving to the *Wall Street Journal*.) Leen called that list the crown jewels. It showed every time a police gun had been fired between 1994 and 1997, accounting for 464 incidents involving 576 officers and 2,271 bullets. "That was very useful," Leen says, "because, it turned out, they literally, in their statistics, did not have as many shootings as we were able to develop from our four streams of information."

Leen talks of "Eureka moments" that occur during investigations— usually early in the data gathering. During Hurricane Andrew, one such moment was the discovery of the pattern showing that "the newer the house, the worse the destruction." The numbers proved that more recent building codes, designed to reduce storm damage levels, were being violated. "When I saw that, I thought, 'You've got it,'" he says of that Miami investigation. In the Washington police probe, as Leen and McGinty saw the data streams all point to the same conclusion—that training lapses and other factors were leading to the high rate of civilian shootings by D.C. police—"I knew we had it, and it would hit like a hydrogen bomb. It would withstand any criticism."

Leen next exercised the "honest man" approach. He went out to find someone with no ax to grind, who simply knew the situation backward and forward. While he won't identify the individual by name, a 2002 book by the *Post* editors Leonard Downie Jr. and Robert G. Kaiser, *The News About the News: American Journalism in Peril*, gives the source as former D.C. deputy chief Bob Klotz. "He just laid it out to me," says Leen of his source: standards were steadily slipping and being abused. Initially the rule was not to shoot unless an officer was threatened by a weapon. That had deteriorated to a possible threat from what appeared to be the flash of a weapon and then just a flash of movement. Leen asked the source about the car shooting incidents. Officers shoot at cars to stop them, Leen was told, and that is against procedure. The assurances of such a high-ranking expert carried weight with the reporter. "There was a problem with police shootings in the District," his source told him. Leen adds, "If he had said there wasn't, I'm not sure what I would have done."[4]

A Break for Monica

When news broke about Monica Lewinsky's relationship with President Bill Clinton, it stalled the *Post*'s shooting investigation. The paper assigned Leen to join others on that story while McGinty plugged away at the police data gathering. The paper used a Freedom of Information Act request to the District's corporation counsel to obtain a list of five years of cases in which the city had defended thirty-one police shootings. Leen selected thirteen for close examination, and McGinty pulled them from Superior Court. Next came a March 13 memo in which McGinty summarized the cases, hinting at what investigative editor Rick Atkinson called "a clear sense of human drama and shattered lives behind our statistical scaffold." One question in McGinty's memo: "Is it acceptable for an officer to step in front of a car, then shoot the driver if he fails to stop?"

By month's end, meetings resumed on the police story, and Leen soon broke free of Lewinsky duty. Marilyn Thompson, who had been away for a time, rejoined Atkinson in investigative editing. Possible approaches for narrowing the story were discussed: concentrate on car shootings—which seemed particularly egregious to Leen—or focus on the peak year of police shootings, 1995. They decided to keep the focus broad and not pick one year or one type of incident.

For the first time, they also discussed a time frame for the series. "This is gigantic," Leen said to Atkinson and Thompson. "How big do you want to make it? Three months? Six months? Nine months? I'll never forget what they said, because it made me so proud to work at the *Washington Post*. Rick and Marilyn said, 'Don't put a limit on it; do what you think needs to be done.'"

If Bob Woodward calls teaming the creation of a "perfect journalistic brain," Jeff Leen compares it to the planning of a perfect bank robbery. "You need an inside man, you need a safecracker, you need a driver." The *Post* team added an investigative specialist with police department knowledge, Sari Horwitz, and a recent *Chicago Tribune* hire, David Jackson. They also gained an office nickname: Teamcop.

An electronic database version of the "crown-jewel" shootings printout was created, and three years of data quickly yielded a shocking new statistic: D.C. averaged roughly one car shooting per month by police officers. The number "floored criminologists and law enforcement experts we interviewed," according to a summary of the investigation that Atkinson prepared later. Another court file the *Post* discovered listed more than six hundred suits that alleged excessive force used by D.C. police officers over four years—nearly half of them settled. "This gift horse, however, implied that non-shooting, excessive force was widespread in the District and caused us to broaden our investigation again," according to the Atkinson summary.

How to treat the question of brutality continued to be a sticky issue for what was essentially a story about shootings. From June through August the discussion was over whether the brutality element detracted from the central gunplay line of the story. Less data supported the brutality charges, and team members worried that investigating beatings could stretch the informal deadline they had set. In the end, brutality was retained as a critical part of the project; it illustrated a "continuum of force" principal by which the department operated—and trained its new officers. Shootings grew from that.

Elements of the story were divvied up. Leen took the overall case pattern, the elements of shootings into cars, and problems with the Glock sidearm. Jackson took all other shooting cases. Horwitz took the issue of brutality. Leen made a presentation for executive editor Len Downie and managing editor Steve Coll. It wasn't easy for Leen. "I was the new guy," he says. "I was nervous and had a pretty dry mouth." But their response was a tonic. "Steve said it was a great project, just go and do it."

Publisher Donald Graham—who once had been a policeman—visited the team about the cop story he was hearing about. "It wasn't one of these pro-forma visits," says Leen. "He asked great questions. He was 100 percent behind it. I was just blown away by that." In Leen's experience at the *Herald*, he says, the publisher's only involvement with investigations had been to cut their budgets.

A "Good Shooting"

Sari Horwitz had started as an intern in 1984. "Like so many journalists I came into journalism and was inspired by Watergate, and Bob Woodward, and wanted to be a political journalist and uncover some huge scandal in the country," she says. When she was offered the "the cop shop" she balked, and it took Ben Bradlee to persuade her to take it. "If you want to write about real life, about love and hate and greed and the human condition, go on the police beat," she remembers being told by the then-executive editor. She did, and she loved it. "I was on the night police beat for a while, which is where I really began to learn how to make sources. It was a significant time in the District, because the murder rate went soaring. And all kinds of things were going on in the city that were really fascinating. One was that Congress decided to give more money to the D.C. police to fight crime, but only if they could get a thousand more officers on the street by a certain deadline."[5]

A related problem—deteriorating training—became a Horwitz specialty. A tipster from the police union suggested that she look at the police academy, where people were being pushed through, "people that are unqualified." Her reporting bore that out, but only because her years of experience allowed here to get her information confirmed. "You have to be on the beat for a couple of years, and do enough stories so that they see you on the crime scene," she says. "You have to be out at the retirement parties and funerals. It's slow going, and sometimes you make them mad and they cut you off."

And things were not always easy getting police stories approved by editors either, even at the *Post*. One idea for a three-part series on "dangers in the future" posed by this group of deficient trainees was rejected. "It was very frustrating," she says, "and it's a very tricky thing to talk about." But about the same time, Horwitz took a year off and had a baby and came back to another beat when she returned in the 1990s. (She had felt "sweet satisfaction," she adds, when two other *Post* reporters pulled together their own police training story along the lines she had envisioned, using some material she provided. Their work was a finalist for the 1995 Investigative Pulitzer Prize.)

Called in 1998 to join the police shootings team, Horwitz saw a great opportunity to dig through old files she had kept at home. "I went back in my basement and found the old notebooks, including one that said, 'This officer is a lawsuit waiting to happen.'" Teamcop would find a place for that example in the series. Horwitz was assigned to develop a story on a "good shooting," one in which all the rules were followed, and the shots fired were clearly necessary. "That turned out to be a very good idea," Horwitz says. "Police work is complicated, and there's a really tough time on the streets, and we needed to tell that story, too."

The good shooting story also gave her a chance to get back to her first love in journalism: reporting about people. "At first I was frustrated that it was such a dry story. All they had was statistics, and I wanted to get at the human story," she says. When she found the perfect "shooter" for her case, though, he did not want to cooperate. Officer Keith DeVille had fired on a person who had suddenly, shockingly shot DeVille's partner point-blank in the head. "He had witnessed that, and had to respond," Horwitz says. "And in the gunfight that ensued, he killed the suspect. He was never the same. His marriage fell apart. He ended up drinking. He said no to me three times. No, no, no."

She managed to change his mind, leading to an emotional interview. "He broke down in tears," Horwitz says. (Something nearly brought the reporter to tears too: in the middle of their talk, her tape recorder jammed, leaving her to try to restructure her notes later. "I don't think I've used a tape recorder since," she says.) But DeVille's story would be one of the highlights of the series.

As the reporting progressed, summaries of sixteen shooting cases were collected and sent to several experts in the use of police force. "Expert" quotes were avoided for publication for fear of populating the story with "talking heads." But privately experts confirmed their assessments. Editors continually encouraged the team to spend time with the police, who were about to be grilled in the series. Horwitz and other reporters went on ride-alongs with officers and shot the Glock at the firing range.

In studying the Glock's problems, Leen had another Eureka moment. Reading through a lawsuit, he found a quote in a deposition describing policeman Frederick Broomfield's accidental shooting by his roommate, Officer Juan "Jay" Martinez Jr. Martinez had been unloading a Glock in his bedroom when Broomfield entered the room to ask Martinez how he wanted his chicken cooked, and the gun went off. "I looked down and I seen smoke coming from my crotch and then after that, you know, I looked at Jay and I said, 'Damn, Jay.' Then my leg started shaking and I fell." The case provided one of many macabre moments in the series.

Scooped by *City Paper*

Teamcop was clearly developing synergy. "We worked very, very closely for several months, at a rapid clip and under the scrutiny of the paper, the police department and the legal community. Our team worked because we trusted each other with moral questions and reportorial dilemmas alike," wrote Dave Jackson later.[6] "And on those last weekends when there was only Dominoes pizza to glue our frayed souls together, we enjoyed each others' company." Horwitz agrees. "I'd come in and say something, and Dave would push me to go further on it," she says.

A six-page e-mail to editor Len Downie and managing editor Steve Coll laid out the plan for a series targeted for the week of November 15, and reporters were asked to "defend" the leads they had constructed. In mid-October the two editors received a note on "home-stretch issues"— photos, layout, and a length suggestion of a six-day package. Drafts of the main stories for the first three days were provided.

Then came a crisis—one all too familiar to reporters and editors working on long-term projects. The team discovered that the rival *City Paper* was preparing a story on what was to be Jackson's third-day lead article. The lawyer who was a Jackson source, it seems, had been talking to both papers. "We're driving a real big battleship, while the *City Paper* is like a speedboat," says Leen. "The story came out, and it was over 200 inches long, and I have to say they did a pretty good job on it." The *Post* cut back the Jackson story to a long sidebar and shortened the entire series to five days. It took a while for the team to bounce back. "I don't know if David Jackson ever did recover," says Leen, "although he ended up doing a great day-three story."

Teamcop went through a final November 9 checklist. Graphics were refined, and everything was in order for Sunday the 15th. Then on Saturday President Bill Clinton called for an attack against Iraq. Just as suddenly the attack was canceled. After a heart-stopping meeting between Atkinson and Coll, the Sunday run date for the police series was reconfirmed. "Summer into fall was very intense," says Horwitz. "There was some question toward the end: Should we have four pieces or five pieces in the series? And some people—especially me, working on the last piece—felt very strongly we needed that last piece. Others thought, How do we keep people reading?"

The way was to write it compellingly. After the overview, the second day covered shootings into cars; the third, problems with police investigations of shootings; the fourth, the Glock and training issues; and the fifth, brutality and the "continuum of force." The first-day story, carrying all four bylines, ran under the headline "D.C. Police Lead Nation in Shootings; Lack of Training, Supervision Implicated as Key Factors." It began:

> The District of Columbia's Metropolitan Police Department has shot and killed more people per resident in the 1990s than any other large American city police force.
>
> Many shootings by Washington police officers were acts of courage and even heroism. But internal police files and court records reveal a pattern of reckless and indiscriminate gunplay by officers sent into the streets with inadequate training and little oversight, an eight-month Washington Post investigation has found.

Washington's officers fire their weapons at more than double the rate of police in New York, Los Angeles, Chicago or Miami. Deaths and injuries in D.C. police shooting cases have resulted in nearly $8 million in court settlements and judgments against the District in the last six months alone.

"We shoot too often, and we shoot too much when we do shoot," said Executive Assistant Chief of Police Terrance W. Gainer, who became the department's second in command in May.[7]

Unlike Ben Bradlee, who says he relishes the moment when a big story actually rolls off the press, Leen finds publication of a long-planned series anticlimactic. "We have this pattern, and when people see it they're not going to believe it," he says. But for the team, the pattern has been old news for months. When Leen had first seen the police database he realized that they could not even keep track of their shootings. "That's what sustained me when we took the hit from the David Jackson story being scooped," he says.

Investigative journalism isn't for everyone, Sari Horwitz cautions. "Lots of reporters don't want to do this. It's tedious. You've got to go through boxes and boxes to find the needle in the haystack." But for a reporter who is not driven by the need for a daily deadline or byline, the rewards are great. "The thing we have is the luxury of time, which a daily reporter doesn't have," she says.

"I don't think any of us were thinking of a prize, but we were so excited by the story," Horwitz adds. "We were excited when the new police chief said to the mayor, 'We're going to go back and look at all these shootings.' And we said, 'Whoa, this story actually made something happen.' I certainly had never been on a story with that kind of impact before." New training procedures were installed across the thirty-five-hundred-officer police force, and investigation techniques were revised. The changes were strictly monitored. In 1998, thirty-two people had been shot by D.C. policemen, twelve fatally. In 2000, the number killed had fallen to one.

1999—The *Washington Post* for its series that identified and analyzed patterns of reckless gunplay by city police officers who had little training or supervision.[8]

"Invisible Lives, Invisible Deaths"

Not long after the *Post* won its 1999 gold medal, Jeff Leen was named an editor on the investigative staff. "I'd been a reporter for twenty years," he says. "I asked myself, Where do I go from the police-shooting series? I thought, If I don't take that editing job, I'm going to get a boss I don't like."[9] His first assignment as editor was prickly. Marilyn Thompson— who had taken over as chief investigative editor after Rick Atkinson left to write a book—handed Leen a draft of Kate Boo's story on institutions for the mentally retarded and told him he should consider putting a different lead on it.

Leen remembers picturing how his meeting with Boo might go. "I'm going to end up telling her about putting a new lead on this thing she's been working on for a year?" Leen and Boo had lunch. "They think you should change the lead," Leen said. Boo, a 1988 Barnard College Phi Beta Kappa graduate, replied, "Who's they?" Welcome to the world of editing at the *Post*.

Things would turn out very well for the Boo piece "Invisible Lives." But the work on that draft also began a year-long process that eventually led to a second project, delving into the heartbreaking world of D.C. homes for the mentally retarded: "Invisible Deaths." By the end of 2000, the stories would lead to the closure of group homes and would prompt federal and local investigations. City officials would be fired and several officials would be indicted. "These stories began in the dark," was the way Len Downie's Pulitzer nomination letter started. And in more ways than one that was the truth.[10]

Kate Boo had been covering the *Post's* poverty beat, working late nights on a series on welfare reform. A non-driver, she sometimes relied on friends for a ride, and one evening her driver friend had to make a stop at one of the District's homes for the mentally retarded. Boo was shocked by what she saw. "The home had no electricity and it was just swarming with bugs," she says. "And everybody was just sitting around this table, with deformities—physical deformities, mental deformities. . . . It was just so different from my perception." Boo, like many Washingtonians, had thought that various reforms over the years had turned such homes into model institutions.

Once the welfare reform story was reported, she chose mental institutions for her next project. She began to see that her first visit had only revealed shadows of what was really wrong. Legal reforms had clearly not done much to improve the situation in institutions. "You could burn somebody or rape somebody, whatever, and the institutions would never be penalized because there was this minor bylaw that hadn't been passed," she says.[11] Boo started visiting homes. She interviewed staffers. She met the residents. She was hooked.

Elroy was one of 1,100 "beneficiaries" of the publicly funded, community-based group homes. Elroy's home, like others in the system, operated under a lucrative contract with entrepreneur Rollie Washington, who lived on a so-called manor farm. Elroy, DeWitt Stith, and others from the home also worked at the farm. They received $5 a day cleaning horse stalls and doing other menial labor as part of what Washington called "reality therapy." Boo followed Elroy's and Stith's lives closely, and she delved into Rollie Washington's business. She established that Elroy had been repeatedly raped in the house and had become suicidal.

One of her reporting techniques was the impromptu visit. Showing up at Rollie Washington's farm on a Saturday, she managed to get him to sit down and talk. "His general position was the essential point of the story: that I'm every bit as good as the District needed," says Boo. "There it was." Some unscheduled visits to homes led to calls to police, who kept her out. For others, though, she saw what she needed to see.

Boo and her editors set certain standards for the story as she reported. It needed to show that past reforms were not working and also that employees were being abusive. Many reporters aim to concentrate on how taxpayers' money is being squandered, and that makes a good story, she says. "But that's never been the thing for me." Her first goal is to write about people and what happened to them. "The second part is about profit," she says. "That's the way it should be in my mind."

By concentrating on Elroy, DeWitt, and others, she achieved the personal emphasis she sought, although the financial picture was hardly lost. Her first story—headlined, in part, "Who Cares?"—began:

Elroy lives here. Tiny, half-blind, mentally retarded, 39-year-old Elroy. To find him, go past the counselor flirting on the phone. Past the broken chairs, the roach-dappled kitchen and the housemates whose neglect in this group home has been chronicled for a decade in the files of city agencies. Head upstairs to Elroy's single bed.

"You're in good hands," reads the Allstate Insurance poster tacked above his mattress—the mattress where the sexual predator would catch him sleeping. Catch him easily. The door between their rooms had fallen from its hinges. Catch him relentlessly—so relentlessly that Elroy tried to commit suicide by running blindly into a busy Southeast Washington street.[12]

"One of the nice things about investigative for me was that there was trust," says Boo. The editors knew she was working hard and gave her the time she needed.

Still, when it came to convincing editors that a reporter had the facts, the *Post's* Janet Cooke legacy remained alive at the paper—especially for stories on poverty issues. Cooke's 1980 "Jimmy's World" story, after all, had been a poverty story: the wrenching tale of a supposed eight-year-old heroin addict.[13] One lesson that the *Post* had learned from that embarrassing episode was that in writing about obscure people with no voice of their own, standards must be just as high as for profiling public figures.

"Because at the *Post* I worked in the ghetto—and Janet Cooke worked in the ghetto—you just have to presume in poverty reporting that it's going to be challenged, that you must get your ducks in a row. That's not just in this series, it's in all the work I've ever done in the inner city," says Boo. In this case, Boo found sources to back up everything she heard from the retarded individuals. "The burden of proof has to come from elsewhere—from the public record, or admissions from the people who did the wrongdoing themselves. Then it's fair."

In early story development, Boo says, Rick Atkinson helped her shape the project to describe the system rather than one home or one individual case. "The next thing was realizing who was running the homes, and the kind of accountability they had," according to Boo. Working through the *Post* lawyers, she filed Freedom of Information Act requests. She followed up on the reports that Elroy had been raped and tried to commit suicide. "The records were saying everything was well and good. It was clear that a false paper trail was being created," she says.

She persisted in trying to get confirmation that Elroy was raped and finally got it. Yes, the manager of the group homes told her, adding the nuance that the sexual predator who victimized him "was incessant." The manager told her that "whatever this guy's taking . . . is better than Viagra!"

Boo kept detailed documentary backup for the story's claims, both about specific cases and about the financial peculiarities of the whole system. "I love documents," she says. "It's a great shy-person's kind of journalism. It's this great intellectual game. What was the relationship of this person, who bought the house for that person. It's a way of seeing the bigger picture."

Boo got along especially well with the paper's attorneys. "The *Post* lawyers are in a class by themselves in terms of caring about justice, as opposed to caring about not getting sued," she says. Plus working with lawyers reminds reporters of the value of accuracy on details in the story. "With these kinds of stories, one mistake can take out two thousand facts."

Unlike most reporters, Boo is "anti-series," she says. Her "Invisible Lives" project was intended as one story, she says, but had to run as a two-parter because of the sheer amount of information.

The Letdown—and Another Series

Then came the letdown after the story was in print. "There was a superficial level of outrage," says Boo. "And I got all of that." There were letters to the editor and statements from officials that heads would roll. But Boo felt stymied by the lack of real action. "What really *means* something is if they actually do something about it," she says. "What I care about is if they change the friggin' law." It was almost as if the first day's headline— "Who Cares?"—described the reaction to the series as well. "As always when you write about poverty issues, there's a hue and cry, and things go back to normal."

Jeff Leen loved the first series for its lyrical writing and its passion for social justice. With some reporters, passion colors the final product. "She's probably the only person who could pull that off," says Leen. "She is so meticulous and fair-minded and precise, and so intelligent,

THE *POST* RINGS TWICE

that it amplifies and raises up her work, and doesn't get in the way of it. She combines these things that most people think are oil and water—incongruous."

All along he had been intrigued by a sidebar that appeared with the first story. It offered just a hint, he thought, of the stark and inhuman end to which Boo's subjects' lives came. "Now," he told her, "you have to do the deaths." The reporter was not thrilled at the thought. "Nobody wanted to read about it in the first place; nobody's going to want to read about it again," she recalls thinking. So why did she keep at it, aiming for a December run date? "In a way I did it because I didn't know what else to do." In the end she found that Leen was right. "It took the deaths to make people care," she says.

The project, focusing on what happens after individuals from the homes die, was also broken into two parts. Boo found official records showing an unrealistically low number of deaths among the institutional-ized people—eleven in six years. (Eventually she obtained an admission from the city that the number was 116.) The lives of some of the deceased had simply been "erased." Further, manipulation of medical records led to some victims of fatal abuse being listed as dying of natural causes.

One example was Frederick E. Brandenburg, who Boo proved had been mistakenly drugged and left to die by a careless attendant. His body was then illegally moved and cremated. When she inquired, Boo was told that an autopsy had been declined by Brandenburg's sisters because they were Jehovah's Witnesses. When she tracked the sisters down, however, one was Baptist, and the other was Catholic.

In the end, Boo says, it helped with her reporting on the Branden-burg story that she was a native Washingtonian, familiar with the city. When she received a call from the person who had shredded the records, the caller was reluctant to talk or give a name. "I knew from the phone exchange exactly where he was, and I knew the one bar in that neighbor-hood, and I said, 'I'll meet you there.'" At the meeting, she was told that employees were rewarded for such shredding. "When I had that, I knew that they couldn't get out of it," she says.

Leen admits to being choked with emotion at times during his edit-ing of Boo's copy. "I still think this was probably the finest series I ever edited," he says. The first story carried the headline "Lives Erased Without a Word." It began:

> The corpse measured 66 inches from blue toes to jutting ears. In a beige house on Tenley Circle, a dentist-entrepreneur lugged this cargo down the stairs into the basement and laid it to rest by the washer.
>
> The body in plaid pajamas was that of a 57-year-old retarded ward of the District of Columbia. On the streets outside the city-funded group home where he had lived and died, kids sometimes called him Retard-O. Inside, he sweetened the hours by printing the name his mother gave him before she gave him up. Frederick Emory Brandenburg. He blanketed old telephone directories with that name, covered the TV Guides the home's staffers tossed aside. He glutted the flyleaves of his large-print Living Bible. The immensity of the effort made his hands shake, but the habit seemed as requisite as breath. In this way Brandenburg, whose thick-tongued words were mysteries to many, impressed the fact of his existence on his world.
>
> In January 1997, that existence was obliterated by his caretakers.[14]

During production week Leen asked managing editor Steve Coll for an extra page. "The project was supposed to be three open pages," but for special graphics and subheadlines that were being planned, four pages were needed. Coll's response: "You got it." Leen says, "There wasn't even a blink."[15]

Read It and Weep

But making it into print was a whole other story. On production night, Leen and Boo stayed late in the office, carefully defusing potential problems. There were lots of them. What made the layout tricky was that the subheads and cutlines for the piece were specially designed, with intricate computer coding. Care had to be taken to avoid losing paragraphs when the story "turned" from column to column. As Leen and Boo watched during the evening, type got dropped and was restored with difficulty. When the situation was finally solved, a cheer went up. Leen took Boo to a Burger King on K Street before each went home. Leen turned in for the night satisfied with "the best story I've ever edited in my career."

The next morning Boo was staying with her parents, her ritual when a story was finished. "We always do that," she says, "because I say that I'll get to see you one last night before I go to libel jail." Her father read the story first the next morning. There was a problem, he said. Not libel, but something in the way the story just stopped flowing. Kate read in horror. Missing were several blocks of type, including that hard-earned explanation of how the authorities had lied about Brandenburg being cremated because his next-of-kin were Jehovah's Witnesses. "I read it that Sunday morning and wept," she recalls.

Leen got her first call. "Kate was devastated. She was saying that people said it ruined the project. It doesn't make sense. Talk about a crisis. I didn't know what to say. I told her that at some point this is going to seem like a very small matter," he says. "I didn't even know if that was true."

The post-mortem on the printing glitch—"it would have taken a presidential commission to figure it out," says Leen—showed a typesetting error in the pagination system. A well-meaning technician had apparently seen a small problem during the press run after Leen and Boo went home. The technician made a "fix" and the delicately balanced layout imploded. No one caught it. "We did have 30,000 copies that were just perfect," says Leen.

By 2005, Boo had almost forgotten about it—almost. Looking at the two-part series as a whole, she is proud of the impact it had in the community. Did it occur to her that it might win a Pulitzer? "As a reporter you don't think about that," says Boo, who eventually moved to *The New Yorker* magazine and who in 2013 was named to the Pulitzer Prize board.[16] There she has helped with selecting winners from among the best of twenty-first-century American journalism—and with steering the Pulitzer Prizes into their second century.

2000—The *Washington Post,* notably for the work of Katherine Boo that disclosed wretched neglect and abuse in the city's group homes for the mentally retarded, which forced officials to acknowledge the conditions and begin reforms.[17]

AFTERWORD

A New Voice of the South

One month after the *Post and Courier* won the 2015 Pulitzer Prize for Public Service, my visit to its Charleston, South Carolina newsroom revealed a mix of continuing celebration and concern about whether legislative inaction would blunt the impact of its project.

"Till Death Do Us Part" had opened with a shocking summary of the situation that the reporters and editors were trying to change: "More than 300 women were shot, stabbed, strangled, beaten, bludgeoned, or burned to death over the past decade by men in South Carolina, dying at a rate of one every 12 days while the state does little to stem the carnage from domestic abuse."[1] The Pulitzer board had praised the staff for putting the issue on the South Carolina agenda, but one of the project's lead reporters, Doug Pardue, had a starker assessment. The work "may ultimately be meaningless if the state's General Assembly doesn't pass the domestic violence law reforms bill it has on its table," Pardue said in his own paper's news story about its Pulitzer.[2] Even in publicity's glare, the legislature balked at limiting the right of convicted spousal abusers to keep firearms, for example. (*Post and Courier* research showed that 70 percent of the murdered women were gunned down.)

My first Charleston interview was with Pierre Manigault, chairman of the anachronistically named Evening Post Industries, his family-controlled company that owned the 212-year-old paper. (Delivered mornings, it reached 82,000 households, 88,000 on Sunday.) When he took over for his father in 2004 he saw the *Post and Courier* as a community beacon but soon developed a grander view. "Charleston was already the cultural capital of the South," he told me, "and I didn't see why we couldn't be the best paper in the South—the new voice of the South, really."[3]

P. J. Browning, who joined as publisher in 2012, had seen investing in Web-based news and presentation as key to enlarging its reach, as long as its reporting power also grew. "Digital opens up the world to us," she said. "It would have been an awfully lofty goal to think we could be the new voice of the South in print," where financial constraints were more daunting.[4] Manigault and Browning both favored hiring Mitch Pugh as executive editor in March 2013, bringing him from Iowa's *Sioux City Journal*, a Lee Enterprises property. The chairman thought Pugh had "a real vision for quality investigative reporting." From the St. Louis-born candidate's perspective, meanwhile, the attraction to Charleston was ownership's commitment to improving coverage *and* online technology. "They were willing to invest in the paper in a way Lee just couldn't," in part because of Lee's heavy debt, Pugh told me. "It almost felt too good to be true."

It *was* true. Corporate support came quickly for Pugh's drive to reinstitute the paper's enterprise reporting function. (The paper already ran quality investigative pieces and feature stories—including two of reporter Tony Bartelme's projects nominated for Pulitzers in 2011 and 2013[5]— but one-person efforts had replaced team projects.) The veteran reporter Glenn Smith, who would join Pardue in leading the domestic violence investigation and would cowrite the stories with him, loved the new digital capability. "In the past we'd do these great stories that would land on junky websites," Smith told me. "Yes," Pardue agreed, "we really brought it all together."[6]

The digital editor Laura Gaton and the newly hired interactive editor J. Emory Parker had just finished the online revamping when a story came along that seemed perfect for an extensive digital presentation. A September 2013 study from the national Violence Policy Center ranked the state as having the highest rate of women killed by men, drawing Smith and Pardue's attention. "Once again we were at the top of a list you didn't want to be at the top of," said Pardue, who had written previously about areas where South Carolina was statistically backward.[7] Mitch Pugh teamed Pardue with "faith and values" reporter Jennifer Berry Hawes to do some basic reporting. Smith was teamed with courts reporter Natalie Caula Hauff, who was asked to develop data for the story—a task that Pardue, Smith, and Pugh knew would be critical to explaining a complex issue like the prevalence of domestic violence in their state.

Their major goal was to analyze the characteristics of this murder plague, illustrate it with cases, and propose solutions. The paper's archives helped them calculate a total of 330 women killed in the last decade. In breaking down elements of the crimes, they found that 70 percent involved firearms—a statistic that raised special controversy in a state where gun rights are often considered sacred. "Having the data was the backbone of the project," said Pugh. "We didn't make a value judgment saying 70 percent of these murders were with guns. It was just the fact."

A second goal was for the reporters to think like their readers. "I've lived here for twenty-some-odd years, and Doug and Glenn have too. We're familiar with this state," said Hawes, originally from Chicago, who was assigned to do most of the victim interviews. "But from the perspective of native South Carolinians there are few things more repugnant than a Yankee coming down here and telling them all the things wrong with their culture and way of life. We had to take a nuanced approach; we talked long and hard about the phrasing of things."

Merry Christmas

Later in September, as Pardue and Hawes were seeking to understand the reasons for the state's bad record, they stumbled onto the series' eventual headline. During an interview, the director of a women's shelter noted factors that included South Carolina's extremely rural population, poverty, and strong gun culture. In a strange way "it has to do with love," she added, "and then there's that religion thing." Pressed to elaborate, she described how fundamentalist Christian men often consider themselves totally dominant in a relationship. "Till death do us part," the director added. "That phrase kind of hung out there," Hawes told me. "And Doug and I thought, Well that's it."[8]

Still, progress was slow in creating a database and finding women to interview, mainly victims of near-fatal attacks. Then, a Christmas present: the nonprofit, Emeryville, California–based Center for Investigative Reporting had received a six-figure grant that included a provision for aiding South Carolina journalism.[9] As Mitch Pugh remembered it, the CIR director Mark Katches called one late December day and asked the editor, "Can you help us spend this money?" Sure, Pugh answered, and the two agreed that the *Post and Courier*'s domestic violence project—in need of a sophisticated database—was a good candidate. By midyear the grant would pay tens of thousands of dollars for training in California with CIR data experts and editors.

Meanwhile, Natalie Hauff kept assembling domestic-violence data, and Jennifer Hawes developed her interviewing approach. "To me that's the strength of any story: the humanity of it. Here we were finding victims everywhere, horrific story after horrific story, and all different on some level. Some were poor, some rich, some black, some white," Hawes said. The diversity of victims and killers became part of the theme.

She started with relationship building. Interviews succeed if women feel "they can trust you, and your motivation is just to share it, and not paint them as something they're not, and not to sensationalize," Hawes said. "You're holding their sacred story in your hands." She learned early that brutalized women didn't want to be called victims. "I referred to them as survivors." She often worked through an intermediary—a pastor or friend—to avoid the feel of a cold call and to "give women the room to say no."

A major barrier was the embarrassment that survivors felt if they had been in abusive relationships for years and couldn't explain why. "There is an inherent accusation there, especially if there are children involved," Hawes noted, and she tried to factor that into her questioning. "I'd often go the route of asking, 'What is it that people don't understand?'" Sometimes that produced insights: that a boyfriend controlled her money, or that leaving a husband could be more dangerous than staying—for the woman or for her children. It helped them to know they wouldn't be alone in the story. "Having multiple people involved with interviews gave them comfort in numbers," said Hawes, and some eventually formed survivor groups.

Interviews filmed for online use would be especially compelling. Natalie Hauff, who had come to the paper from the Charleston ABC television affiliate, helped Emory Parker and videographer Chris Hanclosky produce clips with the polished look of movie trailers.

Pardue and Smith's story drafts began to take shape—they often passed copy from one to the other for tweaking—and Pugh and managing editor Rick Nelson edited. The first story's opening was seen as critical, and an anecdotal beginning quickly gave way to the idea of laying out the extent of the murderous drama going on in their state. "We thought, 'Why don't we just come right out of the box with this and hit people over the head, rather than bury it?'" Smith said.

When the team traveled to California for a June visit with the investigative reporting nonprofit, with the CIR grant taking care of travel and training expenses, Katches was impressed. "These were some of the best first drafts I'd seen come my way, the work of a well oiled team," he told me from his office at Portland's *Oregonian*, where he became editor in mid-2014.

Still, fine-tuning helped. An original draft had started; "More than 300 women were slaughtered by their loved ones in South Carolina," according to Katches's notes. (The *Post and Courier* reporters already had decided against using "slaughtered" after getting negative reactions from women on the staff.) "My suggestion was to replace that with all the forms of death: they were shot, stabbed, strangled, bludgeoned, or burned to death by men in South Carolina," said the editor, who was one of several CIR experts to review drafts. And no longer were the killers called "loved ones." The CIR database senior editor Jennifer LaFleur worked closely with Hauff, giving the project another lift. While there, Hauff came up with the idea of a separate story to examine how state legislators were killing reform bills. A powerful series element began to take shape: comparative timelines that tracked the dates of negative actions in the capital against the mounting statewide death toll, murder by murder.

The Netflix Model

When staffers returned to Charleston, interviews and data collection took on a new energy. An August run date for the series was planned.

Digital editor Gaton and interactive editor Parker helped integrate the data and video into a powerful seven-part package with interactive material that went beyond the developing five-part print series. The decision was made to release the entire online package before the opening print article would run in Charleston. Using what they called a Netflix model, Gaton said, the entire series was released in one interactive package that let the online audience read each piece at will. The early release meant that *Buzzfeed, Huffington Post,* and other outlets ran the news, with a link to the *Post and Courier* website, before local print subscribers saw it— something that in the past would have been seen as breaking a cardinal rule of print publishing. "Now it's becoming the standard," Gaton said. "Everything starts with putting it online first." The move paid off in online readership, helping build eight million page views for August 2014, a 60 percent increase over the same month the year before.

After reading advanced drafts, Katches remembered, he told his CIR associates that the work was worthy of a Pulitzer Prize. He was prescient. Meeting in February 2015, the Pulitzer public service jury nominated the *Post and Courier* as a finalist along with the *Wall Street Journal* and the *Boston Globe.* When the full Pulitzer board named it the 2015 winner, the Charleston paper had its first Pulitzer since winning for editorial writing ninety years earlier, when it was known as the *News and Courier.*[10]

The Pulitzer jurors hadn't paid attention to how the newspaper released the project early through social media, an approach that seems to be gaining popularity in the pursuit of national recognition for major projects. But the jury did admire its collaboration with the Center for Investigative Reporting. "We all thought the paper was smart to invite the CIR to help train and advise it, and the digital database of those killed was an important reporting tool," said the jury chair Scott Kraft, deputy managing editor of the *Los Angeles Times.* The paper's Pulitzer entry wasn't hurt because the series led to no changes in the law, said another juror, Josh Meyer, with Northwestern University's National Security Journalism Initiative. "It had a powerful impact," he added, "in the sense that it took what had become an accepted part of life and turned it into a problem that could no longer be denied."[11]

As it happened, several weeks after my May 2015 *Post and Courier* visit the legislature passed, and Governor Nikki Haley signed, a bill that reflected many of the recommendations in the publication's series, including taking guns from convicted wife-abusers.[12] Then in June, the *Post and Courier* again showed that a new voice of the South had emerged—with extraordinary coverage after a young, white, racist gunman massacred nine black Bible study participants meeting in a historic Charleston church. In the ninety-ninth awarding of the Pulitzer Prizes, once again the gold medal had gone to a news organization that was making a difference.

2015—The *Post and Courier*, Charleston, S.C., for "Till Death Do Us Part," a riveting series that probed why South Carolina is among the deadliest states in the union for women and put the issue of what to do about it on the state's agenda.[13]

PULITZER GOLD NUGGETS

The decision to abbreviate certain Pulitzer-winning accounts for this appendix, rather than to include longer versions in the book's main section was often difficult. A few cases here deserve entire books of their own. But because *Pulitzer's Gold* attempts to showcase the development of a century of American journalism, it was necessary to limit parts I, II, and III to give a sense of flow. Here, summaries of other winners appear in chronological order under the Pulitzer board's citation. The descriptive handiwork of such citations varies; sometimes quite florid, they also can be terse or say almost nothing at all.

The main sources for these descriptions are the entries themselves and supporting material in Columbia University's Pulitzer Prize archives, along with comments from jurors. Links to each year's prizes can be found at www.pulitzer.org, the website of the Pulitzer Prizes. Other sources are as noted, with special attention to *Editor and Publisher* magazine.

No Pulitzer Prize in public service was given in 1917, 1920, 1925, or 1930.[1]

1923—*Memphis Commercial Appeal* for its courageous attitude in the publication of cartoons and the handling of news in reference to the operations of the Ku Klux Klan.

As a southern paper, the *Memphis Commercial Appeal* took special risks launching a campaign against the Ku Klux Klan in the early 1920s. Cartoonist

James Alley produced several cartoons that ridiculed Klan members, including one from December 1922 that pictured a Klan member in full regalia reading a book titled *Law Enforcement*. For the first time there was real competition for the Public Service Prize. Jurors forwarded five nominees to the board.

1924—*New York World* for its work in connection with the exposure of the Florida peonage evil.

Herbert Bayard Swope, the executive editor of the *New York World*, moved on from his pursuit of the Ku Klux Klan (the gold medal winner in 1922) to direct his paper in taking on another social travesty: the use of prison camps in Florida and other southern states to punish people for minor or even nonexistent law violations, a system known as peonage. A Swope credo was that one should "boil over whenever wrong is done the little fellow."[2] As an illustration, his newspaper took up the case of Martin Tabert, a North Dakota boy who had left the farm to seek work in Florida, traveling by rail without a ticket. When he was arrested and could not pay the $25 fine, Tabert was thrust among prisoners leased out by a local sheriff to a lumber camp. There he was horsewhipped to death, although his family was told he had died of malaria and pneumonia. When North Dakota tried in vain to get the death investigated in Florida, Swope's *World* took over his case, tracking down fellow inmates, including one from Brooklyn who had kept a diary. Reporter Samuel Duff McCoy worked the story for two months, finding that a Florida state senator owned a turpentine camp that benefited from convict labor.

1926—*Columbus* (Ga.) *Enquirer Sun* for the service which it rendered in its brave and energetic fight against the Ku Klux Klan; against the enactment of a law barring the teaching of evolution; against dishonest and incompetent public officials and for justice to the Negro and against lynching.

The Pulitzer board picked the *Enquirer Sun* from seventeen public service entries. The Columbus paper's submission was mainly a series of opinion pieces written by editor Julian LaRose Harris. Opposition to the Ku Klux Klan was prominent among the articles, but other topics were covered too. One column opposed those who stood against teaching evolution. (The Scopes Monkey Trial in Tennessee had captivated the nation in the summer of 1925, pitting Clarence Darrow against William Jennings Bryan.)

1928—*Indianapolis Times* for its work in exposing political corruption to Indiana, prosecuting the guilty and bringing about a more wholesome state of affairs in civil government.

The anti-corruption work of the *Indianapolis Times* had a Ku Klux Klan connection. The paper exposed illegal activities involving the governor and a former state treasurer and also ties the two had to a former Grand Dragon of the Klan and "political dictator of the state." Both the governor and the former treasurer were indicted. The board vote overruled the Columbia faculty jury, which had recommended the *Minneapolis Tribune* for a campaign to improve farming methods.

1929—*New York Evening World* for its effective campaign to correct evils in the administration of justice, including the fight to curb "ambulance chasers," support of the "fence" bill, and measures to simplify procedure, prevent perjury and eliminate politics from municipal courts; a campaign which has been instrumental in securing remedial action.

The lead series in the wide-ranging *New York Evening World* entry was written by reporter William O. Trapp and exposed ambulance-chasing lawyers while another urged legislation against the fencing of stolen property. Selection of the *Evening World* was bitterly protested by the Philadelphia *Sunday Transcript*, which claimed that "the whole enterprise upon which the award was made to the *New York World* was originated by the *Sunday Transcript*." The Philadelphia paper "certainly will not compete in any contest so long as it is under the Columbia University and the City of New York," the paper said. Two years later, though, the *Transcript* was back with another public service entry.

1931—*Atlanta Constitution* for a successful municipal graft exposure and consequent convictions.

Solicitor General John A. Boykin of the Atlanta Judicial Circuit wrote to support the *Atlanta Constitution*: "For many months there had been veiled allusions and undercover rumors of wholesale graft in the city government of Atlanta, but not until the *Constitution* courageously called for a sweeping investigation was my office able to obtain evidence upon which I could lay the situation before the grand jury." The paper's own nomination letter was written by the *Constitution* director of news and Pulitzer board member Julian LaRose Harris, who had moved from Georgia's *Columbus Enquirer Sun*. The board picked the *Constitution* over the jury's first choice, the *Louisville Times*, which worked to save the Cumberland Falls in a state park.[3]

1932—*Indianapolis News* for its successful campaign to eliminate waste in city management and to reduce the tax levy.

The *Indianapolis News* won for an eighteen-month effort to rein in city government spending under the pressures of the Great Depression. The state legislature passed laws denying jurisdictions the right to boost their expenses, and the paper said its effort would produce an estimated savings of $12 million in a state budget of $156 million.

1933—*New York World-Telegram* for its series of articles on veterans relief, on the real estate bond evil, the campaign urging voters in the late New York City municipal election to "write in" the name of Joseph V. McKee, and the articles exposing the lottery schemes of various fraternal organizations.

APPENDIX

The Scripps-Howard-owned *New York World-Telegram* won for an entry that covered a range of issues, some of them Depression-related. The centerpiece was a campaign calling attention to federal mismanagement of World War I veterans' bonuses. Disabled veterans were often treated unfavorably compared to some who had seen no battlefield duty. Legislation was proposed to change veterans' compensation and boost dependent pay for families of killed soldiers. Jurors said: "When others were pussyfooting, the *World-Telegram*, in the open, assailed evil where it found it. We believe it has followed in the footsteps of the editor whose benefaction established the prize for public service."

1935—The *Sacramento* (Calif.) *Bee* for its campaign against political machine influence in the appointment of two Federal judges in Nevada.

Selection of the *Sacramento Bee*, which was on the reporting jury's list, was for associate editor Arthur B. Waugh's investigation of the qualifications of two of President Franklin Roosevelt's federal judge nominees in Nevada. Waugh showed that Judge Frank H. Norcross, named to the circuit court of appeals, and William Woodburn, named to replace Norcross on the federal district bench, were associates of crime boss George Wingfield, who had masterminded the closure of a chain of banks in Nevada and was implicated in looting several companies. The appointments were dropped, and Nevadans overthrew the Wingfield machine in the fall elections.

1936—The *Cedar Rapids* (Iowa) *Gazette* for its crusade against corruption and misgovernment in the State of Iowa.

Publisher Verne Marshall used Iowa's *Cedar Rapids Gazette* to report on bootleggers, illegal slot machine operators, crooked state authorities, and Democratic Party campaign fund contributors who were involved in payoffs to public officials. The *Gazette*'s stories started a six-month grand jury inquiry into gambling and liquor violations, much of it across the state in Sioux City. Marshall and the *Gazette* defended themselves against several libel suits during the reporting. In leading a campaign against Iowa graft, according to a May 9, 1936, account in *Editor and Publisher*, he "testified before grand juries, dug up evidence, interviewed possible witnesses, wrote news stories of sweeping charges of graft in the state and stinging page one articles." *Editor and Publisher* noted that the Iowa Supreme Court quashed thirty-one indictments stemming from the reporting and suggested that "one of the major reasons for disqualification of the indictments was payment of $700 by the Gazette" to a special prosecutor in the case.[4]

1939—The *Miami Daily News* for its campaign for the recall of the Miami City Commission.

The *Miami Daily News* successfully fought for a landmark recall of the city commissioners, who had tried to double their own salaries and botched a harbor development project. Meanwhile commissioners paid off attorneys, created funds to remunerate campaign workers, and solicited a $250,000 bribe from a utility company president—until the president took out a newspaper ad announcing: "I Won't Pay a Bribe." At one point the paper started a front-page series called "Speaking of Termites," attacking the city commission majority for "boring from within." The newspaper helped the recall campaign collect 20,000 signatures in a city with only 36,000 registered voters.

1940—*Waterbury* (Conn.) *Republican & American* for its campaign exposing municipal graft.

The *Waterbury Republican & American* had spent ten years investigating the mayor and city controller under publisher William J. Pape and editor E. Robert Stevenson. Exposing wrongdoing had taken that long because officials had severely limited access to city records. The city government had also fought back using devious means. At one point the paper reported finding a Dictaphone hidden in the fireplace of Pape's office—to record his conversations—and documented that the city had underwritten the spying with monthly payments to an investigator. The paper found indications of voting list padding and illicit financial dealings. Eventually Mayor H. Frank Hayes and city controller Daniel J. Leary were sentenced to the maximum prison terms of ten to fifteen years.

1942—*Los Angeles Times* for its successful campaign which resulted in the clarification and confirmation for all American newspapers of the right of free press as guaranteed under the Constitution.

Publisher Harry Chandler's *Los Angeles Times*, long known for its anti-union stands, California boosterism, and a sensationalist streak, fought with the Los Angeles County Bar Association over the right of the press to comment on court proceedings. Acting on a bar association petition, a judge had issued contempt citations declaring that publishing the editorials had interfered with the dispensation of justice. The *Times* could have paid a small fine and simply stopped such commentary. But it chose to fight. The bar association was upheld by higher courts all the way to the Supreme Court, which ruled for the *Times*. Justices said there must be "clear and present danger" to the administration of justice before contempt citations are issued and the press is restrained. It was, in a way, a strange time for a First Amendment victory. "For the time being, the issue was set aside because American newspapers as a whole had accepted a voluntary program of self-censorship during World War II out of concern for national security," wrote Pulitzer Prize historian John Hohenberg.

1943—*Omaha* (Neb.) *World-Herald* for its initiative and originality in planning a state-wide campaign for the collection of scrap metal for the war effort. The Nebraska plan was adopted on a national scale by the daily newspapers, resulting in a united effort which succeeded in supplying our war industries with necessary scrap material.

The *World Herald*'s campaign to collect scrap metal for the war effort had a significant impact, producing 103 pounds of scrap metal per person in its circulation area over three weeks in the summer of 1942. It also sparked a national scrap drive involving newspaper publishers from coast to coast. That effort, called the Nebraska Plan, produced enough scrap to ensure full operation of U.S. steel mills for war production during the winter of 1942.

1945—*Detroit Free Press* for its investigation of legislative graft and corruption in Lansing, Michigan.

Closely following political graft in Michigan's state capital during World War II, the *Detroit Free Press* turned its attention to Republican boss Frank D. McKay—suspected of using Lansing as a base for involvement in criminal activity. The criminal case against him had become bogged down because prosecution was left in the hands of a McKay associate. Veteran *Free Press* crime reporter Kenneth McCormick, just back from a Nieman Fellowship at Harvard, wrote stories about the need for a special prosecutor, and the *Free Press* editorials took that position. When one was named, indictments followed. But before McKay was indicted, one witness against him, State Senator Warren G. Hooper, was assassinated in a small Michigan town. The murder is unsolved to this day. McCormick's story on the killing, early in 1945, couldn't be part of the Pulitzer entry, but the Hooper killing made the Pulitzer board aware of how great the danger facing McCormick and the *Free Press* had been.

1946—*Scranton Times* for its fifteen-year investigation of judicial practices in the United States District Court for the middle district of Pennsylvania, resulting in removal of the District Judge and indictment of many others.

The *Scranton Times* assistant city editor George H. Martin, who discovered irregularities while he was doing routine federal courts rounds, learned that a seventy-three-year-old federal judge, Albert W. Johnson, was taking bribes in the courthouse. Crime-fighting Tennessee congressman Estes Kefauver said the judge was "selling justice" and called his case "the most corrupt situation that could possibly exist in any federal court." The judge resigned, was denied his pension, and was finally indicted for conspiracy to defraud the United States and obstructing justice.

1947—*Baltimore Sun* for its series of articles by Howard M. Norton dealing with the administration of unemployment compensation in Maryland, resulting in convictions and pleas of guilty in criminal court of ninety-three persons.

The *Baltimore Sun* reporter Howard M. Norton wrote a series of eighteen articles on problems with Maryland's unemployment compensation system. Assigned to study the system, he explored lax controls governing payouts and excessive costs of plan administration. Part of the reason for the high cost was that racketeers and cheats were taking advantage of loopholes. The Maryland General Assembly proposed changes in the law, and a number of people abusing the system were convicted or pleaded guilty to charges. Norton became the first individual to be named in the citation accompanying the Public Service Prize. After that, naming one or more reporters became an option for the Pulitzer board. Between 1947 and 2015 it named reporters fourteen times, although the approach is becoming more common. Individuals were named ten times between 1990 and 2015.

1949—*Nebraska State Journal* for the campaign establishing the "Nebraska All-Star Primary" presidential preference primary which spotlighted, through a bi-partisan committee, issues early in the presidential campaign.

A civic project by the Lincoln-based *Nebraska State Journal* created an "All-Star Primary" as a new element in the presidential election campaign.

The brainchild of editor Raymond A. McConnell Jr., the presidential preference primary filled a void in the presidential nominating system and prompted a review of a primary election approach that had been created during the Andrew Jackson administration. The new primary, managed by a bi-partisan committee, allowed names to be entered on the ballot without the permission of the individuals proposed by the committee.[5]

1951—The *Miami Herald* and *Brooklyn Eagle* for their
crime reporting during the year.

The *Miami Herald* and the *Brooklyn Eagle* had independently fought organized crime for years. The *Herald*'s stories concluded a seven-year campaign that resulted in the removal of both the Dade County and Broward County sheriffs and broke a national gambling syndicate in Miami Beach that used wire communications illegally. The *Eagle* reporter Ed Reid exposed Brooklyn rackets and their connections to police. The paper sparked an investigation by the district attorney that led to numerous indictments.

1955—*Columbus* (Ga.) *Ledger* and *Sunday Ledger-Enquirer* for their
complete news coverage and fearless editorial attack on widespread
corruption in neighboring Phenix City, Ala., which were effective
in destroying a corrupt and racket-ridden city government. The
newspaper exhibited an early awareness of the evils of lax law
enforcement before the situation in Phenix City erupted into murder.
It covered the whole unfolding story of the final prosecution of the
wrong-doers with skill, perception, force and courage.

The *Ledger* and the *Sunday Ledger-Enquirer* investigated vice-ridden Phenix City, Alabama, across the Chattahoochee River. The work gained national attention when Alabama's crusading attorney general nominee, Albert L. Patterson, was gunned down in a parking lot in June 1954. Reporters had also been attacked by thugs. The investigation was largely done by Carlton Johnson, who had been detached from duties as city editor to take over the Phenix City staff, along with assistant city editor Thomas J. Sellers Jr. and county court house reporter Ray Jenkins. Eighty-seven racketeers and corrupt politicians had been imprisoned, indicted, or become fugitives from justice by the time of the award submission.

1956—*Watsonville* (Calif.) *Register-Pajaronian* for courageous exposure
of corruption in public office, which led to the resignation of a
district attorney and the conviction of one of his associates.

The seven-thousand-circulation *Watsonville Register-Pajaronian*, south of San Francisco, became suspicious of the city's new district attorney. During their investigation, a reporter and photographer assigned by editor Roy Pinkerton discovered the D.A. visiting a gambler in a midnight meeting. When noticed by a thug in the gambler's employ, the two journalists were held at gunpoint, and the camera was destroyed. As disclosures poured out, community support developed. The California attorney general began an investigation, and the D.A. resigned just as he was about to be tried for malicious misconduct.[6]

1957—*Chicago Daily News* for determined and courageous public
service in exposing a $2,500,000 fraud centering in the office of the
State Auditor of Illinois, resulting in the indictment and conviction
of the State Auditor and others. This led to the reorganization of State
procedures to prevent a recurrence of the fraud.

The *Chicago Daily News*—and George Thiem, who had helped the paper win a gold medal in 1950—targeted state auditor Orville L. Hodge based on a tip from a reader who said the respected millionaire businessman was involved in illegal activities. Hodge had been mentioned as a possible Republican candidate for governor. But twenty-one reporters and other staffers, with Thiem in charge, dug into Hodge's affairs and unearthed a

$2.5 million fraud that eventually sent him and assistant Edward Epping to prison, along with the bank president who had facilitated their crimes. During the pressure-filled investigation, the paper said that two city editors had suffered heart attacks while directing coverage.[7]

1959—*Utica* (N.Y.) *Observer-Dispatch and Utica Daily Press* for their successful campaign against corruption, gambling and vice in their home city and the achievement of sweeping civic reforms in the face of political pressure and threats of violence. By their stalwart leadership of the forces of good government, these newspapers upheld the best tradition of a free press.

The Gannett-owned *Utica Observer-Dispatch* and the *Utica Daily Press* fought a campaign against corruption, gambling, and vice, upsetting powerful forces in the community. Many local leaders did not want the city's image tarnished by association with crime. The common council tried to levy a 5 percent tax on newspaper advertising to send a message to the editors. But the papers—published separately at the time but later combined—did not give up and ran more than eighty editorials attacking law enforcement lapses and suggesting that taxpayers were being defrauded. They used the Gannett News Service resources, including Albany bureau chief Jack Germond. The *Daily Press* city editor Tony Vella and city hall reporter William Lohden also were involved in the coverage, a job that was made harder because city officials had declared a news blackout against the two papers. Sweeping reforms were approved, and a number of crime figures were indicted and jailed.[8]

1960—*Los Angeles Times* for its thorough, sustained and well-conceived attack on narcotics traffic and the enterprising reporting of Gene Sherman, which led to the opening of negotiations between the United States and Mexico to halt the flow of illegal drugs into southern California and other border states.

The *Los Angeles Times* editor Nick Williams and city editor Taylor Trumbo put reporter Gene Sherman on the track of Mexican narcotics smugglers after they noticed a pattern in several drug seizures. Sherman wrote an eight-part series on Mexican narcotics smuggling after a seven-month investigation that took him through Tijuana, Tecate, Nogales, and Juarez to Mexicali and El Paso. He estimated that 75 percent of southern California's heroin and 99 percent of its marijuana had been imported from Mexico. State and federal inquiries sprang from the investigation, and the United States and Mexico began discussing measures for increasing enforcement to reduce drug trafficking.[9]

1961—*Amarillo* (Tex.) *Globe-Times* for exposing a breakdown in local law enforcement with resultant punitive action that swept lax officials from their posts and brought about the election of a reform slate. The newspaper thus exerted its civic leadership in the finest tradition of journalism.

A phone tip to the *Amarillo Globe-Times* editor Thomas H. Thompson led to a meeting in a bar during which he was told he could have "information that would blow the top off the court house" if the tipster could be protected. The source, private detective Armand James Chandonnet, revealed that he had worked for county judge Roy Joe Stevens and knew of bribe taking and other wrongdoing by the judge. The string of stories in the paper—some by John Masterman and Don Boyett, working under city editor Paul Timmons—led to various legal proceedings against Stevens. He was acquitted but was disbarred and left the state. State legislation was enacted to close loopholes that Judge Stevens had used to go free at trial.[10]

1962—*Panama City* (Fla.) *News & Herald* for its three-year campaign against entrenched power and corruption, with resultant reforms in Panama City and Bay County.

The *News & Herald*, with its six-person news operation, ran a three-year campaign against illegal gambling and moonshining operations supported by political corruption. The paper's campaign—under executive editor and editorial writer Edwin B. Callaway and managing editor Bob Brown—relied on the reporting work of W. U. "Duke" Newcome. When the state did not take action on the paper's reports, editors went to newly elected governor Farris Bryant. Together they hatched a plan for digging out the entrenched crime. State investigators and the *News & Herald* reporters worked together on a long-term basis, with the paper agreeing to withhold publication until results were in. Eventually a former sheriff and police chief, among others, were indicted.[11]

1965—*Hutchinson* (Kans.) *News* for its courageous and constructive campaign, culminating in 1964, to bring about more equitable reapportionment of the Kansas Legislature, despite powerful opposition in its own community.

The *Hutchinson News* took the side of voters who had been disenfranchised by politicians through faulty district apportionment in the state legislature. When the *News*, under editor John McCormally, began its campaign for reapportionment, Kansas did not use a strict population basis for determining votes. That left many people poorly represented and locked politicians in for reelection. The same was true in many other states. The Supreme Court's landmark 1962 *Baker vs. Carr* ruling had mandated fair, population-based reapportionment in setting districts. By then, however, the *Hutchinson News* had already proposed how Kansas could achieve that end. The paper had brought suit in the state courts, with board chairman John P. Harris, publisher Peter MacDonald, and McCormally leading the drive. It also made the case on its editorial pages. The Kansas courts ruled in the newspaper's favor in 1964 and changed the basis of the state senate apportionment.[12]

1966—The *Boston Globe* for its campaign to prevent confirmation of Francis X. Morrissey as a Federal District Judge in Massachusetts.

The *Boston Globe*, under editor Thomas Winship, successfully campaigned to prevent Judge Francis X. Morrissey's confirmation as a federal district judge. Morrissey had been a political worker for Joseph P. Kennedy and had been sponsored first by President John Kennedy and then by his brother, Edward M. "Ted" Kennedy, the Massachusetts Democratic senator. The *Globe*'s reporting was the work of a team spearheaded by political editor Robert L. Healey. It examined Judge Morrissey's legal qualifications, found them wanting, and eventually questioned his veracity. The *Globe* thought the appointment "another example of politically inspired actions which had attained for Massachusetts a reputation of operating without a civic conscience in public matters." But then reporters turned up apparent discrepancies in his testimony to a congressional subcommittee. In one they showed that Morrissey had not attended Boston College Law School as he claimed. When the *Globe*'s reporting drew national attention, opposition in the Senate grew, and Morrissey eventually requested that President Lyndon Johnson withdraw his name.[13]

1967—The *Milwaukee Journal* for its successful campaign to stiffen the law against water pollution in Wisconsin, a notable advance in the national effort for the conservation of natural resources.

1967—*Louisville Courier-Journal* for its successful campaign to control the Kentucky strip mining industry, a notable advance in the national effort for the conservation of natural resources.

The *Louisville Courier-Journal* and the *Milwaukee Journal* won for unrelated environmental campaigns in their states. The *Courier-Journal* had launched a drive to preserve Kentucky's natural beauty with a special 1964 section, "Kentucky's Ravaged Land." It followed up that work in 1965 and 1966. In 1966, the state assembly reacted and passed a tough strip-mining control law. The *Milwaukee Journal*'s Public Service Prize—its first since 1919, when it campaigned against World War I "Germanism" in

Wisconsin—was aimed at water pollution. A three-part series in its Picture Journal section used color photographs to show the effects of polluted water. The Wisconsin legislature cited the series when it passed a $300 million water pollution control law.[14]

1968—The *Riverside* (Calif.) *Press-Enterprise* for its exposé of
corruption in the courts in connection with the handling
of the property and estates of an Indian tribe in California,
and its successful efforts to punish the culprits.

Reporter George Ringwald of the *Press-Enterprise* focused on cases of apparent judicial and legal abuse involving the large Palm Springs-area land-holdings of about a hundred members of the Agua Caliente tribe of Native Americans. The tribal members were represented by court-appointed guardians and conservators who were responsible to the Department of Interior's Bureau of Indian Affairs. Ringwald learned that some judges were being paid as executors of estate wills for tribal members. Meanwhile fellow judges rubber-stamped the lucrative arrangements. Eventually the Interior Department and the state judicial qualifications commission were both investigated.[15]

1971—The *Winston-Salem* (N.C.) *Journal and Sentinel* for coverage
of environmental problems, as exemplified by a successful campaign
to block strip mining operations that would have caused irreparable
damage to the hill country of northwest North Carolina.

The *Winston-Salem Journal and Sentinel* covered the plans for a strip-mining enterprise after a reader tipped the paper that a New York company, Gibbsite Corporation, was buying up mineral leases in North Carolina's remote Surry County. Reporter Arlene Edwards found that thousands of acres of mineral leases had been optioned to the company. It planned to strip-mine for alumina, which is processed into aluminum. Public opposition grew and the paper added reporters Joe Goodman, Jesse

Poindexter, Raleigh correspondent Joe Doster, and state editor Jack Tra-
wick to the project. At mid-year Gibbsite said it was letting its options
expire. Editor and publisher Wallace Carroll, formerly of the *New York
Times*, was a Pulitzer board member the year the *Journal and Sentinel* won.
One little-discussed element of gold medal winning is the staff exodus.
Joe Goodman noted that "when the prizes started showing up in '71, hell,
your whole staff is out there looking for jobs. I sure as hell was. So come,
say, '72, everybody's gone." Some went to Gene Roberts's *Philadelphia
Inquirer*, which had an eye for Pulitzer winners. It also had John Carroll as an *Inquirer* editor. Carroll, later the *Los Angeles Times* editor, was
Wallace Carroll's son.[16] (John Carroll noted that his father kept battling
for the environment after retiring in 1974, leading editors in a successful
campaign against Duke Power Company's damming of the New River.
When his parents died, John Carroll said, their ashes were spread on the
river's still-pristine waters.)

1975—The *Boston Globe* for its massive and balanced coverage
of the Boston school desegregation crisis.

As many northern cities faced high-pressure decisions about how to
implement court-ordered integration, the *Boston Globe* took an approach
to news coverage that alienated everybody. It reported the story from all
sides. Angry white parents were stoning buses that carried black children
to segregated south Boston schools. Senator Edward Kennedy, trying to
calm the situation, was pelted with tomatoes and eggs at a rally, where
someone yelled, "You're a disgrace to the Irish." The *Globe* also tried to
calm things—leading some blacks to see it as too accepting of racism—
but it was unquestionably thorough. Editor Thomas Winship and executive editor Jack Driscoll deployed sixty reporters, and in direct charge
of this dispassionate coverage was the assistant managing editor for local
news, Robert H. Phelps, a former chief of the paper's Spotlight Team. The
fairer the *Globe* was, the nastier the repercussions. Groups of parents who
favored all-white schools broke windows at the paper's offices. Rifle shots
were fired and bomb threats received. The *Globe* installed steel shutters.

Pulitzer Prize administrator John Hohenberg wrote in a discussion of its winning work: "Do not look for elegant writing in the *Globe*'s reportage. What went into the paper, day after day and week after week, was the guts of the best kind of newspaper journalism in this land—an unemotional, impartial, immensely detailed and thoroughly honest and accurate report of what was going on in the schools, the streets, the entire community."[17]

1980—*Gannett News Service* for its series on financial
contributions to the Pauline Fathers.

Three Gannett News Service journalists—Tallahassee bureau chief John M. Hanchette, state editor William F. Schmick, and GNS national staffer Carlton A. Sherwood—examined financial mismanagement within the Pauline Fathers, an order of the Roman Catholic Church. All three had Catholic backgrounds, and Sherwood had once been a news editor of the *Catholic Star-Herald* in Camden, New Jersey. The investigation involved more than 200,000 miles of travel to Italy, Poland, Hungary, England, and seventeen U.S. states. The result was an eighteen-day series showing that officials had squandered millions of dollars of loans and charitable donations at the order once known as the Order of St. Paul the First Hermit. As many as 2,500 elderly Catholics were victims, having invested in bonds sold by the Pauline Fathers ostensibly to build a devotional shrine in Kittanning, Pennsylvania. Angry responses came from the Paulines, but a papal investigation confirmed many of the claims in the series, and those who invested in the bonds were repaid in full. It was the first instance of a Public Service Prize going to a news service.[18]

1982—The *Detroit News* for a series by Sydney P. Freedberg and David
Ashenfelter which exposed the U.S. Navy's cover-up of circumstances
surrounding the deaths of seamen aboard ship and which
led to significant reforms in naval procedures.

The *Detroit News* assigned reporter Sydney P. Freedberg, a second-year staffer just a few years out of Radcliffe College, to do a piece on the death of sailor Paul Trerice. He was a Navy enlisted man who had died under mysterious circumstances. In reporting reminiscent of what the *Lufkin News* had done five years earlier—to win the 1977 gold medal—Freedberg and assistant news editor David Ashenfelter revealed another military cover-up. The Navy told the family that an accident had occurred while Trerice was being punished aboard the carrier USS *Ranger* in the Pacific. The two journalists set out to find the truth, and their reporting led to the discovery that the sailor had died of heat stroke and a heart attack brought on by the mental and physical torment inflicted while he was being punished for a minor rule infraction. It was not the accident that the Navy had described. Further, the reporters found that the military routinely deceived families to protect itself from embarrassment and possible liability. "The Navy's initial lies were an effort to shield grieving families from the anguish that the gory details might cause," says Freedberg. "It started out as a humane policy." But the deception had gotten out of hand.[19]

1983—The *Jackson* (Miss.) *Clarion-Ledger* for its successful campaign supporting Governor Winter in his legislative battle for reform of Mississippi's public education system.

The *Jackson Clarion-Ledger* explored why Mississippi's public schools "didn't make the grade," and editorials proposed solutions that fit with what reform-minded governor William Winter was doing. Reporter Nancy Weaver's project was first put on hold during an ownership change that made Gannett its owner. New executive editor Charles Overby took charge and assigned more than a half-dozen other staffers to work with Weaver on what turned out to be a six-month investigation. Overby managed both the news and editorial components. It had been twenty-nine years since the state legislature's last major improvement in the education system, and not even compulsory education was required. Mississippi's management of desegregation had also hurt school financing and led to white children withdrawing from public schools. Weaver worked with reporters Fred Anklam Jr. and Cliff Tryens, among others, to produce a twenty-four-day series titled "Mississippi schools, Hard lessons." Lee Cearnal was the project editor, and editorials were written by editorial director Dave Hardin, who helped analyze reform options. Results included new taxes passed by the voters to support schools, a mandatory attendance law, and the first state-supported kindergartens.[20]

1984—*Los Angeles Times* for an in-depth examination of
southern California's growing Latino community by a
team of editors and reporters.

Describing its twenty-seven-part series on the Latino experience in southern California, the Pulitzer board cited the series for "enhancing understanding among the non-Latino majority of a community often perceived as mysterious and even threatening." Seventeen Latino reporters, editors, and photographers had been assigned to the project under editors George Ramos and Frank Sotomayor. They interviewed one thousand people and polled nearly fifteen hundred in a survey covering social, cultural, and political issues. By most accounts, the series got its start after a number of Latino reporters brought an idea to William F. Thomas, who had been promoted from Metro editor to editor in 1971. But Thomas noted that the genesis was an earlier *Times* series on the experience of African Americans in Los Angeles that led Latino reporters to propose their project.[21]

1986—The *Denver Post* for its in-depth study of "missing children,"
which revealed that most are involved in custody disputes
or are runaways, and which helped mitigate national
fears stirred by exaggerated statistics.

The *Denver Post's* project stemmed from reporter Diana Griego's skepticism about government statistics on missing children—statistics that helped create the widespread belief that thousands of American children were kidnapped and murdered each year by strangers. With reporter Louis Kilzer, she worked under deputy Metro editor Charles R. Buxton Jr. to produce a series called "The Truth About Missing Kids." Later Kilzer and reporter Norman Udevitz found a Denver fundraising firm that solicited money on behalf of a missing children's organization but turned little of the proceeds to charity. Eventually the agency was shut down by authorities. A polling firm hired by the *Post* suggested that public perceptions in Denver exaggerated the threat to children, which accompanying *Post* projects illustrated. "Our reporting exposed a myth and told the truth about one of America's most emotionally charged issues," the *Post* editor David Hall said after the prize was announced.[22]

1989—*Anchorage Daily News* for reporting about the high incidence of alcoholism and suicide among native Alaskans in a series that focused attention on their despair and resulted in various reforms.

Thirteen years after the *Anchorage Daily News* won the 1976 gold medal for its study of the Teamsters Union in the state, the paper took on a daunting social issue: rampant alcoholism and suicide among native Alaskans. Howard Weaver, a reporter on the Teamster series, had become managing editor. "We were older and smarter, and there was that Pulitzer Gold Medal on the wall," he says. "That amplifies your voice, which is a wonderful consequence." The paper used its new Macintosh computer to create a database of rural deaths, drawing from all the press releases put out by Alaska state troopers in recent years, and calculated how many were accidental or alcohol-related or suicides. It was data no one had ever compiled before, says Weaver. Among the challenges: alcohol and suicide were "subjects about which people are always in complete denial, whether it's in Manhattan, New York, or Manhattan, Kansas, or in Alaska." The paper was extremely sensitive to the native communities in its coverage, telling of dashed dreams and disappointments but also capturing the nobility of individuals and their culture. In a technique eerily predictive of the "Portraits of Grief" that the *New York Times* would design after the September 11, 2001, tragedy, the Anchorage paper prepared full pages of personal notices about the native Alaskans who had died in recent years but whose deaths had gotten no news coverage.

1994—The *Akron (Ohio) Beacon Journal* for its broad examination
of local racial attitudes and its subsequent effort to promote
improved communication in the community.

The *Akron Beacon Journal* launched a year-long study of racial attitudes under the heading "A Question of Color." Through it the paper looked at how housing, education, economic opportunity, and crime were affected by race. Managing editor Glenn Guzzo said, "All these are intractable problems and what we found is that you can't talk about solving these problems unless you also address the issue of race." The paper produced twelve separate series, one per month for the entire year, examining different elements of race in the community. The 1992 Los Angeles riots prompted the series, Guzzo said, after "we recognized that the supposed progress in race relations we have made in the last decade maybe hadn't come as far as we'd believed." The *Beacon Journal* committed twenty-nine staffers to the project for the year. The community responded with 22,000 individuals and scores of organizations offering to help improve race relations.[23]

1995—The *Virgin Islands Daily News*, St. Thomas, for its disclosure of
the links between the region's rampant crime rate and corruption in
the local criminal justice system. The reporting, largely the work of
Melvin Claxton, initiated political reforms.[24]

Investigating widespread crime in the territory, the *Virgin Islands Daily News* reporter Melvin Claxton identified numerous issues: the ease of criminals getting guns, law enforcement corruption and incompetence, inept criminal prosecutions, light sentencing by judges, and inadequacies with probation. A six-month investigation drew on statistical analyses showing that of 25,000 violent crimes reported over four years ending in 1993, only 1,400 cases had gone to court, and fewer than 10 percent of reported crimes were even investigated. It resulted in a ten-day series exposing money misspent on the prison system. "The territory spends more than any state—$5,000 a year—to house and feed a juvenile inmate. That is more than 10 times the amount experts say it costs to run preventive programs that would keep them straight," wrote Claxton, an Antigua native.[25]

2001—The *Oregonian*, Portland, for its detailed and unflinching examination of systematic problems within the U.S. Immigration and Naturalization Service, including harsh treatment of foreign nationals and other widespread abuses, which prompted various reforms.[26]

Based on an attorney's tip, the *Oregonian* reporter Julie Sullivan wrote of a fifteen-year-old Chinese client who had been granted political asylum in the United States but who nonetheless had been held in a county jail for eight months because of bureaucratic miscues within the federal Immigration and Naturalization Service. Visiting the juvenile jail, Sullivan found a scared teenager surrounded by murderers and other hardened criminals. Not naming her, Sullivan called her "the girl who cries," which is what the guards caller her. Soon other victims were found trapped within the overall jail population. The stories caught the attention of Amanda Bennett, managing editor/enterprise, and editor Sandra Mims Rowe, who decided to have the paper look at the INS—and the questionable activities of Portland INS district director David Beebe—from a national perspective. Bennett decided that the story "was about the INS being capricious, arbitrary, and possibly acting illegally—and doing things to people for which they had no recourse." Sullivan was teamed with fellow reporter Richard Read, who had won the 1999 Explanatory Reporting Pulitzer for "The French Fry Connection," analyzing the Asian economic crisis by tracing how regionally grown potatoes made their way to a McDonald's outlet in Singapore.[27] The pair's team was then widened to include former Washington correspondent Brent Walth and Kim Christensen. (Later, at the *Los Angeles Times*, Christensen would be part of the King/Drew and the Bell teams, responsible for the paper winning the 2005 and 2011 Public Service Prizes, respectively.) Bennett's nomination letter to the Pulitzer board said: "There are services to the public that only a newspaper can perform. Over and over again throughout the year, the paper righted clear-cut wrongs that small-town mayors, petition-writers, colleagues, business people, corporations, school children, federal judges—even members of Congress—were unable to right."[28]

NOTES

Reintroduction: Refining *Pulitzer's Gold*

1. Gerry Lanosga, "Pulitzer's Gold Review," *Journalism* (February 2010): 126–27, available at http://www.academia.edu/727759/Book_Review_Roy_J._Harris_Jr._Pulitzers_Gold_Behind_the_Prize_for.

2. "Who Killed the Newspaper?" *The Economist*, August 26–September 1, 2006, 9–10 and 52–54.

3. Daniel Akst, "Nonprofit Journalism," *Carnegie Reporter* 3, no. 3 (Fall 2005): 20–29.

4. Jack Shafer, "The Pulitzer Prize Scam." Politico.com, April 20, 2015, available at http://www.politico.com/magazine/story/2015/04/2015-pulitzer-prizes-jack-shafer-column-117151_full.html?print#.VWm4LsaT3gV.

5. Yong Z. Volz and Francis L. F. Lee, "What Does It Take for Women Journalists to Gain Professional Recognition?: Gender Disparities among Pulitzer Prize Winners, 1917–2010." *Journalism and Mass Communication Quarterly* (April 2013): 248–266.

6. Roy J. Harris Jr., "How e-Pulitzers Can Elevate Journalism," *Christian Science Monitor*, April 23, 2009.

7. Jim Amoss, e-mail to author, June 24, 2014.

8. Paul Steiger, telephone interview with author, May 12, 2014.

9. Bob Woodward, e-mail to author, March 5, 2014.

1. A Medal for All Seasons, 2013–2014:
From Police Speeding to NSA Spying

1. Sally Kestin and John Maines, interview with author, February 13, 2014.

2. John Hohenberg, *The Pulitzer Prizes: A History of the Awards in Books, Drama, Music, and Journalism Based on the Private Files Over Six Decades* (New York: Columbia University Press, 1974), 18–20.

3. Basic information on the Pulitzer Prizes, current and past, is found at http://www.pulitzer.org.

4. One discussion of French's medals is in Michael Richman, "The Medals of Daniel Chester French," in *The Medal in America*, ed. Alan M. Stahl, 150–153 (Coinage of the Americas Conference at the American Numismatic Society, New York, September 26–27, 1987).

5. Ben Bradlee Sr., interview with author, October 13, 2005.

6. "History of the Guardian," *Guardian*, http://www.theguardian.com/gnm -archive/2002/jun/06/1.

7. Michael Gartner, telephone interview with author, April 3, 2006.

8. Bob Woodward, interview with author, October 12, 2005.

9. Howard Saltz, interview with author, February 13, 2014.

10. Willie Fernandez, interview with author, February 13, 2014.

11. "Speeding Cops: Special *Sun Sentinel* Investigation," video, http://www .sun-sentinel.com/videogallery/75051368/SPEEDING-COPS-SPECIAL-SUN -SENTINEL-INVESTIGATION.

12. Peter Bhatia, telephone interview with author, April 17, 2013. Quoted in Roy J. Harris Jr., "Pulitzer Surprise: The *Sun Sentinel's* Rise to a Gold Medal," *Columbia Journalism Review*, April 18, 2003, http://www.cjr.org/behind_the_news /pulitzer_surprise_the_sun_sent.php?page=all.

13. Paul Ingrassia, telephone interview with author, March 14, 2014.

14. Paul Tash, interview with author, February 10, 2014.

15. The *Sun Sentinel* stories are available on the Pulitzer website at http://www.pulitzer.org/citation/2013-Public-Service; all the year's prizes at http://www .pulitzer.org/awards/2013.

16. Paul Steiger, telephone interview with author, May 12, 2014.

17. The *Guardian's* first story: Glenn Greenwald, "NSA Collecting Phone Records of Millions of Verizon Customers Daily," *Guardian*, June 6, 2013, http://www .theguardian.com/world/2013/jun/06/nsa-phone-records-verizon-court-order.

18. Laura Poitras, e-mails to author, March 19 to July 3, 2014.

19. Bart Gellman, telephone interview with author, May 14, 2014.

20. Janine Gibson, telephone interview with author, May 9, 2014.

21. Glenn Greenwald, *No Place to Hide: Edward Snowden, the NSA, and the U.S. Surveillance State* (New York: Henry Holt, 2014), 21.

22. Ibid., 20.

23. The Pulitzer winning work on Dick Cheney is at http://www.pulitzer.org /citation/2008-National-Reporting.

24. Jeff Leen, telephone interview with author, May 16, 2014.

25. Sale of the Washington Post to Amazon.com founder Jeff Bezos for $250 million closed in the fall of 2013, http://www.washingtonpost.com/business /economy/washington-post-closes-sale-to-amazon-founder-jeff-bezos/2013/10/01 /fca3b16a-2acf-11e3-97a3-ff2758228523_story.html.

26. Martin Baron, telephone interview with author, May 21, 2014.

27. On the Pulitzer website at http://www.pulitzer.org/files/2014/public-service /guardianus/01guardianus2014.pdf.

28. Glenn Greenwald, Ewen MacAskill, and Laura Poitras, "Edward Snowden: The Whistleblower Behind the NSA Surveillance Revelations," *Guardian*, June 9, 2013, original version preserved on Pulitzer website at http://www.pulitzer.org /files/2014/public-service/guardianus/04guardianus2014.pdf.

29. "NSA Whistleblower Edward Snowden: 'I Don't Want to Live in a Society That Does These Sort of Things'—Video," *Guardian*, http://www.theguardian.com /world/video/2013/jun/09/nsa-whistleblower-edward-snowden-interview-video.

30. "NSA Files: Decoded: What the Revelations Mean for You," *Guardian*, http://www.theguardian.com/world/interactive/2013/nov/01/snowden-nsa-files -surveillance-revelations-decoded#section/1.

31. The website for the documentary is at https://citizenfourfilm.com/. Andrew Pulver, "Edward Snowden Documentary Citizenfour Wins Oscar," *Guardian*, February 22, 2015, http://www.theguardian.com/film/2015/feb/23/edward-snowden -documentary-citizenfour-wins-oscar.

32. Barton Gellman and Greg Miller, "'Black Budget' Revealed," *Washington Post*, August 30, 2013, original version preserved on Pulitzer website at http:// www.pulitzer.org/files/2014/public-service/washpost/09washpostnsa2014.pdf.

33. Ibid.

34. Michael Connelly, telephone interview with author, April 28, 2014.

35. Pulitzer Public Service 2014 jury report, made available to author upon request.

36. Michael Kinsley, "Eyes Everywhere," *New York Times*, May 22, 2014, http://www.nytimes.com/2014/06/08/books/review/no-place-to-hide-by-glenn -greenwald.html.

37. Jay Rosen, "To the Snowden Story System a Crowning Pulitzer Might Have Gone," *PressThink*, April 14, 2014, http://pressthink.org/2014/04/to-the-snowden -story-system-a-pulitzer-might-have-gone/.

38. "Pulitzer Prize Renews Debate Over Controversial NSA Surveillance Reporting," *PBS Newshour*, April 14, 2014, http://www.pbs.org/newshour/bb /pulitzer-renews-debate-nsa-surveillance-reporting/.

39. Bart Gellman, e-mail with author, May 18, 2015.

40. Text of Martin Baron's Lehigh talk is available at http://www.washington post.com/pr/wp/2014/05/19/marty-baron-gave-a-commencement-speech-today -talked-about-tough-decisions-as-an-editor/.

41. The *Washington Post* and the *Guardian-U.S.* stories are available on the Pulitzer website at http://www.pulitzer.org/citation/2014-Public-Service; all the year's prizes at http://www.pulitzer.org/awards/2014.

2. The Most Prized Pulitzer: The "Germ of an Idea" Takes Root

1. The quote was attributed to Philip Graham often and in various forms, including by editors and correspondents at the time of his death on August 3, 1963. According to *Morrow's International Dictionary of Quotations* (1982), Graham apparently used the "first rough draft of history" line to describe both newspapers and *Newsweek* when the Washington Post Co. purchased that magazine. A fuller discussion of the possibility that Graham drew the language from Alan Barth, a *Post* editorial writer from the 1940s to the 1970s, is in Jack Shafer, Slate.com, August 30, 2010, http://www.slate.com/articles/news_and_politics/press_box/2010/08 /who_said_it_first.single.html. The connection of news and history had been made by others, including Mark Twain in the first volume of the autobiography published years after his death in 1910. Twain wrote: "News is history in its first and best form . . . history is the pale and tranquil reflection of it."

2. Quoted in an e-mail from Catherine J. Mathis, *New York Times*, January 30, 2006.

3. Ben Bradlee, *A Good Life: Newspapering and Other Adventures* (New York: Touchstone, 1995), 365–366.

4. Bradlee, interview with author, October 13, 2005.

5. Gary Pruitt, interview with author, November 15, 2005.

6. Original in the Joseph Pulitzer papers, August 1902, Columbia University Rare Manuscripts area, Butler Library. Also cited in John Hohenberg, *The Pulitzer Prizes: A History of the Awards in Books, Drama, Music, and Journalism Based on the Private Files Over Six Decades* (New York: Columbia University Press, 1974), 10.

7. W. A. Swanberg, *Pulitzer: The Life of the Greatest Figure in American Journalism and One of the Most Extraordinary Men in Our History* (New York: Scribner's, 1967), 44.

8. Quoted in Seymour Topping, "Pulitzer biography," on Pulitzer website at http://www.pulitzer.org/biography.

9. Swanberg, *Pulitzer*, 374.

10. Hohenberg, *The Pulitzer Prizes*, 9–11.

11. The Alfred Nobel story is often told. One reference is available at http://www.britannica.com/EBchecked/topic/416842/Alfred-Bernhard-Nobel, which calls this explanation for Nobel's action the "most plausible assumption" that may be made about the reason for Nobel's creation of the Nobel Prizes.

12. A full account of Pulitzer's establishment of the prizes is in Hohenberg, *The Pulitzer Prizes*, 9–27.

13. David Shaw, *Press Watch: A Provocative Look at How Newspapers Report the News* (New York: Macmillan, 1984), 191. For the *Los Angeles Times*, he covered the Pulitzer Prizes more closely than did any other journalist. His Pulitzer stories are summarized in *Press Watch*, chap. 7.

14. Columbia purchased the Liberty Window—installed in the old World Building to memorialize Joseph Pulitzer's campaign to build the Statue of Liberty's platform—from New York City for $1. It is dedicated to Herbert Bayard Swope, who helped arrange the deal. The city had condemned the World Building to improve access to the Brooklyn Bridge. See the footnote in Hohenberg, *The Pulitzer Diaries*, 313.

15. Howard Weaver, interview with author, November 15, 2005.

16. Geneva Overholser, interview with author, December 1, 2005.

17. Board member biographies are on the Pulitzer website at http://www.pulitzer.org/board/2015.

18. For a fuller description of one Sig Gissler-led Pulitzer Prize day, see Roy J. Harris Jr., "The Eye of the Pulitzer Storm," *Poynter.org*, April 6, 2005, http://www.poynter.org/uncategorized/38806/the-eye-of-the-pulitzer-storm/.

19. For a description of Pulitzer Day, see Harris, "The Pulitzers That Got Away," *Poynter.org*, April 6, 2004, http://www.poynter.org/uncategorized/21905/the-pulitzers-that-got-away/.

3. A Newsroom Challenged, 2002: The *New York Times* and 9/11

1. Gerald Boyd, telephone interview with author, February 2, 2006.

2. David Barstow, interview with author, September 9, 2005.

3. Christine Kay, interview with author, November 29, 2005.

4. Jonathan Landman, e-mail to author, March 27, 2006.

5. Allan Siegal, e-mail to author, March 14, 2006.

6. New York Times, *Portraits 9/11/01* (New York: Times Books: Henry Holt, 2002), ix.

7. Howell Raines, foreword to *Portraits 9/11/01*, vii.

8. Lengthy report on Jayson Blair ran May 11, 2003, headlined "Reporter Who Left the Times Left Long Trail of Deception." The *New York Times* archive is found at http://www.nytimes.com/2003/05/11/us/correcting-the-record-times -reporter-who-resigned-leaves-long-trail-of-deception.html.

9. An account is in "Newsroom Celebrates 'Days of Legend,'" *Ahead of the Times* 10, no. 2 (April 2002).

10. A ten-year retrospective on "Portraits of Grief" was produced by the *Times*. It is described in Harris, "'Portraits of Grief' Ten Years Later," *Poynter.org*, August 31, 2011, http://www.poynter.org/latest-news/top-stories/144274/portraits-of-grief-10-years -later-lessons-from-the-original-new-york-times-911-coverage/. A retrospective on the 2002 Breaking News Pulitzer Prize winner, the *Wall Street Journal*, is described in Harris, "How the *Wall Street Journal*'s Improvised 9/11 Battle Plan Helped It to a Pulitzer," *Poynter.org*, September 6, 2011, http://www.poynter.org/news/mediawire/144936 /how-the-wall-street-journals-improvised-911-battle-plan-helped-it-to-a-pulitzer/.

11. On the Pulitzer website at http://www.pulitzer.org/citation/2002-Public -Service; all the year's prizes at http://www.pulitzer.org/awards/2002.

4. Epiphany in Boston, 2003: The *Globe* and the Church

1. On the Pulitzer website at http://www.pulitzer.org/citation/2001-Breaking -News-Reporting.

2. The first in a series of author interviews with Martin Baron and other *Globe* staff members was April 7, 2003, in the newsroom, the day its Pulitzer was announced.

3. Eileen McNamara's stories appeared in the *Globe* on July 22 and July 29, 2002.

4. Jonathan M. Albano, e-mail with author, January 17, 2006.

5. Walter V. Robinson, "Shining the Globe's Spotlight on the Catholic Church," *Nieman Reports* (Spring 2003): 56.

6. A Spotlight report prepared for Robinson and the author by Timothy Leland, the team's founder, March 5, 2006. The discussion of *Newsday*'s influence is also found in Robert F. Keeler, *Newsday: A Candid History of the Respectable Tabloid* (New York: Arbor House/Morrow), 431–432.

7. Walter V. Robinson, interview with author, November 3, 2005.

8. Michael Rezendes, interview with author, November 3, 2005.

9. Matt Carroll, interview with author, November 2, 2005.

10. Sacha Pfeiffer, interview with author, October 11, 2005.

11. Robinson, "Shining the Globe's Spotlight," *Nieman Reports* (Spring 2003): 56.

12. On the Pulitzer website at http://www.pulitzer.org/archives/6729.

13. More on the *Globe* Pulitzer announcement by Harris, "A Prized Moment for the Globe, and the Pulitzers," *Poynter*, April 7, 2003, http://www.poynter.org /uncategorized/9638/a-prized-moment-for-the-globe-and-the-pulitzers/.

14. Thomas Farragher, interview with author, November 2, 2005.

15. On the Pulitzer website at http://www.pulitzer.org/archives/6736.

16. Michael Paulson, interview with author, November 7, 2005.

17. Cover letter, Baron to Pulitzer Prizes, undated, 2003.

18. The 2003 Pulitzer Prize nomination submitted by the *Globe* quoted from Greeley, "The Tipping Point," July 7, 2002, his review of 2002 *Globe* book *Betrayal*, http://www.boston.com/globe/spotlight/abuse/stories2/070702_betrayal_review .htm.

19. Sandra Mims Rowe, interview with author, November 16, 2005.

20. Elizabeth Mehren, "Reporting Stories with Children as Victims of Priests," *Nieman Reports* (Spring 2003): 55. http://niemanreports.org/articles/reporting -stories-with-children-as-victims-of-priests/.

21. "Pope Creates Tribunal to Hold Bishops Accountable," *Boston Globe*, June 11, 2015, http://www.bostonglobe.com/news/nation/2015/06/10/pope-francis -creates-tribunal-investigate-bishops-accused-violating-sex-abuse-policy /XH5FfiLEB4gRoiaMbLo4IO/story.html.

22. Michael Paulson, in an e-mail with author, May 23, 2015, cited Daniel Burke, "How to Really Measure the 'Francis Effect,'" *CNN.com*, March 13, 2014, http:// www.cnn.com/2014/03/08/living/pope-francis-effect-boston/; a sample of one *Globe* follow-up story is Michael Rezendes, "Top Vatican Prosecutor Failed to Report Abuser," November 23, 2014, http://www.bostonglobe.com/metro/2014/11/22 /vatican-new-top-prosecutor-abusive-priests-implicated-past-failure-stop-notorious -abuser-donald-mcguire/gPaBPJUdvuTy5PSTlιj5sM/story.html.

23. A description of the Spotlight motion picture planning is here http://www .imdb.com/title/tt1895587/.

24. Steve Kurkjian, interview with author, November 3, 2005.

25. Bob Woodward, interview with author, October 12, 2005.

26. On the Pulitzer website at http://www.pulitzer.org/citation/2003-Public -Service; all the year's prizes at http://www.pulitzer.org/awards/2003.

5. From *Times* to *Times*, 2004–2005: Rivals Win in New York and Los Angeles

1. David Barstow, interview with author, September 9, 2005.

2. Walter V. Robinson, interview with author, January 12, 2006. He served on the investigative reporting jury. The *San Francisco Chronicle*'s Robert J. Rosenthal, a

public service juror, was interviewed by the author for "The Pulitzers that Got Away," http://www.poynter.org/uncategorized/21905/the-pulitzers-that-got-away/.

3. Pulitzer Prize investigative jury report, 2004, from the Pulitzer Prize files, Columbia University.

4. David Barstow, "When Workers Die: A Trench Caves In," *New York Times*, December 21, 2003, on the Pulitzer website at http://www.pulitzer.org /archives/6838; "U.S. Rarely Seeks Charges for Deaths in Workplace," *New York Times*, December 22, 2003, at http://www.pulitzer.org/archives/6839.

5. On the Pulitzer website at http://www.pulitzer.org/citation/2004-Public -Service; all the year's prizes at http://www.pulitzer.org/awards/2004.

6. Section describing the *Los Angeles Times* King/Drew project reflects interviews with the author at the *Times* office, primarily on May 25, 2005. Interviews were with John Carroll, Julie Marquis, Mitchell Landsberg, Tracy Weber, Charles Ornstein, and Steve Hymon.

7. On the Pulitzer website at http://www.pulitzer.org/awards/1971.

8. Tracy Weber, Charles Ornstein, and Mitchell Landsberg, "Deadly Errors and Politics Betray a Hospital's Promise," *Los Angeles Times*, December 5, 2004, on the Pulitzer website at http://www.pulitzer.org/archives/6935.

9. On the Pulitzer website at http://www.pulitzer.org/citation/2005-Public -Service; all the year's prizes at http://www.pulitzer.org/awards/2005.

6. The Storm Before the Calm, 2006:
The *Times-Picayune* and the *Sun Herald*'s Summer of Katrina

1. The 1997 prizes are on the Pulitzer website at http://www.pulitzer.org /citation/1997-Public-Service and http://www.pulitzer.org/citation/1997-Editorial -Cartooning.

2. The "Washing Away" series appeared in the *Times-Picayune* from June 23 to 27.

3. Jim Amoss, "The Story of Our Lives," *Quill* (April 2006): 27.

4. Butch Ward, "From Biloxi and New Orleans: The Stories Behind the Pulitzers," *Poynter*, April 17, 2006, http://www.Poynter.org.

5. Mark Fitzgerald, "Jim Amoss, E&P's 2006 Editor of the Year," *Editor and Publisher*, February 1, 2006, http://editorandpublisher.com.

6. Ward, "From Biloxi and New Orleans."

7. Fitzgerald, "Jim Amoss, E&P's 2006 Editor of the Year."

8. Scott Hawkins, telephone interview with author, July 7, 2006.

9. Stan Tiner, interview with author, March 30, 2006.

10. Amoss, "The Story of Our Lives," 28.

11. Mark Schleifstein, interview with author, May 29, 2006.

12. Times-Picayune story, "Rape. Murder. Fights," on the Pulitzer website at http://www.pulitzer.org/archives/7087.

13. Michael Perlstein, interview with author, May 30, 2006.

14. Amoss, interview with author, May 30, 2006.

15. Peter Kovacs, interview with author, May 30, 2006.

16. "Tropical Cyclone Report," National Hurricane Center, December 20, 2005, updated August 10, 2006.

17. Amoss, interview.

18. Gene Roberts and Hank Klibanoff, *The Race Beat: The Press, the Civil Rights Struggle, and the Awakening of a Nation* (New York: Knopf, 2006). http://www .pulitzer.org/works/2007-History.

19. Gene Roberts, telephone interview with author, August 2, 2006.

20. Janet Coates, telephone interview with author, April 21, 2006.

21. Tiner, interview.

22. The *Sun Herald*, August 31, 2005, edition on the Pulitzer website at http:// www.pulitzer.org/archives/7056.

23. Tiner, interview.

24. More detail in Harris, "Shared Glory for Pulitzer's Top Prize," *Poynter*, April 17, 2006.

25. On the Pulitzer website at http://www.pulitzer.org/citation/2006-Public -Service; all the year's prizes at http://www.pulitzer.org/awards/2006.

7. Stocks and Soldiers, 2007–2008: The *Journal* on Options, the *Post* on Walter Reed

1. Mark Maremont, interview with author, April 30, 2007.

2. Charles Forelle and James Bandler, "The Perfect Payday: Some CEOs Reap Millions by Landing Stock Options When They Are Most Valuable," *Wall Street Journal*, March 18, 2006, on the Pulitzer website at http://www.pulitzer.org /archives/7196.

3. Dan Kelly, telephone interview with author, May 4, 2007.

4. Holman W. Jenkins Jr., "The Backdating Witch Hunt," *Wall Street Journal*, June 21, 2006, http://www.wsj.com/articles/SB115085169575385877.

5. Emily Steel, "Wall Street Journal Wins a Pair of Pulitzers," *Wall Street Journal*, April 17, 2007, http://www.wsj.com/articles/SB117673531050871312.

6. Paul Steiger, telephone interview with author, May 12, 2014.

7. On the Pulitzer website at http://www.pulitzer.org/citation/2007-Public -Service; all the year's prizes at http://www.pulitzer.org/awards/2007.

8. Dana Priest and Anne Hull, interview with author, November 6, 2008, and telephone interview with Priest, September 23, 2009.

9. Al Tompkins, "Anatomy of a Pulitzer," *Poynter*, April 8, 2008, http://www.poynter.org/latest-news/top-stories/88125/anatomy-of-a-pulitzer-qa-with-hull-and-priest/.

10. Priest and Hull, interview with author.

11. Lori Robertson, "Uncovering the Misery at Walter Reed," *American Journalism Review*, April/May 2007, http://ajrarchive.org/Article.asp?id=4295.

12. Priest, follow-up interview with author, March 13, 2014. The topic of whether this was an undercover operation is discussed in Brooke Kroeger, *Undercover Reporting: The Truth About Deception* (Evanston, Ill.: Northwestern University Press, 2012), 3–9.

13. Michel du Cille died in December 2014 on assignment for the *Post* in Liberia, http://www.washingtonpost.com/local/obituaries/2014/12/11/04e06b78-8189-11e4-8882-03cf08410beb_story.html.

14. Priest and Hull, interview with author.

15. Tompkins, "Anatomy of a Pulitzer."

16. Priest and Hull, interview with author.

17. On the Pulitzer website at http://www.pulitzer.org/archives/7813.

18. Tompkins, "Anatomy of a Pulitzer."

19. Robert Gates, *Duty: Memoirs of a Secretary at War* (New York: Knopf, 2014), 110–111.

20. On the Pulitzer website at http://www.pulitzer.org/citation/2008-Public-Service; all the year's prizes at http://www.pulitzer.org/awards/2008.

8. Prizing Youth, 2009–2010: The *Las Vegas Sun* and the *Bristol* (Va.) *Herald Courier*

1. Drex Heikes, interview with author at *Los Angeles Times*, January, 14, 2014.

2. Alexandra Berzon, series of telephone interviews with author, April 16 to September 23, 2009.

3. On the Pulitzer website at http://www.pulitzer.org/archives/8381.

4. Michael Kelley, telephone interview with author, March 19, 2014.

5. David Clayton, telephone interview with author, April 20, 2014. Some quotes appeared in Harris, "What Happened in Vegas: A Pulitzer Shines on the Sun," *Poynter*, April 21, 2009, http://www.poynter.org/uncategorized/95349/what-happened-in-vegas-a-pulitzer-shines-on-the-sun/.

6. Neil Brown and David Boardman, telephone interviews with author, April 20, 2009.

7. Brian Greenspun, telephone interview with author, May 26, 2014.

8. On the Pulitzer website at http://www.pulitzer.org/citation/2009-Public -Service; all the year's prizes at http://www.pulitzer.org/awards/2009.

9. Daniel Gilbert, Skype interview with author, April 20, 2014.

10. J. Todd Foster, telephone interview with author, April 12, 2010. Some quotes appeared in Harris, "Pulitzer Alchemy Turns Methane Gas to Public Service Gold," *Poynter*, April 13, 2010, http://www.poynter.org/news/mediawire/102025 /pulitzer-alchemy-turns-methane-gas-to-public-service-gold/.

11. Paul Provonost, telephone interview with author, April 12, 2010.

12. Rebecca Blumenstein, telephone interview with author, June 4, 2014.

13. Jim Maxell, telephone interview with author, May 12, 2014.

14. On the Pulitzer website at http://www.pulitzer.org/citation/2010-Public -Service; all the year's prizes at http://www.pulitzer.org/awards/2010.

9. The Tradition Survives, 2011–2012: Return of the *L.A. Times* and the *Philadelphia Inquirer*

1. University of Southern California Annenberg School Director's Forum, August 24, 2010, accessible at https://www.youtube.com/watch?v=_YXt30g_rfE.

2. Kimi Yoshino, Shelby Grad, Steve Marble group interview with at the *Times* office with author, January 15, 2014.

3. Ruben Vives, interview with author, June 6, 2011. Vives and Jeff Gottlieb both interviewed with the author at the *Times* office June 6 and again January 15, 2014.

4. Marble, group interview with author.

5. Davan Maharaj, interview with author, January 15, 2014.

6. Russ Stanton, telephone interview with author, April 18, 2011.

7. Kim Christensen, telephone interview with author, January 22, 2014.

8. Christopher Goffard, "How Bell Hit Bottom," *Los Angeles Times*, December 28, 2011, on the Pulitzer website at http://www.pulitzer.org/archives/9213.

9. James Rainey, "On the Media: An Unlikely Duo Wins Pulitzer for Bell Coverage," *Los Angeles Times*, April 19, 2011, http://articles.latimes.com/2011 /apr/19/entertainment/la-et-onthemedia-20110419.

10. Shelby Grad, group interview with author.

11. On the Pulitzer website at http://www.pulitzer.org/citation/2011-Public -Service; all the year's prizes at http://www.pulitzer.org/awards/2011.

12. Bill Marimow, interview with author at *Inquirer*, March 13, 2014.

13. Stan Wischnowski, interview with author, March 13, 2014.

14. John Sullivan, interview with author at *Washington Post*, March 12, 2014.

15. Kristen Graham and Sue Snyder, interviews with author, March 13, 2014.

16. Mike Leary, telephone interview with author, March 6, 2014.

17. Sullivan, interview with author, confirmed by Snyder.

18. John Sullivan, Susan Snyder, Kristen A. Graham, and Dylan Purcell, "Climate of Violence Stifles City Schools," *Inquirer*, March 27, 2011, on the Pulitzer website at http://www.pulitzer.org/files/2012/public_service/assault01.pdf.

19. Arizona State University press release, January 27, 2012, http://cronkite .asu.edu/node/1503; also Andrew Beaujon and Julie Moos, "New Owners Bring Bill Marimow Back to The Philadelphia Inquirer," *Poynter*, April 4, 2012, http://www.poynter.org/latest-news/mediawire/169100/new-owners -bring-bill-marimow-back-to-the-philadelphia-inquirer/.

20. Mike Armstrong, "Inquirer Wins Pulitzer Prize for School Violence Series," *Philly.com*, April 16, 2012, http://articles.philly.com/2012-04-17/news/31355824_1 _south-philadelphia-high-school-inquirer-district-and-state-data; also Marimow interview by author, March 13, 2014.

21. On the Pulitzer website at http://www.pulitzer.org/awards/2012; all the year's prizes at http://www.pulitzer.org/awards/2012

10. First Gold, 1917–1919: The Great War, Brought Home

1. John Hohenberg, *The Pulitzer Prizes: A History of the Awards in Books, Drama, Music, and Journalism Based on the Private Files Over Six Decades* (New York: Columbia University Press, 1974), 28–31.

2. Meyer Berger, *The Story of the New York Times* (New York: Simon and Schuster, 1951), 153. Also cited in W. A. Swanberg, *Pulitzer: The Life of the Greatest Figure in American Journalism and One of the Most Extraordinary Men in Our History* (New York: Scribner's, 1967), 300.

3. Berger, *The Story of the New York Times*, 160–161.

4. Ibid., 202–205.

5. The *Times* used that spelling of what it would later call Serbia.

6. Berger, *The Story of the New York Times*, 253–254.

7. Michael Richman, "The Medals of Daniel Chester French," in Alan M. Stahl, ed., *The Medal in America* (New York: Coinage of the Americas Conference at The American Numismatic Society, September 26–27, 1987), 150–153.

8. Arthur S. Ochs, letter to Pulitzer Advisory Board, July 8, 1920, provided to author by the *New York Times*.

9. All the year's Pulitzer Prizes are at http://www.pulitzer.org/awards/1918.

10. Pulitzer Prize jury reports, 1919.

11. Robert W. Wells, *The Milwaukee Journal: An Informal Chronicle of Its First One Hundred Years* (Milwaukee: Milwaukee Journal, 1982), 116.

12. All the year's Pulitzer Prizes are at http://www.pulitzer.org/awards/1919.

II. Reporting on the Roaring, 1920–1929: Charles Ponzi and an Ohio Editor's Murder

1. This emerges from the collected letters of Joseph Pulitzer II, located in the Library of Congress. They feature his frequent communications with other board members, often before they met to decide on winners.

2. John Hohenberg, *The Pulitzer Prizes: A History of the Awards in Books, Drama, Music, and Journalism Based on the Private Files Over Six Decades* (New York: Columbia University Press, 1974), 33.

3. Ibid., 41–42; Pulitzer jury report, 1921.

4. Mitchell Zuckoff, *Ponzi's Scheme: The True Story of a Financial Legend* (New York: Random House, 2005), 43.

5. Ibid., 36–37.

6. Ibid., 95.

7. Ibid., 96.

8. Ibid., 120–139.

9. From the *Post*'s 1921 Pulitzer entry; also Zuckoff, *Ponzi's Scheme*, 160.

10. Zuckoff, *Ponzi's Scheme*, 183–187.

11. Ibid., 209–229.

12. Ibid., 255–272.

13. Ibid., 299–313.

14. All the year's Pulitzer Prizes are at http://www.pulitzer.org/awards/1921.

15. Hohenberg, *The Pulitzer Prizes*, 39–40.

16. Ibid., 91.

17. E. J. Kahn Jr., *The World of Swope: A Biography of Herbert Bayard Swope* (New York: Simon and Schuster, 1965), 233.

18. Ibid., 240–242; Alfred Allan Lewis, *Man of the World, Herbert Bayard Swope: A Charmed Life of Pulitzer Prizes, Poker and Politics* (Indianapolis: Bobbs-Merrill Company, Inc., 1978), 94.

19. From the 1922 Pulitzer entry.

20. Lewis, *Man of the World*, 94.

21. Pulitzer jury report, April 18, 1922.

22. All the year's Pulitzer Prizes are at http://www.pulitzer.org/awards/1922.

23 Helen Bloom, New York University, *News Workshop* newsletter, January 1965.

24. John Bartlow Martin, "Murder of a Journalist," *Harper's* (September 1946), 274.

25. From the 1927 Pulitzer entry.

26. John Hohenberg, *The Pulitzer Prize Story* (New York: Columbia University Press, 1959), 47–48; also Bloom, New York University *News Workshop* newsletter.

27. All the year's Pulitzer Prizes are at http://www.pulitzer.org/awards/1927.

28. Joseph Pulitzer II, Collected Papers, Library of Congress. His letters show he kept close track of the numbers of awards the *World* papers and the *Post-Dispatch* won each year.

29. Pulitzer II, Collected Papers. From a letter to Columbia's Nicholas Murray Butler, dated April 13, 1928.

30. Pulitzer II, Collected Papers. Letter from executive secretary Robert A. Parker to the Pulitzer Advisory Board, November 14, 1929.

31. Telegram from JP II to brother Ralph, dated August 6, 1929, one of several in the JP II papers on this subject.

12. From Depression to Wartime, 1930–1945: Corruption and the Dust Bowl

1. The case is summarized in John Hohenberg, *The Pulitzer Prize Story* (New York: Columbia University Press, 1959), 50–55.

2. From the Pulitzer Prize archives, 1934. Also republished in Hohenberg, *The Pulitzer Prize Story*, 51–52.

3. Seven-page Robert Ruhl letter, "Public Service Award," undated, in the Pulitzer Prize archive.

4. Pulitzer jury report, March 6, 1934.

5. Pulitzer II, Collected Papers. Letter from Ralph Pulitzer to Pulitzer II.

6. Pulitzer jury report, 1934.

7. All the year's Pulitzer Prizes are at http://www.pulitzer.org/awards/1934.

8. From the 1938 Pulitzer entry.

9. All the year's Pulitzer Prizes are at http://www.pulitzer.org/awards/1938.

10. From the *Times*'s cover letter with the entry.

11. An April 8, 1943, *Times* article noted the *Harvard Crimson* comments.

12. All the year's Pulitzer Prizes are at http://www.pulitzer.org/awards/1944.

13. A Handful of Gold, 1936–1952: The *Post-Dispatch* Makes Its Mark

1. This chapter reflects work for the James C. Millstone Memorial Lecture delivered by the author to the Missouri Historical Society and the *Post-Dispatch* staff, September 9, 2002; published as "The Gold Medal Crusade Years," Saint Louis University School of Law, 2002. Summarized in Harris, "An Era of Crusaders," *Quill* (May 2003).

2. St. Louis Post-Dispatch, *The Story of the St. Louis Post-Dispatch*, 6th ed. (St. Louis: St. Louis Post-Dispatch, 1954), 5, 10.

3. Discussed in Daniel Pfaff, *Joseph Pulitzer II and the Post-Dispatch* (University Park: Pennsylvania State University Press, 1991), 154–167.

4. Pfaff, *Joseph Pulitzer II and the Post-Dispatch*, 37–39. More detail in Pfaff, "Pulitzer Journalism and Public Service," James Yeatman Lecture, St. Louis, November 10, 2006.

5. Pfaff, *Joseph Pulitzer II*, 227–228.

6. Louis Starr, "Reminiscences of Ben Reese," Oral History Research Office, (New York: Columbia University, 1957).

7. As published daily on the *St. Louis Post-Dispatch* editorial page.

8. Louis Starr, "Reminiscences of Ben Reese."

9. Ibid.

10. Selwyn Pepper, interview with author, June 29, 2002; also from the 1937 Pulitzer entry.

11. Wayne Leeman, interview with author, June 29, 2002.

12. Pulitzer II, Collected Papers.

13. Pulitzer jury report, 1937.

14. All the year's Pulitzer Prizes are at http://www.pulitzer.org/awards/1937.

15. Pfaff, *Joseph Pulitzer II*, 212–213.

16. *Post-Dispatch* Pulitzer entry, 1941.

17. All the year's Pulitzer Prizes are at http://www.pulitzer.org/awards/1941.

18. Pepper, interview.

19. Quoted matter taken from *Post-Dispatch* 1948 Pulitzer entry.

20. Pfaff, *Joseph Pulitzer II*, 225–226.

21. All the year's Pulitzer Prizes are at http://www.pulitzer.org/awards/1948.

22. *Post-Dispatch* Pulitzer entry, 1950.

23. "Chicago, St. Louis Dailies Win Pulitzer Gold Medals," *Editor and Publisher*, May 6, 1950, 7.

24. "Reporters Reveal Work Behind Payroll Expose," *Editor and Publisher*, August 27, 1949, 24.

25. Cited in the *Post-Dispatch* Pulitzer entry, 1950.

26. All the year's Pulitzer Prizes are at http://www.pulitzer.org/awards/1950.

27. "Theodore C. Link Dies; Investigative Reporter," *Post-Dispatch*, February 14, 1974.

28. The *Post-Dispatch* Pulitzer entry, 1952.

29. All the year's Pulitzer Prizes are at http://www.pulitzer.org/awards/1952.

14. A New Stew of Issues, 1953–1969:
Little Rock, the Suburbs, and Firsts for Women

1. Ray Erwin, "2 Weeklies Win Pulitzer Prizes for Anti-KKK War," *Editor and Publisher*, May 9, 1953, 9.

2. Associated Press account, May 5, 1943.

3. All the year's Pulitzer Prizes are at http://www.pulitzer.org/awards/1953.

4. Discussed in Robert Keeler, *Newsday: A Candid History of the Respectable Tabloid* (New York: Arbor House/Morrow, 1990), 46–50.

5. Ibid., 196–198. Because individual reporters were rarely discussed in connection with the Public Service Prize, there is no good way to document this.

6. Ibid., 199–203, is the source for most information on Greene.

7. Bob Greene, telephone interview with author, March 3, 2006.

8. Keeler, *Newsday: A Candid History*, 208.

9. Ray Erwin, "3 Pulitzer Prizes Awarded for Exclusive Exposes: Newsday Wins Gold Medal for Track and Labor Racket Stories," *Editor and Publisher*, May 9, 1954, 13.

10. All the year's Pulitzer Prizes are at http://www.pulitzer.org/awards/1954.

11. Ray Erwin, "Pulitzer Prizes Awarded for the Little Rock Story," *Editor and Publisher*, May 10, 1958, 11. Also the *Arkansas Gazette* Pulitzer entry, 1958.

12. Gene Roberts, interview with author, November 30, 2005.

13. The *Gazette* Pulitzer entry; also quoted in John Hohenberg, *The Pulitzer Prize Story* (New York: Columbia University Press, 1959), 102. The chapter's initial September 9 *Arkansas Gazette* commentary by Ashmore is discussed in Hohenberg, *The Pulitzer Prize Story*, 101.

14. Pulitzer jury report, 1958.

15. Gene Roberts and Hank Klibanoff, *The Race Beat: The Press, the Civil Rights Struggle, and the Awakening of a Nation* (New York: Knopf, 2006). On the Pulitzer website at http://www.pulitzer.org/citation/2007-History.

16. The *Arkansas Gazette Democrat* website, "Arkansas' Past Entwined with Newspaper's Vivid Story," at http://www.arkansasonline.com/tools/newspaper historymain/.

17. All the year's Pulitzer Prizes are at http://www.pulitzer.org/awards/1958.

18. Lois Wille, telephone interview with author, April 3, 2006. Also the *Chicago Daily News* Pulitzer entry, 1957, and "Pulitzer Prizes Awarded For Crusades, Enterprise," *Editor and Publisher*, May 11, 1963, 12.

19. All the year's Pulitzer Prizes are at http://www.pulitzer.org/awards/1963.

20. Ray Erwin, "St. Petersburg Times Wins Public Service Pulitzer," *Editor and Publisher*, May 9, 1964, 12; also Cortland Anderson, "Gold Medal Stories Save

Florida Taxpayers Millions," and Robert Sherrill, "Tipsters Whisper Secrets, and He ROARS," *Editor and Publisher*, 13.

21. The *Tampa Bay Times* website at http://www.tampabay.com/company /about-us/times-history.

22. All the year's Pulitzer Prizes are at http://www.pulitzer.org/awards/1964.

23. The *Los Angeles Times* obituary, February 23, 2014, at http://www.latimes .com/local/obituaries/la-me-bill-thomas-20140224-story.html#page=1.

24. William F. Thomas, interview with author, May 28, 2005.

25. The *Los Angeles Times* Pulitzer entry, 1969. Other accounts of coverage are in *Editor and Publisher*, May 10, 1969, 9; *Los Angeles Times*, May 6, 1969, 1.

26. All the year's Pulitzer Prizes are at http://www.pulitzer.org/awards/1969.

15. Secret Papers, Secret Reporting, 1972:
The Pentagon Papers and the *Times*

1. Reston comments opening the chapter quoted in John Hohenberg, *The Pulitzer Prizes: A History of the Awards in Books, Drama, Music, and Journalism Based on the Private Files Over Six Decades* (New York: Columbia University Press, 1974), 293.

2. Harrison E. Salisbury, *Without Fear or Favor: An Uncompromising Look at the New York Times* (New York: Ballantine, 1980), 230.

3. Butterfield, telephone interview with author, March 11, 2006.

4. Ben Bradlee, *A Good Life: Newspapering and Other Adventures* (New York: Touchstone, 1995), 310.

5. Salisbury, *Without Fear or Favor*, 166–167.

6. Ibid., 47–93. Salisbury's account takes the reader through Daniel Ellsberg's process in making Sheehan the outlet for the Pentagon Papers.

7. Salisbury, *Without Fear or Favor*, 122.

8. Ibid., 118–124.

9. Ibid., 127–133, reviews the William Bayard Hale interview with Kaiser Wilhelm, described in chapter 10 of this volume. The Bay of Pigs precedent is discussed at 148–164.

10. Ibid., 165–205.

11. Floyd Abrams, *Speaking Freely: Trials of the First Amendment* (New York: Viking, 2005), 12.

12. Butterfield, interview.

13. From the *Times* Pulitzer entry, 1972.

14. John Lynch, Vanderbilt University Television News Archive, Nashville, Tennessee, e-mail to author, April 17, 2006.

15. Salisbury, *Without Fear or Favor*, 231–247, has detailed speculation about Nixon's reaction.

16. Abrams, *Speaking Freely*, 12. Abrams cites a number of books describing the Nixon administration reaction to the Pentagon Papers, including David Rudenstine's *The Day the Presses Stopped*; Richard Reeves's *President Nixon: Alone in the White House*; and John Prados and Margaret Pratt Parker's *Inside the Pentagon Papers*, citing transcripts of telephone conversations between Nixon and aides.

17. Salisbury, *Without Fear or Favor*, 240–247.

18. Abrams, *Speaking Freely*, 17–18.

19. Bradlee, *A Good Life*, 313–317.

20. Butterfield, interview.

21. Abrams, *Speaking Freely*, 30–31.

22. Ibid., 37.

23. Ibid., 44–45.

24. John Hohenberg, *The Pulitzer Prize Story II, 1959–1980* (New York: Columbia University Press, 1980), 155.

25. Pulitzer jury report, March 10, 1972; also Hohenberg, *The Pulitzer Prizes*, 308.

26. Daniel Pfaff, *No Ordinary Joe: A Life of Joseph Pulitzer III* (Columbia, Mo.: University of Missouri Press, 2005), 288. Pfaff cites a January 24, 1972, note from Ben Bradlee in the papers of Pulitzer III.

27. Hohenberg, *The Pulitzer Prize Story II*, 157.

28. Bradlee, *A Good Life*, 323.

29. The *New York Times* maintains a Pentagon Papers online archive at http://topics.nytimes.com/top/reference/timestopics/subjects/p/pentagon_papers/index.html; all the year's Pulitzer Prizes are at http://www.pulitzer.org/awards/1972.

16. All the Editor's Men, 1973: Watergate and the *Post*

1. Bob Woodward, interview with author, October 12, 2005.

2. Carl Bernstein and Bob Woodward, "40 Years After Watergate Nixon Was Far Worse Than We Thought," *Washington Post*, June 8, 2012, http://www.washingtonpost.com/opinions/woodward-and-bernstein-40-years-after-watergate-nixon-was-far-worse-than-we-thought/2012/06/08/gJQAlsioNV_story.html.

3. Presidential recording on file at the Miller Center, University of Virginia, Charlottesville, http://millercenter.org/presidentialrecordings/rmn-525-001.

4. Woodward, interview with author.

5. Kept in Rare Manuscripts Room, Butler Library, Columbia University, New York.

6. Woodward, interview.

7. Howard Simons, Washington Post 1973 Pulitzer nominating letter, January 29, 1973.

8. American Society of News Editors panel, April 3, 2012, "The Digital Age and Investigative Journalism," http://www.c-span.org/video/?305299–1/digital-age-investigative-journalism.

9. The accounts of the *Post*'s Watergate coverage here are largely from Carl Bernstein and Bob Woodward, *All the President's Men* (New York: Simon and Schuster, 1974); and Bradlee, *A Good Life: Newspapering and Other Adventures* (New York: Touchstone, 1995), 324–384, supplemented by Woodward and Bradlee interviews with the author. When articles are quoted, the source is the *Post*'s Pulitzer entry, 1973.

10. Robert G. Kaiser, "Ben Bradlee, Legendary Washington Post Editor, Dies at 93," *Washington Post*, October 21, 2014, http://www.washingtonpost.com/national/ben-bradlee-legendary-washington-post-editor-dies-at-93/2014/10/21/3e4cc1fc-c59c-11df-8dce-7a7dc354d1b1_story.html.

11. Katharine Graham, *Personal History* (New York: Random House, 1997), 461.

12. Woodward, interview.

13. Bradlee, interview.

14. Woodward, interview.

15. Ibid.

16. Ibid

17. Anthony Marro, telephone interview with author. His evaluation of key Watergate stories covered in March 2005 University of Texas seminar.

18. Woodward, interview.

19. Carl Bernstein and Bob Woodward, comments at American Society of News Editors, "The Digital Age."

20. Bernstein and Woodward, *All the President's Men*, 170–198.

21. Woodward, interview.

22. Bradlee, *A Good Life*, 341. For his discussion of the reporting error, in which "our Watergate machine blew a fuse," see 337–343.

23. From the *Post* Pulitzer Prize entries, 1973.

24. The best accounts of how the *Post*'s Watergate entry was received in the Pulitzer competition are in three John Hohenberg works: *The Pulitzer Prize Story II: 1959–1980* (New York: Columbia University Press, 1980), 208–237; *The Pulitzer Prizes: A History of the Awards in Books, Drama, Music, and Journalism Based on the Private Files Over Six Decades* (New York: Columbia University Press, 1974), 313–38; and *The Pulitzer Diaries: Inside America's Greatest Prize* (Syracuse, N.Y.: Syracuse University Press, 1997), 265–272.

25. Pulitzer jury report, March 8, 1973, provided by Pulitzer Prize office.

26. Woodward, interview.

27. Hohenberg, *The Pulitzer Prize Story II*, 223.

28. Hohenberg, *The Pulitzer Prizes*, 315.

29. Bradlee, interview. A discussion that falls just short of that declaration is in *A Good Life*, 367–368.

30. Woodward, interview.

31. Seymour Topping, telephone interview with author, March 11, 2006.

32. Roberts, interview.

33. Topping, telephone interview.

34. Cited in Graham, *Personal History*, 404.

35. American Society of News Editors, "The Digital Age."

36. Woodward, interview.

37. The *Washington Post*'s archive of its original Watergate articles is at http://www.washingtonpost.com/wp-dyn/politics/specials/watergate/articles/; all the year's Pulitzer Prizes are at http://www.pulitzer.org/awards/1973.

38. Anthony Marro, University of Texas seminar transcript, March 23, 2005.

39. Woodward, interview.

40. Other works examining the legacy in journalism of the *Post*'s Watergate coverage include Michael Schudson, *Watergate in American Memory: How We Remember, Forget, and Reconstruct the Past* (New York: Basic Books, 1992); Jon Marshall, *Watergate's Legacy and the Press; The Investigative Impulse* (Evanston, Ill.: Northwestern University Press, 2011); and Alicia C. Shepard, *Woodward and Bernstein: Life in the Shadow of Watergate* (Hoboken, N.J.: Wiley, 2007).

41. Marro, University of Texas seminar transcript. An appraisal of Woodward and Bernstein by Seymour Hersh who covered Watergate for the *New York Times* can also be found in "Watergate Days," the *New Yorker*, June 13, 2005. http://www.newyorker.com/magazine/2005/06/13/watergate-days.

42. Roberts, interview.

17. In Watergate's Shadow, 1970–1978: *Newsday*, the *Inquirer*, and Davids vs. Goliaths

1. Michael Schudson, *Watergate in American Memory: How We Remember, Forget, and Reconstruct the Past* (New York: Basic Books, 1992), 110.

2. Jon Marshall, *Watergate's Legacy and the Press* (Evanston, Ill.: Northwestern University Press, 2011), 43.

3. Robert F. Keeler, *Newsday: A Candid History of the Respectable Tabloid* (New York: Arbor House/Morrow, 1990), 192–209.

4. Ibid., 311–315.

5. Ibid., 199–203.

6. Bob Greene, telephone interview with author, March 3, 2006.

7. Ibid.

8. Geraldine Shanahan, interview with author, November 29, 2005.

9. Marro, telephone interview.

10. Keeler, *Newsday: A Candid History*, 430.

11. Marro provided a transcript of *Newsday* anniversary party, September 26, 2002.

12. Pulitzer jury report, 1970.

13. Greene, telephone interview; story also told in Keeler, *Newsday: A Candid History*, 431.

14. All the year's Pulitzer Prizes are at http://www.pulitzer.org/awards/1970.

15. Greene, telephone interview; story also told in Keeler, *Newsday: A Candid History*, 431.

16. Marro, telephone interview.

17. Keeler, *Newsday: A Candid History*, 511.

18. Marro, telephone interview.

19. Ibid.

20. Pulitzer jury report, 1974.

21. The Arizona Project brought many top reporters together on the same story under the auspices of the new Investigative Reporters and Editors, or IRE, which describes the background on its website at http://www.ire.org/about/history/. An article written after Greene's death is Harris, "Remembering *Newsday*'s Bob Greene," *Poynter*, April 11, 2008, at http://www.poynter.org/uncategorized/88228/remembering-newsdays-bob-greene/.

22. All the year's Pulitzer Prizes are at http://www.pulitzer.org/awards/1974.

23. The 1973 movie *Serpico*, with Al Pacino, tells the story, http://www.imdb.com/title/tt0070666/.

24. Howard Weaver, interview with author, November 15, 2005. The section is based largely on his account, along with the 1976 *Anchorage Daily News* Pulitzer entry and jury report.

25. *Anchorage Daily News*, December 20, 1975, from Pulitzer entry.

26. All the year's Pulitzer Prizes are at http://www.pulitzer.org/awards/1976.

27. Joe Murray, telephone interview with author, March 3, 2006. Based on the accounts of Murray and Ken Herman, with material from the *Lufkin News*'s 1977 Pulitzer entry. A 2001 report titled "A Case Study Analysis and Quarter-Century Perspective of a Story that Won the Pulitzer Prize," by Dr. Wanda Mouton, Department of Communication, Stephen F. Austin State University, Nacogdoches, Texas, contains additional detail.

28. Ken Herman, telephone interview with author, March 7, 2006.

29. *Lufkin News*, March 16, 1976, in Pulitzer entry, 1977.

30. *Lufkin News*, April 4, 1976.

31. All the year's Pulitzer Prizes are at http://www.pulitzer.org/awards/1977.

32. Harrison Salisbury quoted in *Columbia Journalism Review* (May/June 2003).

33. Gene Roberts, interview with author, November 30, 2005.

34. Steve Lovelady, interview with author, November 29, 2005.

35. Bill Marimow, telephone interview with author, March 13, 2006.

36. Gene Roberts, interview.

37. The *Inquirer* series ran from April 24 to 27, from Pulitzer entry, 1978.

38. All the year's Pulitzer Prizes are at http://www.pulitzer.org/awards/1978.

18. Mightier Than the Snake, 1979: The *Point Reyes Light* on Synanon

1. While it may surprise that this is a New Age quotation, and not much older, *Morrow's International Dictionary of Contemporary Quotations* (New York: William Morrow, 1982) is among the references crediting Dederich as its originator, circa 1969.

2. Dave Mitchell, Cathy Mitchell, and Richard Ofshe, *The Light on Synanon: How a Country Weekly Exposed a Corporate Cult—and Won the Pulitzer Prize* (New York: Seaview Books, 1980), 4, 22. (Initial chapter quote on page 280.)

3. Dave Mitchell, interview with author, November 18, 2005.

4. Paul Morantz, telephone interview with author, October 25, 2005.

5. *Point Reyes Light*, September 28, 1978, from Pulitzer entry.

6. Mitchell, Mitchell, and Ofshe, *The Light on Synanon*, 181.

7. Ibid., 191–203.

8. Paul Morantz, telephone interview. Also follow-up telephone interview, May 24, 2014.

9. Dave Mitchell, interview.

10. Cathy Mitchell, telephone interview with author, December 20, 2005.

11. Tess Elliot, telephone interview with author, May 22, 2014.

12. Paul Morantz with Hal Lancaster, *Escape: My Lifelong War Against Cults* (Pacific Palisades, Calif.: Cresta Publications, 2013).

13. All the year's Pulitzer Prizes are at http://www.pulitzer.org/awards/1979.

19. Everybody's Business, 1980–1989:
Considering the Company View

1. Howard Weaver, interview with author.

2. Richard A. Oppel, telephone interview by author, April 3, 2006. This section is based largely on the *Charlotte Observer* 1981 Pulitzer entry.

3. The letter from the textile industry executive was included by Oppel in the *Observer's* cover letter for its 1981 Pulitzer Prize entry.

4. All the year's Pulitzer Prizes are at http://www.pulitzer.org/awards/1981.

5. Charles Shepard, in Kendall J. Wills, *The Pulitzer Prizes 1987* (New York: Simon and Schuster, 1988), 21–24. Wills put together four books for Simon and Schuster from 1988 to 1991, each a compendium of Pulitzer-winning journalism for the prior year.

6. Richard Oppel, telephone interview.

7. All the year's Pulitzer Prizes are at http://www.pulitzer.org/awards/1988.

8. Mark J. Thompson, telephone interview with author, March 27, 2006. The section is also based on the *Star-Telegram* Pulitzer entry, 1985.

9. All the year's Pulitzer Prizes are at http://www.pulitzer.org/awards/1985.

10. Andrew Schneider, telephone interview with author, April 2, 2006. The section also reflects material from the *Pittsburgh Press* Pulitzer entry for 1986, along with another account, in Wills, *The Pulitzer Prizes 1987*, written by Matthew Brelis and Schneider, 22–25.

11. All the year's Pulitzer Prizes are at http://www.pulitzer.org/awards/1987.

12. John Hohenberg, *The Pulitzer Diaries: Inside America's Greatest Prize* (Syracuse, N.Y.: Syracuse University Press, 1997), 22. Discussions of several attempts to expand the reach of the Pulitzer Prize are also found in Joseph Pulitzer II, Collected Papers, Library of Congress. Daniel W. Pfaff's biographies of both Pulitzer II and Pulitzer III give additional detail in their relationship.

13. In David Shaw, *Press Watch: A Provocative Look at How Newspapers Report the News* (New York: Macmillan, 1984); the chapter 7 discussion of the prizes, 178–214, is based on a *Los Angeles Times* series on the Pulitzers.

14. Hohenberg, *The Pulitzer Prize Story II*, 151–158.

15. Ibid., 222–228.

16. Gene Patterson, telephone interview with author, April 19, 2006. Patterson died in January 2013, http://www.tampabay.com/news/obituaries/former-times-editor-eugene-patterson-who-championed-civil-rights-and/1270371.

17. Roberts, interview with author.

18. Jack Fuller, telephone interview with author, March 23, 2006.

19. Michael Gartner, telephone interview with author.

20. The Nature of Things, 1990–1998:
The Scientific and the Sordid

1. J. Douglas Bates, *The Pulitzer Prize: The Inside Story of America's Most Prestigious Award* (New York: Birch Lane Press, 1991), especially 209–211, focuses on the Pulitzer process for 1990.

2. Also following the year 1990 in Pulitzers was Kendall J. Wills, *The Pulitzer Prizes 1990* (New York: Simon and Schuster), 2–6, offering the basis for much of this section.

3. Douglas Martin, "William, Coughlin, 101, Editor, Dies; His Newspaper Exposed Fouled Water," *New York Times*, May 12, 2014, http://www.nytimes.com/2014/05/13/business/media/william-coughlin-91-dies-editor-exemplar.html.

4. All the year's Pulitzer prizes are at http://www.pulitzer.org/awards/1990.

5. Gilbert Gaul, interview with author, October 13, 2005. See also Wills, *The Pulitzer Prizes 1990*, 31–33.

6. Geneva Overholser, interview with author, December 1, 2005. This account balances the views of editor Overholser and reporter Jane Schorer. References to articles are from the *Register*'s 1991 Pulitzer entry.

7. Jane Schorer Meisner, telephone interview with author, April 3, 2006.

8. *Des Moines Register*, February 25, 1990, from Pulitzer archives. The series was made available electronically by the *Register* for an article in *Parade* magazine, April 12, 2013, at http://www.desmoinesregister.com/article/20130216/CAROUSEL/104120006/Pulitzer-Transcript&template=artinteractive. The entire *Parade* article is at http://communitytable.com/4953/parade/4-memorable-pulitzer-prize-winning-stories-of-the-last-25-years/.

9. Michael Gartner, telephone interview with author.

10. All the year's Pulitzer Prizes are at http://www.pulitzer.org/awards/1991.

11. Tom Knudson, interview with author, November 16, 2005.

12. Pulitzer jury report, 1992.

13. All the year's Pulitzer Prizes are at http://www.pulitzer.org/awards/1992.

14. Account based largely on the *Miami Herald* Pulitzer entry, 1992.

15. Pete Weitzel, telephone interview with author, April 4, 2006.

16. Pulitzer Public Service jury report, 1993.

17. All the year's Pulitzer Prizes are at http://www.pulitzer.org/awards/1993.

18. Melanie Sill, telephone interview with author, April 4, 2006. Also *Editor and Publisher*, "80th Annual Pulitzer Prizes," April 13, 1996, 9.

19. *News and Observer*, February 19, 1994, on the Pulitzer website at http://www.pulitzer.org/archives/5893.

20. *News and Observer* winning entry on the Pulitzer website at http://www.pulitzer.org/citation/1996-Public-Service. The Pulitzer organization first made

winning entries available online in 1995. All the year's prizes at http://www.pulitzer
.org/awards/1996.

21. Mark Schleifstein, interview with author, April 6, 2006. Also the *Times-
Picayune* Pulitzer entry, 1997.

22 Peter Kovacs, interview with author, May 30, 2006.

23. Jim Amoss, interview with author, May 30, 2006.

24. Public Service jury report, 1998.

25. On the Pulitzer website at http://www.pulitzer.org/works/1997-Public
-Service; all the year's prizes at http://www.pulitzer.org/awards/1997.

26. On the Pulitzer website at http://www.pulitzer.org/archives/6166.

27. Mike Maidenberg, telephone interview with author, April 11, 2006.

28. On the Pulitzer website at http://www.pulitzer.org/archives/6165.

29. On the Pulitzer website at http://www.pulitzer.org/archives/6169.

30. Maidenberg, telephone interview.

31. Mike Jacobs, "Four Lessons of Newspapering . . . Come Hell and High
Water," *Poynter*, June 18, 2003, http://www.Poynter.org, June 18, 2003, from
American Society of Newspaper Editors speech.

32. Maidenberg, telephone interview.

33. James Naughton, e-mail to author, April 4, 2006.

34. Grand Forks Herald Public Service entry on the Pulitzer website at http://
www.pulitzer.org/citation/1998-Public-Service; all the year's prizes at http://www
.pulitzer.org/awards/1998.

21. The *Post* Rings Twice, 1999–2001: Police Shootings and Shameful Homes

1. Jeffrey M. Leen, interview with author, October 12, 2005.

2. Bob Woodward, interview with author.

3. The December 23, 1997, memo was summarized in a later recap of the *Post*
police project, prepared in December 1998 by Rick Atkinson and others. That
recap, titled "Deadly Force: The Making of The Post's Police Project," was provided to the author by Jeff Leen.

4. Jeff Leen, interview.

5. Sari Horwitz, interview with author, October 12, 2005.

6. David Jackson comments quoted in December 1998 Atkinson memo.

7. Jeff Leen, Jo Craven (McGinty), David Jackson, Sari Horwitz, *Washington
Post*, November 15, 1998, on the Pulitzer website for 1999 at http://www.pulitzer
.org/archives/6276.

8. On the Pulitzer website at http://www.pulitzer.org/citation/1999-Public
-Service; all the year's prizes at http://www.pulitzer.org/awards/1999.

9. Leen, interview.

10. The *Washington Post* Pulitzer entry, 2000.

11. Katherine Boo, interview with author, October 12, 2005.

12. Boo, "Invisible Lives: D.C.'s Troubled System for the Retarded," *Post*, March 14, 1999; on the Pulitzer website at http://www.pulitzer.org/archives/6369.

13. A corrected archival piece appears on a *Washington Post* website at http://www2.uncp.edu/home/canada/work/markport/lit/litjour/spg2002/cooke.htm.

14. Boo, "Invisible Deaths: The Fatal Neglect of D.C.'s Retarded," *Post*, December 5, 1999; on the Pulitzer website at http://www.pulitzer.org/archives/6376.

15. Leen, interview. Coll, who left the *Post* in 2005, joined the Pulitzer board in 2012. Coll became dean of the Columbia University Graduate School of Journalism in July 2013. On the Columbia website at http://www.journalism.columbia.edu/news/797.

16. On the Pulitzer website at http://www.pulitzer.org/boo_collins_press_release.

17. On the Pulitzer website at http://www.pulitzer.org/citation/2000-Public-Service; all the year's prizes at http://www.pulitzer.org/awards/2000.

Afterword: A New Voice of the South

1. "Till Death Do Us Part," digital version posted August 19, 2014, *Post and Courier*, Charleston, South Carolina, http://www.postandcourier.com/tilldeath/.

2. Andrew Knapp, "Post and Courier Wins Pulitzer for Domestic Abuse Series," *Post and Courier*, April 20, 2015, http://www.postandcourier.com/article/20150420/PC16/150429937/1005/post-and-courier-wins-pulitzer-prize. Also discussed in Harris, "Post and Courier's Ninety-Year Pulitzer Drought Ends with Public Service Gold," Poynter.org, April 21, 2015, http://www.poynter.org/news/mediawire/338069/post-and-couriers-90-year-pulitzer-drought-ends-with-public-service-gold/.

3. Pierre Manigault, interview with author, May 30, 2015.

4. P. J. Browning, telephone interview with author, June 4, 2015.

5. On the Pulitzer website at http://www.pulitzer.org/faceted_search/results/Bartelme.

6. Mitch Pugh, Doug Pardue, and Glenn Smith, interview with author, May 30, 2015.

7. Pardue, telephone interview with author, April 20, 2015.

8. Jennifer Berry Hawes, interview with author, May 30, 2015; http://www.postandcourier.com/tilldeath/.

9. Information on the Center for Investigative Reporting is at https://www.revealnews.org/about-us/.

10. "1925 Pulitzer Winner: The Plight of the South," *Post and Courier*, April 25, 2015, http://www.postandcourier.com/article/20150425/PC1002/150429514. Noted on the Pulitzer Prize website at http://www.pulitzer.org/awards/1925.

11. Scott Kraft, e-mail to author, June 3, 2015. An interview with juror Josh Meyer of Northwestern University appears in Harris, "Post and Courier's Ninety-Year Pulitzer Drought Ends with Public Service Gold," Poynter.org; Josh Meyer, e-mail to author, April 21, 2015. The seven jury members are listed here: http://www.pulitzer.org/jurors/2015-Public-Service.

12. Cynthia Roldan, "Signing Ushers in Stiffer Penalties, Gun Ban for Domestic Violence Crimes," *Post and Courier*, June 4, 2015, http://www.postandcourier.com/article/20150604/PC1603/150609697/1180/haley-signs-bill-toughening-penalties-for-criminal-domestic-violence.

13. On the Pulitzer website at http://www.pulitzer.org/citation/2015-Public-Service; all the year's prizes at http://www.pulitzer.org/awards/2015.

Appendix: Pulitzer Gold Nuggets

1. Links to all the year's Pulitzer Prizes for these four years and for all other years mentioned in this appendix can be found by searching the year at http://www.pulitzer.org/awards.

2. E. J. Kahn Jr., *The World of Swope: A Biography of Herbert Bayard Swope* (New York: Simon and Schuster, 1965).

3. Case discussed in John Hohenberg, *The Pulitzer Prize Story* (New York: Columbia University Press, 1959), 69–70.

4. "Iowa Daily's Expose Stirred State: Prize Campaign Against Graft Brought Resignations, One Trial, Many Indictments, Although Latter Were Dismissed on a Technicality," *Editor and Publisher*, May 9, 1936, 5.

5. Discussed in "'All-Star Primary' Wins Pulitzer Medal," *Editor and Publisher*, May 7, 1949, 7.

6. Hohenberg, *The Pulitzer Prize Story*, 45.

7. Ibid., 66–68. Also Ray Erwin, "Pulitzer Gold Medal Given for Exposure of Fund Fraud," *Editor and Publisher*, May 11, 1957, 13.

8. Ray Erwin, "Utica Papers Win Pulitzer Medal for Crime Exposure," *Editor and Publisher*, May 12, 1958, 12.

9. Gene Sherman, "Prize-Winning Series Background Described," *Los Angeles Times*, May 3, 1960. Also Ray Erwin, "Exposes of Civic Sins Win 5 Pulitzer Prizes," *Editor and Publisher*, May 7, 1960, 15.

10. Thomas H. Thompson, "First Failure, Then Sweeping Victory in Gold Medal Expose," *Editor and Publisher*, May 6, 1961, 59.

11. Ray Erwin, "Crusades Versus Corruption & Collusion Win Pulitzers," *Editor and Publisher*, May 12, 1962, 11–12.

12. Ray Erwin, "Hutchinson News Wins Public Service 'Pulitzer,'" *Editor and Publisher*, May 8, 1965, 12.

13. See "Boston Globe Wins The Pulitzer Prize," *Boston Globe*, May 3, 1966, 1. Also Ray Erwin, "Boston Globe Wins Pulitzer Gold Medal," *Editor and Publisher*, May 7, 1966, 13.

14. Ray Erwin, "Louisville and Milwaukee Win Pulitzer Gold Medals," *Editor and Publisher*, May 6, 1967, 11.

15. Newton H. Fulbright, "Crusade for Indians Wins Pulitzer Medal," *Editor and Publisher*, May 11, 1968, 11.

16. Frank V. Tursi, *The Winston-Salem Journal: Magnolia Trees and Pulitzer Prizes* (Winston-Salem, N.C.: John F. Blair and Winston-Salem Journal, 1996), 191–195. Also "Pulitzers Again Applaud Crusade for Environment," *Editor and Publisher*, May 8, 1971, 10.

17. "Globe Wins Pulitzer Gold Medal for Hub School Busing Coverage," *Boston Globe*, May 5, 1975, 1; Hohenberg, *The Pulitzer Prize Story II*, 287; stories excerpted, 286–291.

18. Lenora Williamson, "Pulitzer for Public Service Won by Gannett News," *Editor and Publisher*, April 19, 1980, 11.

19. Sydney Freedberg, telephone interview with author, March 29, 2006; Lenora Williamson, "Detroit News Wins Pulitzer Gold Medal," *Editor and Publisher*, April 17, 1982. Story also references from the *Detroit News* Pulitzer entry.

20. Lenora Williamson, "Jackson Clarion-Ledger Tops Pulitzers," *Editor and Publisher*, April 23, 1983, 16–17.

21. William F. Thomas, telephone interview with author, March 23, 2003; David Shaw, "Times Wins 2 Pulitzers," *Los Angeles Times*, April 17, 1984; Lenora Williamson, "L.A. Times Wins Pulitzer Prize for Public Service," *Editor and Publisher*, April 21, 1984.

22. Lenora Williamson, "Denver Post Wins the Pulitzer Prize for Public Service with In-Depth Study of Missing Children Statistics," *Editor and Publisher*, April 26, 1986, 16.

23. Tony Case, "78th Annual Pulitzer Prizes," *Editor and Publisher*, April 16, 1994, 9–10.

24. First year that Pulitzer Prizes post winning work on its website; Daily News entry at http://www.pulitzer.org/citation/1995-Public-Service; all the year's prizes at http://www.pulitzer.org/awards/1995.

25. Tony Case and Dorothy Giobbe, "Tiny Virgin Island Daily News Wins for Public Service," *Editor and Publisher*, April 22, 1995, 17–8; also "After the

Pulitzers," November 4, 1995, and Ryan Frank, "Three Tips for Project Reporting" on a talk byMelvin Claxton at the 2002 National Writers Workshop, Portland, Oregon.

26. Oregonian Pulitzer entry on the Pulitzer website at http://www.pulitzer .org/citation/2001-Public-Service; all the year's prizes at http://www.pulitzer.org /awards/2001.

27. Richard Read, "French Fry Connection," on the Pulitzer website at http:// www.pulitzer.org/works/1999-Explanatory-Reporting.

28. Sandy Rowe, Julie Sullivan, and Richard Read interviews with author, November 16, 2006; Richard Read, "The Oregonian Investigates Mistreatment of Foreigners," *Nieman Reports* (Winter 2001): 27–29.

BIBLIOGRAPHY

Books

Abrams, Floyd. *Speaking Freely: Trials of the First Amendment.* New York: Viking, 2005.

Aucoin, James L. *The Evolution of American Investigative Journalism.* Columbia: University of Missouri Press, 2006.

Bates, J. Douglas. *The Pulitzer Prize: The Inside Story of America's Most Prestigious Award.* New York: Birch Lane, 1991.

Bent, Silas. *Newspaper Crusaders: Neglected Story.* Westport, CT: Greenwood, 1970.

Berger, Meyer. *The Story of the New York Times.* New York: Simon and Schuster, 1951.

Bernstein, Carl, and Bob Woodward. *All the President's Men.* New York: Simon and Schuster, 1974.

Boston Globe. *Betrayal: The Crisis in the Catholic Church.* By the Investigative Staff. Boston: Little, Brown and Company, 2002.

Bradlee, Ben. *A Good Life: Newspapering and Other Adventures.* New York: Touchstone, 1995.

Daly, Christopher B. *Covering America: A Narrative History of a Nation's Journalism.* Amherst: University of Massachusetts Press, 2012.

Davis, Elmer. *History of the New York Times, 1851–1921.* New York: Classic Books, 1922.

Downie, Leonard Jr., and Robert G. Kaiser. *The News about the News: American Journalism in Peril.* New York: Knopf, 2002.

Ellison, Sarah. *War at the Wall Street Journal: Inside the Struggle to Control an American Business Empire.* New York: Houghton Mifflin Harcourt, 2010.

France, David. *Our Fathers: The Secret Life of the Catholic Church in an Age of Scandal.* New York: Broadway Books, 2004.

Fuller, Jack. *What Is Happening to the News: The Information Explosion and the Crisis in Journalism.* Chicago: University of Chicago Press, 2010.

Gates, Robert. *Duty: Memoirs of a Secretary at War.* New York: Knopf, 2014.

Graham, Katharine. *Personal History.* New York: Random House, 1997.

Greenwald, Glenn. *No Place to Hide: Edward Snowden, the NSA, and the U.S. Surveillance State.* New York: Henry Holt and Company, 2014.

Harris, Roy J. Jr. *Pulitzer's Gold: Behind the Prize for Public Service Journalism.* Columbia: University of Missouri Press, 2007. *Pulitzer's Gold* website at http://www.pulitzersgold.com.

Hohenberg, John. *The Pulitzer Diaries: Inside America's Greatest Prize.* Syracuse, NY: Syracuse University Press, 1997.

——. *The Pulitzer Prizes: A History of the Awards in Books, Drama, Music, and Journalism Based on the Private Files Over Six Decades.* New York: Columbia University Press, 1974.

——, ed. and annot. *The Pulitzer Prize Story.* New York: Columbia University Press, 1959.

——, ed. and annot. *The Pulitzer Prize Story II: 1959–1980.* New York: Columbia University Press, 1980.

Kahn, E. J. Jr. *The World of Swope: A Biography of Herbert Bayard Swope.* New York: Simon and Schuster, 1965.

Keeler, Robert F. *Newsday: A Candid History of the Respectable Tabloid.* New York: Arbor House/Morrow, 1990.

Kroeger, Brooke. *Undercover Reporting: The Truth About Deception.* Evanston, IL: Northwestern University Press, 2012.

Lewis, Alfred Allan. *Man of the World, Herbert Bayard Swope: A Charmed Life of Pulitzer Prizes, Poker and Politics.* Indianapolis: Bobbs-Merrill Company, 1978.

Lewis, Anthony. *Written Into History: Pulitzer Prize Reporting of the Twentieth Century from the New York Times.* New York: Times Books, 2002

Marshall, Jon. *Watergate's Legacy and the Press: The Investigative Impulse.* Evanston, IL.: Northwestern University Press, 2011.

Merritt, Davis. *Knightfall: Knight Ridder and How the Erosion of Newspaper Journalism Is Putting Democracy at Risk.* New York: Amacom, 2005.

Mindich, David T. Z. *Tuned Out: Why Americans under 40 Don't Follow the News.* Oxford: Oxford University Press, 2004.

Mitchell, Dave, Cathy Mitchell, and Richard Ofshe. *The Light on Synanon: How a Country Weekly Exposed a Corporate Cult—and Won the Pulitzer Prize.* New York: Seaview Books, 1980.

Mnookin, Seth. *Hard News: The Scandals at the New York Times and the Future of American Media.* New York: Random House, 2004.

Morantz, Paul, with Hal Lancaster. *Escape: My Lifelong War Against Cults.* Pacific Palisades, CA: Cresta Publications, 2013.

Morris, James McGrath. *Pulitzer: A Life in Politics, Print, and Power.* New York: HarperCollins, 2010.

Morrow's International Dictionary of Contemporary Quotations. New York: William Morrow, 1982.

New York Times. *Portraits 9/11/01.* New York: Times Books: Henry Holt and Co., 2002.

Pfaff, Daniel W. *Joseph Pulitzer II and the Post-Dispatch.* University Park: Pennsylvania State University Press, 1991.

———. *No Ordinary Joe: A Life of Joseph Pulitzer III.* Columbia: University of Missouri Press, 2005.

Plante, Thomas G., ed. *Sin Against the Innocents; Sexual Abuse by Priests and the Role of the Catholic Church.* Westport, CT: Praeger, 2004.

Roberts, Gene, and Hank Klibanoff. *The Race Beat: The Press, the Civil Rights Struggle, and the Awakening of a Nation.* New York: Knopf, 2006.

Rothmyer, Karen. *Winning Pulitzers: The Stories Behind Some of the Best News Coverage of Our Time.* New York: Columbia University Press, 1991.

St. Louis Post-Dispatch. *The Story of the St. Louis Post-Dispatch,* 6th ed. Revised and supplemented by Richard G. Baumhoff. St. Louis: Pulitzer Publishing Co., 1954.

Salisbury, Harrison E. *Without Fear or Favor: An Uncompromising Look at the New York Times.* New York: Ballantine Books, 1980.

Schudson, Michael, *Discovering the News: A Social History of American Newspapers.* New York: Basic Books, 1978.

———. *Watergate in American Memory: How We Remember, Forget, and Reconstruct the Past.* New York: Basic Books, 1992.

Serrin, Judith and William, eds. *Muckraking! The Journalism That Changed America.* New York: The New Press, 2002.

Shaw, David. *Press Watch: A Provocative Look at How Newspapers Report the News.* New York: Macmillan, 1984.

Shepard, Alicia C. *Woodward and Bernstein: Life in the Shadow of Watergate.* Hoboken, NJ: Wiley, 2007.

Snyder, Louis L., and Richard B. Morris, eds. *A Treasury of Great Reporting.* New York: Simon and Schuster, 1949.

Starkman, Dean. *The Watchdog That Didn't Bark: The Financial Crisis and the Disappearance of Investigative Journalism.* New York: Columbia University Press, 2014.

Stephens, Mitchell. *A History of News: From the Drum to the Satellite*. New York: Viking, 1988.

Streitmatter, Rodger. *Mightier Than the Sword: How the News Media Have Shaped History*. Boulder, CO: Westview Press, 1997.

Swanberg, W. A. *Pulitzer: The Life of the Greatest Figure in American Journalism and One of the Most Extraordinary Men in Our History*. New York: Scribner's, 1967.

Tursi, Frank V. *The Winston-Salem Journal: Magnolia Trees and Pulitzer Prizes*. Winston-Salem, NC: John F. Blair and Winston-Salem Journal, 1996.

Wells, Robert W. *The Milwaukee Journal: An Informal Chronicle of Its First One Hundred Years*. Milwaukee: Milwaukee Journal, 1982.

Wendt, Lloyd. *The Wall Street Journal: The Story of Dow Jones and the Nation's Business Newspaper*. Chicago: Rand McNally and Co., 1982.

Williams, Paul N. *Investigative Reporting and Editing*. Englewood Cliffs, NJ: Prentice-Hall, 1978.

Wills, Kendall J. *The Pulitzer Prizes, 1987, 1988, 1989, 1990* (4 volumes), New York: Simon and Schuster, 1987–1990.

Zuckoff, Mitchell. *Ponzi's Scheme: The True Story of a Financial Legend*. New York: Random House, 2005.

Articles, Periodicals, and Websites

"1925 Pulitzer Winner: The Plight of the South," *Post and Courier*, April 25, 2015, http://www.postandcourier.com/article/20150425/PC1002/150429514. Noted on the Pulitzer Prize website at http://www.pulitzer.org/awards/1925.

Akst, Daniel. "Nonprofit Journalism." *Carnegie Reporter* 3, no. 3 (Fall 2005): 20–29, http://carnegie.org/publications/carnegie-reporter/single/view/article/item/138/.

American Journalism Review. Published bimonthly by the University of Maryland. Online at http://AJR.org, College Park, Maryland.

Amoss, Jim. "The Story of Our Lives." *Quill* (April 2006): 26–29.

Armstrong, Mike. "Inquirer Wins Pulitzer Prize for School Violence Series." *Philly.com*, April 16, 2012, http://articles.philly.com/2012–04–17/news/31355824_1_south-philadelphia-high-school-inquirer-district-and-state-data.

Barstow, David. "When Workers Die: A Trench Caves In." *New York Times*, December 21, 2003.

——. "U.S. Rarely Seeks Charges for Deaths in Workplace." *New York Times*, December 22, 2003.

Beaujon, Andrew, and Julie Moos. "New Owners Bring Bill Marimow Back to The Philadelphia Inquirer." *Poynter*, April 4, 2012.

Bernstein, Carl, and Bob Woodward. "40 Years After Watergate Nixon Was Far Worse Than We Thought." *Washington Post*, June 8, 2012, http://www.washing tonpost.com/opinions/woodward-and-bernstein-40-years-after-watergate-nixon -was-far-worse-than-we-thought/2012/06/08/gJQAlsioNV_story.html.

Bloom, Helen. *News Workshop*. New York University Department of Journalism newsletter, January 1965.

Burke, Daniel. "How to Really Measure the 'Francis Effect,'" CNN.com, March 13, 2014, http://www.cnn.com/2014/03/08/living/pope-francis-effect-boston/.

The Economist. "Who Killed the Newspaper?" *The Economist*, August 26, 2006, http://www.economist.com/node/7830218.

Editor and Publisher. Published monthly. Magazine dates to 1884 as *The Journalist* and as *Editor and Publisher* since 1901. Online at http://www.Editorand Publisher.com. New York.

Erwin, Ray. "2 Weeklies Win Pulitzer Prizes for Anti-KKK War." *Editor and Publisher*, May 9, 1953.

——. "3 Pulitzer Prizes Awarded for Exclusive Exposes: Newsday Wins Gold Medal for Track and Labor Racket Stories." *Editor and Publisher*, May 9, 1954.

——. "Pulitzer Prizes Awarded for the Little Rock Story," *Editor and Publisher*, May 10, 1958.

——. "St. Petersburg Times Wins Public Service Pulitzer." *Editor and Publisher*, May 9, 1964.

Forelle, Charles, and James Bandler. "The Perfect Payday: Some CEOs Reap Millions by Landing Stock Options When They Are Most Valuable." *Wall Street Journal*, March 18, 2006.

Fitzgerald, Mark. "Jim Amoss, E&P's 2006 Editor of the Year." *Editor and Publisher*, February 1, 2006, http://www.EditorandPublisher.com.

Gellman, Barton, and Greg Miller. "'Black Budget' Revealed." *Washington Post*, August 30, 2013.

Goffard, Christopher. "How Bell Hit Bottom." *Los Angeles Times*, December 28, 2011.

Greeley, Andrew M. "The Tipping Point," July 7, 2002, *Globe* http://www.boston .com/globe/spotlight/abuse/stories2/070702_betrayal_review.htm.

Greenwald, Glenn. "NSA Collecting Phone Records of Millions of Verizon Customers Daily," *Guardian*, June 6, 2013, http://www.theguardian.com /world/2013/jun/06/nsa-phone-records-verizon-court-order.

Greenwald, Glenn, Ewen MacAskill, and Laura Poitras. "Edward Snowden: The Whistleblower Behind the NSA Surveillance Revelations," *Guardian*, June 9, 2013.

The Guardian. "History of the Guardian." *Guardian*, http://www.theguardian .com/gnm-archive/2002/jun/06/1.

———. "NSA Files: Decoded: What the Revelations Mean for You," *Guardian*, http://www.theguardian.com/world/interactive/2013/nov/01/snowden -nsa-files-surveillance-revelations-decoded#section/1.

———. "NSA Whistleblower Edward Snowden: 'I Don't Want to Live in a Society That Does These Sort of Things'—Video," *Guardian*, http://www .theguardian.com/world/video/2013/jun/09/nsa-whistleblower-edward -snowden-interview-video.

Harris, Roy J. Jr. The Poynter Institute. http://www.poynter.org/author /royharris/.

Entries in a continuing series about the Pulitzer Prizes on www.poynter.org include: "Post and Courier's 90-Year Pulitzer Drought Ends with Public Service Gold," April 21, 2015; "Looking at the Pulitzers… with Pride," April 21, 2015; "Predicting the Pulitzers: Will a Magazine Win?" April 16, 2015; "Pulitzer Preview: Snowden Factor and More on Prize Prospects for Monday," April 11, 2014; "Winners to Watch For," April 14, 2013, and April 13, 2012; "'Portraits of Grief' 10 Years Later," August 31, 2011; "Handicapping the Pulitzers," April 18, 2012; "This Year's Pulitzer Game: I've Got a Secret," March 4, 2011; "New Year Ends Rush to Publish Blockbusters, Begins Rush to Enter Pulitzers," January 1, 2010; "In Down Year, Some Entries Up," February 8, 2010; "Pulitzer Alchemy Turns Methane Gas to Public Service Gold," April 13, 2010; "What Happened in Vegas: A Pulitzer Shines on the Sun," April 21, 2009; "Remembering Selwyn Pepper of the St. Louis Post-Dispatch," September 7, 2008; "Remembering Bob Greene," April 11, 2008; "When Two Were Two Many Pulitzers," April 9, 2008; "Hard Target Journalism: An Excerpt from Pulitzer's Gold," March 19, 2008; "Whatever Happened to Pulitzer Surprises," April 23, 2007; "Pounding the Pulitzer Beat," April 12, 2007; "Shared Glory for Pulitzer's Top Prize," April 17, 2006; "The Pulitzers That Got Away," April 6, 2004; "Prizes and Rumors of Prizes," April 6, 2005; "The Eye of the Pulitzer Storm," April 2, 2005; and "A Prize Moment for the Globe, and the Pulitzers," April 7, 2003.

———. "5 Myths about the Pulitzer Prizes." *Washington Post*, April 13, 2014. http://www.washingtonpost.com/opinions/five-myths-about-the-pulitzer -prizes/2014/04/11/c62b42de-bc3c-11e3-96ae-f2c36d2b1245_story.html.

———. "Why the Pulitzer Prizes Still Matter." *Columbia Daily Spectator*, March 2, 2012. http://columbiaspectator.com/2010/03/01/why-pulitzer-prizes-still-matter.

———. "How e-Pulitzers Can Elevate Journalism." *Christian Science Monitor*, April 23, 2009. http://www.csmonitor.com/Commentary/Opinion/2009 /0423/p09s03-coop.html.

———. "The Pulitzers—and Charles Ponzi." *Los Angeles Times*, April 18, 2009. http://articles.latimes.com/2009/apr/18/opinion/oe-harris18.

——. "Journalism at Its Very Best." *Christian Science Monitor*, April 2, 2008. http://www.csmonitor.com/Commentary/Opinion/2008/0402/po9so1-coop .html.

——. "An Era of Crusaders." *Quill* (May 2003). Society of Professional Journalists.

——. *The Gold Medal Crusade Years*. Saint Louis University Law School, St. Louis, 2002.

——. "Pulitzer Surprise: The *Sun Sentinel*'s Rise to a Gold Medal." *Columbia Journalism Review*, April 18, 2003, http://www.cjr.org/behind_the_news /pulitzer_surprise_the_sun_sent.php?page=all.

Hull, Anne, and Dana Priest. "Creating an Investigative Narrative." *Nieman Reports* (Summer 2008), 57–62. http://www.Nieman.harvard.edu/reportsitem .aspx?id+100033.

Investigative Editors and Reporters. *IRE Extra Extra Blog*. http://www.ire.org /blog/extra-extra/.

IRE Journal. Published bimonthly since 1978 by Investigative Reporters and Editors. Columbia, Missouri. http://www.IRE.org.

Jacobs, Mike. "Four Lessons of Newspapering . . . Come Hell and High Water." *Poynteronline*, June 18, 2003. http://www.Poynter.org.

Jenkins, Holman W., Jr. "The Backdating Witch Hunt." *Wall Street Journal*, June 21, 2006, http://www.wsj.com/articles/SB115085169575385877.

Kaiser, Robert G. "Ben Bradlee, Legendary Washington Post Editor, Dies at 93." *Washington Post*, October 21, 2014, http://www.washingtonpost.com /national/ben-bradlee-legendary-washington-post-editor-dies-at-93 /2014/10/21/3e4ccıfc-c59c-11df-8dce-7a7dc354dıbı_story.html.

Kinsley, Michael. "Eyes Everywhere." *New York Times*, May 22, 2014, http://www .nytimes.com/2014/06/08/books/review/no-place-to-hide-by-glenn -greenwald.html.

Knapp, Andrew. "Post and Courier Wins Pulitzer for Domestic Abuse Series," *Post and Courier*, April 20, 2015, http://www.postandcourier.com/article/20150420 /PC16/150429937/1005/post-and-courier-wins-pulitzer-prize.

Lanosga, Gerry. "Pulitzer's Gold Review." *Journalism* (February 2010): 126–27. http://www.academia.edu/727759/Book_Review_Roy_J._Harris_Jr. _Pulitzers_Gold_Behind_the_Prize_for.

Martin, John Bartlow. "Murder of a Journalist." *Harper's* (September 1946): 271–282.

Mehren, Elizabeth, Walter V. Robinson, and Steve Kurkjian. "Journalist's Trade: Investigating Scandal in the Catholic Church." *Nieman Reports* (Spring 2003): 52–61.

Newseum. *On the Media* program. Dana Priest Anne Hull, and author. January 19, 2009. Washington, D.C. http://www.newseum.org/events_edu/event _archive/reporting.aspx?item_HARRo90110&style+d.

New York Times. "Ahead of the Times" newsletter, Volume 10, No. 2, April 2002.

New York Times. Vietnam War archive, accessed May 24, 2015. http://topics
.nytimes.com/top/reference/timestopics/subjects/v/vietnam_war/index.html.

PBS. "Pulitzer Prize Renews Debate Over Controversial NSA Surveillance
Reporting." *PBS Newshour*, April 14, 2014, http://www.pbs.org/newshour/bb
/pulitzer-renews-debate-nsa-surveillance-reporting/.

Post-Dispatch. "Theodore C. Link Dies; Investigative Reporter." *Post-Dispatch*,
February 14, 1974.

Poynter.org. The website of the Poynter Institute, a school for journalists and
teachers. http://www.Poynter.org.

Pulitzer Prizes website. http://www.Pulitzer.org. Columbia University, New York.

Quill. Published ten times per year by the Society of Professional Journalists.
Online at http://www.spj.org. Indianapolis.

Rainey, James. "On the Media: Against the Odds, Vegas Paper Wins." *Los Angeles
Times*, April 22, 2009.

——. "On the Media: An Unlikely Duo Wins Pulitzer for Bell Coverage."
Los Angeles Times, April 19, 2011, http://articles.latimes.com/2011/apr/19
/entertainment/la-et-onthemedia-20110419.

Read, Richard. "The Oregonian Investigates Mistreatment of Foreigners."
Nieman Reports (Winter 2002): 27–29.

Richman, Michael. "The Medals of Daniel Chester French." In *The Medal in
America*, ed. Alan M. Stahl, 150–153. Coinage of the Americas Conference at
the American Numismatic Society, New York, September 26–27, 1987.

Robertson, Lori. "Uncovering Misery at Walter Reed." *American Journalism
Review* (April/May 2007): 10–12. http://www.AJR.org/Article.asp?id=4295.

Robinson, Walter V. "Shining the Globe's Spotlight." *Nieman Reports* (Spring
2003): 55–59.

Roldan, Cynthia. "Signing Ushers in Stiffer Penalties, Gun Ban for Domestic
Violence Crimes," *Post and Courier*, June 4, 2015, http://www.postandcourier
.com/article/20150604/PC1603/150609697/1180/haley-signs-bill
-toughening-penalties-for-criminal-domestic-violence.

Rosen, Jay. "To the Snowden Story System a Crowning Pulitzer Might
Have Gone." *PressThink*, April 14, 2014, http://pressthink.org/2014/04
/to-the-snowden-story-system-a-pulitzer-might-have-gone/.

Shafer, Jack. "Who Said It First? Journalism Is the First Rough Draft of History."
Slate.com, August 30, 2010, http://www.slate.com/articles/news_and_politics
/press_box/2010/08/who_said_it_first.single.html.

——. "The Pulitzer Prize Scam." Politico.com, April 20, 2015,
http://www.politico.com/magazine/story/2015/04/2015-pulitzer-prizes-jack
-shafer-column-117151_full.html?print#.VWm4LsaT3gV.

Steel, Emily. "Wall Street Journal Wins a Pair of Pulitzers." *Wall Street Journal*, April 17, 2007, http://www.wsj.com/articles/SB117673531050871312.

Sullivan, John, Susan Snyder, Kristen A. Graham, and Dylan Purcell. "Climate of Violence Stifles City Schools." *Inquirer*, March 27, 2011.

"Till Death Do Us Part." *Post and Courier*, August 19, 2014, http://www.post andcourier.com/tilldeath/.

Tompkins, Al. "Anatomy of a Pulitzer." *Poynter*, April 8, 2008, http://www.poynter .org/latest-news/top-stories/88125/anatomy-of-a-pulitzer-qa-with-hull-and -priest/.

Volz, Yong Z., and Francis L. F. Lee. "What Does It Take for Women Journalists to Gain Professional Recognition?: Gender Disparities among Pulitzer Prize Winners, 1917–2010." *Journalism and Mass Communication Quarterly* (April 2013): 248–266. http://jmq.sagepub.com/content/90/2/248.

Ward, Butch. "From Biloxi and New Orleans: The Stories Behind the Pulitzers." *Poynteronline*, April 17, 2006. http://www.Poynter.org.

——. "Journalism in Recovering Communities: Lessons from Grand Forks." *Poynteronline*, August 31, 2005. http://www.Poynter.org.

Washington Post. Watergate archive, accessed May 24, 2015. http://www.washing tonpost.com/wp-dyn/politics/specials/watergate/articles/.

Weber, Tracy, Charles Ornstein, and Mitchell Landsberg. "Deadly Errors and Politics Betray a Hospital's Promise." *Los Angeles Times*, December 5, 2004.

Unpublished Material

Carroll, John. "Last Call at the ASNE Saloon." Speech delivered at American Society of Newspaper Editors convention, Seattle, April 26, 2006.

Cohen, Murray. "The Crusade Against Election Fraud by the Post-Dispatch and Star-Times of St. Louis in 1936." M.A. thesis, University of Missouri, Columbia, Missouri, 1953.

Columbia University. The Pulitzer Prizes, jury reports from 1917. Maintained in the Journalism Building, Pulitzer Prize office, New York.

——. Pulitzer Prize archive of entries and supporting documentation. Microfilm, Lehman Library, New York.

——. Rare Manuscripts. Butler Library, New York.

Dessauer, Philip Edward. "A Contemporary Study of the 1938–1940 Campaign for Smoke Control by the St. Louis Post-Dispatch." M.A. thesis, University of Missouri, Columbia, Missouri, 1940.

French, Daniel Chester. Family Papers. Library of Congress, Washington, D.C., Reel 20, 222–237.

Hudson, Berkley. "Hambone and the Ku Klux Klan in 1922: James P. Alley's Cartoons of a Southern White Conservative Mentality and the Pulitzer Prize." Excerpted from notes by Hudson, University of Missouri, Columbia, Missouri, 2006.

Marro, Anthony. "Watergate & The Press." Working paper, University of Texas, March 23, 2005.

Mouton, Wanda. "A Case Study Analysis and Quarter-Century Perspective of a Story that Won the Pulitzer Prize." Working paper, Department of Communication, Stephen F. Austin State University, Nacogdoches, Texas, 2001.

Nappier, Teresa A. "Ben Reese: Managing the St. Louis Post-Dispatch." M.A. thesis, University of Missouri, Columbia, Missouri, August 1993.

New York Times. Communications from the Times files, including letter exchanges between Arthur S. Ochs and Nicholas Murray Butler, June–July 1920.

Pfaff, Daniel W. "Pulitzer Journalism and Public Service." Lecture, James Yeatman Lecture, St. Louis, November 10, 2006.

Pulitzer, Joseph II. Collected Papers. Library of Congress, Containers 167–169.

Starr, Louis W. "Reminiscences of Ben Reese," Oral History Research Office, Columbia University, New York, 1957.

———. Joseph Pulitzer II Oral History. From interviews conducted October 7, 1954. Columbia University, New York, 1957.

INDEX

33494038R00271

Made in the USA
Middletown, DE
15 July 2016